O

THE MINDS OF MASS MURDERERS

In both cases, the compulsion involved a psychological penalty. In prison, unable to carry out his Coastal Kills, Gaskins had to be sedated for fits of rage and depression. In the year before his arrest, Frederick West was treated by his doctor for depression. There was a sense in which both were at the end of their tether. West's daughter Mai told policewomen that she had learned that her sister was buried in the garden from her father, who liked to make "jokes" about it . . .

O

—from THE KILLERS AMONG US
Book 1
Motives Behind Their Madness

O

O

ALSO BY COLIN WILSON

Written in Blood: The Criminal Mind and Method
Written in Blood: Detectives and Detection
Written in Blood: The Trail and the Hunt

PUBLISHED BY
WARNER BOOKS

THE KILLERS AMONG US

MOTIVES BEHIND THEIR MADNESS

COLIN WILSON
author of *Written in Blood*
& DAMON WILSON

WARNER BOOKS

A Time Warner Company

Originally published in Great Britain by Robinson Publishing Ltd.
under the title, *A Plague of Murder*.

WARNER BOOKS EDITION

Cover design by Mike Stromberg
Cover photos courtesy of AP/Wide World Photos

Warner Books, Inc.
1271 Avenue of the Americas
New York, NY 10020

Visit our Web site at
www.warnerbooks.com

Ⓦ A Time Warner Company

Printed in the United States of America

First Warner Books Printing: October, 1996

10 9 8 7

O

Contents

Introduction: The Mind of the Serial Killer

1. THE 1960s

2. THE 1970s

3. THE 1980s AND 1990s

4. 1995: THE CASE OF FRED AND ROSE WEST

CONTENTS

THE KILLERS AMONG US

INTRODUCTION

WHEN JACK THE RIPPER KILLED FIVE PROSTITUTES IN THE EAST End of London in 1888, he became instantly the world's most infamous, and also its best-known murderer. He was not the world's most prolific killer, nor the first to mutilate his victims. France's Gilles de Rais murdered and mutilated more than fifty children. Hungary's Countess Elizabeth Bathory murdered an unknown number of servant girls—the number certainly ran into dozens—to take baths in their blood, and is known to have bitten chunks out of their flesh. But the enduring fascination of the Ripper lay in the mystery of his identity, and in his obvious desire to shock, to spit into the face of society. He was also one of the first examples of what we now call a sex killer, and therefore, of what is now labeled a serial killer.

The Killers Among Us could be about all those who have killed large numbers of people—in which case, it would have to include the Nazis, and Mafia contract killers, and insane gunmen who go on a rampage and shoot anyone who crosses their path, and terrorists who blow up public buildings. But it is not, because serial killers are different.

The term "serial killer" was invented in 1978 by FBI agent Robert Ressler to describe obsessive "repeat killers" like Jack the Ripper. Before that, they were called "mass murderers," an ambiguous phrase, since it included criminals like the Frenchman Landru "Bluebeard" who murdered women for their money. Ressler coined the new term because of the increasing number of American multiple sex killers—like Albert DeSalvo, Ted Bundy, Dean Corll, John Gacy and Henry Lee Lucas—whose crimes had achieved worldwide notoriety. Since then, cases like that of the Milwaukee "cannibal" Jeffrey Dahmer and the Russian Andrei Chikatilo have made it clear that he was right: there is a fundamental difference between serial killers and other types of murderers.

What drives a man to become a serial killer? One answer—as we shall see in this book—is that their self-esteem is often so low that killing is a way of asserting that they exist. In some cases, the killing has no sexual component. Donald Harvey, an American nursing orderly, was sentenced in 1987 for murdering twenty-four people, mostly elderly hospital patients. It emerged later that Harvey had been sexually abused by two adults since he was a child and warned that his mother would be harmed unless he kept silent. Years as a passive object of lust led to the total destruction of his self-esteem; killing hospital patients was his way of asserting that he was a "doer," a mover, not a nonentity.

In most cases of serial murder there is an element of this kind of self-assertion. Many such killers are naturally "dominant"—members of what zoologists call "the dominant 5 percent"—but find themselves in a situation in which they feel passive and impotent. Psychologically speaking, such killers can differ as radically as the American Henry Lee Lucas, who confessed to 360 murders that were basically motivated by sex, and the British nurse Beverley Allitt, who killed children in hospital out of some strange sense of inadequacy.

The same inadequacy can be seen in the case of Jeffrey Dahmer, who drugged and murdered males he lured back to his Milwaukee apartment, and the Russian Andrei Chikatilo, whose sexual impotence vanished only when he was inflicting multiple stab wounds on his victims.

The desire to inflict pain is an element that links many serial killers. This sadism may or may not have been present early in their lives but could have developed as a result of sexual obsession. Here we encounter one of the strangest and most difficult psychological mysteries connected with the serial killer. Many men, from Casanova and the anonymous Victorian who wrote *My Secret Life* to H. G. Wells and Bertrand Russell, have experienced a desire to sleep with every attractive woman they see; the urge seems to be as uncomplicated as an angler's desire to catch a fish. Yet in others this urge can get out of control and turn into the need to inflict pain and humiliation. One of the most horrific examples of the sadistic rape syndrome was Donald "Pee Wee" Gaskins. He was imprisoned for murdering nine people, thought to be business acquaintances with whom he had quarreled. Later it was revealed that he was probably the worst serial killer of this century; he killed consistently and regularly over a number of years, the result of an abnormal and overdeveloped sexual urge. In 1991 he went to the electric chair having confessed to killing over 120 victims.

Gaskins explained that he acted when a boiling rage, like hot lead, welled up from somewhere deep inside. Other serial killers acted only when drunk, or under the influence of drugs. One man, Steve Wilson, killed two prostitutes in a motel in Los Angeles in 1944, cutting them up in the manner of the original Ripper. He told the psychiatrist that he had strong sadistic tendencies which only emerged when he was drunk—his first wife had left him because he liked to creep up on her when she was naked and cut her buttocks with a razor; he would then apologize and kiss the wounds. Wilson was executed in the San Quentin gas chamber in September 1946.

Many other serial killers have committed their murders when drunk—two notable cases being the Briton Dennis Nilsen and Jeffrey Dahmer from Milwaukee. All three—Wilson, Nilsen and Dahmer—have one thing in common: a traumatic childhood. When Steve Wilson was 5, he and his siblings were placed in an orphanage. Dennis Nilsen's father was a violent drunk and Nilsen was farmed out to his grandparents. Jeffrey Dahmer's parents quarreled violently for years before finally separating, and Dahmer complained that his childhood was loveless. The seeds of serial murder are planted in childhood, in a sense of neglect and occasionally of downright abuse. Since this rarely happens in higher-income families, the majority of serial killers are working class, and the few who are not (Dahmer's father was an electrical engineer) are neglected and emotionally deprived.

Can a head injury turn a man into a killer? As we shall see during the course of this book, many serial killers have sustained serious and damaging head injuries early in life.

Dr. Jonathan Pinckus, a neurologist from Georgetown University in Washington, DC, cites a case of a killer who had been involved in a serious car accident at the age of 16, in which the front of his head came into violent collision with the roof of the car. He was unconscious for several days and spent many weeks in intensive care. His family noted that his behavior changed after the accident, and that he developed an explosive temper. In due course, he committed a particularly violent double murder, stabbing both victims more than a hundred times. Sentenced to death, he showed no remorse—or any other emotion—about the murder, and no feeling about his impending execution. A brain scan subsequently showed areas of scar tissue in both frontal lobes of the brain; the damage had occurred when his head hit the car roof and his brain had surged forward against the front of the skull.

The brain has the consistency of jelly and is easily damaged. Behind the prefrontal lobes lies an area called the limbic system, which is concerned with feeling, emotion and such responses as aggression. The prefrontal lobes seem to be the part of the brain that inhibits violent responses. But sometimes, when patients have sunk into a state of permanent fear or depression, they can be "cured" by an operation which severs the connections between the prefrontal lobes and the rest of the brain; it is called lobotomy, a procedure once widespread but now discredited as a treatment for mental illness. The lobotomized patient ceases to experience tension; in fact, he usually turns into a contented cow, incapable of emotion.

Pinckus's diagnosis was that the accident had been the equivalent of a lobotomy operation, destroying the killer's normal feelings and preventing the prefrontal lobes from doing their work of inhibiting violent explosions of emotion.

Other killers perform the equivalent of a lobotomy operation on themselves. Subjected to emotional torment in childhood, they learn the trick of switching off their feelings so that nothing can hurt them. Two obvious examples in this book are Jeffrey Dahmer and Andrei Chikatilo, both apparently gentle and normal people, both incapable of any feeling except for themselves. Such people find that sex restores their ability to feel; in effect, it makes them feel "more alive." The other person is unimportant; they have little or no empathy with their fellow human beings. There is a sense in which killers such as Jack the Ripper, Andrei Chikatilo and Jeffrey Dahmer are aliens from another world.

Albert DeSalvo, the Boston Strangler, was one of those possessed of a manic sex drive—his wife testified that he was capable of sex a dozen times a day. DeSalvo estimated that he had raped or sexually attacked about two thousand women;

on one occasion he raped four women in one day, then unsuccessfully attacked a fifth. It is hard for a normal human being to understand sexual desire on such a scale. Sexual excitement is like hunger or thirst; it creates physical discomfort until it is satisfied. For most of us, it then goes away and only reappears after a reasonable interval. For DeSalvo the hunger reappeared almost as soon as it was satisfied, creating a permanent state of discomfort like a stone in a shoe.

The purpose of this book is to explore the mind of the serial killer through examples and case histories. They are chronicled from the beginning of the 1960s to the mid-1990s, when one policeman declared, "there may be as many as five thousand of them out there." (A second volume of *The Killers Among Us*, subtitled *Sex, Madness, and Murder*, will trace the phenomenon back to the beginning of the nineteenth century, when the first serial killers emerged.)

The period following the Second World War saw a decline in the murder rate, but it rose steeply during the fifties. The crime figures always fall during and immediately after wars, but it soon became clear that something strange was happening. An increasing number of murderers seemed to be in the grip of a compulsion to kill, from Christie with his private morgue at 10 Rillington Place to the German Werner Boost who killed courting couples and violated the women. In Britain, the most traumatic crimes of the sixties were the Moors murders, and the most frightening thing about them was that Ian Brady was an articulate and intelligent "criminal outsider" who shared Sade's obsession with "the forbidden" and quoted Dostoevsky. Before the end of the decade, Charles Manson would also preach a philosophy that justified murder. But it was the seventies that saw the emergence of serial murder in Robert Ressler's sense, with sex criminals like Dean Corll, John Gacy and Henry Lee Lucas, who killed on an unprecedented scale. And in the eighties and nineties, cases like the Atlanta murders, the Green River killer, the Paris "phantom," the Night Stalker, the Milwaukee cannibal, the "Red Ripper" and the Gloucester "house of horror" revealed that serial murder is a disease that criminologists have not yet even begun to understand.

This book is an attempt to throw some light on the problem by tracing its history and development.

the evidence of the bullet, she explained that she wanted to see if she could kill a man "and not worry about it afterwards."

Now in fact, it is obvious that no crime is really "motiveless." Penny Bjorkland's shooting may have been motivated by childhood abuse. Norman Smith's random sniping may have been a form of sexual aggression, like that of a later New York serial killer, David Berkowitz, known as "Son of Sam." And the murder committed by Leopold and Loeb was clearly an act of *ego-assertion*. They felt that they were immensely superior to their fellow students, but it was necessary to *do* something to prove it to themselves.

I saw in this type of "motiveless crime" an ominous portent for the future. And this feeling crystallized when I read of a mass murder that took place in Mesa, Arizona, on November 13, 1966, when an 18-year-old student named Robert Benjamin Smith walked into a hairdressing parlor called the Rose-Mar College of Beauty, ordered four young women and a 3-year-old girl to lie face downward on the floor, then shot them all in the back of the head. Asked why he did it, Smith said: "I wanted to get known, to get myself a name." He added: "I knew I had to kill a lot of people to get my name in the newspapers all over the world."

Such a motive seems absurd and incomprehensible—until we recall the Greek Herostratus, who in 356 BC burnt down the temple of Artemis at Ephesus "to make his name immortal." In 1938 Sartre wrote a story called "Herostratus" about a man who decided to shoot half a dozen people at random for the same reason (the first of the "crazy gunmen").

Now, as most contemporary psychologists acknowledge, the hunger for self-esteem is one of the most basic human urges. The first to develop this notion as a basis for psychotherapy was Freud's disciple (later his opponent) Alfred Adler, who argued that man has turned his physical inferiority to animals to his advantage by developing his *brain*. And in the same way, physically weak individuals compensate for their inferiority to stronger ones by developing their intelligence. This becomes their source of "superiority" and self-esteem. Adler suggested that the "inferiority complex" is the most basic cause of neurosis.

The American psychologist Abraham Maslow found himself torn between the Freudian explanation of neurosis (sexual repression) and the Adlerian (inferiority) until it struck him that *both* play a fundamental role. Maslow reconciled them by creating his theory of the "hierarchy of needs."

What Maslow suggested, briefly, is this. If human beings are at the bottom of the social scale, their chief desire is just to stay alive—to have the basic means of subsistence. A man who has been half-starved since birth feels that if only he could have three good meals a day, he would be ecstatically happy. But if this level of need is satisfied, the next emerges: for security, a roof over one's head (every tramp daydreams of retiring to a cottage with roses round the door). If *this* level is satisfied, the next emerges—the sexual level: not just the need for sex, but for love, for companionship. And if this level is satisfied, the next need emerges: to be *recognized* and respected: in other words, the need for self-esteem. And if this level is satisfied, a final level sometimes (though not always) emerges: what Maslow called "self-actualization"—creativity: not necessarily writing novels or symphonies, but the need to do something well merely for the sake of doing it well. Even stamp collecting counts as self-actualization.

Cases like that of Robert Smith made me aware that a new level of crime was beginning to emerge as a successor to "the age of sex crime": what might be called the crime of self-esteem. This was followed by the insight that in the past two centuries, society itself has passed through the levels of Maslow's hierarchy of needs. In the days of the *Newgate Calendar* (1774), that immense compilation of criminal cases, sex crime was virtually unknown; criminals were too busy merely staying alive to bother about rape. When rape did occur it was often treated with remarkable leniency: in the *Encyclopedia*, I cite a nineteenth-century record that mentions a man being sentenced to death for stealing a loaf of bread, and a man who received two weeks in jail for raping a servant girl.

In the Victorian age, with its higher level of prosperity, Maslow's second level emerges: crime committed for domestic security. Belle Gunness epitomizes it perfectly: what she wanted was not just cash, but the ideal home and the social security that goes with it.

The third level of need, the sexual level, begins to emerge in the second half of the nineteenth century, and is symbolized by Jack the Ripper. The age of sex crime had begun.

And now, in the late 1950s and early 1960s, we see the emergence of the next level: self-esteem. This is the ultimate motivation of Peter Manuel, Werner Boost, Melvin Rees.

But at this point, a serious objection occurs. These three men were, after all, sex criminals. Yet we only have to compare them with "sex maniacs" like Earle Nelson, Harvey Glatman or Heinrich Pommerencke—or even Ed Gein—to see that there is a major difference. The typical rapist killer is suffering from a kind of sexual starvation, and he "steals" sex as a starving man might steal food. He recognizes it as wrong, but the compulsion is overwhelming. The self-esteem killer denies that what he is doing is wrong. Like some bomb-throwing revolutionary, he feels that society is somehow to blame—or God, or the laws of nature. It is true that he is a sex criminal, but sex is no longer the basic driving force. What such men are really interested in is power, self-esteem. Sartre catches it perfectly in a scene in "Herostratus" in which the hero goes to a prostitute and simply makes her remove her clothes and walk about the room, while he sits in an armchair, fully clothed, holding a revolver in his lap. He explains elsewhere in the story that he never indulges in sexual intercourse; he feels this would be a kind of surrender to a woman who is his inferior.

Here, suddenly, we can grasp the reason for the sadism involved in so many modern sex crimes. The sex is inextricably entangled with the craving for self-esteem, for personal "superiority." And as soon as we see this, we can also see that this throws a new light on the fantasies of the Marquis de Sade. Sade had a keen sense of his own intellectual superiority, yet it was being continually challenged by those in authority. Sade's novels are *authoritarian* daydreams rather than sexual daydreams. This is why he devotes as much time to intellectual argument as to sexual fantasy. We may see Sade as an "in-betweener," someone who is in between two levels of Maslow's hierarchy, sex and self-esteem.

Maslow's hierarchy also suggests why so many burglars urinate and defecate in the course of robbery. As a crime, burglary belongs to the lower levels of Maslow's hierarchy—the need for subsistence and security. But the sexual level is also beginning to emerge, and it is sexual excitement that prompts the urge to "do something dirty" as well as merely stealing property. Lowering the trousers is essentially a sexual act. And here again, the crime involves *two* adjacent levels of Maslow's hierarchy, and the criminal may be seen as an "in-betweener."

Maslow's "hierarchy" is about *human evolution*. And this in turn explains why human beings are capable of so much more violence and cruelty than animals: in man, this evolutionary urge is far more acute and painful.

And what of Maslow's next level, self-actualization? We can also see the increasing emergence of this level in the latter part of the twentieth century: for example, in the increasing interest in the "expansion of consciousness," in yoga, in "occultism," in the "psychedelic revolution" and virtual real-

ity. Now it can be found in any town or village anywhere—
even the small Cornish village where I live has a yoga group.

Now, self-actualizers do not commit crimes—at least, not
murder. For example, there is no known example of a writer
or artist committing a premeditated murder. (A few have
killed men in duels, or—like the composer Gesualdo, who
caught his wife in bed with a lover—in a fit of jealousy; but
never a coldly calculated killing.) Shaw underlined the point
by observing that we judge an artist by his highest moments,
a criminal by his lowest. Once a man has decided that he is an
artist—one of the "unacknowledged legislators of the
world"—then he has achieved a level of self-esteem at which
crime is no longer a valid option. There is a sense in which he
feels "above" society as Sartre's Herostratus feels "above"
sex with prostitutes.

There is, nevertheless, a point at which sex, self-esteem and
self-actualization mingle rather uncomfortably. The level of
self-actualization, is, for example, the religious level, and
there are many examples of religious prophets and "messiahs" who are still entangled in the need for sex and self-
esteem. The usual assumption is that such men are simply
confidence tricksters who prey on the gullible, like Sinclair
Lewis's Elmer Gantry. But this is not necessarily true. Many
possess a genuine urge to self-transcendence, but still mixed
with sex and self-esteem urges. Edward Wilson, who preferred to be called Brother Twelve, possessed remarkable religious gifts, which emerge clearly in his writings.[1] But as
soon as he became a successful prophet, he engaged in seduction and became a kind of power-maniac, who finally absconded with the money collected from his disciples. The
Rev. Jim Jones, who ordered nine hundred disciples to com-

[1]See *Brother Twelve*, by John Oliphant (McClelland and Stewart, Toronto,
1991).

mit mass suicide in Guyana in 1978, also seems to have started out with genuine religious inspiration. So did Jeffrey Lundgren, a breakaway Mormon who started a religious community in Kirtland, Ohio, in the 1980s. Lundgren invented a ceremony called Intercession, in which female disciples had to dance naked in front of him, while he masturbated into their panties, explaining that his shedding of semen was analogous to Christ's shedding of his blood for the redemption of sin. Lundgren eventually ordered his followers to murder a family of five disciples, whom he accused of backsliding, and was sentenced to death in 1990.[2]

A certain skepticism is inevitable in considering such cases; it is easier to dismiss such "messiahs" as confidence men. Yet unless we can grasp that genuine "self-actualization" needs can be entangled with sex and self-esteem needs, we fail to grasp an important aspect of what has been happening since the 1960s. When the Charles Manson "family" came to trial in 1970, the general public was thoroughly confused by Manson's attempt to turn the trial into an indictment of bourgeois society. Manson explained: "You made my children what they are." Asked if she thought the killing of eight people was unimportant, Susan Atkins countered by asking if the killing of thousands of people with napalm was important. It looked like thoroughly muddled logic. Yet it is only necessary to read some of the interviews Manson has given in prison, or watch them on videotape, to recognize that Manson still believes that his "philosophy" was really about self-actualization, and that the murders were intended as a kind of violent protest against a society that denied him self-actualization. Again, on October 9, 1970, an ecology enthusiast named John Linley Frazier murdered eye surgeon Victor Ohta

[2]*The Kirtland Massacre*, by Cynthia Statter Sasse and Peggy Murphy (Willder, Donald I. Fine Inc., New York, 1991).

and his family, leaving behind a note that declaimed against those who "misuse the natural environment," and concluding: "Materialism must die or mankind will stop."

It is also worth bearing in mind that Frazier, like the Manson family—and most of the hippies in the 1960s—spent a great deal of his time on "acid trips." And one of the effects of psychedelic drugs is to produce visions of "transcendence" which authorities like Aldous Huxley, Timothy Leary and Arthur Koestler agree to be valid, rather than some kind of drug-induced delusion. On the other hand, drugs are clearly a short cut to "expanded states of awareness," which explains why such states are usually unstable.

This also explains why criminals like Manson and Frazier are so puzzling and difficult to place: because they are "in-betweeners," existing uneasily between the levels of self-esteem and self-actualization.

It seems likely that this is also the key to one of the most sensational murder cases of the decade: The "Moors murders"— a case that, as journalist Fred Harrison commented, "has tormented the psyche of a nation." On April 19, 1966, Ian Brady, 28, and Myra Hindley, 23, appeared in court in Chester, accused of three murders: two of children, Lesley Ann Downey and John Kilbride, one of a teenage boy, Edward Evans. They were also believed to have killed Pauline Reade, 16, and Keith Bennett, 12, but the bodies had not been found.

What produced the sense of shock was that a young girl— and apparently one who loved animals and children—should have participated in the sex murder of children. Commentators on the case seemed divided between those who thought Brady a hypnotic Svengali, and those who thought they were probably both equally bad. In his introduction to *The Trial of Ian Brady and Myra Hindley*, Jonathan Goodman makes it clear that he simply regards Brady as a monster. More insight is provided by Jean Ritchie in *Myra Hindley: Inside the Mind of a Murderess* (1988), who seems to have based part of her account on interviews with Brady's foster parents.

Ian Brady—christened Ian Duncan Stewart—was born on January 2, 1938 in Glasgow; his mother, 28-year-old Margaret Stewart, worked as a waitress in hotel tea-rooms; his father was a Glasgow journalist, who died three months before Ian's birth. Margaret Stewart did her best to support the child, farming him out to babysitters when she had to work in the evening, but finally advertised for a full-time "childminder." Mary and John Sloan took him into "their warm and friendly home," where his mother, who now called herself Peggy, came to visit him every Sunday, bringing him clothes and presents. So it hardly seems that Ian Brady can be classified with Carl Panzram as someone who was subjected to childhood neglect and brutality.

Jean Ritchie has one highly significant story to tell: how, at the age of 9, he was taken on a picnic to the shores of Loch Lomond.

For Ian it was a day of discovery. He discovered in himself a deep affinity with the wild, rugged and empty scenery around the lake. He was moved by the grandeur of the hills, awed by the vastness of the sky. When it was time to go home, the family found him halfway up one of the hills, standing still absorbing something—who knows what?—from the strange, open, inspiring scenery around him. It was an unusual Ian who came down the hill, one who babbled happily about his day out to his foster sisters . . .

This story sounds as if it came from the Sloan family, and it is supported by other comments from those who knew him: for example, Lord Longford, who visited him in prison. The

latter is also on record as saying that Brady knew his Tolstoy
and Dostoevsky better than anyone he had known. Others
have spoken of his interest in Nietzsche. This hardly sounds
like the sadistic psychopath described by Goodman.

What most writers on the case seem agreed upon is that
Brady was—as Jean Ritchie puts it—"a loner, an outsider."
He was also a highly dominant child at school, a born leader,
who seems to have embarked on burglary at an early age (9
has been quoted)—not, as in the case of Panzram, out of envy
of contemporaries from wealthier backgrounds, but simply
out of devilment.

When he was 10, the family were moved from the Gorbals
to a new council estate at Pollock, with—as Jean Ritchie
says—"indoor bathroom and lavatory, a garden and nearby
fields." At the age of 11 he started attending Shawlands Academy, a school for above-average pupils, but seems to have
taken a certain pleasure in misbehaving, perhaps in reaction
against richer schoolmates.

At the age of 13 he came before a juvenile court for burglary, but was bound over; nine months later, he was again
bound over for the same thing. At 16 he appeared again before a Glasgow court with nine charges against him. This time
he was put on probation on condition that he joined his
mother in Manchester. Margaret Stewart had moved there
when her son was 12, and had married a meat porter named
Patrick Brady, whose name Ian was to take.

His stepfather found him a job in the fruit market. He was
still a loner, spending hours in his room reading. But in November 1955, he was again in court, this time on a charge of
aiding and abetting. A lorry driver had asked him to load some
stolen lead onto his lorry. The scrap dealer gave him away to
the police, and he in turn implicated Brady. In court, Brady
pleaded guilty, expecting a fine for such a trivial offense—
after all, everybody in the market was "on the fiddle." But be-

cause he was on probation, the judge decided that severity was called for. To his bewilderment—and rage—Brady was remanded to Strangeways jail to await his sentence.

There he spent three months among professional criminals, and deliberately cultivated fences, cracksmen, even killers. He had made up his mind that society was going to get what it deserved. This reaction—reminiscent of Joseph Smith, Carl Panzram, Peter Manuel and Werner Boost—is typical of the high-dominance male faced with what he considers outrageous injustice. The two-year Borstal sentence that followed only confirmed the decision—particularly when, in an open Borstal at Hatfield, he found himself in further trouble. He had been selling home-distilled liquor and running a book on horses and dogs. One day, after getting drunk and having a fight with a warder, he was transferred to an altogether tougher Borstal housed in Hull prison. This, says Jean Ritchie, "was where he prepared himself to become a big-time criminal." The aim was to become wealthy as quickly as possible, so he could enjoy the freedom he dreamed about. This was why he studied bookkeeping in prison—to learn to handle money.

Three months in Strangeways and two years in Borstal had turned a youth with a minor criminal record and a tendency to bookishness into an antisocial rebel. Even taking into account the fact that he had been on probation, the ineptitude of the law seems incredible.

He was released at the end of two years, but remained on probation for another three. When he was released, he returned home to Manchester, as he had to under the terms of the probation. But Fred Harrison, the journalist who interviewed Brady in prison, and who wrote a book on the case,[1]

[1] *Brady and Hindley: Genesis of the Moors Murders* (Ashgrove Press, Bath 1986).

has an interesting passage that makes it clear that Brady soon became actively involved in crime. He speaks of a Borstal friend named Deare, who delivered a stolen Jaguar to Manchester—not to Brady but to another man. The car was to be used in a "job." The other man, says Harrison, made the mistake of not getting rid of the Jaguar after the "job," and was arrested. He gave Deare's name to the police. Deare subsequently vanished, and Harrison suggests that Brady was responsible. Now in fact, Gilbert Deare was still around at the time of Brady's arrest for the Moors murders, and died some time later in a drowning accident. On this topic, Harrison is inaccurate. But the significance of the passage is that it makes clear that Brady was involved in crimes that required a getaway car soon after he returned to Manchester, and that he had at least two accomplices. What is also clear is that Brady spent a great deal of time "casing" banks and building societies, watching the transportation of money.

But apart from one brush with the law for being drunk and disorderly, Brady managed to stay out of trouble. His probation officer obliged him to take a laboring job in a brewery, which he understandably detested. In 1959, at the age of 21, he succeeded in changing this for something less disagreeable; the bookkeeping training led to a job as a stock clerk with Millwards Ltd., a small chemical firm. He was a careful and neat worker, although inclined to be unpunctual, and to slip out of the office to place bets with a local bookmaker. But he remained a loner, spending the lunch hour alone in the office, reading books which included *Mein Kampf* and other volumes on Nazism.

What seems clear, then, is that Ian Brady was turned into a criminal by a sense of injustice. Whether this attitude was justified is beside the point; given his background, and the two years in Borstal, it was inevitable. Although a loner as a child, he was by no means an outcast among his contemporaries, who regarded him as a daredevil. His brushes with the law had been infrequent, and he was treated leniently until the lead episode. In the Manchester fruit market he was "on the fiddle"—like everyone else—but was basically prepared to settle down. The decision to remand him to Strangeways was the true origin of the Moors murders.

Among writers on the case there has been a fairly concerted effort to represent Brady as a mindless devotee of violent comics and book with titles like *The Kiss of the Whip*. This is clearly inaccurate, since his reading included *Crime and Punishment* and *Thus Spake Zarathustra*, as well as Sade's *Justine* (the early "non-pornographic" version of 1787). Fred Harrison records that Brady discovered *Crime and Punishment* in the Manchester public library in 1958, around the time of his twentieth birthday. Its hero, Raskolnikov, justifies his murder of an old woman by explaining that he asked himself what Napoleon would have done in his place—if, instead of having the opportunity to prove himself at Toulon at the age of 25, he had been a poor student in St. Petersburg, who had to make his own opportunities?

This seems, in many ways, to be the key to Brady's personality. Since childhood he had never doubted that he was a "somebody." Nietzsche talks about "how one becomes what one is." But *how* could he find a way of becoming "somebody"? Beethoven never had any doubt that he was a composer, Nietzsche that he was a philosopher, Dostoevsky that he was a writer, Einstein that he was a scientist. All of them had difficult early struggles—Einstein even worked as a clerk in a patent office—but they had a sense of purpose, of what Sartre calls a "project." What was Brady's "project"? To some extent it had been determined by those early forays into burglary to obtain pocket money. He wanted the opportunity to live as he wanted, to go where he wanted, at any time he felt inclined. That seemed to point to a career in crime. His aim was to make a large sum of money from robbery, then probably to retire abroad.

The second major influence was Hitler's *Mein Kampf*. Anyone who wonders how an antisemitic tirade could have exercised such an immense influence on a whole generation should push aside preconceptions and try reading it, as I did in my late teens. Its keynote is reasonableness, and it reminds us that when Albert Speer first went to hear Hitler speak, expecting a ranting maniac, he was amazed to discover a man who talked quietly and rationally, almost pedantically. Hitler begins by speaking of his father, the son of a poor cottager, who set out from his home village at the age of 13, with a satchel on his back and three gulden in his pocket, to launch himself into the strange, unknown world of Vienna. He became a civil servant, then retired at 56 and became a farmer.

Hitler goes on to speak of himself.

It was at this time I began to have ideals of my own. I spent a good deal of time playing about in the open, on the long road from school, and mixing with some of the roughest of the boys, which caused my mother many anxious moments. All this tended to make me the opposite of a stay-at-home. I gave no serious thought to a profession; but I was certainly out of sympathy with the kind of career my father had followed. I think that an inborn talent for speaking now began to develop . . . I had become a juvenile ringleader who learned well and easily at school, but who was rather difficult to manage.

Every word must have struck Brady as a reflection of himself.

Hitler's father was determined that he should become a civil servant; Hitler was equally determined that he would not. The conflict began when Hitler was 11, and became more bitter when, at the age of 12, he decided to become an artist.

Then, in his early teens, his father and his mother died in quick succession. He was left in poverty. And so, like his father, he was forced to go to Vienna to seek his fortune.

By this point the reader is hooked. Hitler's description of his sufferings and poverty in Vienna are simple and undramatized. And when he goes on to speak of a corrupt society, rotten with injustice and poverty, it seems that he is speaking common sense. Suddenly, it is possible to see how Hitler exercised such an immense influence on his audiences; they felt he was simply articulating what they had always felt. He goes on to conjure up a family of seven living in a dark basement, where every minor disagreement turns into a quarrel. Sometimes the father assaults the mother in a fit of drunken rage. All religious and political and humanistic values seem an illusion. The truth is simply the brutal struggle to survive. A child brought up in such an environment is totally antiauthoritarian. When he leaves school he is cynical and resentful. And he soon ends up in a reformatory, which completes his education in self-contempt and criminality . . .

Hitler goes on to describe how, working in the building trade, he first came up against trade unionism and Marxism. When told he had to join the union, he refused. As he got to know his fellow workers better, he knew he could never "join" them; they struck him as too stupid. Finally, when they threatened to throw him from the scaffolding, he left. By that time he had come to despise socialism, which seemed to him the glorification of the mediocre.

According to Hitler, it took him a long time to recognize the connection between socialism and the Jews. At first he was simply disgusted by the antisemitic press. Then he began to recognize the part played by Jews in socialism, particularly Marxism. It was Marxism that aroused his most furious disgust, with its dislike of entrepreneurs and—by implication—of individual enterprise. Dostoevsky had expressed the same disgust with socialism in *The Possessed* (a book that Brady read five times). Hitler ends his second chapter by stating ominously that "should the Jew, with the aid of his Marxist creed, triumph over the people of this world, his crown will be the funeral wreath of humanity . . ."

It becomes possible to see why Hitler's doctrine achieved such enormous influence. Since the collapse of communism in Russia, most people can acknowledge that they share his sentiments about Marxism. What Hitler was proposing to put in its place was a purified German nationalism based upon the greatness of the German cultural heritage—Goethe, Beethoven, Nietzsche, Wagner . . . The result is a highly potent brew which, when distilled into films like Leni Riefenstahl's *Triumph of the Will*, seems to offer a simple and seductive solution to all the problems of the modern world.

There was another element in Brady that Fred Harrison was the first to bring out: a curious black romanticism associated with death. Harrison described how Brady became an atheist at the age of 12, when he prayed that his pet dog would not die, and his prayers remained unanswered. Two years later, cycling to a job interview, he felt giddy and halted in the doorway of a newsagent's shop. There he saw "a green, warm radiation, not unattractive to the young man who tried to steady himself. The features were unformed but still recognizable. Ian knew that he was looking at The Face of Death . . . he instantly knew that his salvation was irrevocably bound to its demands. 'I'll do it a favor, and . . . it will do me favors.' The bond with death was fused by the green radiation."

For two years Brady worked quietly at Millwards, reading, learning German and playing records—including Hitler speeches—and almost certainly continued to keep in touch with ex-Borstal friends and plan "jobs." Then, on Monday January 16, 1961, an 18-year-old shorthand typist named Myra Hindley came to work at Millwards, and Ian Brady dictated her first letter. She was four and a half years younger than Brady, a completely normal working-class girl, not bad-looking, with a blonde hair-do and bright lipstick, interested in boys and dancing. She had been born a Catholic, brought up a Protestant, and returned to Catholicism when she was 16. When she was 4, the birth of a sister made the home too cramped, and she went to live with her grandmother nearby. This was not particularly traumatic since she could spend as much time as she liked at her home around the corner.

At school she received good marks and wrote poetry and excellent English essays. She played the mouth organ and was known as a high-spirited tomboy.

She had been engaged but had broken it off, finding the boy "immature." This was one of the problems for working-class girls at that time, whose notions of male attractiveness were formed by cinema and television—hard-bitten heroes with strong jaws, or charismatic rebels like James Dean and Elvis Presley. By contrast, the youths they met at dance halls seemed commonplace and boring.

Ian Brady was certainly not that. He had slightly sulky good looks reminiscent of Elvis Presley, and a dry and forceful manner. His self-possession was intriguing. So was his total lack of interest in her. Myra's infatuation blossomed, and she confided it to her red diary. "Ian looked at me today." "Wonder if Ian is courting. Still feel the same." "Haven't spoken to him yet." Then: "Spoken to him. He smiles as though embarrassed." On August 1: "Ian's taking sly looks at me at work." But by November: "I've given up with Ian. He goes out of his way to annoy me . . ." Then, on December 22, 1961: "Out with Ian!" They went to see the film *King of Kings*, the life story of Jesus. Just over a week later, on the divan bed in her gran's front room, Ian Brady and Myra Hindley became lovers. "I hope Ian and I love each other all our lives and get married and are happy ever after."

Many books on the Moors murder case imply that Brady's attitude towards her was cold and manipulative. In fact, it seems to have been exceptionally close. Myra was overawed and fascinated by her lover. She declared later: "Within months he had convinced me there was no God at all: he could have told me the earth was flat, the moon was made of green cheese and the sun rose in the west, I would have believed him." Brady is on record as saying that the relationship was so close that they were virtually telepathic. They spent every Saturday night together, went on for visits to the moors on Ian's motorbike, taking bottles of German wine, read the same books, and went to see his favorite films, such as *Compulsion*, based on the Leopold and Loeb murder case.

Now he had a female partner, but the central problem remained: how to escape the boring rut of working-class existence, and find a more fulfilling way of life. According to Fred Harrison, it was early in 1963—after they had been lovers for a year—that Brady suggested that the two of them should collaborate on robbing a bank or a store. But this raises some obvious questions. Brady already had at least two criminal contacts; it is unlikely that he took a year to tell Myra about them, and about his plans for a payroll robbery. It seems far more likely that she knew about these plans from the beginning. At all events, it is clear from her later admissions to Detective Chief Superintendent Topping that he had no trouble persuading her to participate.

For a payroll robbery it would be necessary to possess a car. Myra began to take driving lessons, and passed her test at the first attempt. Also at about this time, Brady took up photography, and bought a camera with a timing device. He took photographs of Myra in black crotchless panties; she photographed him holding his erect penis; then, using a timing device, they photographed themselves having sexual intercourse. The intention, apparently, was to make money selling the pictures.

In April 1963, he wrote to her that he would be surveying an "investment establishment" (i.e., bank or building society) in the Stockport Road. In June 1963, Brady moved into the house of Myra's gran, and Myra acquired a car, a second hand minivan. It was then, according to Harrison, that he began to talk to her about committing a murder.

In a letter to the press in January 1990, Brady wrote that the murders were "the product of an existentialist philosophy, in tandem with the spiritualism of Death itself." What seems clear is that crime had become a form of dark romanticism, and that this philosophy was based on Nietzsche, Dostoevsky and Sade.

The first "Moors murder," that of Pauline Reade, happened on July 12, 1963, a month after Brady had moved in with Myra. The only account we have of the murder is from the confession Myra Hindley made to Topping in January 1987. According to Myra, she picked up Pauline Reade—who was 16—in the minivan, and asked her to help her come and look for an expensive glove which she had lost at a picnic on Saddleworth Moor. She offered her a pile of gramophone records in exchange. When they had been on the moor about an hour, Brady arrived on his motorbike, and was introduced as Myra's boyfriend. Brady and Pauline then went off to look for the glove, while Myra waited in the car. Later Brady returned to the car, and took her to Pauline's body. Her throat had been cut and her clothes were in disarray, indicating rape. They then buried the body with the spade that Myra had brought in the back of the van.

In his open letter of 1990, Brady claimed that Myra had been involved in the actual killing, and had also made some kind of sexual assault on Pauline Reade. On the whole, his account sounds the more plausible. Myra's account of the murders invariably has her elsewhere at the time, and Topping admits that Myra told the truth only in so far as it suited her.

It seems clear that Brady was now totally in the grip of the criminal-outsider syndrome. The plans for the payroll robbery—or robberies—were well advanced. And so were plans for more murders. The one thing we know for certain about sex crime is that it is addictive. The satisfaction in all sex derives from the "forbidden," but the forbiddenness is diluted by the need for mutual consent; rape—possessing a woman without her consent—is like undiluted corn liquor. Few rape killers have succeeded in stopping of their own accord. But it is also important to grasp that the murders were only a part of Brady's "agenda."

In October 1963, three months after the murder of Pauline Reade, Ian Brady made the acquaintance of 16-year-old David Smith, the husband of Myra's sister Maureen (who was now also working at Millwards). Smith was a big youth who had been a member of a street gang and had been in trouble with the law. Soon David and Maureen took a trip to the Lake District with Ian and Myra, where they sailed on Windermere. While not homosexual, Smith experienced an emotional attraction to males; soon he was almost as completely under Brady's spell as Myra was.

On Saturday, November 23, Ian Brady and Myra Hindley drove to the small market town of Ashton-under-Lyne. A 12-year-old boy named John Kilbride had spent Saturday afternoon at the cinema, then went to earn a few pence doing odd jobs for stallholders at the market. It began to get dark and a fog came down from the Pennines. At that moment, a friendly lady approached him and asked him if he wanted a lift. It seemed safe enough, so he climbed in. It was the last time he was seen alive. Later, Brady was to take a photograph of Myra kneeling on his grave on the moor.

On June 16, 1964, 12-year-old Keith Bennett set out to spend the night at his grandmother's house in the Longsight district. When his mother called to collect him the following morning, he had failed to arrive. Like John Kilbride, Keith Bennett had accepted a lift from a kind lady. His body has never been found.

Meanwhile, David Smith's admiration for his mentor was steadily increasing. Brady took him up to Saddleworth Moor and they engaged in pistol practice—Myra had obtained two pistols by the expedient of joining the Cheadle Rifle Club. Myra was not entirely happy about this intimacy; her attitude to Smith had an undertone of hostility; in fact, both of them were getting sick of the Smiths. She was glad when her gran was rehoused in Wardle Brook Avenue, in the suburb of Hattersley, in September 1964, and she and Ian moved into the little house at the end of a terrace. Nevertheless, Ian continued to consolidate his influence over David. If he was going to rob banks, a partner would be needed. Soon David Smith was recording in a notebook sentences like: "God is a disease, a plague, a weight round a man's neck" and "Rape is not a crime, it is a state of mind. God is a disease which eats away a man's instincts, murder is a hobby and a supreme pleasure." Soon he and Brady were "casing" banks and drawing up elaborate plans.

One day Brady asked him: "Is there anyone you hate and want out of the way?"

Smith mentioned several names, including an old rival named Tony Latham. After some discussion, they settled on Tony Latham as the murder victim. But first, Brady explained, he would need a photograph. This was no problem. Smith had a Polaroid camera, and he knew the pub where Latham drank. The next evening, Ian and Myra drove him to the pub, then drove away. Unfortunately, Smith had forgotten to insert the film, and when he went into the toilet to develop the photograph, found the camera empty.

When he went out to Wardle Brook Avenue to confess his failure, Brady seemed to take it casually enough. In reality he did not believe Smith was telling the truth and was alarmed. Now, suddenly, David Smith was a potential risk. If he had participated in the murder of Tony Latham, he would have been bound to Ian and Myra. Now Brady began to think seriously about removing him. Oddly enough, it was Myra who dissuaded him. "It would hurt Mo" (Maureen).

On December 26, 1964, there was another murder. Like the others, this was planned in advance. Myra had arranged for her grandmother to stay the night with an uncle at Dunkinfield. At about six o'clock that evening, she picked up 10-year-old Lesley Ann Downey at a fair in Hulme Hall Lane. In her "confession" to Topping, Myra gave her own version of what happened. They took Lesley back to the house in Wardle Brook Avenue, and switched on a tape recorder. Myra claims that she was in the kitchen when she heard the child screaming. Brady was squeezing her neck and ordering her to take off her coat. Lesley was then made to undress, and to assume various pornographic poses, while Brady filmed her. On the tape, Myra can be heard ordering her to "put it in, put it in tighter," presumably referring to the gag that appears in the photographs. Lesley screams and asks to be allowed to go home. At this point, Myra claims she was ordered to go and run a bath; she stayed in the bathroom until the water became cold. When she returned, Lesley had been strangled, and there was blood on her thighs. The following day they took the body to the moors and buried it.

In his open letter to the press, Brady denies that Myra played no active part in the murder. "She insisted upon killing Lesley Ann Downey with her own hands, using a two foot length of silk cord, which she later used to enjoy toying with in public, in the secret knowledge of what it had been used for."

Brady had killed approximately once every six months since July 1963: Pauline Reade, John Kilbride, Keith Bennett,

Lesley Ann Downey. For some reason, July 1965 went by—as far as we know—without a further murder. But in September, Brady decided to kill out of sequence. The aim seems to have been to cement David Smith's membership of the "gang" (which fairly certainly involved other people besides himself and Myra). According to Smith, during a drunken session on September 25, Brady asked Smith: "Have you ever killed anybody? I have—three or four. The bodies are buried up on the moors."

Two weeks later, on October 6, Smith turned up at Wardle Brook Avenue—he was now living close by, in a council flat in Hattersley—hoping to borrow some money, but they were all broke. Brady had already suggested that they should rob an electricity board showroom, and the robbery had been planned for two days later. Smith's urgent need for money to pay the rent suggested that now was the time to "cement" him beyond all possibility of withdrawal. (It seems unlikely that this robbery would involve only three of them—after all, Smith was totally inexperienced.)

Towards midnight, Myra called at her sister's flat with a message for their mother, then asked David Smith to walk her home. As he stood waiting in the kitchen—expecting to be offered a drink—there was a scream from the sitting room, and Myra called "Dave, help him!" As Smith ran in, Ian Brady was hacking at the head of a youth who was lying on the floor. In spite of blow after blow, the youth continued to twist and scream. Finally, when he lay still, Brady pressed a cushion over the face and tied a cord around the throat to stop the gurgling noises. Brady handed Smith the hatchet. "Feel the weight of that." Smith's fingers left bloodstained prints on the handle.

Gran called down to ask what the noise was about, and Myra shouted that she had dropped a tape recorder on her foot.

When the room had been cleaned up, the body was carried upstairs between them—Brady commented: "Eddie's a dead weight." The victim was 17-year-old Edward Evans, who had been picked up in a pub that evening.

They all drank tea, while Myra reminisced about a policeman who had stopped to talk to her while Brady was burying a body. After this, Smith agreed to return with an old pram the next day, and help in the disposal of Edward Evans.

When he arrived home Smith was violently sick. And when he told Maureen what had happened, it was she who decided to go to the police.

At eight o'clock the next morning, a man dressed as a baker's roundsman knocked on the door of 16 Wardle Brook Avenue. Myra answered the door, still rubbing the sleep out of her eyes. The man identified himself as a police officer, and said he had reason to believe there was a body in the house. Brady was on the divan bed in the living room, writing a note to explain why he was not going to work that day. Upstairs, the police demanded to see into a locked room. When Myra said the key was at work, a policeman offered to go and fetch it. At this, Brady said: "You'd better tell him. There was a row here last night. It's in there." Under the window in the bedroom there was a plastic-wrapped bundle. Two loaded revolvers were found in the same room.

David Smith told the police that Brady had stored two suitcases in the left luggage at Manchester Central Station, and these were recovered. (The cloakroom ticket was later found where Brady had described it—in the spine of a prayer book.) These proved to contain pornographic photographs—including nine of Lesley Ann Downey—the tape of Lesley Ann pleading to be allowed to leave, various books on sex and torture, and wigs, coshes and notes on robbing banks. Other photographs led them to dig on the moors, where the bodies of Lesley Ann Downey and John Kilbride were recovered.

* * *

On May 6, 1966, Ian Brady and Myra Hindley were both sentenced to life imprisonment. There had been no confession—this was to come many years later, Brady to the journalist Fred Harrison, and then Myra to Topping. At the time, Brady maintained that Lesley had been brought to the house by two men, who had taken her away after taking the photographs. It was not until July 1987 that Brady returned to the moor, under police escort, and tried—without success—to help locate the body of Keith Bennett. Pauline Reade had already been located, with the help of Myra's confession.

It is easy to understand why the Moors murders have "tormented the psyche of a nation" for more than a quarter of a century. Like the Jack the Ripper murders, they seem to embody some of our worst nightmares about human cruelty. Brady has often been described as "Britain's most hated murderer." But our business is not to dwell on the horror, but to try to understand how it came about.

After she attended the trial, Pamela Hansford Johnson wrote a book about it called *On Iniquity*. Her argument was that Brady and Hindley seemed totally "affectless," totally without feeling. This view sounds plausible enough until we recall that both killers had an enormous affection for animals, and that when she learned that her dog had died in police custody, Myra burst out: "They're just a lot of bloody murderers." She was equally upset by the death of her sister Maureen's baby. And Brady's affection for his mother and stepmother—as well as for Myra—indicates that he possessed the same human feelings as the rest of us. Harrison reveals that after the arrest, he did his best to dissociate Myra from the crimes.

In fact, from the criminological view, the main interest of the Moors case is that it reveals so clearly the basic psychological patterns of a certain type of antisocial behavior.

One of the fundamental problems of human beings, particularly in adolescence, is to discover "who they are." The certainties of childhood are behind them; they face an adult world in which they have to play an active part. But unless they happen to be lucky enough to have clear "role models," or to have acquired some basic enthusiasm (like art or science) in childhood or early teens, their identity remains a kind of blank, like a gap on a census form, waiting for someone to fill in a name.

In the case of a dominant male, the question is particularly acute. Biological studies have established that approximately one in twenty of any animal group is "dominant"—that is, 5 percent. The dominant 5 percent are, on the whole, natural leaders. They crave a means of expressing their dominance. Those of purely physical dominance may establish a place in life by sheer force of personality. In childhood, Brady seems to have established this kind of dominance over his contemporaries. But in his teens, it ceased to be so simple. Fred Harrison comments: "Ian Brady knew that he was special. He did not *feel* the same way as ordinary people . . ." The word "outsider" turns up with monotonous regularity. An American serial killer, Douglas Clark, expressed it in another way: "I march to a different drummer."

Although Brady's background was less stressful than that of Panzram, it is clear that the two years in Borstal produced much the same effect as Panzram's early periods of imprisonment: a feeling that "authority" was the enemy, and that the insult would not be forgotten or forgiven.

The years of his late teens, when he read Dostoevsky, Nietzsche, Sade, and *Mein Kampf*, were a period of intellectual ferment in which he seems to have begun to perceive the outline of his "real identity." The influence of *Mein Kampf* can hardly be underestimated. Even its title—my struggle—helps to explain the profound influence it still exercises among youthful right-wingers who would indignantly reject the label of "Naza thugs." To these enthusiasts, it is a kind of archetypal Hollywood success story, the autobiography of an "outsider" with all the cards stacked against him, who somehow succeeded in imposing his own vision on the world. And certainly, it is as impossible to deny Hitler's intelligence as to deny Brady's. Moreover, with his admiration of Goethe, Beethoven, Nietzsche, Wagner, it is also impossible to deny that he must be described as an "idealist."

The fly in the ointment is, of course, the racism. Any normally intelligent person knows that it is impossible to generalize about any racial group. Yet Hitler's "conspiracy" theory about Zionism and Marxism looks plausible because there is undoubtedly an element of truth in it. Swallow that particular gnat, and you are ready to swallow the camel of antisemitism and black inferiority. And then suddenly everything looks marvelously simple. It is merely necessary to embrace nationalism and racial purity to have a marvelously clear vision of a utopian society in which "outsiders" are not suppressed and ignored.

This kind of oversimplification is not confined to "fascists." Bernard Shaw tells how, as a poverty-stricken young man, he attended a lecture by the socialist Henry George and bought a copy of his book *Progress and Poverty*. It had upon him exactly the same effect as *Mein Kampf* on Ian Brady.

Thus a bee, desperately striving to reach a flower bed through a window pane, concludes that he is the victim of evil spirits or that he is mad, his end being exhaustion, despair and death. Yet if he only knew, there is nothing wrong with him; all he has to do is to go out as he came in, through the open window or door . . . Your born Communist begins like the bee on the pane. He worries himself and everybody else until he dies of peevishness, or is led by some propagandist pamphlet . . . to investigate the structure of our society. Immediately everything becomes clear to him. Property is theft; respectability founded on property is blasphemy; marriage founded on property is prostitution; it is easier for a camel to go through the eye of a needle than for a rich man to enter the kingdom of heaven. He now knows where he is, and where this society that has so intimated him is.

Shaw swallowed socialism; Brady swallowed Nazism. As it happened, Shaw's socialism did not lead him to acts of violence because, as a born writer, he was an instinctive self-actualizer. But many members of Red Brigades and People's Liberation Armies use socialism as a justification for acts of violence, even murder—all in the name of the future utopia.

With *Mein Kampf*, Brady had a creed, but not an identity. It was the relationship with Myra that seems to have caused this to crystallize. The German jurist Rosenstock-Huessy said: "Even a man who believes in nothing needs a girl to believe in him." Quite apart from the sexual drive—which is usually overpowering in those of high dominance—the admiration of a member of the opposite sex is like a mirror in which a man can see his own face.

But the "mirror" also represents a call to action, a demand that the dominant male should *assert* his identity. So far he may have been content to regard "society" from a distance, the aloof outsider, happy to nurse his own sense of superiority, and to daydream of the world at his feet. But when a girl accepts his dominance, it becomes urgently necessary to *do* something to justify her admiration. The ideal would be something that brings instant wealth and fame.

Now, unlike Shaw, Brady had no means of achieving this. Under different circumstances, he might have turned his latent rebelliousness to account in the manner of Sade and Jean

Genet—in literature of defiance. Unfortunately, although highly articulate (and the winner of essay prizes at school) Brady had never seen himself as a writer. Neither had he ever developed any early enthusiasm—for science, for art, for acting—that might have offered an outlet for his frustrated energies. But the two years in Borstal had offered him a kind of identity: as a criminal. As he read Nietzsche and *Mein Kampf*, he conceived himself as a kind of samurai, one who stands out from society because of his self-discipline and will-power.

With Myra, a normal girl of medium dominance who regarded him as a superior being, the need for a "project" became urgent. It had to be crime, but not petty crime: something more like the Great Train Robbery. And meanwhile, while he looked around for the right opportunity, the philosophy of crime had to be put into effect on a smaller scale.

The murder of Pauline Reade was clearly a watershed. He obviously regarded it as an act of self-creation, Nietzsche's "how one becomes what one is." It involved not only dominance and self-assertion, but also risk and danger—almost like Russian roulette. After the murder, there could be no doubt who he was: he was the man who had the courage to set himself apart from society, to do what others did not dare to do, to take a risk that might bring him to the gallows. (At that time there was still capital punishment in England.) Like Raskolnikov's murder, it was a "definitive act," an act as meaningful as a monk's vows of renunciation or a general's attempt at a *coup d'état*. Now, in a sense, there could be no going back. The face that looks out of the police photograph seems to express that attitude: the eyes staring straight into the camera, the mouth firm but slightly contemptuous.

Yet in just over two years, an unexpected problem arose. Harrison records it in Brady's own words: "I felt old at 26. Everything was ashes. I felt there was nothing of interest—nothing to hook myself onto. I had experienced everything."

Lord Byron had similarly declared that his early initiation into sex—by a maidservant at the age of 9—was responsible for his later tendency to satiety and melancholy: "having anticipated life."

But the problem is simpler than that. Everyone is familiar with it. Experience is "interesting" only in so far as we put a certain effort, a certain *attention*, into it. If I really want to enjoy an experience, the best way is to think about it in advance, to build up anticipation, so that when it actually happens, I give it my full and complete attention. If I approach my experience in a casual way, taking it for granted, it soon palls. If we do not wish to be subject to this law of diminishing returns, we have to put as much into experience as we get out of it. This explains the apparently irrational behavior of saints and ascetics, starving themselves and sleeping on bare boards. A man who is starving finds a crust and a glass of water as delicious as the most expensive meal, because discomfort has *stretched* his attention. This stretching of attention is like stretching a spring, or pulling back a rifle bolt: it charges the mind with vital energy. And if he could learn this trick of "stretching" his attention, he could enjoy everything with the same intensity, even at the age of 90. Conversely, a youth of 16 can experience boredom and satiety by habitually relaxing the attention, taking experience for granted.

Sex is a particularly interesting case in point. Because the appetite is so powerful, we assume that it is analogous to the appetite for food, which is basically physical. In fact, as we have seen, it is almost entirely "mental," based on a sense of "forbiddenness." A man who badly wants a girl can work up an "appetite" so powerful that she seems like a goddess, an embodiment of the eternal feminine, and the very thought of possessing her produces a foretaste of ecstasy. But because sex contains such a large mental component, it can collapse into boredom if the element of "preparedness," of focused attention, is neglected.

Sex crime is particularly subject to this law of diminishing returns. Just as the starving man imagines that three good meals a day would leave him totally satisfied, just as the tramp imagines that a country cottage would make him blissfully happy, so a sex-starved man imagines that a certain sexual abundance would bring total fulfillment. All three are mistaken, because as soon as one level of need is fulfilled, another opens up.

In Brady's case, the problem was complicated by the need to crystallize a sense of identity and purpose—Maslow's self-esteem level. He was intelligent, determined, strong-willed— but was not sure what to *do* with these qualities—a situation that must have reminded him of one of his favorite fictional characters, Dostoevsky's Stavrogin in *The Possessed*. At the age of 23, Brady urgently needed a "project." And the only project he had been trained in was crime.

Matters were further complicated by his almost Wordsworthian mysticism about nature. (He has stated that *The Prelude* is one of his favorite poems.) Harrison describes how, when he wanted to talk about the murders, Brady only wanted to tell him about a childhood trip to Oban and Tobermory, which he had found enchanting. He also records that David Smith had difficulty in sharing Brady's sense of beauty in miles of black peat moors. Such an obsession obviously belongs to Maslow's self-actualizing level. And what distinguishes the self-actualizer—or "outsider"—is a tormented need for self-expression.

In short, Ian Brady was a powder-keg waiting to explode. All that was needed was a match. Myra Hindley provided the match; the moment he met her, *some* kind of violence became inevitable.

The reason for this lies in the psychology of what has been

called *folie à deux*. In most murders involving two killers—other cases are Leopold and Loeb and Fernandez and Beck—there is almost invariably a leader and a follower, one of high dominance, one of medium dominance.

Maslow was also one of the first to grasp the immense significance of patterns of dominance behavior. It all sprang from his observation of monkeys in the Bronx Zoo in the mid-1930s. He was at this time puzzling about the relative merits of Freud and Adler: Freud with his view that all neurosis is sexual in origin, Adler with his belief that man's life is a fight against the feeling of inferiority, and that his mainspring is his "will-to-power." In the Bronx Zoo, he was struck by the dominance behavior of the monkeys and by the non-stop sex. He was puzzled that sexual behavior seemed so indiscriminate: males mounted females or other males; females mounted other females and even males. There was also a distinct "pecking order," the more dominant monkeys bullying the less dominant. There seemed to be as much evidence for Freud's theory as for Adler's. Then, one day, a revelation burst upon Maslow. Monkey sex *looked* indiscriminate because the more dominant monkeys mounted the less dominant ones, whether male or female. Maslow concluded, therefore, that Adler was right and Freud was wrong—about this matter at least.

Since dominance behavior seemed to be the key to monkey psychology, Maslow wondered how far this applied to human beings. He decided to study dominance behavior in human beings and, since he was a young and heterosexual male, decided that he would prefer to study women rather than men. Besides, he felt that women were usually more honest when it came to talking about their private lives. In 1936, he began a series of interviews with college women; his aim was to find out whether sex and dominance are related. He quickly concluded that they were.

The women tended to fall into three distinct groups: high-dominance, medium-dominance and low-dominance, the high-dominance group being the smallest of the three. High-dominance women tended to be promiscuous and to enjoy sex for its own sake—in a manner we tend to regard as distinctly masculine. They were more likely to masturbate, sleep with different men, and have lesbian experiences. Medium-dominance women were basically romantics; they might have a strong sex drive, but their sexual experience was usually limited. They were looking for "Mr. Right," the kind of man who would bring them flowers and take them out for dinner in restaurants with soft lights and sweet music. Low-dominance women seemed actively to dislike sex, or to think of it as an unfortunate necessity for producing children. One low-dominance woman with a high sex drive refused to permit her husband sexual intercourse because she disliked children. Low-dominance women tended to be prudes who were shocked at nudity and regarded the male sexual organ as disgusting. (High-dominance women thought it beautiful.)

Their choice of males was dictated by the dominance group. High-dominance women like high-dominance males, the kind who would grab them and hurl them on a bed. They seemed to like their lovers to be athletic, rough and unsentimental. Medium-dominance women liked kindly, home-loving males, the kind who smoke a pipe and look calm and reflective. They would prefer a romantic male, but were prepared to settle for a hard worker of reliable habits. Low-dominance women were distrustful of all males, although they usually wanted children and recognized that a man had to be pressed into service for this purpose. They preferred the kind of gentle, shy man who would admire them from a distance for years without daring to speak.

But Maslow's most interesting observation was that *all* the women, in all dominance groups, preferred a male who was slightly more dominant than themselves. One very high-dominance woman spent years looking for a man of superior dominance—meanwhile having many affairs; and once she found him, married him and lived happily ever after. However, she enjoyed picking fights with him, provoking him to violence that ended in virtual rape; and this sexual experience she found the most satisfying of all. Clearly, even this man was not *quite* dominant enough, and she was provoking him to an artificially high level of dominance.

The rule seemed to be that, for a permanent relationship, a man and woman needed to be in the same dominance group. Medium-dominance women were nervous of high-dominance males, and low-dominance women were terrified of medium-dominance males. As to the males, they might well show a sexual interest in a woman of a lower dominance group, but it would not survive the act of seduction. A medium-dominance woman might be superficially attracted by a high-dominance male; but on closer acquaintance she would find him brutal and unromantic. A high-dominance male might find a medium-dominance female "beddable," but closer acquaintance would reveal her as rather uninteresting, like an unseasoned meal. To achieve a personal relationship, the two would need to be in the same dominance group. Maslow even devised psychological tests to discover whether the "dominance gap" between a man and a woman was of the right size to form the basis of a permanent relationship.

It was some time after writing a book about Maslow (*New Pathways in Psychology*, published in 1972) that it dawned on me that this matter of the "dominance gap" threw an interesting light on many cases of partnership in crime. The first case of the sort to arouse my curiosity was that of Albert T. Patrick, a scoundrelly New York lawyer who, in 1900, persuaded a manservant named Charles Jones to kill his employer with chloroform. Jones had been picked out of the gutter by his employer, a rich old man named William Rice, and had every reason to be grateful to him. Yet he quickly came under Patrick's spell and took part in the plot to murder and defraud. The plot misfired; both were arrested. The police placed them in adjoining cells. Patrick handed Jones a knife saying "You cut your throat first and I'll follow . . ." Jones was so completely under Patrick's domination that he did not even pause to wonder how Patrick would get the knife back. A gurgling noise alerted the police, who were able to foil the attempted suicide. Patrick was sentenced to death but was eventually pardoned and released.

How did Patrick achieve such domination? There was no sexual link between them, and he was not blackmailing Jones. But what becomes very clear from detailed accounts of the case is that Patrick was a man of extremely high dominance, while Jones was quite definitely of medium dominance. It was Patrick's combination of charm and dominance that exerted such a spell.

It struck me that in many cases of duo-murder (partnership in murder), one of the partners is usually high-dominance and the other medium—as already noted, Loeb and Leopold even referred to themselves as "master and slave." It is true that the Lonely Hearts murders—Fernandez and Beck—are slightly less simple: Fernandez *was* the dominant one of the pair, with his belief that he could hypnotize women and seduce them by magic; yet it was Martha who dragged him into murder. And in the Moors case, Myra's chin alone reveals that she was a woman of fairly high dominance, so Brady's claim that she took an active role in the murders sounds plausible. Yet it is still perfectly obvious that Brady was the dominant one, and that Myra was putty in his hands.

The simple truth seems to be that in most cases of *folie à deux*, neither partner would be capable of murder if it were not for the stimulus of the other. Some strange chemical reaction seems to occur, like a mixture of nitric acid and glycerine that makes nitroglycerine.

One of the most interesting examples of the syndrome was the Thurneman case, which occurred in Sweden in the 1930s. Dr. Sigvard Thurneman was a psychiatrist—and a hypnotist—who saw himself as a kind of Professor Moriarty. Between 1930 and 1936, a series of robberies and murders occurred in the area of Sala, near Stockholm. A man named Eriksson was found shot in a frozen lake. A wealthy mining official named Kjellberg was found, together with his housekeeper, in his burnt home, shot in the head, and a safe full of wages had been forced. A woman named Blomqvist was found in her burnt home, her jewelry missing. But when, in June 1936, a quarryman carrying the payroll was murdered, an elderly man heard the shot, and saw an American car driving away.

Newspaper publicity led the thieves to panic and abandon the car by the roadside; it then became clear that its number plates had been altered by a professional. This man was tracked down in a routine investigation of garages, and implicated his employer, a man named Hedstrom. Hedstrom denied it, but as soon as the police left, rang a number in Stockholm—Dr. Sigvard Thurneman. The police had tapped his phone, and went to call on Thurneman—a young man in his late twenties with a receding chin and a high forehead, not unlike the pictures of Moriarty. He flatly denied knowing anything about the crimes.

It was Hedstrom who decided to confess, when one of the murder guns was found in his garage. He and Thurneman had met at the University of Uppsala, where Thurneman had been fascinated by hypnosis and occultism. Thurneman had also spent a great deal of time planning "perfect crimes." The first victim, Eriksson, had become one of Thurneman's patients, and had been regularly hypnotized for nervous problems. He had agreed to take part in a robbery, but had changed his mind at the last moment; this is why he had been killed. A number of crimes—including the murders and several robberies—had then been committed by Hedstrom and other patients of Thurneman.

Faced with Hedstrom's confession, Thurneman decided to tell everything. He even wrote an autobiography in prison, telling the whole incredible story of his domination of the gang by hypnosis. It might be used by Adlerian psychologists as a classic demonstration of the way that physical inferiority—Thurneman was a sickly and undersized child—can lead to over-compensation. Thurneman had studied yoga, then occultism, and finally become a cult leader. He seduced underage girls under hypnosis then disposed of them in the white slave trade. A bisexual, he caused one of his male lovers to commit suicide by hypnotic suggestion. He induced a deep trance in another gang member and injected a fatal dose of poison.

His aim was to become a millionaire and retire to South America, and at the time of his arrest he was planning to rob a Stockholm bank by blowing it open with a huge quantity of dynamite.

Thurneman and four accomplices were sentenced to life imprisonment, but Thurneman soon became unmistakably insane, and was transferred to a criminal lunatic asylum.

Here we have a very clear parallel with the Brady case—in some ways, Thurneman was what Brady might have hoped to become, if his career had not been cut short by David Smith's decision to go to the police.

A curiously similar case took place in Copenhagen in 1951, when a man named Palle Hardrup killed two bank officials in the course of an unsuccessful hold-up. The police were tipped off that the real killer was a man named Bjorn Nielsen, who had absolute and total control of Hardrup, whom he had met in prison. Faced with Nielsen in the police interrogation room, Hardrup seemed to go into a trance, in which he insisted that Nielsen had nothing to do with the crime. But a policeman noticed that Nielsen was holding up two crossed fingers. Hardrup's wife also stated that Nielsen had gained total ascendancy over her husband, and that he had done this through hypnosis. She told how Nielsen had stripped her and flogged her with a leather belt, while her normally admiring husband looked on.

In police custody, Hardrup periodically improved—until he received a letter from Nielsen signed with an X, at which he would revert to his trance-like insistence that he alone was guilty. A police psychiatrist was able to establish that Hardrup had been hypnotically conditioned to go into a trance when he saw an X.

Finally, kept away from Nielsen—and Xs—Hardrup suddenly demanded paper, and wrote a confession describing how Nielsen had become his "master" through hypnosis, and now, under Nielsen's orders, he had committed an earlier robbery and handed Nielsen the complete proceeds—£5,000. The police were able to establish that this had been paid into Nielsen's bank the day after the robbery.

In court, with Nielsen's blazing eyes fixed upon him, Hardrup withdrew his confession, but the jury—who had noted this change of demeanor—decided that Nielsen was the real culprit, and sentenced him to life imprisonment. Hardrup was placed in a psychiatric hospital.

In these two cases involving hypnosis, we seem to be in the presence of the archetypal criminal daydream: to be able to commit crime by proxy, and to have complete control of the human robot who is the instrument of the super-criminal. The assumption that underlies the daydream is expressed by Harry Lime, in Graham Greene's *The Third Man*, in the scene on the

Big Wheel in Vienna. When the hero reproaches him with selling adulterated life-saving drugs that actually cause death, Lime points to the people "moving like black flies" on the ground, and asks: "Would you really feel any pity if one of those dots stopped moving for ever? If I said you can have twenty thousand pounds for every dot that stops, would you really tell me to keep my money?" Sade's argument is basically identical: human beings are fundamentally selfish. We cannot feel love—or even interest—towards people we have never met. So why pretend that all men are brothers? Why not accept the truth: that we all care for "number one," and only care for others in so far as it suits us?

There is an obvious element of truth in this, or someone as intelligent as Sade—or Brady—would not have been taken in by it. But it misses the essential point. Self-actualization is basically about the *control of consciousness*. It brings a curious sense of power over oneself, and an awareness of the immense *meaningfulness* of the external world. Such moments bring the recognition that our usual notions about consciousness are based on a misconception: upon the notion that consciousness proceeds automatically, like a television picture, and that the "you" that watches it is essentially *passive*. Moments of intensity—and even the sexual orgasm must be included—make us aware that we are "in control": that we can alter the brightness, the color, even the speed at which it moves. We are affected by great music, great poetry, great art, because the artist has somehow learned the trick of inducing these moods of intensity and control. It is as if he has changed a black-and-white picture on television into color.

Now, as Sade noted, there are other ways of achieving this sense of control. One of them is sex. Another is manipulating other people. Even eating and drinking can bring this sensation of heightened control. (It is significant that when Sade was confined to the lunatic asylum, he overate until he be-

normal sexual assault. But four of her front teeth were missing. Oddly enough, the teeth had not been knocked out by a blow, but deliberately forced out; a piece of one of them was found lodged in her throat. Medical investigation also revealed the presence of male sperm in her throat. Here, then, was the cause of death; she had been choked by a penis, probably in the course of performing an act of fellatio. The missing teeth suggested that the killer had repeated the assault after death. It was established that she had disappeared some days before her body was found. Where, then, had her body been kept? Flakes of paint found on her skin suggested the answer, for it was the type of paint used in spraying cars. Clearly, the body had been kept somewhere near a car spraying plant, but in some place where it was not likely to be discovered by the workers.

The "nude murders" became a public sensation, for it now seemed likely that they were the work of one man. Enormous numbers of police were deployed in the search for the sprayshop, and in an attempt to keep a closer watch on the areas in which the three victims had been picked up—around Notting Hill and Shepherds Bush. Perhaps for this reason, the killer decided to take no risks for several months.

The body of the fourth victim—Mary Fleming, aged 30—found on July 14, confirmed that the same man was probably responsible for all four murders. Her false teeth were missing; there was sperm in her throat; and her skin showed traces of the same spray paint. She had vanished three days earlier.

Her body was found, in a half-crouching position, near a garage in Acton, and the van was actually seen leaving the scene of the crime. A motorist driving past Berrymede Road, a cul-de-sac, at 5:30 in the morning, had to brake violently to avoid a van that shot out in front of him. He was so angry that he contacted the police to report the incident. If he had made a note of the van number, the nude case would have been solved.

A squad car that arrived a few minutes later found the body of Mary Fleming in the forecourt of a garage in the cul-de-sac.

The near-miss probably alarmed the killer, for no more murders occurred that summer. Then, on November 25, 1964, another naked body was found under some debris on a car park at Hornton Street, Kensington. She was identified as Margaret McGowan, 21, a Scot. Under the name Frances Brown, she had been called as a witness in the trial of Stephen Ward, and Ludovic Kennedy described her (in his book on the trial) as a small, bird-like woman with a pale face and fringe. Margaret McGowan had disappeared more than a month before her body was found, and there were signs of decomposition. Again, there were traces of paint, and a missing front tooth indicated that she had died in the same way as the previous two victims.

The last of the stripper's victims was a prostitute named Birdie O'Hara, 28. She was found on February 16, 1965, in some undergrowth on the Heron Trading Estate, in Acton. She had last been seen on January 11, in the Shepherds Bush Hotel. The body was partly mummified, which indicated that it had been kept in a cool place. As usual, teeth were missing, and sperm was found in the throat. Fingermarks on the back of her neck revealed that, like the other victims, she had died in a kneeling position, bent over the killer's lap.

Detective Chief Superintendent John du Rose was recalled from his holiday to take charge of the investigation in the Shepherds Bush area. The Heron Trading Estate provided the lead they had bee waiting for. Investigation of a paint spray shop revealed that this was definitely the source of the paint found on the bodies—chemical analysis proved it. The proximity of a disused warehouse solved the question of where the bodies had lain before they were dumped. The powerful spray guns caused the paint to carry, with diminishing intensity, for several hundred yards. Analysis of paint on the bodies enabled experts to establish the spot where the women must have been concealed: it was underneath a transformer in the warehouse.

Yet even with this discovery, the case was far from solved. Thousands of men worked on the Heron Trading Estate. (Oddly enough Christie had been employed there.) Mass questioning seemed to bring the police no closer to their suspect. Du Rose decided to throw an immense twenty-mile cordon around the area, to keep a careful check on all cars passing through at night. Drivers who were observed more than once were noted; if they were seen more than twice, they were interviewed. Du Rose conducted what he called "a war of nerves" against the killer, dropping hints in the press or on television that indicated the police were getting closer. They knew he drove a van; they knew he must have right of access to the trading estate by night. The size of the victims—who were all short women—suggested that the killer was under middle height. As the months passed, and no further murders took place, du Rose assumed that he was winning the war of nerves. The killer had ceased to operate. He checked on all men who had been jailed since mid-February, all men with prison records who had been hospitalized, all men who had died or committed suicide. In his book *Murder Was My Business*, du Rose claims that a list of twenty suspects had been reduced to three when one of the three committed suicide. He left a note saying that he could not bear the strain any longer. The man was a security guard who drove a van, and had access to the estate. At the time when the women were murdered, his rounds included the spray shop. He worked by night, from 10 p.m. to 6 a.m. He was unmarried.

Another serial killer of the 1960s provides an interesting—and virtually unique—illustration of the same mechanism.

Between June 1962 and January 1964 the city of Boston, Massachusetts was terrorized by a series of murders that achieved worldwide publicity. The unknown killer, who strangled and sexually abused his victims, became known as the Boston Strangler. The first six victims were elderly women, whose ages ranged from 55 to 85.

On June 4, 1962 55-year-old Anna Slesers was found in her apartment in the Back Bay area of Boston. She had been knocked unconscious with a blunt instrument—later determined to be a lead weight—and then strangled. The body, clad only in an open housecoat, was lying on its back with the legs apart. No semen was found in the vagina, but she had evidently been sexually assaulted with some hard object such as a soda bottle. The apartment had been ransacked.

Two weeks later on June 30, 68-year-old Nina Nichols failed to call back a friend after a telephone conversation had been interrupted by a ring at the doorbell. The friend asked the janitor to check her apartment. Nina Nichols was lying on the bedroom floor, strangled with a stocking, her legs open in a rape position. Her killer had also bitten her. Medical examination revealed that she had been sexually assaulted with a wine bottle after death. There was semen on her thighs, but not in the vagina.

Two days later, on Monday, July 2, neighbors of a 65-year-old retired nurse named Helen Blake, who lived in Lynn, north of Boston, became anxious at not having seen her for two days, and sent for the police. Helen Blake was lying face downwards on her bed, a stocking knotted around her throat. Again, there was dried semen on her thighs but not in the vagina. Mrs. Blake had apparently been killed on the previous Saturday, the same day as Nina Nichols.

On August 21, Mrs. Ida Irga, 75, was found dead in her apartment. Death was due to manual strangulation, after which a pillow case had been tied round her neck. She had been sexually assaulted with some hard object, and bitten. It was estimated that she had been dead for two days.

The last of the elderly victims was 67-year-old Jane Sullivan, another nurse. She was found in a kneeling position in the bathtub, her face in six inches of water. She was a powerful Irishwoman, and had evidently put up a tremendous fight—her assailant must have been very strong to overpower her. Two stockings were knotted around her neck. She had been killed on the day after Ida Irga, but the body was not found for more than a week; consequently it was impossible to determine whether she had been raped, but she had been sexually assaulted with a broom handle.

Boston was in a state of hysteria, but as weeks went by without further stranglings, it slowly subsided. A hot summer was succeeded by a very cold winter. In the early evening of December 5, 1962 two girls rang the doorbell of the apartment they shared with a 20-year-old black girl, Sophie Clark, and were surprised when she failed to answer. They let themselves in, and found Sophie lying on the floor; she was naked and in the rape position. She had been strangled with nylon stockings knotted round her neck. Medical examination established that she had been raped, and a semen stain on the carpet beside the body indicated that her killer had later masturbated over her. This was the first case in which rape was unquestionably established, and it led to the speculation that her killer was a second Boston Strangler, one who preferred young girls.

Three weeks later, on the last day of 1962, a businessman stopped his car outside the apartment of his secretary at 515 Park Drive and blew his horn. When she failed to come down, he assumed that she had already left, but when he found that she was not at the office, he rang the superintendent of her apartment building to ask him to check on her apartment. Patricia Bissette, 23, was lying in bed, covered with the bedclothes. She had been strangled with stockings, and medical examination established that she had been raped.

On February 18, 1963 a German girl named Gertrude Gruen survived an attack by the Strangler. A powerfully built man with a beaky nose, about five feet eight inches tall, knocked on her door and told her he had been sent to do work in her apartment. She was suffering from a virus, and only allowed him in after some argument. The man removed his coat and told her that she was pretty enough to be a model. Then he told her she had dust on the back of her dressing gown; she turned, and he hooked a powerful arm round her neck. She fought frantically, and sank her teeth into his hand until they bit to the bone. The man pushed her away, and as she began to scream, he ran out of the apartment.

The police were excited when the girl reported the attack—and then frustrated when they discovered that the shock had wiped all traces of the Strangler's face from her memory.

A month later, on March 9, 1963, the Strangler killed another elderly victim. Sixty-nine-year-old Mrs. Mary Brown lived in Lawrence, an industrial town twenty-five miles from Boston. The fact that her breasts had been exposed and a fork stuck in one of them should have suggested that she had been murdered by the "Phantom" (as the press had now labeled the killer). However, because her skull had been beaten to a pulp with a piece of brass piping, she was not recognized as a Strangler victim—it was assumed that she had disturbed a burglar. In fact, she had been manually throttled.

The next victim was also nontypical. On May 9, 1963 a friend of 23-year-old graduate student Beverly Sams was puzzled when she failed to answer the telephone, and borrowed a key from the building supervisor. Beverly had been stabbed in the throat, and a stocking knotted around her neck. She was naked, and her legs spreadeagled and tied to the bed supports. Medical examination revealed that she had been raped.

Four months later, on September 8, friends of 58-year-old divorcee, Evelyn Corbin, wondered why she failed to keep a lunch appointment and let themselves into her flat. Evelyn Corbin was lying almost naked on the bed, nylon stockings knotted around her throat and her panties rammed into her mouth. There was semen in her vagina and in her mouth.

On November 23, 1963, the day President Kennedy was assassinated, the Strangler killed his next victim in Lawrence. She was Joanne Graff, a Sunday school teacher. She had been strangled with stockings and raped.

The final victim was strangled on January 4, 1964. She was 19-year-old Mary Sullivan, who was found by roommates when they came back from work. She was sitting on the bed, her buttocks on the pillow, her back against the headboard. Her knees had been parted, and a broom handle inserted into her vagina. Semen was running from the corner of her mouth. A card saying "Happy New Year" had been propped against her foot. The killer had placed her body in a position where it would be seen as soon as anyone opened the door.

The murders ceased; but a rapist who became known as The Green Man—because he wore green clothes—began operating over a wide area that included Massachusetts, Connecticut, New Hampshire and Rhode Island. On one occasion he raped four women in a single day. He gained entrance to the apartment—sometimes forcing the lock with a strip of plastic—and often threatened the victim with a knife. When she was stripped, he would caress her with his hands and mouth; then, if he judged she wanted him to, he "raped" her. (He was later to insist that the "Green Man" had never raped an unwilling woman.) He was never physically violent, and had even been known to apologize before he left.

On the morning of October 27, 1964 a young married woman was dozing in bed after her husband had gone to work when a man entered the bedroom. He was dressed in green trousers, a green shirt, and wore green sunglasses, and he insisted that he was a detective. After seizing her by the throat he threatened her with a knife. He tore off her nightclothes, stuffed a pair of panties into her mouth, and tied her wrists and ankles to the bedposts. Then he kissed and bit her from head to foot, finally ejaculating on her stomach. His sexual appetite was obviously enormous; he continued to abuse her sexually for a great deal longer before he seemed satisfied. Then, after apologizing, he left. The girl called the police immediately, and went on to describe her assailant in such detail that a police artist was able to make a sketch of his face. As one of the detectives was studying it, he commented: "This looks like the Measuring Man." The "Measuring Man" had been a harmless crank named Albert DeSalvo, who had been arrested in 1960 for talking his way into girls' apartments claiming to represent a modeling agency. If the girl indicated that she might be interested in modeling, he would take her measurements with a tape measure. After that he would thank her politely and leave. The aspiring model would never hear from him again, and it was this that made some of them so indignant that they reported him. The police were baffled, since there seemed to be no obvious motive—although some girls admitted that they had allowed him to raise their skirts to measure from the hip to the knee. On a few occasions, he had allowed himself an intimate caress; but if the girl protested, he immediately apologized. One girl, as he crouched with his hand on her panties, had said: "I'd better get these clothes off or you won't get the right measurements," and stripped. On this occasion, as on a number of others, the "Measuring Man" had ended up in bed with the girl.

On March 17, 1960 a police patrol that had been set up to trap the "Measuring Man" saw a man acting suspiciously in a backyard in Cambridge, Mass., and arrested him. Girls identified him as the "Measuring Man," and he finally admitted it—claiming that he did it as a kind of lark, in order to make himself feel superior to college-educated girls. In May 1961

DeSalvo was sentenced to serve two years in the Middlesex County House of Correction. He served eleven months before being released. He had told a probation officer that he thought there was something wrong with him—that he seemed to be wildly oversexed, so that he needed intercourse six or more times a day. No one suggested that he needed to see a psychiatrist.

Albert DeSalvo had clearly graduated from caressing girls as he measured them to rape. He was arrested on November 5, 1964 and identified by some of his victims. On February 4, 1965 he was committed to the Bridgewater State Hospital, a mental institution in Massachusetts.

Bridgewater had—and still has—many sexual psychopaths in residence, and many spoke freely about their exploits, particularly in the group therapy sessions. Albert DeSalvo was not reticent about his own sexual prowess, which was apparently considerable. He described how, in the summer of 1948, when he was 17, he had worked as a dishwasher in a Cape Cod motel, and spent much time swimming and sunbathing on the beach. There were many college girls there, and they found the powerfully built youth attractive. Word of De-Salvo's amazing sexual prowess soon spread. "They would even come up to the motel sometimes looking for me and some nights we would spend the whole night doing it down on the beach, stopping for a while, then doing it again . . . "

Possibly because he encountered a certain skepticism—he had a reputation as a boaster—DeSalvo began hinting that he had done far more serious things than raping a few women. Only one of his ward-mates took him seriously: a murderer called George Nassar. At first, Nassar also thought DeSalvo was merely boasting—particularly when he confided that he was the Boston Strangler. What finally convinced him was DeSalvo's detailed knowledge of the crimes. "He knows more about them stranglings than the cops."

Nassar knew there was a large reward for the Boston Strangler, and he spoke to his attorney, F. Lee Bailey, who had achieved fame when he obtained freedom for Dr. Sam Sheppard, accused of murdering his wife. Bailey was also skeptical—there are endless fake confessions to almost every widely publicized murder—but when he went to see DeSalvo on March 4, 1965, he soon realized that this sounded authentic. DeSalvo was not a man of high intelligence—although bright and articulate—and it seemed unlikely that he could have read and memorized newspaper accounts of the murders. He even mentioned a murder that no one knew about— an old lady of 80 or so who had died of a heart attack as he grabbed her. In fact, DeSalvo's account enabled the police to identify her as 85-year-old Mary Mullens who had been found dead in her Boston apartment two weeks after the murder of Anna Slesers, the first Strangler victim. DeSalvo's descriptions of other murder scenes made it clear that he knew details that had never been published. Most important of all, he knew exactly what the Strangler had done to various victims. This information had been deliberately suppressed, giving rise to all kind of wild rumors of torture and perversion. DeSalvo knew, for example, precisely what position Mary Sullivan—the last victim— had been left in, and that she had a broom handle inserted into her vagina; and he was able to describe in precise detail the rooms of most of the victims.

There were some odd complications. Several witnesses who had seen a man entering apartment buildings where stranglings had taken place failed to identify DeSalvo as the man. And two women who had seen the Strangler—including Gertrude Gruen, the German girl who had fought him off— not only failed to identify DeSalvo, but identified George Nassar as the strangler. Yet DeSalvo's incredibly detailed knowledge of the crimes finally convinced most of those involved with the case that he alone was the Boston Strangler.

In the long run, all this proved irrelevant. Albert DeSalvo stood trial for the Green Man rapes, and in 1967 was sentenced to permanent detention in the Walpole State Prison, where he could receive psychiatric treatment. On November 26, 1973 DeSalvo was found dead in his cell, stabbed through the heart. No motive was ever established, and whoever was responsible was never caught.

In January 1964, while the Boston Strangler was still at large, the assistant attorney-general of Massachusetts, John S. Bottomly, decided to set up a committee of psychiatrists to attempt to establish some kind of "psychological profile" of the killer. One of the psychiatrists who served on that committee was Dr. James A. Brussel, the man who had been so successful in describing New York's "Mad Bomber." When he attended his first meeting, Brussel discovered that there was a sharp division of opinion within the committee. One group believed that there were two stranglers, one of whom killed old women, and the other young girls; the other group thought there was only one strangler.

It was at his second meeting of the committee—in April 1965—that Brussel was hit by a sudden "hunch" as he listened to a psychiatrist pointing out that in some cases, semen was found in the vagina, while in others it was found on the breasts, thighs, or even on the carpet. When it came to his turn to speak, Brussel outlined the theory that had suddenly come to him "in a flash."

"I think we're dealing with one man. The apparent differences in M.O., I believe, result from changes that have been going on in this man. Over the two-year period during which he has been committing these murders, he had gone through a series of upheavals . . ."

The first five victims, said Brussel, were elderly women, and there was no semen in the vaginas. They had been manipulated in other ways—"a type of sexual molestation that might be expected of a small boy, not a man." A boy gets over his sexual obsession with his mother, and transfers his interest to girls of his own age. "The Strangler . . . achieved this transfer—achieved emotional puberty—in a matter of months." Now he wanted to achieve orgasm inside younger women. And with the final victim, Mary Sullivan, the semen was in her mouth and over her breasts; a broom had been inserted in the vagina. The Strangler was making a gesture of triumph and of defiance: "I throw my sex in your face."

This man, said Brussel, was a physically powerful individual, probably in his late twenties or early thirties, the time the paranoid reaction reaches its peak. He hazarded a guess that the Strangler's nationality was Italian or Spanish, since garrotting is a method used by bandits in both countries.

Brussel's final "guesses" were startlingly to the point. He believed that the Strangler had stopped killing because he had worked it out of his system. He had, in effect, grown up. And he would finally be caught because he would be unable to resist talking about his crimes and his new-found maturity.

The rest of the committee was polite but skeptical. But one year later, Brussel was proved correct when DeSalvo began admitting to George Nassar that he was the Boston Strangler.

In 1966, Brussel went to Boston to interview DeSalvo. He had been half-expecting a misshapen monster, and was surprised to be greeted by a good-looking, polite young man with a magnificent head of dark hair. (Brussel had even foretold that the Strangler would have well-tended hair, since he was obsessed by the impression he made on women.) Brussel found him charming, and soon realized how DeSalvo had talked his way into so many apartments; he seemed a thoroughly nice young man. Then what had turned him into a murderer? As usual, it proved to be the family and childhood background. DeSalvo's father was the worst kind of brute. He beat his wife and children mercilessly—on one occasion he broke his wife's fingers one by one. He beat one son with a hosepipe so badly—for knocking over a box of fruit—that the boy was not allowed on the beach all summer because he was covered in black and yellow bruises. He often brought a prostitute home and had sex with her in front of the children. Their mother was also less than satisfactory. She was indifferent and self-preoccupied, and had no time for the children. As a child Albert had been a "loner," his only real friend a dog that lived in a junkyard. He developed sadistic compulsions at an early age. He and a playmate called Billy used to place a dog and cat in two compartments of an orange crate and starve them for days, then pull out the partition, and watch as the cat scratched out the dog's eyes. But, like so many psychopaths (Albert Fish and Gary Heidnik, for example) he could display considerable charm and make himself liked.

The real key to DeSalvo was sex. From an early age he was insatiable, "walking around with a rail on most of the time, ready to take on any broad or fag come along, or to watch some broad and masturbate . . . thinking about sex a lot, more than anything, and needing it so much all the time. If only somebody could've seen it then and told me it was not normal, even sick . . ." DeSalvo is here exaggerating; a large proportion of healthy young males go around in much the same state. DeSalvo's environment offered a great deal of sexual stimulus. He participated in sex games with his brothers and sisters when he was 5 or 6 years old. At the age of 8 he performed oral sex on a girl at school, and was soon persuading girls to do the same for him. Albert DeSalvo was turned into a sexual psychopath by the same kind of "hothouse environment" that had nurtured Albert Fish. Combined with the lack of moral restraint that resulted from his family background, his tremendous sex urge soon led him to rape—his own estimation was that he had raped or assaulted almost two thousand women. During the course of the Green Man attacks, he raped four women in a single day, and even then tried to pick up a fifth. This was something that Brussel had failed to recognize. The Strangler had not been "searching for his potency"—he had always been potent. During his teens, a woman neighbor had asked him if it was true that he had a permanent erection, and when he modestly admitted it, invited him into her apartment. "She went down on her knees and blowed me and I come almost right off and she said: 'Oh, now you went and come and what am I going to have to get screwed with?,' and I said: 'Don't worry, I'll have a hard on again in a few minutes.'" When he left her, she was exhausted, but he was still unsatisfied. It was not potency DeSalvo was searching for, but emotional stability.

Yet Brussel was undoubtedly correct about the main thing: that DeSalvo's murders were part of an attempt to grow up. The murders of elderly women were acts of revenge against the mother who had rejected him; but the murder of the young black girl Sophie Clark signaled a change. When he knocked on her door DeSalvo had no idea that she would be so young—he was looking for elderly women, like his mother. Her white dress and black stockings excited him. He talked his way into her apartment by claiming to be a workman sent to carry out repairs—the method he invariably used—then, when she turned her back, hooked his arm round her neck and squeezed until she was unconscious. After that he raped her, then strangled her. The experience taught him that he preferred young girls to older women, and caused the change in his method.

Yet from the beginning, DeSalvo suffered from the same problem as so many sex killers: self-division. A month before he killed Anna Slesers—the first victim—DeSalvo talked his way into the apartment of an attractive Swedish girl, claiming that he had been sent to repair the ceiling. "She was laughing and she was very nice. An attractive, kind woman." In the bathroom she turned her back on him, and DeSalvo hooked his powerful forearm round her neck. As he began to squeeze, he saw her face in the bathroom mirror, "the look of awful fear and pain." "And I see myself, the look on my own face . . . and I can't do it. I take my arm away." The girl asked him what he was going to do, and he admitted that he was going to rape her and possibly kill her. "I tell you now that I was ashamed—I began to cry." He fell on his knees in front of her and said: "Oh God, what was I doing? I am a good Catholic man with a wife and children. I don't know what to do . . . Please call the police." The girl told him to go home. "She was a kind person and she was trying to be good to me. But how much better it would have been if she had called the police right then and there." The episode is an interesting confirmation of a theory advanced by Brussel to his fellow committee members: that the Strangler only attacked women who turned their backs on him, because it seemed a form of "rejection."

After killing Sophie Clark, he came very close to sparing his next victim, Patricia Bissette. "She was very nice to me, she treated me like a man—I thought of doing it to her and I talked myself out of it." She offered him coffee, and when he offered to go out and get some doughnuts, told him she had food there. "Then it was as good as over. I didn't want it to happen but then I knew that it would." After he had throttled her into unconsciousness and was raping her, "I want to say that all the time I was doing this, I was thinking about how nice she had been to me and it was making me feel bad. She had treated me right, and I was doing this thing to her . . ."

At other times, Mr. Hyde took over—as in his next murder, that of Mary Brown in Lawrence. This murder was not, at the time, recognized as one of the Strangler's crimes, because its ferocity seemed untypical. DeSalvo described how he had knocked on the door and explained to the gray-haired lady who answered that he had come to paint the kitchen. She let him in without question. In his pocket, DeSalvo had a piece of brass pipe that he had found in the hallway. "As she walked to the kitchen, her back was to me. I hit her right on the back of the head with the pipe . . . this was terrible, and I don't like talking about it. She went down and I ripped her things open, showing her busts . . . she was unconscious and bleeding . . . I don't know why but then I hit her again on the head with the pipe. I kept on hitting and hitting her with the pipe . . . this is like out of this world . . . this is unbelievable . . . oh, it was terrible . . . because her head felt like it was all gone . . . terrible . . . then I took this fork and stuck it into her right bust." As in so many other cases, DeSalvo was unable to say why he did it. (Similarly, he had been unable to explain why he rifled the apartments after committing the murders: he was not looking for anything specific and apparently took nothing.) What he failed to recognize was that, like so many other serial killers, he had been taken over—literally possessed—a sadistic compulsion, the sheer joy of destruction. Yet even as he did it, he continued to feel "This is terrible."

DeSalvo never succeeded in overcoming his feeling of guilt. He intimidated the tenth victim, 23-year-old Beverly Sams, with a knife; she made him promise not to rape her, because she was afraid of pregnancy. When he had her lying on the bed, DeSalvo decided to gag her. "Then I thought that I wouldn't want a broad like that, with her stupid ideas to see me, so I tied a blindfold over her eyes." When she recovered consciousness and discovered that he was raping her, she called him an animal. This enraged him enough to make him stab her. When he could kill like this—giving rein to his resentment—he experienced no guilt.

The last victim, Mary Sullivan, tried to reason with him, to talk him out of rape. Her words struck home. "I recall thinking at the time, yes, she is right, I don't have to do these things any more now . . . I heard what this girl is saying and it stayed with me." At the time he was angry, and hit her several times. As he tied her up and prepared to rape her, he realized "I would never be able to do it again." After raping her, he strangled her manually, while she struggled to get up. "This is what I don't like to talk about. This is killing me even to talk about." After death, her face looked "surprised and even disappointed with the way I had treated her." Then DeSalvo propped her up against the head of the bed, straddled her chest, and masturbated so that the sperm would strike her face. "She is sitting there with the stuff on her nose and mouth and chin. I am not in control of myself. I know that something awful has been done, that the whole world of human beings are shocked and will be even more shocked." He went into the kitchen and fetched a broom, then inserted it into her vagina, "not so far as to hurt her . . . you say it is funny that I worry about hurting her when she is already dead, but that is the truth . . . I do not want to hurt her." And, after leaving the apartment, "as far as I was concerned it wasn't me. I can't explain it to you any other way." When Brussel later pressed him to explain why Mary Sullivan was his final victim, he admitted that she had reminded him of his daughter: Dr. Jekyll was back in control.

That he would now remain in control was demonstrated in a sensational manner. In February 1967, a month after being sentenced to life imprisonment, DeSalvo and two more inmates escaped from the Bridgewater mental institution. The city of Boston was plunged into panic. Interviewed by the press, Brussel was unconcerned. He pointed out that DeSalvo had left a note behind, apologizing for taking unauthorized leave, and explaining that he was only doing so to draw attention to the fact that he was receiving no psychiatric treatment. He promised that he would harm nobody. Brussel stated that he was sure DeSalvo would honor his promise. In fact, DeSalvo gave himself up after only thirty-six hours. His protest failed in its purpose—he was transferred to the virtually escape-proof Walpole Prison, but still failed to receive any psychiatric treatment.

At least Brussel had proved his point. The Boston Strangler had raped and murdered his way to a kind of maturity.

While the Boston Strangler was still at large, an unusual case of serial sex murder was taking place behind the Iron Curtain.

In July 1964, the communist regime in Poland was getting prepared to celebrate the twentieth anniversary of the liberation of Warsaw by Russian troops; a great parade was due to take place in Warsaw on the 22nd. On July 4, the editor of *Przeglad Polityczny*, the Polish equivalent of *Pravda*, received an anonymous letter in spidery red handwriting: "There is no happiness without tears, no life without death. Beware! I am going to make you cry." Marian Starzynski thought the anonymous writer had him in mind, and requested police protection. But on the day of the big parade, a 17-year-old blonde, Danka Maciejowitz, failed to arrive home from a parade organized by the School of Choreography and Folklore in Olsztyn, one hundred and sixty miles north of Warsaw. The next day, a gardener in the Olsztyn Park of Polish Heroes discovered the girl's body in some shrubbery. She had been stripped naked and raped, and the lower part of her body was covered with Jack-the-Ripper-type mutilations. And the following day, the 24th, another red-ink letter was delivered to *Kulisy*, a Warsaw newspaper: "I picked a juicy flower in Olsztyn and I shall do it again somewhere else, for there is no holiday without a funeral." Analysis of the ink showed that it had been made by dissolving red art paint in turpentine.

On January 16, 1965, the Warsaw newspaper *Zycie Warsawy* published the picture of a pretty 16-year-old girl, Aniuta Kaliniak, who had been chosen to lead a parade of students in another celebration rally the following day. She left her home

in Praga, an eastern suburb of Warsaw, and crossed the river
Vistula to reach the parade. Later, she thumbed a lift from a
lorry driver, who dropped her close to her home at a cross-
roads. (The fact that a 16-year-old girl would thumb a lift like
this indicates that the level of sex crime in Poland must be a
great deal lower than in England or the U.S.) The day after the
parade, her body was found in a basement in a leather factory
opposite her home. The killer had removed a grating to get in.
The crime had obviously been carefully planned. He had
waited in the shadows of the wall, and cut off her cry with a
wire noose dropped over her head. In the basement, he had
raped her, and left a six-inch spike sticking in her sexual organs (an echo of the Boston Strangler). While the search went
on another red-ink letter advised the police where to look for
her body.

Olszytn and Warsaw are one hundred and sixty miles apart;
this modern Ripper differed from his predecessor in not sticking to the same area. Moreover, he was a man with a strong
dramatic sense: the selection of national holidays for his
crimes, the letters philosophizing about life and death.

The Red Spider—as he had come to be known, from his
spidery writing—chose All Saints' Day, November 1, for his
next murder, and Poznan, two hundred kilometers west of
Warsaw, as the site. A young, blonde hotel receptionist, Janka
Popielski, was on her way to look for a lift to a nearby village,
where she meant to meet her boyfriend. Since it was her holiday, the freight terminal was almost deserted. Her killer
pressed a chloroform-soaked bandage over her nose and
mouth. Then he removed her skirt, stockings and panties, and
raped her behind a packing shed. After this, he killed her with
a screwdriver. The mutilations were so thorough and revolt-
ing that the authorities suppressed all details. The Red Spider
differed from many sex killers in apparently being totally un-
interested in the upper half of his victims. Janka was stuffed

into a packing case, where she was discovered an hour later. The police swooped on all trains and buses leaving Poznan, looking for a man with bloodstained clothes; but they failed to find one. The next day, the Poznan newspaper *Courier Zachodni* received one of the now-notorious letters in red ink, containing a quotation from Stefan Zeromsky's national epic *Popioly* (1928): "Only tears of sorrow can wash out the stain of shame; only pangs of suffering can blot out the fires of lust."

May Day, 1966, was both a communist and a national holiday. Marysia Galazka, 17, went out to look for her cat in the quiet suburb of Zoliborz, in northern Warsaw. When she did not return, her father went out to look for her. He found her lying in the typical rape position, with her entrails forming an abstract pattern over her thighs, in a tool shed behind the house. Medical evidence revealed that the killer had raped her before disemboweling her.

Major Ciznek, of the Warsaw Homicide Squad, was in charge of the case, and he made a series of deductions. The first was that the Red Spider was unlikely to confine himself to his well-publicized murders on national holidays. Such killers seek victims when their sexual desire is at maximum tension, not according to some preconceived timetable. Ciznek examined evidence of some fourteen other murders that had taken place since the first one in April 1964, one each in Lublin, Radom, Kielce, Lodz, Bialystock, Lomza, two in Bydgoszcz, five in the Poznan district. All places were easily reached by railway; the *modus operandi* was always the same. Every major district of Poland within four hundred kilometers of Warsaw was covered. Ciznek stuck pins in a map and examined the result. It looked as if Warsaw might be the home of the killer, since the murders took place all round it. But one thing was noticeable. The murders extended much farther south than north, and there were also more of them to the south. It rather looked as if the killer had gone to Bialystock, Lomza and Olsztyn as a token gesture of extending his boundaries. Assuming, then, that the killer lived somewhere south of Warsaw, where would this be most likely to be? There were five murders in the Poznan district, to the west of Warsaw. Poznan is, of course, easily reached from Warsaw. But where in the south could it be reached from just as easily? Cracow was an obvious choice. So was Katowice, twenty miles or so from Cracow. This town was also at the center of a network of railway lines.

On Christmas Eve, 1966, Cracow was suddenly ruled out as a possibility. Three servicemen getting on a train between Cracow and Warsaw looked into a reserved compartment and found the half naked and mutilated corpse of a girl on the floor. The leather miniskirt had been slashed to pieces; so had her abdomen and thighs. The servicemen notified the guard, and a message was quickly sent to Warsaw, who instructed the train-driver to go straight through to Warsaw, non-stop, in case the killer managed to escape at one of the intervening stations. A careful check of passengers at Warsaw revealed no one stained with blood or in any way suspicious. But the police were able to locate the latest letter from the killer, dropped into the post slot of the mail van on top of all the others. It merely said: "I have done it again," and was addressed to *Zycie Warsawy*. It looked as if the Red Spider had got off the train in Cracow, after killing the girl, and dropped the letter into the slot.

The girl was identified as Janina Kozielska, of Cracow. And the police recalled something else: another girl named Kozielska had been murdered in Warsaw in 1964. This proved to be Janina's sister Aniela. For Ciznek, this ruled out Cracow as the possible home of the killer. For he would be likely to avoid his home territory. Moreover, there surely had to be some connection between the murders of the two sisters . . .

The compartment on the Cracow–Warsaw train had been booked over the telephone by a man who said his name was Stanislav Kozielski, and that his wife would pick up the tickets. Janina had paid 1,422 zloty for them—about twenty-five pounds. Janina had come to the train alone and been shown to her compartment by the ticket inspector. She said that her husband would be joining her shortly. The inspector had also checked a man's ticket a few moments later, but could not recall the man. It was fairly clear, then, that the Red Spider knew the girl well enough to persuade her to travel with him as his wife, and had probably paid for the ticket. He had murdered her in ten minutes or so, and then hurried off the train.

Ciznek questioned the dead girl's family. They could not suggest who might have killed their daughter, but they mentioned that she sometimes worked as a model—as her sister had. She worked at the School of Plastic Arts and at a club called The Art Lovers Club.

Ciznek recollected that the red ink was made of artist's paint dissolved in turpentine and water; this looked like a lead.

The Art Lovers Club proved to have one hundred and eighteen members. For an Iron Curtain country, its principles were remarkably liberal; many of its members painted abstract, tachiste and pop-art pictures. Most of them were respectable professional men—doctors, dentists, officials, newspapermen. And one of them came from Katowice. His name was Lucian Staniak, and he was a 26-year-old translator who worked for the official Polish publishing house. Staniak's business caused him to travel a great deal—in fact, he had bought an *ulgowy bilet*, a train ticket that enabled him to travel anywhere in Poland.

Ciznek asked if he could see Staniak's locker. It confirmed his increasing hope that he had found the killer. It was full of knives—used for painting, the club manager explained. Staniak daubed the paint on with a knife blade. He liked to use red paint. And one of his paintings, called "The Circle of Life," showed a flower being eaten by a cow, the cow being eaten by a wolf, the wolf being shot by a hunter, the hunter being killed by a car driven by a woman, and the woman lying with her stomach ripped open in a field, with flowers sprouting from her body.

Ciznek now knew he had his man, and he telephoned the Katowice police. They went to Staniak's address at 117 Aleje Wyzwolenia, but found no one at home. In fact, Staniak was out committing another murder—his last. It was a mere month after the train murder— January 31, 1967—but he was impatient at the total lack of publicity given to the previous murder. So he took Bozhena Raczkiewicz, an 18-year-old student from the Lodz Institute of Cinematographic Arts, to a shelter built at the railway station for the use of stranded overnight travelers, and there stunned her with a vodka bottle. In accordance with his method when in a hurry, he cut off her skirt and panties with his knife. He had killed her in a few minutes between six o'clock and six twenty-five. The neck of the broken bottle had a clear fingerprint on it.

Staniak was picked up at dawn the next day; he had spent the night getting drunk. His fingerprints matched those on the bottle. He was a good-looking young man of twenty-six. And when he realized that there was no chance of escape, he confessed fully to twenty murders. He told the police that his parents and his sister had been crossing an icy road when they were hit by a skidding car, being driven too fast by the young wife of a Polish Air Force pilot. The girl had been acquitted of careless driving. Staniak had seen the picture of his first victim in a newspaper, and thought she looked like the wife of the pilot; this was his motive in killing her. He had decided against killing the wife of the pilot because it would be traced back to him.

Sentenced to death for six of the murders—the six described here—Staniak was later reprieved and sent to the Katowice asylum for the criminally insane.

Staniak, like Brady, is an example of the relatively new phenomenon of the "high IQ killer." It is true that Landru, Kürten and Rees were men of some intelligence; but where murder was concerned, the intelligence was overruled. Like Earle Nelson and Fritz Haarmann, they were simply driven by a compulsion to violate. By comparison, Rees, Brady and Staniak represent a new level of motivation in serial killers. The desire to violate is less than compulsive, but they use their intelligence to justify it, asking themselves—in an almost philosophical spirit—"Why not?"

The same pseudo-Sadeian logic lay behind a series of murders that created panic on the campuses of Michigan in the late 1960s.

At nine o'clock on a warm Sunday evening, a man relaxed on his front porch in Ypsilanti, Michigan, enjoying the first cool breeze of the day. He recognized the attractive, slightly built brunette who was strolling towards him as Mary Fleszar, the niece of one of his workmates; she was a college student who lived in an apartment on the next corner. As she walked past him, a car slowed down, and a young man leaned out of the window and spoke to her—it sounded as if he was asking if she wanted a lift. Mary shook her head and walked on. The car turned at the next corner. A few moments later, to the man's surprise, the car reappeared from the same direction, shot past the girl, and pulled into a private driveway, blocking her path. Once again the driver seemed to be trying to persuade her to get in, but the girl again shook her head, and walked around the rear of the car. The driver backed out and drove off down the street. As the man watched anxiously, ready to intervene, he saw that Mary was within yards of the front door of her apartment block; she was obviously safe now . . .

Twenty-four hours later—July 19, 1967—Mary's flatmate rang the girl's home. Mary had apparently gone out for a breath of air the previous evening, only ten minutes after returning home, and had not been back since.

At first the police were unconcerned, pointing out that most 19-year-old college students were old enough to look after themselves, and often took off for the night without telling anyone. Mary's parents protested that she was a quiet, studious girl, and that she had walked out in the clothes she stood up in.

The day after the police had issued a missing person report, a detective tracked down the neighbor who had seen Mary accosted by the young man. He was able to say that the car was an old model, that it looked like a Chevrolet, and that it was bluish gray.

From then on, investigations led nowhere. The Fleszars came to accept that their daughter was dead—no other theory made sense. Fortunately, they were a deeply religious family, and their faith enabled them to accept their loss as the will of God.

Four weeks after Mary's disappearance, on August 7, 1967, two teenage boys were trying to repair a tractor in a field near Superior Township, two miles north of Ypsilanti. When they heard a car door slam, they looked at one another with mischievous smiles, and crept off into the brush towards the broken-down farmhouse at the edge of the field. Because it afforded shelter from the main road, the spot had become a lovers' lane. But before the boys reached the area favored by courting couples, they heard a car start up and drive away. In the clearing near the old farmhouse, they found fresh tire tracks. They also observed a nauseating smell. A few yards farther on they discovered its source—a fly-infested mass of rotten meat that looked like a dead animal. A closer look revealed that, although the extremities of the limbs were missing, it had an oddly human appearance.

The local police who hurried to the scene—and who at first assumed the boys had found a dead deer—soon recognized it as a human body. The Ypsilanti pathologist, Dr. H. A. Scovill, was able to tell them that it was of a female, and that she had been baking in the hot sun for many weeks. A careful search of the area failed to discover the victim's clothing. But fifty yards away, in dense weeds, a policeman found a female sandal. Later the same afternoon, the Fleszars identified it as their daughter's.

The autopsy on the remains revealed that the girl had been stabbed in the chest and abdomen about thirty times—obviously by someone in a frenzy.

Two days later, a blue-gray Chevrolet pulled up in front of the Moore Funeral Home, where Mary's remains were awaiting burial, and a powerfully built, good-looking young man got out. In the reception, he explained that he was a friend of the Fleszar family, and would like to take a photograph as a keepsake for the parents. When told that was impossible, he shrugged and left. But the girl behind the desk noticed that he was not carrying a camera . . .

When, almost a year later, at the beginning of another hot July, a student at Eastern Michigan University telephoned to report that her flatmate was missing, the Ypsilanti police had a sense of *déjà vu*. The circumstances were oddly similar to those of the disappearance of Mary Fleszar. Joan Schell, a 20-year-old art student, had returned to her apartment on the evening of Sunday July 2—a mere three blocks from Mary's apartment—and decided to go out again. She wanted to get into nearby Ann Arbor, to spend the night at the flat of a girlfriend. In fact, her boyfriend had telephoned to say he had arrived in town unexpectedly and was waiting there for her. Her roommate accompanied her to catch the 10:30 bus from in front of the university. Three quarters of an hour later, it was clear that she had missed it. At that point, a two-tone red car had pulled up, and a young man climbed out and called "Want a ride?" He looked about 20, and was wearing an East Michigan University sweatshirt. And since there were also two other young men in the car, Joan decided it was safe enough. Seconds later, Joan was in the back seat. But as the door closed, she called that she would telephone as soon as she reached her friend's flat in Ann Arbor. And when, two and a half hours later, she failed to call, the flatmate decided to ring the police.

Five days later, two workmen at a construction site in Ann Arbor were taking a breather from digging storm drains when one of them wrinkled up his nose. "Can you smell something?" He began looking in the high weeds. A moment later he called: "It's a dead girl."

The sex of the corpse was obvious since her blue miniskirt and white underslip had been tugged up around her neck. The torso was covered with a mass of wounds. The pathologist who was called to the scene reported that she had been stabbed to death, and had been dead for some time, perhaps a week. What intrigued the police was the evidence that the body had lain in its present location for less than twenty-four hours. This was revealed by the fact that parts of the body that had been exposed to the sun were nevertheless still fresh and undecayed, while the underside was tough and leathery. The pathologist also noted signs that the victim had been raped.

Joan Schell's body was identified through the clothing she was wearing. A few days later, the missing boyfriend—with whom she had intended to spend the night—was located and questioned. But he had a perfect alibi. He had been waiting at the flat of Joan's girlfriend in Ann Arbor during the crucial hours following her abduction.

But enquiries among the university students revealed a possible clue. At least two of them believed they had seen Joan late on the night she vanished, walking with a young man. And although neither of them was prepared to be positive, both thought it was an Eastern Michigan University student named John Norman Collins.

The detectives lost no time in interviewing Collins. He proved to be a well-built, handsome youth of 21 with short dark hair, who was majoring in education. But he flatly denied being with Joan Schell. He had spent the weekend at home in the Detroit suburb of Center Line, and had not returned to his room near the campus until early Monday morning. He did not even know Joan Schell, although she lived just across the street. The detectives decided that John Collins was either innocent or a superb liar. Besides, there was the problem of the car containing *three* men. And since the identifications of him had not been positive, he was allowed to go.

As in the case of Mary Fleszar, the investigation soon ran out of leads. It was ten months later, on March 21, 1969, that a 13-year-old schoolboy returned home at 7:15 in the morning to tell his mother that he had found a gift-wrapped present in a shipping bag near the cemetery. A note on the package said: "I love you, Jane." Together, mother and son returned to the spot where he had found it. Outside the cemetery, near the gate, she saw something covered with a yellow raincoat. It was a girl's body, lying on its back. Although the skirt had been pulled up above the waist, and the pantyhose rolled down, it was fully clothed. A few hours earlier, the Ypsilanti police had received a missing person report on 23-year-old Jane Mixer, a law student at the University of Michigan. A check with a photograph in the yearbook revealed that this was the victim.

Jane had been due home that weekend, a semester recess. She had telephoned her parents in Muskegon, a few hours away, to say that she had succeeded in finding someone to give her a lift, but had never arrived. Jane had been shot in the back of the head and then strangled. A sanitary pad that was still in place indicated why there had been no sexual attack.

Four days later, on Tuesday March 25, 1969, a construction worker in Ann Arbor, working close to the spot where Joan Schell's body had been found, tripped over an arm that was sticking out of a batch of weeds. It was the body of a young girl, lying in a rape position; a branch had been jammed into the vagina, and the head and body showed signs of a brutal beating. She was identified as 16-year-old Maralynn Skelton, and investigation revealed that she was a known drug user—and dealer—whose relations with her family were strained. She had vanished on Friday—the day Jane Mixer's body had been found—when hitch-hiking, on her way to see her boyfriend. It seemed likely that she had been picked up by her killer. The newspapers had no doubt whatever that the killer was the man they were now calling "the Ypsilanti Coed Slayer."

Other than that, there were no clues—no witnesses, no leads. The police were encountering total frustration. So far they had not even succeeded in finding the exact spot where any of the victims had been killed.

In that respect, at least, their luck was about to change.

Two victims in four days suggested that the Ypsilanti killer was being driven by an increasing obsession, and that unless he was caught soon, the time between the murders would grow shorter.

That fear was confirmed when, three weeks later, early on the morning of April 16, 1969, the body of another young girl was found. She was a teenager, and she was wearing only a white blouse and a white bra, pushed up around her neck. She had been strangled with black electrical flex, and her full breasts had been slashed again and again. It looked like the sadistic frenzy the police had come to associate with the Ypsilanti coed slayer. An early morning motorist had seen the body lying at the side of a country road near Ypsilanti, in a patch of weeds.

The girl proved to be the youngest victim yet: 13-year-old Dawn Basom, a junior high-school student. She had gone out to see friends early on the previous evening, and had failed to return home.

The police launched a thorough search of the area, and soon found both her shoes, at different locations near the body. The local sheriff, Douglas Harvey, decided to keep the discovery of the body secret, and to stake out the area in case the killer returned. But at the news conference he gave a few hours later, an embarrassed young reporter admitted that it was already too late: he had learned of the discovery from a policeman, and had promptly telephoned it to his office.

Yet the fact that the body had been found so soon after Dawn's disappearance filled Sheriff Harvey with a sense of getting close to the killer. He ordered the search for her clothes to be extended over a wider area. And a few hours later, a deputy looking through rubble at a deserted farmhouse not far from Dawn Basom's home found a bright orange sweater—the one Dawn had been wearing when she left home. The place was full of empty beer bottles and used condoms—it was obviously a site used by lovers. And in the basement, police discovered Dawn's blouse, and a length of the same black electrical flex that had been used to strangle her.

They had found where Dawn had been murdered, but there were no clues to her killer: no tire marks, footprints or anything else that might provide a lead. But a week later, when the investigation was already marking time, another clue was found in the farmhouse: a cheap gold-plated earring that was identified as belonging to Dawn. It had undoubtedly not been there a few days earlier. The only conclusion was that the co-ed killer was deliberately taunting the police with their failure to catch him. Two weeks later, on May 16, the barn at the farm site caught fire. A reporter looking over the smoking ruins the next day found five purple lilac blossoms lying nearby; they were fresh, as if newly cut. Five blossoms, five murders.

The coed slayer obviously had a liking for deserted farms. On the afternoon of Monday, June 9, 1969, three teenage boys taking a short cut through a disused farmyard saw a body lying beside the path. It was a girl, and her torn clothes were scattered around her. The pathologist hazarded a guess that she was in her early twenties, and that she had been dead for less than a day. She had been shot in the head and stabbed repeatedly before her throat had been cut. The sheer frenzy of the attack was the signature of the coed slayer.

Because of the remoteness of the spot, Sheriff Harvey again decided to order a news blackout. And once again he was frustrated: one of the teenagers who had found the body had phoned the news to a local radio station that had a standing offer of $25 for news items.

The girl was identified as Alice Elizabeth Kalom, a student from Kalamazoo who was taking a design course in Ann Arbor. She had last been seen at a party for a local rock musician in the early hours of the previous Sunday morning, and left to walk home. The coed slayer had obviously offered her a lift.

Four murders in three months caused panic in the local community; reward money of $42,000 was offered for information. The police were heavily criticized; yet they knew that they had done everything possible to catch the killer. So far, two news leaks had frustrated their best hope of catching him. Sheriff Harvey was determined that it wouldn't happen again.

On July 23, 1969, the campus police at Eastern Michigan University received a phone call telling them that an 18-year-old student named Karen Sue Beineman had failed to appear at dinner or in her room after curfew. By this time, the Ypsilanti police were ready to act instantly in the case of a missing girl. Karen's roommates told them that she had last been seen around midday, on her way to a downtown wig shop.

Joan Goshe, the proprietress of the wig shop, had an interesting story to tell. The girl had come in to pick up a small headpiece that had been made for her. As she paid $20 for it, she made the comment that she had done two foolish things in her life: bought a wig, and accepted a lift on a motorcycle from a complete stranger—the young man who was now waiting outside. Joan Goshe had commented that accepting lifts from strangers was not safe these days. But she had to admit that the young man *looked* decent enough—good-looking, with short dark hair. He was wearing a horizontal-striped sweater. A few minutes later, Karen had roared off on the back of his motorcycle. An assistant in the Chocolate House next door was able to identify it as a Triumph.

Another girl student who was interviewed described how a good-looking young man in a horizontal-striped sweater had recently tried hard to persuade her to go for a ride on his motorbike, but had only shrugged good-humoredly when she declined.

Four days later, a doctor and his wife out for an afternoon walk found Karen Sue Beineman's body in a wooded gully not far from their suburban home. The naked corpse lay on its belly as if rolled over the edge. As soon as Sheriff Harvey received the call, he gave orders for a news blackout. Like most of the other victims, Karen had been strangled and brutally beaten. Medical examination revealed that she had been raped and that her panties had been stuffed into her vagina. One curious fact noted by the medical examiner was that there were human hair-clippings stuck to the panties.

That night, the gully was surrounded by police officers, and in the place of Karen Sue Beineman lay a store mannequin.

Towards midnight, a storm broke, and the watchers did their best to keep out of sight while bitten by gnats and soaked by the rain. Shortly after midnight, one of the policemen thought he saw a man running out of the gully; the heavy rain had prevented him from seeing him earlier. He tried to contact colleagues on his walkie-talkie, but the rain had made it inoperative. By the time he had made his way to other watchers on the main road, the man was already far away. They heard an engine start up, and a car drive away. The police followed, but they were too late. What had happened, they realized, was that the killer had made his way back to the "body," found it was a mannequin, and left at top speed. To the frustrated police, the luck of the coed slayer seemed inexhaustible.

In fact, it had already run out. Descriptions of the young man on the motorbike had led a young campus policeman, Larry Mathewson, to note their similarity to one of his former fraternity fellows, John Norman Collins, the student who had already been interviewed in connection with the death of Joan Schell. He succeeded in borrowing a photograph of Collins from a fellow student, and showed it to Joan Goshe, the wigshop owner. Both Joan Goshe and her assistant identified it as the young man who had been waiting for Karen Sue Beineman on his motorcycle.

The Sunday evening after the stake-out, two young policemen called on John Norman Collins at the pleasant, wooden frame house at 619 Emmet Street that he shared with his friend Arnold Davis. They were enthusiastic but inexperienced, and one of them tried to shock Collins into an admission by telling him that he had been the last person seen with Karen Sue Beineman. Collins said there must be some mistake. When the police asked if he was willing to take a lie-detector test, he flushed and said: "I guess so."

When he got back to his room after the interview, Collins told Davis indignantly that the police had accused him of being the coed slayer. But Davis was later to describe how, the following evening, Collins emerged from his bedroom with a box covered in a blanket. As he opened the door for Collins, Davis glimpsed its contents: women's shoes and clothing, and a woman's bag. Collins returned later without the box.

On the evening of Tuesday July 29, 1969, Police Corporal David Leik returned from a twelve-day holiday with his wife Sandra, and three young sons. The following morning, Mrs. Leik carried a basket of washing down to the machine in the basement, and was mildly annoyed to notice patches of black paint on the concrete floor. Her husband denied all knowledge of it, and was puzzled to realize that the paint had the dull finish of spray paint. There had been a can of black spray paint in the basement, but it had gone.

His wife pointed out that some washing powder and a bottle of ammonia were also missing. Only one person could have taken them: her nephew, who had kept an eye on the house and fed the dog in their absence. But why should he spray black paint on the floor?

They were still puzzling about it when the telephone rang. It was the police station down on Michigan Avenue, and the sergeant asked if David Leik would mind coming over immediately. Half an hour later, Leik was talking to Sergeant Chris Walters, who lost no time in explaining why he needed to see him so urgently:

"That nephew of yours, John Collins. He's the prime suspect in these coed murders."

Leik was incredulous; Collins was like a younger brother.

But when Walters had outlined the strength of the evidence, and mentioned that Collins had backed down from taking a lie-detector test, the shaken Leik had to acknowledge that there was very powerful evidence that his nephew could be the coed slayer.

He decided against telling his wife; although only ten years Collins's senior, Sandra seemed to regard him as a son. But late that night, Leik tiptoed down to the basement and scraped off some of the black paint with a knife. Underneath, there was a stain that looked ominously like blood.

Early the next morning, while his wife and children were still asleep, Leik hurried to the police station to report his find; he returned to find his wife on the telephone to Collins. "John wants to know if you've found anything about that black paint yet." "Not yet," said Leik. Then, when she had hung up, he tried to tell her, as gently as possible, that her sister's youngest son was almost certainly the coed killer. Sandra was shattered by the news, and cried uncontrollably for a long time.

The lab men arrived two hours later. After erecting flood-lights, they scraped fragments of the brown stain on to paper, and tested it with benzidine solution. If it had been blood, the benzidine should have turned blue-green; in fact, it remained transparent.

One forensic expert remarked: "It *looks* like a varnish stain."

Leik clapped a hand to his forehead. "Oh my God! Of course! I used varnish on some window shutters . . . I'm sorry."

"Don't be sorry. What I'd like to know is why someone covered up varnish stains with spray paint."

As the lab men went on studying the floor, one of them peered into the space next to the washing machine. What he saw was hair—tiny clippings of human hair. Leik explained that his wife cut the children's hair in the basement. He looked stunned when the lab man explained that tiny clippings of hair had been found inside the panties that the killer had stuffed into Karen Sue Beineman's vagina.

A closer examination of the floor revealed tiny brown spots that looked like—and proved to be—bloodstains. They also proved to be of human origin.

That afternoon, David Leik and Police Captain Walter Stevens called on John Collins. Collins looked shaken when told he was the prime suspect, and when Stevens told him that the stains on the basement floor had been varnish, he burst into tears. They expected a confession; but Collins pulled himself together, and continued to deny knowing anything about Karen Sue Beineman. Later the same day, after laboratory examination had revealed that the bloodstains were of the same type as Karen's, John Norman Collins was placed under arrest.

A search of Collins's rooms failed to reveal anything incriminating; the detectives cursed when his roommate Arnold Davis told them of the box that Collins had disposed of on the previous Monday evening. It had almost certainly contained evidence to tie Collins to the earlier murders. Examination of the basement furnace revealed nothing but ashes. What it meant was that the only evidence against Collins were the hairs and human bloodstains found in Leik's basement. If these failed to convince a jury—and juries are notoriously unwilling to convict on purely circumstantial evidence—John Collins might still go free. And if Collins had not made the absurd mistake of spraying varnish stains with black paint, the evidence in Leik's basement would never have been discovered.

Collins's friend Arnold Davis provided some interesting insights into the suspected killer. Collins was apparently a habitual thief; this explained how he was able to afford to run four motorcycles—he stole spare parts, even to wheels and engines—in fact, one of the motorcycles was stolen. And more recently, Collins had been committing burglaries with another former roommate, Andrew Manuel—not because he needed the money (he was an indefatigable odd-job man), but simply for fun.

The police wanted to talk to Andrew Manuel for another reason. When Collins's arrest had been broadcast on national news networks, it had mentioned that he had just returned from a trip to California. On June 30, that year, near Salinas, a pretty 17-year-old girl, Roxie Ann Philips, had vanished after telling a friend that she had a date with a man called "John" from Michigan; John and his friend were staying in a camper-trailer. In fact, the trailer had been left behind in Salinas—in the backyard of Andrew Manuel's grandfather. The strangled and battered body of Roxie Ann Philips had been discovered in a ravine on July 13. The trailer-hire company were still trying to recover their property.

Manuel was finally located in Phoenix, Arizona, and charged with burglary and stealing the trailer. He denied knowing anything about any of the murders, although he admitted hastily leaving Ypsilanti when he heard that the police had been asking questions about Collins. Eventually, he was sentenced to five years' probation.

On June 22, 1970, the trial of John Norman Collins opened in the Washtenaw County Building in Ann Arbor before Judge John Conlin. The prosecution, led by William F. Delhey, had finally decided that he would be charged only with the murder of Karen Sue Beineman—it had been impossible to collect enough evidence to risk other charges. The defense, led by Joseph Louisell, an immensely successful lawyer from nearby Detroit, spent two weeks challenging jurors who might be prejudiced, so the actual trial opened on July 20.

It was uphill work for the defense. The wig-shop owner and the assistant from the Chocolate House testified that it had been Collins they saw waiting outside on his motorcycle for

Karen Sue Beineman; Neil Fink, for the defense, questioned them about their eyesight. Roommate Arnold Davis was led to testify that the police had questioned him for sixty hours— the implication being that he had been harassed into testifying against Collins. Corporal David Leik (now a sergeant) was pressed about whether there was any actual evidence that Collins had been in their house while he was away, and had to admit that there was not.

But the heart of the case, as everyone realized, lay in the hair evidence. Walter Holz, a graduate chemist from the Department of Health's Criminalistics Section, testified that the hairs in the girl's panties were identical with those found on the Leik's basement floor; the defense argued that a comparison of sixty-one hairs from the panties and fifty-nine from the floor was inadequate. Similar objections were made to the evidence of other experts on hair. In due course, the defense called its own experts to object that precise identification of hairs was impossible. Louisell also suggested that the hairs in the panties might have been picked up in a girls' dormitory if a brown-haired girl had clipped her bangs, and—when the judge sustained an objection—that they might have been picked up in the wig shop (although Louisell failed to explain how they had found their way under the girl's clothes).

On August 13, 1970, Prosecutor Delhey concluded a brisk summary of the evidence with the remark that common sense dictated a verdict of guilty. Louisell rested his defense on the uncertainty of the hair evidence. But when having lunch with the judge and the prosecutor, he admitted that he expected a guilty verdict. He was correct. On Wednesday August 19, 1970, the jury brought in a unanimous verdict of guilty. Two days later, John Collins was sentenced to life imprisonment— meaning a minimum of twenty years. He heard the sentence with the same impassivity he had shown throughout the trial.

What motivated a personable young student—known as a

good athlete, an excellent student and an "all-American boy"—to kill eight or more young women? The answer is that we do not know. His family background had been unstable. His father left his mother for another woman soon after John Collins' birth in 1947; her second marriage lasted only a year; her third husband turned out to be an alcoholic who beat her and the children—she divorced him when Collins was 9. In his early years at college it suddenly became clear that he was less than honest—he was suspected of taking $40 from the entertainment fund, and of numerous petty thefts. One of his professors suspected him of some "pretty ambitious cheating." So, like so many men who graduate to murder—Landru, Petiot, Smith, Heath—he had a deeply ingrained crooked streak. We can only assume that, as a highly sexed young man, this crooked streak led him to "steal" sex as he had earlier stolen money and motorcycles, and that—as in the case of Ian Brady—he knew how to overrule his conscience with intellectual justifications.

By comparison, the case of another American serial killer of the late 1960s seems like a flashback to the era of Albert Fish and Earle Nelson. Although a brilliant mechanic and something of a genius with electronic equipment, Jerome Henry Brudos was anything but intellectual; his murders were as simple and compulsive as a schoolboy stealing jam tarts.

It was on May 10, 1969, that the police in Portland, Oregon, knew for certain that there was a sex killer at large. A fisherman standing on the Bundy Bridge, which crossed the Long Tom River, saw something that looked like a parcel floating in the water; when he climbed down for a closer view, he realized that it was a bloated corpse, still clad in a coat. The police officers who were dispatched from the Benton County sheriff's office soon confirmed that it was the body of a girl, and that it had been weighted down with a car transmission unit that weighed as much as she did.

The forensic pathologist, Dr. William Brady, estimated that the body had been in the water about two weeks. Cause of death was strangulation with a ligature. Because the body had been immersed for so long, it was impossible to determine whether she had been raped. There was one curious feature that the doctor found hard to explain. A few inches below each armpit there was a needle puncture, surrounded by an area of burn.

It was not difficult to identify the girl. She was 22-year-old Linda Dawn Salee, who had vanished just over two weeks ago, on April 23, after leaving her office job in Portland. Her car had been found in the underground parking garage. She had failed to arrive at the swimming pool, where she was due to meet her boyfriend, who was a lifeguard. Linda had been one of many girls who had vanished in Oregon during the past two years.

Police divers spent the next two days searching the river for clues. It was on the morning of Monday May 12, that one of them located another body, fifty feet from the spot where Linda Salee had been found. This one was also weighted down with a car part—this time a cylinder head. And since the pathologist estimated that the body had been in the water for around two months, this suggested that it was 19-year-old Karen Sprinker, a university student from the Oregon State University in Corvallis, who had vanished on March 27. Her parents soon verified the identification. Karen had been due to meet her mother for lunch in a department store in Salem, Oregon, but had failed to arrive. Her car was found in the parking garage, still locked.

Again, there were some curious—and grisly—features. The body was fully clothed, but the cotton bra had been replaced by a waist-length black bra that was too big. Both breasts had been removed, and in their place were two screwed-up pieces of brown paper. Like Linda Salee, Karen had been strangled with a ligature.

Linda and Karen were only two of a dozen girls who had vanished in Oregon in the past two years. Before the Long Tom River discovery, only one of them had been found: a skeleton lying on the banks of a creek had been identified as that of 16-year-old Stephanie Vilcko, who had vanished from her Portland home in July 1968. But two other cases bore an ominous resemblance to those of Linda and Karen. Linda Slawson, a 19-year-old encyclopedia saleswoman, had failed to return to her Portland home on January 26, 1968. And 23-year-old Susan Jan Whitney had vanished en route from Eugene, Oregon, to McMinnville, south of Portland, on November 26, 1968. Her car was found parked by the highway, incapacitated by a mechanical defect.

The policeman who had been investigating the disappearance of Karen Sprinker was Detective Jim Stovall. Now her body had been found, but he still had no clues to her killer, except that he was probably an electrician—both bodies had been tied with electrical wire—and a car mechanic, an inference based on the car parts used to weight the bodies.

Stovall decided to begin at the Corvallis campus, eighty miles south of Portland, where Karen had been a student. Stovall and his colleague Jim Daugherty took over a room on campus and spent days talking to every girl student in the university. The only possible leads that materialized were several mentions of a stranger who had made a habit of telephoning the hall of residence, asking for various girls by their first names. When a girl answered, he would talk at some length about himself, claiming to be a Vietnam veteran, and giving other details—such as that he was "psychic." He usually asked for a date, but seemed unoffended when refused. It was when one of the girls mentioned that she had agreed to meet the "Vietnam veteran" that Stovall's interest suddenly increased.

The man had seemed interested when she mentioned that she was taking a psychology course, and told her that he had been a patient at the Walter Reed Hospital, where he had learned about some interesting new techniques. When he suggested coming to the dorm for a coffee, the girl agreed.

The man's appearance had been a disappointment. He was overweight, freckled, and looked as if he was in his thirties. He had a round, unprepossessing face and the narrow eyes gave him an oddly cunning look, like a schoolboy who is planning to steal the jam tarts. But he seemed pleasant enough, and they sat in the lounge and talked at some length. Nevertheless, she had the feeling that he was a little "odd." This suddenly came into focus when he placed a hand on her shoulder and remarked: "Be sad." "Why?" "Think of those two girls whose bodies were found in the river . . ." And when he left, he asked her to go for a drive, and when she declined, made the curious comment: "How do you know I wouldn't take you to the river and strangle you?"

Stovall and Daughterty began to feel excited when the girl told them that the "Vietnam veteran" had mentioned that he might call again.

'If he does, would you agree to let him come here? Then call us immediately?'

The girl was reluctant, but agreed when the police told her that they would be there before the man arrived. She merely had to make some excuse to delay him for an hour.

A week later, on Sunday, May 25, the Corvallis Police Department received the call they had been hoping for. The girl told them that the "Vietnam veteran" had telephoned a few minutes ago, asking if he could come over. The girl had told him she wanted to wash her hair, and asked him to make it in about an hour.

When the overweight, freckle-faced man in a tee shirt walked into the lounge of Callaghan Hall, two plain-clothes policemen walked up to him and produced their badges. The man seemed unalarmed; he gave his name as Jerry Brudos, and said that he lived in Salem; the only sign of embarrassment was when he admitted that he had a wife and two children. He was now in Corvallis, he explained, because he was working nearby—as an electrician.

Brudos had committed no offense for which he might be arrested, or even taken in for questioning. But when they escorted him outside to his green Comet station wagon, the policemen made a note of its license number.

A preliminary check on Brudos showed that he was what he claimed to be—an electrician working in Corvallis. But when Stovall looked into his record, he realized that he had a leading suspect. Jerome Henry Brudos, 30 years of age, had a record of violence towards women, and had been in the State Mental Hospital. Moreover, at the time of the disappearance of Linda Slawson, Brudos had lived in Portland, in the area where she was trying to sell encyclopedias.

The first thing to do was to check him out. Stovall called on Brudos at his home in Center Street, Salem, and talked to him in his garage. Stovall's colleague, Detective Jerry Frazier, also went along, and noted the lengths of rope lying around the room, and the hook in the ceiling. He also noticed that one of the ropes was knotted, and the knot was identical to one that had been used to bind the corpses in the river.

This, Stovall decided, had to be their man. Everything fitted. He worked as an electrician and car repairman. He had been working at Lebanon, Oregon, close to the place where Jan Whitney's car had been found. And he had been living close to the place from which Karen Spinker had disappeared in Salem.

There was another piece of evidence that pointed to Brudos. On April 22, a 15-year-old schoolgirl had been grabbed by an overweight, freckled man holding a gun, as she hurried to school along the railroad tracks; she had screamed and succeeded in running away. She immediately picked out the photograph of Jerry Brudos from a batch shown to her by the detectives.

Except for this identification, there was no definite evidence against Brudos. This is why Stovall was reluctant to move against him. But five days after Brudos had been questioned in Corvallis, Stovall realized he could no longer take the risk of leaving him at large. As he was on his way to arrest Brudos for the attempted abduction of the schoolgirl on the railway tracks, he received a radio message saying that Brudos and his family had left Corvallis, and were driving towards Portland. Shortly after this, Brudos's station wagon was stopped by a police patrol car. At first it looked as if Brudos was not inside; but he proved to be lying in the back, hidden under a blanket.

Back at the Salem police station, Brudos was asked to change into overalls. When he removed his clothes, he was found to be wearing ladies' underwear.

When Stovall first questioned Brudos, he failed to secure any admissions. It was the same for the next three days. Stovall did not ask outright if Brudos had murdered the girls; he confined himself to general questions, hoping to pick more clues. But at the fifth interview, Brudos suddenly began to talk about his interest in female shoes and underwear. Then he described how he had followed a girl in attractive shoes, broken into her home through a window, and made off with the shoes. Soon after this, he described how he had stolen the black bra—found on Karen Sprinker's body—from a clothesline. Now, at last, he had virtually admitted the killing. Then, little by little, the rest came out—the curious history of a psychopath who suffered from the curious sexual abnormality for which the psychologist Alfred Binet coined the word fetishism.

In Jerry Brudos's case, it first showed itself when he was five years old, when he found a pair of women's patent leather shoes on a rubbish dump, and put them on at home. His mother was furious and ordered him to return them immediately; instead he hid them and wore them in secret. When his mother found them, he was beaten and the shoes were burned. In first grade at school, he was fascinated by the high-heeled shoes that his teacher kept as spares; one day he stole them and hid them in the schoolyard; they were found and handed back to the teacher. When he later confessed, and she asked him why he did it, he rushed out of the room. The truth was that he could not have told her.

When he was 16—in 1955—he stole the underwear of a girl who lived next door. Then he approached the girl and told her he was working for the police as an undercover agent, and could help her to recover the stolen articles. She allowed herself to be lured into his bedroom on an evening when his family was away. Suddenly, a masked man jumped on her, threatened her with a knife, and made her remove all her clothes. Then, to her relief, he merely took photographs of her with a flashlight camera. At the end of the session, the masked man walked out of the bedroom, and a few minutes later, Jerry Brudos rushed in, claiming that the masked intruder had locked him in the barn. The girl knew he was lying, but there was nothing she could do about it.

In April 1956, Brudos invited a 17-year-old girl for a ride in his car. On a deserted highway, he dragged her from the car, beat her up and ordered her to strip. A passing couple heard her screams, and Brudos actually agreed to accompany them back to their home, where they called the police. His story that the girl had been attacked by "some weirdo" was soon disproved, and he was arrested. The girl next door now came forward, and told her story of the photographic session.

Psychiatrists who examined the young Brudos decided that he was not mentally ill and—in spite of the beating he had administered—had no violent tendencies. Back in his home, police found a large box of women's underwear and shoes. They sent him to the Oregon State Hospital for observation, and he was released after nine months.

A period in the army followed, but he was discharged because of his bizarre delusions—he was convinced that a beautiful Korean girl sneaked into his bed every night to seduce him.

Back in Salem, he attacked a young girl one night and stole her shoes. He did it again in Portland. Then, just as it looked as if nothing could stop him from turning into a rapist, he met a gentle 17-year-old girl who was anxious to get away from home, and who agreed to marry him. She was sometimes a little puzzled by his odd demands—making her dress up in silk underwear and high-heeled shoes and pose for photographs—but assumed that most men were like this.

While his wife was in the hospital having a baby, Brudos followed a girl who was wearing pretty shoes. When he broke into her room that night, she woke up, and he choked her unconscious. Then, unable to resist, he raped her. He left her apartment carrying her shoes.

Now he was like a time bomb, waiting for another opportunity to explode. It happened when an encyclopedia saleswoman knocked on his door one winter evening . . .

Linda Slawson—a slight, plain girl with short-cropped hair—had seen Brudos in his yard in Portland, and asked if he was interested in buying encyclopedias. He had invited her into his garage, explaining that his wife had visitors. And when she bent down to take an encyclopedia from her case, he had knocked her unconscious with a heavy piece of wood.

Then he knelt beside her and strangled her to death. Brudos's mother was upstairs, together with his two children; he sent them out to get supper at a hamburger joint, then hurried back to his garage.

To his delight, the dead girl was wearing pretty underwear. Brudos opened the box of panties and bras he had stolen from clotheslines, and spent the next hour or so dressing and undressing the body like an oversize doll. Oddly enough, he felt no desire to rape her. That night, when his family was asleep, he loaded the body into his station wagon, drove it out to the Willamette River, and tossed it off the bridge, weighted down with part of a car engine. He kept only one part of her—a foot—in the freezer in his garage; he wanted it to try shoes on . . .

That November, he found his second victim. On his way home from work in Lebanon, he stopped beside a car that had broken down on the freeway. The driver was student Jan Whitney, and she had two passengers—two male hippies to whom she had given a lift. Brudos explained that he was a car mechanic, but that unfortunately he did not have his tools with him. He would be glad to go home and get them . . . The three climbed into his station wagon, and were driven to Salem. There the two hippies got out. Back in his garage, Brudos left the girl while he went to check that his wife was not at home—she was going out to visit friends for the evening. Then he moved into the seat behind the unsuspecting girl, looped a leather strap round her neck, and strangled her. After that he placed her in the rear seat of his car and performed an act of anal sex. He spent the next hour or so "playing dolls," dressing and undressing the body, taking photographs, and also committing rape. Finally, he suspended her by the wrists from a hook in the ceiling.

This time Brudos was determined not to dispose of the body the same day; he was enjoying his plaything. For the next two days he hurried down to his garage after work—it was locked, so his family could not wander in—and played dolls again. He even removed one of her breasts, with the intention of making a paperweight, but finally abandoned the idea because the hardener failed to set satisfactorily.

A few days later, his necrophiliac obsession nearly brought about his downfall. He took his family to Portland for Thanksgiving—November 28—leaving the girl hanging in his garage. When he got back, he saw to his alarm that a corner of his garage had been demolished. A car driver had gone out of control and knocked a hole in the wall. The police had come to investigate, but were unable to get into the garage. A policeman who had peered through the hole in the wall had failed to see the body in the dark garage. Brudos lost no time in moving Jan Whitney into the pumphouse before he called the police and allowed them to inspect his garage. That same night he threw her into the Willamette River, weighed down with scrap iron.

After this close shave, Brudos made no more attempts at abduction until the following March. He drove to the Meier and Frank department store in Salem on Saturday the 27th, and was "turned on" by a girl in high-heeled shoes and a miniskirt. He parked and hurried into the store looking for her, but she was nowhere to be seen. But walking back towards his car he saw a pretty girl with long dark hair about to get into her car. He grabbed her by the shoulder, pointed a pistol at her, and said: "Come with me and I promise not to hurt you." Instead of screaming—which would probably have saved her life—Karen Sprinker begged him not to shoot, and accompanied him to his car. Brudos drove her back to his garage, then ordered her out at gunpoint. She told him she would do whatever he liked. Brudos asked her if she was a virgin; she said yes, and added that she was having her period. (This part of the confession confirmed Stovall's belief that he had the right man; Karen's mother had told him that the girl was menstruating.) Brudos made her lie on the floor and raped her. Afterwards, the girl said she had to go to the toilet; Brudos took her into the house and allowed her to use the family bathroom. (His wife was away again.) Then he took her back to the garage and made her pose for pictures—some in her white cotton panties and bra, some in the more "glamorous" stolen underwear and patent leather high-heeled shoes. Finally he tied her hands behind her, placed a rope round her neck, and pulled on it. He asked the girl if it was too tight, and she said it was. Then Brudos pulled her clear of the ground, and watched her suffocate. "She kicked a little and died." Brudos then violated the corpse. Later still he repeated the violation, cut off her breasts, and disposed of her remains in the Long Tom River that same evening, weighted down with a cylinder head.

Linda Salee, a pretty, athletic little girl (only five feet one inch tall) was also walking to her car—her arms loaded with packages—when Brudos approached her, showed her a police badge, and told her he was arresting her for shoplifting. She believed him, and protested that she had sales slips to prove that she had paid for the parcels. Brudos told her he was "taking her in," and drove her back to his garage.

Like Karen Sprinker, Linda Salee behaved with a docility that undoubtedly cost her life. Brudos drove into the garage and closed the doors. Then he told her to follow him, and started across the yard to the house. At this point, Brudos's wife came out on the porch, and Brudos turned and signaled the girl to stand still. A single scream now—or a run for the gate—would have saved her life. Darcie Brudos failed to see her, and her husband took the girl back into the garage and tied her up. Then, incredibly, he went into the house for dinner. By the time Brudos returned—his wife had now gone out—the girl had freed herself, but had not picked up the garage telephone and called the police. "She was just waiting for me, I guess," said Brudos.

Now, too late, she decided to put up a fight. But she was no match for the overweight killer. When he had subdued her, Brudos put the leather strap around her neck and tightened it. The girl asked: "Why are you doing this to me?" Then she went limp. Brudos was in the act of raping her as she died.

Now, to "punish" her, Brudos suspended her by the neck from the hook in the ceiling. He had decided to try an experiment. He stuck two hypodermic syringes into her ribs on either side—these were the two puncture marks that puzzled the pathologist—and attached them to electric wires. When he switched on the current, he was hoping she would dance. "Instead it just burned her."

Brudos kept her for another day, and violated the body just once more. This time he experienced no temptation to cut off the breasts; he did not like pink nipples. ("They should be brown.") Instead he decided to make plastic molds of the breasts; but the epoxy fiber glass somehow failed to work. On the second night, Brudos drove the body away in his station wagon, and dumped it in the Long Tom River, weighted down with a car overdrive unit.

Brudos made these confessions with a certain pedantic precision, as if explaining how to dismantle a gear box; it never seemed to strike him that Detective Jim Stovall might be horrified or sickened. In fact, Stovall went out of his way not to react; he had no wish to interrupt the flow of confession.

Brudos was charged with the murder of Karen Sprinker. The following day, a search warrant was issued, and the detectives entered the empty house—Darcie Brudos had moved away, together with her children. In the attic, police found his collection of shoes, girdles, bras and panties—dozens of them. On the living room shelf there was a replica of a female breast—at least, it looked like a replica until they looked more closely, and saw that it was real, and that it had been made solid with epoxy. In the basement, they found a tool box that contained photographs of the missing girls—some suspended from the hook in the ceiling, others posing for Brudos's camera in underwear. The police were to learn that Brudos had telephoned his wife from prison, and asked her to destroy the contents of the tool box; for once in her life, she had decided to disobey him.

One picture found under the workbench incriminated Brudos beyond all possible doubt. He had photographed the hanging girl reflected in a mirror lying below her on the floor, and had inadvertently caught his own reflection too.

Because Brudos pleaded guilty to four counts of murder, he was sentenced without trial to life imprisonment. When a neighbor alleged that she had seen Darcie Brudos helping her husband to force a woman wrapped in a blanket into her home, Darcie was charged with taking part in the murder of Karen Sprinker. But the jury found her not guilty. By the time she was acquitted, her husband had already started to serve his term of life imprisonment in the Oregon State Penitentiary.

His first year in prison was a difficult one. Sex criminals are detested by other prisoners, and are often kept segregated for their own good. Brudos was not segregated; but he was ignored. No one would talk to him or eat with him. He lost a great deal of weight. When someone managed to give him a hard blow on the side of the head with a bucket of water, he was taken to the prison hospital; but there proved to be no grounds for the suspicion that his eardrum was perforated.

In later years, Brudos's life improved. He proved to have a natural gift for electronics, and was soon virtually running the prison's computer system. The prison authorities have also allowed him, to some small extent, to pursue his lifelong interest in women's shoes and undergarments. His cell has stacks of mail order catalogues full of glossy photographs. Once again, Jerome Henry Brudos is living in his own private world. But now, fortunately, there are no real women who can be forced into helping him act out his fantasies.

Two of the most widely publicized murder cases of the 1960s qualify as mass murders—or "spree killings"— rather than serial killings, but both deserve a brief mention at this point.

On July 13, 1966, 24-year-old Richard Speck knocked on a door in a nurses' hostel in Jeffrey Manor, Chicago, and pointed a gun at the Filipino nurse who opened it. He ordered her into another bedroom where three nurses were sleeping, and bound and gagged them. Speck smelt strongly of alcohol, but he kept assuring the women that he had no intention of hurting them. Five more nurses came in late, and were also bound and gagged. Then, one by one, he took the nurses into the next room. The Filipino, Corazon Amurao, struggled to free herself and tried to persuade the others to attack the man, but no one was prepared to act. Corazon Amurao rolled under a bunk, and lay there, hoping the man would not look for her. Fortunately, he seemed to lose count. When he finally left at 5 a.m. she looked into the next room, and saw that the other eight nurses were dead. She screamed for help from the balcony. Police who entered the hostel soon after found that seven of the girls had been stabbed to death, the eighth strangled. Only one, Gloria Davy, had also been raped and sodomized.

Corazon Amurao described the killer as pockmarked, with a tattoo "Born to raise hell" on his arm. He was quickly identified through a nearby seamen's hiring hall, where he had applied for a berth, and his name and description published in newspapers. Two days later, a doctor attending a patient who had been admitted with slashed wrists recognized the "Born to raise hell" tattoo, and sent for the police.

In court, spectators who had expected to see a monster were astonished to find that the multiple killer looked like a down-at-heel nobody. Psychiatrists learned that Speck had been a delinquent all his life. A man of low self-esteem, he could be modest and agreeable when sober, but became boastful and violent when drunk. A nurse who had dated him said that he seemed to be seething with hatred and resentment. At 20 he had married a 15-year-old girl, whom he had come to hate. He had raped a 65-year-old woman during a burglary, and was believed to be responsible for the murder of a barmaid. He was also in the area of Indiana Harbor when three girls wearing swimsuits vanished one day—their bodies were never found.

Sentenced to a total of six hundred years in jail, Richard Speck died of a heart attack on December 5, 1991, a day before his fiftieth birthday.

Charles Manson, who was sentenced to death in April 1971, may or may not have actually killed anyone, but his followers—known as "the Family"—killed at least nine people, possibly more. (Their prosecutor, Vincent Bugliosi, estimates thirty-five.)

When Charles Manson was released from jail in 1967—at the age of 32—he had spent most of his life in prisons or reformatories. When he came to San Francisco, and found himself among flower children and hippies, all smoking pot and preaching sexual abandon, he felt he had arrived in heaven. Manson, who played the guitar and advocated a rambling philosophy of freedom not unlike that of Aleister Crowley ("Do what thou wilt shall be the whole of the law"), was soon regarded as a kind of guru among the young people of the Haight-Ashbury district, many of whom were runaways. In the following year, surrounded by a crowd of disciples— mostly female—Manson moved into a ranch owned by an old man named George Spahn, who allowed them to live rent free in exchange for stable work and sexual favors from the girls.

One respectable college graduate named Charles Watson fell under Manson's spell and joined the "family." He later described to FBI agent Robert Ressler how Manson preached a philosophy of total abandonment of the ego—"cease to exist"—which was reinforced by sessions with psychedelic drugs and sexual promiscuity. When they were stoned on LSD, Manson would paint word pictures of murder and torture. He dreamed of some tremendous social revolution— "Helter skelter"—in which the pigs (bourgeoisie) would be finally suppressed, and blacks would be exterminated. To some extent, these vengeful dreams were the outcome of his own constantly dashed hopes of achieving fame as a pop musician.

One of the male disciples, Bobby Beausoleil, murdered a drug dealer named Gary Hinman—after Manson had sliced off Hinman's ear. Watson, who now thought of himself as Manson's rival—or at least, chief lieutenant—decided that it was time to assert his own authority, and realize Manson's dreams of slaughter. He agrees that Manson did not specifically *tell* him to go out and kill, but is certain that Manson wanted it. Watson led a band of three female disciples to the house of film actress Sharon Tate on August 8, 1969—her husband Roman Polanski was in Europe, and she had three guests to dinner—an ex-lover and a Polish writer and his mistress. Entering the drive of the house, they shot and killed a teenage boy who was just leaving, then went into the house, bound the four occupants, then shot and stabbed them all to death—Sharon Tate, who was pregnant, was stabbed in the stomach. After the murders, Manson is believed to have gone to the house, to make sure everyone was dead.

That evening, there were two more victims—supermarket owner Leno LaBianca and his wife Rosemary. Manson entered the house first and tied them at gunpoint, then invited in Watson and two female disciples, who stabbed the LaBiancas to death, and wrote "Death to pigs" on the walls in their blood. (The intention was to try to convince the world that the murders were the work of Black Panthers, and to try to start a massacre of blacks by whites.)

Two months later, after the "family" had moved to a deserted ranch in Death Valley, most of them were arrested on suspicion of burning a bulldozer belonging to park rangers. In prison, Susan Atkins, who had been one of the three who killed Sharon Tate, could not resist dropping hints about the murders to fellow prisoners, who in turn told the police.

The trial was one of the longest and most expensive in Los Angeles history (until the Hillside Stranglers a decade later), and ended with seven of the "family"—including Manson and Watson—being sentenced to death or life imprisonment.

Unlike the Moors murders in England, the Manson case aroused a great deal of support for the accused, particularly among the beatnik and hippie population of the west coast. The feeling seemed to be that Manson was a genuine rebel against bourgeois society, and that his plea that this society had "made his children what they were" had some justification. In fact, it is hard to see how Manson was any more justified than Brady. Both were inspired by a kind of mysticism of death and violence—a mysticism that had its roots in the ego. And, in spite of a genuine element of self-actualization, both must be classified as self-esteem killers.

THE 1970s

THE 1970s WAS THE ERA IN WHICH THE GENERAL PUBLIC SUD-
denly became conscious of the problem of the serial killer.
This was due mainly to six cases, five American, one British.
In four out of five of the American cases, the murders reached
double figures. It seemed that violence in the late twentieth
century was spiraling out of control—and that, moreover, the
killers were becoming increasing sadistic. At least the Boston
Strangler and Jerry Brudos had simply murdered and raped
their victims; Dean Corll and the Hillside Stranglers also tortured theirs. All this caused a shock impact not unlike that of
the Jack the Ripper murders on the Victorians.

Dean Corll, a homosexual who was still attached to his
teddy bear, was the first serial killer to create this feeling that
human depravity had reached new depths.

Shortly after 8 a.m. on August 8, 1973, the telephone operator in the Pasadena Police Department received a call from
someone with a boyish voice and a broad Texas accent. "Ya'll
better come on here now. Ah jes' killed a man." He gave the
address as 2020 Lamar Drive.

Within a minute, two squad cars were on their way. Lamar

Drive was in a middle-class suburb of Pasadena—a southeastern suburb of Houston—and 2020 Lamar was a small frame bungalow with an overgrown lawn. Three teenagers were sitting on the stoop by the front door: two boys and a girl. The girl, who was small and shapely, was dressed in clothes that looked even more tattered than the usual teenage outfit. All three were red-eyed, as if they had been crying. A skinny, pimply youth with an incipient blonde moustache identified himself as the one who had made the phone call. He pointed at the front door: "He's in there."

Lying against the wall in the corridor was the naked body of a well-built man, his face caked with blood that had flowed from a bullet wound. There were more bullet holes in his back and shoulder. The bullet in the head had failed to penetrate fully, and the end was sticking out of his skull. He was very obviously dead.

The three teenagers had identified themselves as Elmer Wayne Henley, 17, Timothy Kerley, 16, and Rhonda Williams, 15. Henley, the youth who had made the call, also acknowledged that he had shot his friend, whose name was Dean Arnold Corll. The teenagers were driven off to the Pasadena police headquarters. Meanwhile, an ambulance was summoned to take the corpse to the morgue, and detectives began to search the house.

It was obvious that Corll had moved in recently—the place was only half furnished. The bedroom outside which the corpse was lying contained only a single bed and a small table. It smelt strongly of acrylic paint—the type used in "glue-sniffing." The oddest thing about the room was the transparent plastic sheeting that covered the whole carpet. And lying beside the bed was an eight-foot length of plywood with handcuffs attached to two of its corners, and nylon ropes to the other two. A long hunting knife in its scabbard lay nearby. A black box proved to contain a seventeen-inch dildo—an imitation male sexual organ—and a tube of vaseline. It did not require the powers of a Sherlock Holmes to deduce that these objects were connected with some bizarre sexual ritual in which the victims were unwilling.

The new Ford van parked in the drive produced the same impression. There were navy blue curtains that could be drawn to seal off the whole of the rear portion, a piece of carpeting on the floor, and rings and hooks attached to the walls. There was also a considerable length of nylon rope. In a large box—covered with a piece of carpet—there were strands of human hair. Another similar box in a shed had air-holes drilled in its sides.

Back at the police station, Elmer Wayne Henley was explaining how he came to shoot his friend Dean Corll. He was nervous, and chain-smoked as he made his statement.

He had met Corll, he said, when he had lived in a run-down area of Houston called the Heights. Corll, who was sixteen years his senior, had recently moved into a house that had belonged to his father; it was in Pasadena. On the previous night, he and Timothy Kerley had gone to a glue-sniffing party at Corll's house. But in the early hours of the morning, the two boys had made some excuse to go out and collect Rhonda Williams, who had just decided to run away from home. Rhonda had been in a state of tension and misery ever since her boyfriend had vanished a year ago.

Corll had been furious when the boys arrived back at the house with Rhonda. "You weren't supposed to bring a girl," he yelled, "You spoilt everything." But after a while he seemed to control himself and regain his good humor, and the four of them settled down to glue-sniffing in the living room. Acrylic paint was sprayed into a paper bag, which was then passed around so they could all breathe in the fumes. Within an hour, they were all stretched out unconscious on the floor.

When Wayne Henley woke up, daylight was filtering

through the drawn curtains, and Corll was snapping handcuffs on his wrists; his ankles were tied together. The other two were already handcuffed and bound. As they all began to re-cover their senses and struggle against their bonds, Corll re-vealed that his good humor of a few hours ago had been deceptive. He was seething with resentment and fury. He waved the knife at them and told them he was going to kill them all. "But first I'm gonna have my fun." Then he dragged Henley into the kitchen and rammed a revolver in his belly.

Henley decided that his only chance of escape was to "sweet talk" Corll, persuading him that he would be willing to join in the murder of the other two. It took some time, but finally Corll calmed down and removed the handcuffs. Hen-ley would rape Rhonda while he raped Timothy Kerley. Corll went and picked up Kerley, carrying him to the bedroom like some huge spider. Then he came back and carried off Rhonda. He turned on the portable radio to its top volume to drown any screams or protests.

When Henley went into the bedroom, Corll was naked, and was handcuffing Kerley, who was also naked, to the ply-wood board. Kerley, like Rhonda, was gagged. Corll handed Henley the knife and ordered him to cut off Rhonda's clothes. Rhonda was still dazed from the glue-sniffing, and was only half-aware of what was happening. But Kerley un-derstood, and struggled violently as Corll tried to sexually assault him.

Knowing he was under observation, Henley pretended to rape Rhonda; in fact, he was incapable. But as Kerley thrashed and struggled violently, trying to throw off the heavy man, Henley shouted above the music: "Why don't you let me take her outa here? She don't want to see that." Corll ignored him. Henley jumped to his feet and grabbed the .22 pistol from the night table. "Back off, Dean! Stop it!" Corll lurched to his feet. "Go on Wayne, kill me. Why don't you?" As he lurched towards Henley, the boy fired; the bullet struck Corll in the head, and he staggered past, while Henley fired another shot into his shoulder. As Corll fell through the door and hit the wall of the corridor, Henley emptied the rest of the bullets into his back. Corll slumped down slowly to the floor, resting finally with his cheek and shoulder against the wall.

Henley quickly found the handcuff key and released the two teenagers—Rhonda was still unable to take in what had happened. But when she saw Corll lying in a pool of blood, she began to scream. Henley calmed her, and the three of them dressed—Rhonda making do with her slashed clothes. They discussed what to do next—whether to simply leave the corpse and go away. But it would be found sooner or later, and if neighbors had seen them entering or leaving the house, they would be in serious trouble. So Henley looked up the number of the Pasadena police department and rang them. As the tension relaxed, all three of them found they were unable to stop sobbing.

It took Henley an hour and a half to make his statement. Meanwhile, Kerley was able to confirm the story. But Kerley also mentioned something that intrigued the detectives. "While we were waiting for the police, Wayne told me that if I wasn't his friend, he could have got fifteen hundred dollars for me."

Questioned about the plywood board and the dildo, Henley told the police that Corll liked little boys, and had been paying him to procure them for him. But why, in that case, had Henley decided to kill him? "He made one mistake," said Henley, "He told me that I wouldn't be the first one he'd killed. He said he'd already killed a lot of boys and buried them in the boat shed."

The words made the detectives glance at one another. So far, they had been assuming that this was a simple case of glue-sniffing and sexual perversion, and that Corll's threats to kill the teenagers had been intended to frighten them. Henley's words raised a far more unpleasant suspicion. For nearly three years now, boys had been disappearing in the Heights area of Houston. Some were assumed to be runaways, but in the case of many of them, the parents had ruled it out as impossible—as, for example, in the case of a 9-year-old boy. Now the police had learned that Corll had lived in the Heights area until he moved to Pasadena, and one of his homes had been directly opposite that of the missing 9-year-old . . .

"Where is this boat shed?"

Henley said he wasn't sure; he had been there only once. But it was somewhere in south-west Houston. And now he was able to recollect three of the names that Corll had mentioned: Marty Jones, someone called Cobble, and someone called Hilligiest.

Even now, none of the detectives really believed they were dealing with mass murder. It was more likely that Henley was still under the influence of the "glue." But it had to be checked.

Detective Sergeant Dave Mullican asked Henley: "Can you remember how to get to this boat shed?"

"I think so. It's near Hiram Clark Road."

The first stop was the Houston police headquarters. There Henley was shown pictures of two boys who had been missing since July 27, thirteen days ago. Henley identified them as Charles Cobble, 17, and Marty Jones, 18. The teenagers had shared a room, and both had good school records. Neither had any reason to run away.

The Pasadena detectives—accompanied by two of their Houston colleagues—now headed south to Hiram Clark Road. Another group of detectives were ordered to collect spades and ropes, and to meet them there. It was already late afternoon when the two cars arrived at the rendezvous, and Henley now took over the navigating. This was an area of open fields with cattle grazing in them. Finally, they pulled up beside a barbed wire fence on Silver Bell Street, and Henley pointed out the corrugated iron shed standing well back from the road.

Southwest Boat Storage was virtually a car park for boats, with twenty roofed "stalls." The police cars drove into the compound, and Henley directed them to stall number eleven. "That's Dean's."

The double doors were padlocked, and the lady who lived in a large house next to the compound—a Mrs. Mayme Meynier—told them she had no key: the renters provided their own padlock. When they explained that Dean Corll was dead, she gave them permission to break in.

There was no boat inside: only a half-dismantled car, a bicycle and a large iron drum. The place was like an oven. There were also some cardboard boxes, water containers, and—ominously—two sacks of lime. The earthen floor was covered by two long strips of old carpet. A large plastic bag proved to contain a mixed lot of male clothing, including a pair of red shoes.

Wayne Henley stood at the door, looking inside. Then he walked back towards the cars, sat down on the ground, and buried his head between his knees.

The first task was to move everything out of the shed. While this was being done, a detective noted the registration numbers on the car and the bicycle and radioed them to headquarters. The answer came back quickly: the car had been stolen from a used car lot, and the bicycle belonged to a 13-year-old boy named James Dreymala who had vanished less than a week ago.

Now the place had been emptied, the two strips of carpet were also rolled out. Mullican pointed to a swelling in the floor near the left wall, and told two "trusties"—convicts from the local jail who had been brought along to help—to start digging.

Even with the doors open, the heat was still stifling. Both men were soon perspiring heavily. Six inches down in the sandy earth, they uncovered a white substance.

"That's lime," said Mullican, "Keep digging."

Suddenly, the shed was filled with a sickening stench; the detectives held their noses. The next carefully excavated shovelful revealed a face looking up at them. The younger trusty dropped his spade and rushed outside, making retching noises. A policeman took up the spade and went on clearing the earth. Minutes later, the policemen found themselves looking down at a large plastic bag that contained the body of a boy. He looked about 12 or 13, and was naked. When the bag had been carefully lifted from the ground, it was obvious that the body inside had been recently buried. One of the detectives radioed headquarters to send forensic experts.

Outside, the press was starting to arrive. One radio reporter had allowed Wayne Henley to use his car telephone to call up his mother. They heard him say: "Mama, I killed Dean." Over his own microphone the reporter heard Mrs. Henley said: "Oh Wayne, you *didn't*!" From what followed, it was clear that Henley's mother wanted to rush out to the site; a detective shook his head.

Moments later, as Henley hung up, the body was carried out from the boat shed in its plastic sheeting. The boy was clearly shaken. "It was all my fault." "Why?" asked a detective casually. "Because I introduced him to them boys." And the teenager went on to explain that, during the past two years, he had procured many boys for Dean Corll.

By the time the radio reporter went on the air at six o'clock, a second body had just been discovered. As it began to grow dark, a fire engine with a floodlight and two air-extractors arrived. Soon after that, two more bodies were uncovered. One had been shot in the head, the other strangled with a Venetian blind cord that was still knotted tight around the throat. As the news of the finds was broadcast, crowds of spectators arrived to stare over the barbed wire fence. The air extractors blasted the smell of decaying corpses at them. One reporter had already minted a striking phrase: "There are wall to wall bodies in there."

Mrs. Meynier, the owner of the site, was being questioned about her former tenant. She described him as "the nicest person you'd ever meet," a "gentleman" with a charming smile and dimples. He had never been behind with his $5 a week rent. But recently, she had been baffled when he told her he wanted to rent another stall. Why should he need more space? Surely he already had plenty?

Asked how long Corll had rented the stall, she replied: "Since 1971." The detective turned away muttering: "My God!'

Henley, meanwhile, was also telling reporters how nice Corll could be. His mother liked "ol' Dean" and did not object to their friendship. But as the fourth body was carried out, he became nervous; it was obvious that he was suffering from a glue-sniffing hangover. At ten o'clock he was driven back to the police station. Two hours later, the body count had risen to eight, and the diggers were exhausted. They decided to call it a day.

Back in the Heights, many families with missing teenage sons were now watching their television screens for the printed messages that gave the latest news, and trying to convince themselves that *their* child could not be among those in the boat shed. But for those whose children had known Dean Corll, that was a slender hope. Now the parents found themselves wondering why they had failed to suspect Corll of being a sexual pervert. He and his mother had run a candy factory in the Heights, and Corll was popular with the children because he gave them candy. He also gave them lifts in his white Dodge van.

By midnight, a planeload of reporters from other parts of the country arrived in Houston. And from all over the world, reporters were converging on the corrugated iron boat shed. Dean Corll had been dead for only sixteen hours, but his name had already reached every part of the globe. If the number of his suspected victims was confirmed—and the detectives had a list of forty-two youngsters who had vanished since 1970—he would be America's worst mass murderer to date. Even H. H. Holmes had only confessed to twenty-eight.

Two hours after the lights went out at Southwest Boat Storage on Silver Bell Street, a car containing five people drew up at the barbed wire fence. They identified themselves to the police on guard as the Hilligiest family. Thirteen-year-old David Hilligiest had disappeared more than two years earlier, on May 30, 1971. He had set out for the local swimming pool early that afternoon, and failed to arrive there. On that same day, another local boy, George Malley Winkle, 16, had vanished. The Hilligiests had spent eleven hundred dollars on a private detective, but had failed to find the slightest trace of their son. Now, after telephoning police headquarters, they had learned that Wayne Henley had mentioned David Hilligiest as one of the victims buried in the boat stall. They begged the police guard to allow them to go to the boat stall. The police explained sympathetically that that was impossible; the lights were out and the place was now locked up. They had better go home, get some sleep, and prepare for their ordeal of the next day.

At ten the next morning, after a visit from his mother and a light breakfast, Henley was again sitting opposite Mullican in the Pasadena interrogation room. The rings under his eyes made it obvious that he had slept badly.

"Tell me about the boys you procured."

Henley explained that he had met Corll two years earlier, and that Corll had then offered him $200 each for any boys he could "bring along." For a year he did nothing; then, when he badly needed money, decided to take up the offer. Corll had not actually paid him the full $200 for the first boy he had procured. And he had not paid subsequently.

Now Henley made his most significant admission so far: that he had been present when Corll had killed some of the boys. This suddenly changed the whole situation. The police had been assuming that they were dealing with an insatiable homosexual rapist and a youth he had persuaded to help him find boys. Now it began to look as if Wayne Henley had been an active partner in the murders.

They were interrupted by the telephone. It was the Houston police headquarters. A man named Alton Brooks had turned up at the police station with his 18-year-old son David, explaining that David had known Corll and wanted to talk about it. And David Brooks was now giving a statement that implicated Henley in the murders.

When Mullican hung up, he told the teenager on the other side of the desk: "That was Lieutenant Porter at Houston Homicide. He says he has a boy named David Brooks in there, and Brooks is making a statement about you and Dean Corll."

Oddly enough, Henley looked relieved.

"That's good. Now I can tell you the whole story."

Mullican's next question was: "Did you kill any of the boys yourself?"

Henley answered without hesitation: "Yes, sir."

Mullican did his best to show no emotion during the statement that followed. But it was difficult to look impassive. What Henley was describing was how he had lured some of his own best friends into Corll's lair, witnessed their torture and rape, and then participated in their murders.

It seemed that David Brooks had been Corll's original accomplice, as well as his lover. He had been procuring victims tor Corll long before Henley came along. In fact, Henley was intended to be just another victim when he was taken along to meet Corll in 1971. But Corll soon realized that Henley would be more useful as an accomplice. He had lots of friends, and would do anything for money. In fact, said Henley, he was pretty sure that Corll still planned to kill him sooner or later, because he had his eye on Henley's 14-year-old brother Ronnie, and knew he would have to kill Wayne before he could get his hands on Ronnie . . .

The method of obtaining victims was usually much the same. Corll would drive around with Henley until they saw a likely victim, and Corll would offer him a lift. Since there was already a teenager in the car, the boy would suspect nothing. That was how Dean had picked up that 13-year-old blond kid a few days ago. Dean was parked in front of a grocery store when the kid came past on his bike. Dean called him over and told him he had found some Coke bottles in his van, and the kid could go and collect the deposit on them. The boy (it was 13-year-old James Dreymala) took the bottles and came back a few minutes later with the money. Then Dean remembered that he had a lot more Coke bottles back in his garage, and if the kid would like to come along, he could have them. So James Dreymala allowed Dean to put his bike in the back of the van, and went back to Dean's house on Lamar Street. The boy said he had to ring his father to ask if he could stay out, but the father refused. After the call, Dean "had his fun," then strangled the boy, taking the body out to the boatshed to join the others . . .

At about this time, Mullican heard the latest report from the ooat shed. Four more victims had been found in the past two hours, bringing the total up to twelve. And beside one of them his genitals had been found in a plastic bag. Part of Dean's "fun" was castrating his victims.

Henley's new confession went on for two more hours. It was

rambling and often incoherent, but Mullican gathered that Henley had been present at the murder of at least nine boys. He admitted shooting one of them himself. The bullet had gone up his nose, and the boy had looked up and said: "Wayne, why did you shoot me?" Henley pointed the gun at the boy's head and pulled the trigger again; this time the boy died.

Had Corll buried any bodies in other places beside the boat-shed? Mullican wanted to know. Oh sure, said Henley, there were some on the shores of Lake Sam Rayburn, and more on High Island Beach, east of Galveston . . .

It was now past noon, but it seemed a good idea to bring Wayne Henley and David Brooks face to face. Then get Henley to show them where the bodies were buried at Lake Sam Rayburn.

When they arrived at the Houston police station, Lieutenant Breck Porter took Mullican aside. David Brooks was doing plenty of "confessing," but it was all about Wayne Henley and Dean Corll. According to Brooks he had been merely an innocent bystander.

David Brooks proved to be a tall, round-faced, long-haired youth who wore granny glasses; apparently he had recently married. He looked startled to see Wayne Henley—no one had warned him Henley was on his way. Henley stared across at his former friend. "David, I told 'em everything. You better do the same."

Brooks looked defensive. "I don't know what you're talking about."

'Yes you do. And if you don't tell everything, I'm gonna change my confession and say you was responsible for all of it."

David Brooks said he wanted to talk to his father, and was taken out of the room. Later that day, he was told he was under arrest for being implicated in the murders. He was subdued and tearful as he was led away.

Henley, on the other hand, seemed to have been infused with a new life since his confession. On the way out to Lake Sam Rayburn—a hundred and twenty miles away, in the Angelina National Park—he talked non-stop, and made a number of damaging admissions. "I choked one of them boys until he turned blue, but Dean still had to come and finish him off." When a deputy asked how a decent boy like him could get involved in murder, he made the odd reply: "If you had a daddy that shot at you, you might do some things too."

An hour later he was leading them into the woods on the shores of Lake Sam Rayburn. He was already implicating David Brooks, although not by name. "We picked them up and Dean raped and killed them." Asked by a reporter if there had been any torture, he replied cryptically: "It wasn't what you would really call torture." But he declined to elaborate. Then, refusing to allow reporters and photographers to accompany them, he led the police to the sites of four more bodies. One of them had been buried underneath a board; it emerged later that when Henley and Corll had returned to bury another body, they had found a hand sticking out of the ground, so had re-buried it with the board on top.

Before darkness made further digging impossible, two bodies had been unearthed. The latest news from the boat shed in south Houston was that the digging was now finished, and seventeen bodies—or parts of bodies—had been found. The ones that had not been buried in plastic bags had decayed, so that little but bones remained. The body count so far was nineteen.

The following morning, it rose to twenty-one, with the uncovering of the other two bodies at Lake Sam Rayburn. By mid-morning, the convoy of police and reporters was on its way south to High Island, where Henley insisted there were eight more bodies buried.

The search of the High Island beach turned into a kind of

circus. Three helicopters had arrived with camera crews, and the reporters almost outnumbered the crowds of morbidly fascinated spectators. Henley was in good spirits, offering to race the overweight sheriff up the beach—an offer which, in view of the 90 degree heat, the sheriff politely declined. David Brooks, who had been brought down from Houston, was much more subdued; he sat there much of the time, his arms around his knees, refusing to speak to reporters.

Only two more bodies were found that afternoon, bringing the total up to twenty-three. Later, four more would be unearthed on the beach. The other two mentioned by Henley were never discovered. But even a total of twenty-seven made Dean Corll America's worst mass murderer so far.

While Wayne Henley was helping the police at Lake Sam Rayburn, David Brooks was offering the first complete picture of Corll's career of homicidal perversion in the Houston interrogation room. He still insisted that he had never taken an active part in the killings, but his questioners suspected that this was because he had sworn to his father that he was innocent of murder. Henley, who seems to have been the more truthful of the two, stated that Brooks *had* taken an active part in several murders. The picture that emerged left little doubt that this was true.

Meanwhile, reporters were learning all they could about the background of America's worst mass murderer. For the most part, it proved to be surprisingly innocuous.

Dean Arnold Corll was born on Christmas Day 1939, in Waynesdale, Indiana, the first child of Arnold and Mary Corll, who were in their early twenties. But the parents were temperamentally unsuited; both were strong characters, and their quarrels could be violent. Mary Corll adored her eldest son; Arnold Corll—a factory worker who became an electrician— was a disciplinarian who found children tiresome. When Dean was six, the couple divorced, and Arnold Corll was drafted into the Army Air Force. Mrs. Corll bought a house trailer and drove to join her husband at his base in Tennessee, but the quarrels continued and they separated again. An elderly farm couple agreed to look after the boys—Dean had a younger brother, Stanley—while Mary Corll went out to work.

From the beginning, Dean was an oversensitive loner. Because his feelings were hurt at a birthday party when he was six, he always refused to go to other people's houses. While Stanley played with other children Dean stayed at home.

The Corlls made yet another attempt at reconciliation after the war, and in 1950 drove the trailer to Houston. But the marriage still failed to work out, and they parted again.

At this point, it was discovered that Dean had a congenital heart ailment, and he was ordered to avoid sports. In fact it was hardly necessary; he was not the sporting type.

Life for Mrs. Corll was hard; she worked while the boys went to one school after another. In 1953 she married a travelling clock salesman named Jake West, by whom she had a daughter. They moved to Vidor, Texas, a small town where, as one commentator put it, "the big event is for the kids to pour kerosene on the cat and set it afire." Since he spent so much time without his parents, Dean became intensely protective of his siblings—a kind of surrogate mother.

Now a teenager, Dean took up skin-diving, but had to quit when he fainted one day, and the doctor diagnosed a recurrence of the heart problem. But he was allowed to continue playing the trombone in the school band. He was always quiet, always polite, and never complained or "fussed."

One day, a pecan-nut salesman observed Mrs. West's efficiency at baking pies and asked her why she didn't take up candy making. She liked the idea, and was soon running a candy business in their garage, with Jake West as traveling salesman and Dean as the errand boy and "gofer" ("go fer this, go fer that . . .") He was often overworked, but remained cheerful and uncomplaining. After his graduation from high school at the age of 20, Dean went back to Indiana to be with Jake West's widowed mother, while the family returned to Houston. There the candy business continued to be underfunded. Two years later, when Dean moved back to Houston, he took a job with the Houston Lighting and Power Company, and made candy at nights. Women who worked there were overawed at his industry.

In 1964, Dean Corll was drafted into the army. This seems to have been a watershed in his life, for it was the time when he first realized he was homosexual. No details are available, but it seems obvious that some homosexual affair made him realize what he had so far failed to suspect. Released from the army after eleven months—pleading that his family needed him to work in the candy business—he returned to Houston to find his mother's second marriage in the process of dissolution. Mr. and Mrs. West had become business rivals rather than partners, and when Jake West threw her out of the shop one day, Mary West went off and started one of her own. Dean didn't mind; he had never liked his stepfather.

Now living in an apartment of his own, Dean began making friends with the children of the neighborhood—notably the boys—giving away free candy. Yet when a boy who worked for the company made some kind of sexual advance, Dean was angry and upset, and pleased when his mother dismissed him. Nevertheless, a fellow-worker noticed that another teenage employee always made sure that he was never left alone with Corll.

Dean's mother remained intensely protective, treating him as if he was still a teenager. But he was once again seeing something of his father, for whom he had great admiration.

Meanwhile, Mary West now repeated her error and married yet again—this time a merchant seaman. She found him stupid and coarse, and soon began to suspect he was a psychotic. They divorced—and then re-married. He became neurotically jealous of his wife, and they separated again. But his continual attempts to force his way into the candy factory destroyed her enthusiasm for the place. When a psychic told her to move to Dallas, she took his advice, and divorced the merchant seaman yet again. And Dean, now left alone in Houston, suddenly felt that he was free to do as he liked.

Corll's Mr. Hyde aspect had at first manifested itself simply as a powerful attraction to boys, with whom he enjoyed playing the part of an elder brother. One boy said: "He acted real nice to me. He never tried to mess with me or nothin'." But the desire was there, and Mr. Hyde began to break out when he realized that some boys would permit oral sex in exchange for money. Fourteen-year-old David Brooks was one of these. In fact, he was delighted to have an "elder brother," and became totally emotionally dependent on Corll—so dependent that he made no attempt to denounce him when he learned that he was a killer.

This emotional dependence of David Brooks undoubtedly played a major part in the tragedy that followed. His love for Corll meant that he was willing to subjugate his will to Corll's. And Corll, in turn, was encouraged to give way to his Mr. Hyde personality. It was a case of *folie à deux*.

Brooks was a lonely schoolboy when he met Dean Corll in the Heights in 1969. The two had something in common: their parents had broken up, and they were on their own. Corll's mother had wound up the candy factory she ran with her son's help, and gone off to live in Dallas. Corll had found himself a $5 an hour job with the Houston Lighting and Power Company, and moved his few possessions into a shed. Corll had propositioned Brooks, and the teenager had agreed to allowing Corll to have oral sex for a payment of $5. But their relationship was not purely commercial. Corll was able to give Brooks something he needed badly—affection. Brooks, in turn, worshipped Corll: "Dean was a real good dude," "a brilliant and generous man." And when he returned to Houston in 1970—escaping from his disintegrating family—Brooks began to see a great deal of Corll: during the next three years they often shared rooms for brief periods. By that time, it seems probable that Corll had already committed his first murder. A 21-year-old student from the University of Texas in Austin, Jeffrey Alan Konen, had hitchhiked to his home in Houston on September 25, 1970. He had last been seen at six o'clock in the evening, looking for another lift. It seems probable that it was Corll who picked him up, and invited him back to his apartment at 3300 Yorktown. Konen's body was one of the last of those found—on High Island beach—and was so decomposed that it was impossible to determine cause of death. But the fact that the body had been bound hand and foot suggested that Corll had killed Jeffrey Konen in order to commit sodomy.

What made Corll's murderous mission so easy was the teenage drug culture of the Heights. In the claustrophobic, run-down environment, all the kids were bored and discontented; they felt they were stuck there for life. The mere suggestion of a party was enough to make their eyes light up. They all smoked pot—when they could afford it. They also popped pills—Seconal, Nembutal, phenobarbital, Quaaludes, even aspirin, washed down with beer or Coca Cola. But because it was cheap, acrylic paint was the easiest way of obtaining a quick "high." Although one boy collapsed and died when he tried to play football after a long glue-sniffing session, it made no difference to the others; he was merely "unlucky." Moreover, the possession of "glue" was perfectly legal; and in an environment where a teenager was likely to be searched for drugs at any hour of the day, this went a long way towards making acrylics the most popular form of escape.

The fact that most of the kids were permanently broke conferred another tremendous advantage on a predatory homosexual like Corll. Allowing a "queer" to perform oral sex was an easy and quick way of obtaining a few dollars. There can be no doubt that many of Corll's victims had been back to his room several times before his demand for a more painful form of sex caused them to balk, and led to their deaths. The fact that there *were* a fairly high number of runaways from the Heights meant that occasional disappearances caused little stir.

The central key to the Houston murders is Corll's craving for sexual violation. At some point, oral sex ceased to satisfy him. Brooks admitted: "He killed them because he wanted sex, and they didn't want to." Even Brooks himself seems to have withheld anal sex. He described how, after he had introduced Corll to Wayne Henley, the latter knocked him unconscious as he entered Corll's apartment; Corll then tied him to the bed and sodomized him. This would obviously have been pointless if anal sex had been a normal part of their relationship. Yet in spite of the rape, Brooks continued to worship Corll, and to participate in the murders and disposal of the bodies.

It also seems clear that Corll was in love with Henley. But Henley remained independent. Far more avaricious than Brooks, he became Corll's accomplice for cash. In spite of Henley's denial, there can be no doubt that Corll paid him large sums of money as a procurer. One friend of Henley's later described how Henley had suggested that they should go to Australia together as homesteaders—Henley declared that he would provide the $1,700 they each would need. "Where would you get it?" asked his friend. "I already have it." Henley's later assertion that Corll never paid him is almost certainly an attempt to conceal the appalling truth: that he sold his friends to Corll for $200 each.

By the end of 1970, Corll was firmly in the grip of "Mr. Hyde." Brooks later tried to justify the murders: "Most of the boys weren't good boys. This . . . probably sounds terrible, but most of 'em wasn't no great loss. They was in trouble all the time, dope fiends and one thing or another." This is almost certainly a repetition of something Corll said to Brooks—perhaps on many occasions.

Not long after the murder of Jeffrey Konen, David Brooks walked into Corll's Yorktown apartment unannounced, and found Corll naked. In another room there were two naked boys strapped to a plywood board. Corll demanded indignantly what Brooks was doing there, and ordered him to leave. Later, he told Brooks that he had killed both boys, and offered him a car as the price of his silence. In fact, he gave Brooks a new Corvette. The identity of these two victims has never been established, but they were probably among the bodies found on the High Island beach.

Having accepted the Corvette, Brooks was now an accomplice. He would go "cruising" with Corll and offering lifts to teenage boys. One unknown youth was picked up some time in November 1970, and taken back to Corll's apartment. Corll raped and murdered the boy while Brooks looked on. No further details of this murder—or victim—are known.

Corll's appetite for murder was growing. Many of the boys he used to befriend in the days of the candy factory, and who had always been welcome visitors in his room, now noticed that he was becoming bad tempered and secretive, and they stopped calling round. Many of these boys later insisted that Corll had simply been "nice" to them, without any attempt to make sexual advances. Many others, like David Brooks, had undoubtedly accepted money for oral sex.

On December 15, 1970, Brooks persuaded two boys back to an apartment that Corll had rented on Columbia Street. They were 14-year-old James Eugene Glass, and his friend

Danny Michael Yates, 15. Both had been to church with James Glass's father, and had agreed to meet him later. Glass had already been back to Corll's apartment on a previous occasion, and had taken a great liking to Corll. This time, both boys ended on the plywood board, after which they were strangled. By this time, Corll had decided that he needed somewhere closer than High Island or Lake Sam Rayburn (where his family owned a holiday cabin), so he rented the boat shed on Silver Bell Street. The two boys were buried there.

Corll had apparently enjoyed the double murder so much that he was eager to try it again. Six weeks later, two brothers, 14-year-old Donald Edward Waldrop, and 13-year-old Jerry Lynn Waldrop, were lured to a newly rented apartment at 3200 Mangum Road. (Corll changed apartments frequently, almost certainly to prevent curious neighbors from gossiping about his activities.) The father of the Waldrop boys was a construction worker who worked next door to Corll's new apartment. The boys were also strangled and buried in the boat shed. Brooks admitted: "I believe I was present when they were buried." This was typical of his general evasiveness.

On May 29, 1971, David Hilligiest, 13, disappeared on his way to the swimming pool; his friend, 16-year-old George Malley Winkle, also vanished the same day. Malley was on probation for stealing a bicycle. That same evening, just before midnight, the telephone rang; it was Malley, contacting his mother to tell her that he was in Freeport—a surfing resort sixty miles to the south—with some kids. They would be on their way home shortly. That night, Mrs. Winkle slept badly, with a foreboding that her son was in trouble. When he failed to return, she asked young people in the neighborhood if they had seen him, and learned that he had climbed into a white van, together with David Hilligiest.

The frantic parents spent weeks following up every possible lead. They had posters printed, offering a thousand dollars' reward, and friendly truckers distributed them all over southern Texas. So did a lifelong friend of David Hilligiest's—Elmer Wayne Henley, another child of a broken home. He tried to comfort the Hilligiests by telling them that he was sure nothing had happened to David. A psychic who was consulted by the Hilligiests disagreed: he plunged them into despair by telling them their son was dead.

Ruben Watson, 17, another child of a broken home, went off to the cinema on the afternoon of August 17, 1971, with a few dollars borrowed from his grandmother; he later rang his mother at work to say he would meet her out at 7:30. He never arrived, and she never saw him again. Brooks later admitted being present when Ruben was murdered.

By this time, Wayne Henley had entered the picture. He had become friendly with David Brooks, and Brooks had introduced him to Dean Corll. Henley was intended as a victim, but Corll seems to have decided that he would be more useful as a pimp. The fact that Henley was skinny and pimply may also have played a part in Corll's decision to let him live. The Hilligiests' son Greg—aged 11—came home one day to say that he had been playing an exciting game called poker with Wayne Henley, David Brooks, and an older friend of Henley's who made candy. Dorothy Hilligiest knew the man who made candy—in the previous year, she had gone looking for David, and found him at the candy factory with Malley Winkle and the round-faced man who owned the place. Mrs. Hilligiest had bought a box of candy from him before she took David away . . .

Another friend of Henley's was 14-year-old Rhonda Williams, a shapely girl who was as anxious to escape the Heights as most of its other teenagers. Since she had been sexually assaulted as a child, her attitude to sex was inhibited and circumspect. Like so many Heights teenagers, she was part of a one-parent family—her mother had collapsed and died of a heart attack as she was hanging out the washing. Rhonda craved affection and security, and she seemed to have found it when she met 19-year-old Frank Aguirre. He was slightly cross-eyed, but serious-minded, and was already saving money—from his job in a restaurant—to get married to Rhonda. But on February 24, 1972, Frank Aguirre failed to return home from his work, and was never seen again. He left his pay check uncollected. Rhonda was shattered and went into nervous depression for a year; she was only just beginning to recover on that evening of August 1973 when she informed Wayne Henley that she had decided to run away from home, and Henley took her over to Dean Corll's house in Pasadena to stay the night . . .

On May 21, 1972, 16-year-old Johnny Delome vanished. The body was found at High Island fourteen months later; he had been shot as well as strangled. Johnny Delome must have been the youth that Henley shot up the nose, and then in the head. He was killed at the same time as Billy Baulch, 17, who was also buried at High Island. Six months later, Billy's 15-year-old brother Michael would become another victim of Dean Corll. In the meantime, he had killed another two boys, Wally Jay Simoneaux, 14, and Richard Hembree, 13, on October 3, 1972. Their bodies were found together in the boat shed.

Another victim of 1972 was 18-year-old Mark Scott, whose body was one of those that were never identified; Brooks stated that he was also one of Corll's victims.

And so the murders went on into 1973; Billy Lawrence, 15, on June 11; Homer Garcia, 15, on July 7; Charles Cobble, 17, on July 25, who vanished with his friend Marty Jones, 18, on the same day. The final victim was 13-year-old James Dreymala, lured to Corll's Pasadena house to collect Coke bottles, and buried in the boat shed. There were undoubtedly other victims in 1973, possibly as many as nine. Brooks said that Corll's youngest victim was a 9-year-old boy.

On Monday August 13, five days after the death of Dean Corll, a Grand Jury began to hear evidence against Henley and Brooks. The first witnesses were Rhonda Williams and Tim Kerley, the two who had almost become Corll's latest victims. It was clear that Kerley had been invited to Corll's house by Henley in order to be raped and murdered—this is what Henley meant when he told Kerley that he could have got fifteen hundred dollars for him. He was exaggerating, but was otherwise telling the truth. And when Corll had snarled: "You've spoilt everything," he meant that the arrival of Rhonda Williams now made it impossible to murder Kerley. At that moment, it seems, he thought of a solution: to kill all three teenagers.

Rhonda Williams, it emerged, had decided to run away with Henley, whom she now regarded as her boyfriend. In fact, Corll knew all about the arrangement and had no objection—he himself was planning to move to Colorado, where his mother was living, and to take Henley and Rhonda Williams with him. The fact that he also planned to take an old flame of his pre-homosexual days called Betty Hawkins, as well as her two children, suggests that Corll had decided to give up killing teenagers. But Rhonda had arranged to run away on August 17, nine days later; and when she arrived at Corll's house in the early hours of August 8, he felt that his fun had been spoiled.

After listening to the evidence of various teenagers, the jury indicted Henley and Brooks on murder charges. Henley was charged with taking part in the killing of Billy Lawrence, Charles Cobble, Marty Jones, Johnny Delome, Frank Aguirre and Homer Garcia; Brooks for his part in the murders of James Glass, Ruben Watson, Billy Lawrence and Johnny Delome. Efforts by the lawyers to get bail were turned down.

Houston was stunned by the events of the past week, and criticism of the police department was bitter and uninhibited. The main complaint of the parents of missing teenagers was that they had been unable to get the police to take the slightest interest; they were told that their children were runaways. The Police Chief Herman Short counterattacked clumsily by publicly stating that there had been no connection between the missing teenagers—implying that there would have been little for the police to investigate. The statements of Henley and Brooks—indicating that most of the victims knew one another—flatly contradicted this assertion. Short went on to say that the murders indicated that parents should pay closer attention to the comings and goings of their teenagers, a remark that drew outraged comments from parents like Dorothy Hilligiest, whose children had simply vanished on their way to or from some normal and innocent activity. Short went on angrily to attack the Soviet newspaper *Izvestia*, which had referred to the "murderous bureaucracy" of the Houston police department, pointing out that the Soviet government had a reputation for making dissenters disappear. All this failed to impress the public or the politicians, and Short resigned three months later after the municipal elections.

There was also criticism of the attitude of the police towards the search for more bodies. One of Corll's ex-employees, Ruby Jenkins, had mentioned the interesting fact that, during the last years of the candy factory's existence, Corll was often seen handling a shovel and digging holes. He dug under the floor of his private room in the factory—known jokingly as the "pouting room," because he often retired there to sulk—then cemented over the excavation. He also dug holes near the rear wall of the factory, and on a space that later became a parking lot. He always did this by night. His explanation was that he was burying spoiled candy because it drew bees and bred weevils. No one at the time questioned this curious explanation, or asked him what was wrong with placing the spoiled candy in a plastic bag and dropping it in the trash can. "He had this big roll of plastic sheet, four or five foot wide, and he had sacks of cement and some other stuff back in his pouting room." Clearly, this was something that required investigating. But when the police came along to look at the spots indicated by Ruby Jenkins, they dug only half-heartedly in a few places, and soon gave up. "Lady, this is old cement. There couldn't be any bodies there."

After the finding of bodies 26 and 27—on High Island beach, tied together—the search for more bodies was dropped, even though Henley insisted that two more were buried there. Another curious feature of this final discovery was that there were two extra bones—an arm bone and a pelvis—in the grave, plainly indicating a twenty-eighth victim.

Lieutenant Porter received two calls about bodies on the same morning. A Mr. and Mrs. Abernathy had been camping on Galveston Island—about fifty miles down the coast from High Island—when they saw two men carrying a long bundle over the dunes. Another man had been camping on east Galveston beach when he saw a white car and another car parked near a hole in the beach; a long plastic bundle the size of a body lay beside the hole. There were three men beside the hole. The man identified two from photographs as Dean Corll and Wayne Henley. The third man had long blond hair—like David Brooks. As the campers sat looking at this curious scene in their own car, Henley advanced on them with a menacing expression, and they drove off.

These two events took place in March and June, 1973. In fact, the first 1973 victim identified (from the Lake Sam Rayburn burial site) was Billy Lawrence, who vanished on June 11. It seems unlikely that a man who had been killing as regularly as Corll should allow a seven-month period to elapse between victims (the last known victim of 1972 is Michael Baulch, Billy Baulch's younger brother). The unidentified victims found in the boat shed had obviously been buried much earlier, probably in 1971.

The Galveston authorities flatly declined to allow the Houston police to follow up this lead, refusing to permit digging on their beach.

Meanwhile, the police switchboard in Houston continued to handle hundreds of inquiries about missing teenagers—one mother, whose son had been working with a circus, and had vanished in Houston, was certain that he was one of Corll's victims. In most of these cases, the police were forced to state that they were unable to help.

When Brooks and Henley appeared for their arraignment, there was a heavy guard of armed police—dozens of threatening phone calls had been received from all over Texas. Henley's defense lawyer, Charles Melder, indicated that his defense would be one of insanity. Brooks's attorney, Ted Musick, indicated that he would follow the same line. At the same time, the District Attorney announced that each of the accused would be tried on one charge only: Henley for the murder of Charles Cobble, and Brooks for that of Billy Lawrence.

Since Corll was already dead, and the two accused had already confessed, the trial itself was something of an anticlimax. Its venue was changed, on the insistence of the lawyers, and it opened at San Antonio, Texas, in July 1974, before Judge Preston Dial. Predictably, the jury rejected the insanity defense, and Henley was convicted on nine counts (not including the shooting of Dean Corll), drawing a total sentence of 594 years. Brooks was convicted on only one count, and received life imprisonment. Henley appealed in 1979, and was convicted for a second time.

It is easy to understand the sense of shock produced by the Corll murders—analogous to that felt in England after the

Moors murder case. The impression produced by the evidence is that Corll was a sadistic monster, the kind we would expect to encounter in a horror film, possessed by evil spirits. But our study of other serial killers—like Haarmann and Kürten—makes it clear that nothing is ever as simple as that. The evidence shows that Corll was basically a spoilt brat who always wanted his own way, and that he remained emotionally a child—this aspect of his personality is caught in the notorious photograph that shows him holding a teddy bear.

In fact, like so many serial killers, Corll drifted into it by slow steps—as a man becomes a drug addict or an alcoholic. He wanted young boys; he bought their sexual favors. Then he began raping and killing them. It was a gentle progression down a slope, like walking slowly into a pond . . .

This is also true of another case that received even more publicity than the Corll murders. Ted Bundy is a textbook case of the "high IQ killer."

On January 31, 1974, a student at the University of Washington, in Seattle, Lynda Ann Healy, vanished from her room; the bedsheets were bloodstained, suggesting that she had been struck violently on the head. During the following March, April and May, three more girl students vanished; in June, two more. In July, two girls vanished on the same day. It happened at a popular picnic spot, Lake Sammanish; a number of people saw a good-looking young man, with his arm in a sling, accost a girl named Janice Ott and ask her to help him lift a boat on to the roof of his car; she walked away with him and did not return. Later, a girl named Denise Naslund was accosted by the same young man; she also vanished. He had been heard to introduce himself as "Ted."

In October 1974 the killings shifted to Salt Lake City; three girls disappeared in one month. In November, the police had their first break in the case: a girl named Carol DaRonch was accosted in a shopping center by a young man who identified himself as a detective, and told her that there had been an attempt to break into her car; she agreed to accompany him to headquarters to view a suspect. In the car he snapped a handcuff on her wrist and pointed a gun at her head; she fought and screamed, and managed to jump from the car. That evening, a girl student vanished on her way to meet her brother. A handcuff key was found near the place from which she had been taken.

Meanwhile, the Seattle police had fixed on a young man named Ted Bundy as a main suspect. For the past six years, he had been involved in a close relationship with a divorcee named Meg Anders, but she had called off the marriage when she realized he was a habitual thief. After the Lake Sammanish disappearances, she had seen a photofit drawing of the wanted "Ted" in the *Seattle Times* and thought it looked like Bundy; moreover, "Ted" drove a Volkswagen like Bundy's. She had seen crutches and plaster of Paris in Bundy's room, and the coincidence seemed too great; with immense misgivings, she telephoned the police. They told her that they had already checked on Bundy; but at the suggestion of the Seattle police, Carol DaRonch was shown Bundy's photograph. She tentatively identified it as resembling the man who had tried to abduct her, but was obviously far from sure. (Bundy had been wearing a beard at the time.)

In January, March, April, July and August 1975, more girls vanished in Colorado. (Their bodies—or skeletons—were found later in remote spots.) On August 16, 1975, Bundy was arrested for the first time. As a police car was driving along a dark street in Salt Lake City, a parked Volkswagen launched into motion; the policeman followed, and it accelerated. He caught up with the car at a service station, and found in the car a pantyhose mask, a crow-bar, an icepick and various other tools; there was also a pair of handcuffs.

Bundy, 29 years old, seemed an unlikely burglar. He was a graduate of the University of Washington, and was in Utah to study law; he had worked as a political campaigner, and for the Crime Commission in Seattle. In his room there was nothing suspicious—except maps and brochures of Colorado, from which five girls had vanished that year. But strands of hair were found in the car, and they proved to be identical with those of Melissa Smith, daughter of the Midvale police chief, who had vanished in the previous October. Carol DaRonch had meanwhile identified Bundy in a police line-up as the fake policeman, and bloodspots on her clothes—where she had scratched her assailant—were of Bundy's group. Credit card receipts showed that Bundy had been close to various places from which girls had vanished in Colorado.

In theory, this should have been the end of the case—and if it had been, it would have been regarded as a typical triumph of scientific detection, beginning with the photofit drawing and concluding with the hair and blood evidence. The evidence was, admittedly, circumstantial, but taken all together, it formed a powerful case. The central objection to it became apparent as soon as Bundy walked into court. He looked so obviously decent and clean-cut that most people felt there must be some mistake. He was polite, well-spoken, articulate, charming, the kind of man who could have found himself a girlfriend for each night of the week. Why *should* such a man be a sex killer? In spite of which, the impression he made was of brilliance and plausibility rather than innocence. For example, he insisted that he had driven away from the police car because he was smoking marijuana, and that he had thrown the joint out of the window.

The case seemed to be balanced on a knife-edge—until the judge pronounced a sentence of guilty of kidnapping. Bundy sobbed and pleaded not to be sent to prison; but the judge sentenced him to a period between one and fifteen years.

The Colorado authorities now charged him with the murder of a girl called Caryn Campbell, who had been abducted from a ski resort where Bundy had been seen by a witness. After a morning courtroom session in Aspen, Bundy succeeded in wandering into the library during the lunch recess, and jumping out of the window. He was recaptured eight days later, tired and hungry, and driving a stolen car.

Legal arguments dragged on for another six months—what evidence was admissible and what was not. And on December 30, 1977, Bundy escaped again, using a hacksaw blade to cut through an imperfectly welded steel plate above the light fixture in his cell. He made his way to Chicago, then south to Florida; there, near the Florida State University in Tallahassee, he took a room. A few days later, a man broke into a nearby sorority house and attacked four girls with a club, knocking them unconscious; one was strangled with her pantyhose and raped; another died on her way to the hospital. One of the strangled girl's nipples had been almost bitten off, and she had a bite mark on her left buttock. An hour and a half later, a student woke up in another sorority house when she heard bangs next door, and a girl whimpering. She dialed the number of the room, and as the telephone rang, someone could be heard running out. Cheryl Thomas was found lying in bed, her skull fractured but still alive.

Three weeks later, on February 6, 1978, Bundy—who was calling himself Chris Hagen—stole a white Dodge van and left Tallahassee; he stayed in the Holiday Inn, using a stolen credit card. The following day a 12-year-old girl named Kimberly Leach walked out of her classroom in Lake City, Florida, and vanished. Bundy returned to Tallahassee to take a girl out for an expensive meal—paid for with a stolen credit card—then absconded via the fire escape, owing large arrears of rent. At 4 a.m. on February 15, a police patrolman noticed an orange Volkswagen driving suspiciously slowly, and radioed for a check on its number; it proved to be stolen from Tallahassee. After a struggle and a chase, during which he tried to kill the policeman, Bundy was captured yet again. When the police learned his real name, and that he had just left a town in which five girls had been attacked, they suddenly understood the importance of their capture. Bundy seemed glad to be in custody, and began to unburden himself. He explained that "his problem" had begun when he had seen a girl on a bicycle in Seattle, and "had to have her." He had followed her, but she escaped. "Sometimes," he admitted, "I feel like a vampire."

On April 7, a party of searchers along the Suwanee River found the body of Kimberly Leach in an abandoned hut; she had been strangled and sexually violated. Three weeks later, surrounded by hefty guards, Bundy allowed impressions of his teeth to be taken, for comparison with the marks on the buttocks of the dead student, Lisa Levy.

Bundy's lawyers persuaded him to enter into "plea bargaining": in exchange for a guarantee of life imprisonment—rather than a death sentence—he would confess to the murders of Lisa Levy, Margaret Bowman and Kimberly Leach. But Bundy changed his mind at the last moment and decided to sack his lawyers.

Bundy's trial began on June 25, 1979, and the evidence against him was damning; a witness who had seen him leaving the sorority house after the attacks; a pantyhose mask found in the room of Cheryl Thomas, which resembled the one found in Bundy's car; but above all, the fact that Bundy's teeth matched the marks on Lisa Levy's buttocks. The highly compromising taped interview with the Pensacola police was judged inadmissible in court because his lawyer had not been present. Bundy again dismissed his defense and took it over himself; the general impression was that he was trying to be too clever. The jury took only six hours to find him guilty on all counts. Judge Ed Cowart pronounced sentence of death by electrocution, but evidently felt some sympathy for the good-looking young defendant. "It's a tragedy for this court to see such a total waste of humanity. You're a bright young man. You'd have made a good lawyer . . . But you went the wrong way, partner. Take care of yourself . . ."

Bundy was taken to Raiford prison, Florida, where he was placed on Death Row. On July 2, 1986, when he was due to die a few hours before serial killer Gerald Stano, both were granted a stay of execution.

The Bundy case illustrates the immense problems faced by investigators of serial murders. When Meg Anders—Bundy's mistress—telephoned the police after the double murder near Lake Sammanish, Bundy's name had already been suggested by three people. But he was only one of 3,500 suspects. Later Bundy was added to the list of 100 "best suspects" which investigators constructed on grounds of age, occupation and past record. Two hundred thousand items were fed into computers, including the names of 41,000 Volkswagen owners, 5,000 men with a record of mental illness, every student who had taken classes with the dead girls, and all transfers from other colleges they had attended. All this was programmed into thirty-seven categories, each using a different criterion to isolate the suspect. Asked to name anyone who came up on any three of these programs, the computer produced 16,000 names. When the number was raised to four, it was reduced to 600. Only when it was raised to twenty-five was it reduced to ten suspects, with Bundy seventh on the list. The police were still investigating number six when Bundy was detained in Salt Lake City with burgling tools in his car. Only after that did Bundy become suspect number one. And by that time, he had already committed a minimum of seventeen murders. (There seems to be some doubt about the total, estimates varying between twenty and forty; Bundy himself told the

Pensacola investigators that it ran into double figures.) Detective Robert Keppel, who worked on the case, is certain that Bundy would have been revealed as suspect number one even if he had not been arrested. But in 1982, Keppel and his team were presented with another mass killer in the Seattle area, the so-called Green River Killer, whose victims were mostly prostitutes picked up on the "strip" in Seattle. Seven years later, in 1989, he had killed at least forty-nine women, and the computer had still failed to identify an obvious suspect number one.

The Bundy case is doubly baffling because he seems to contradict the basic assertions of every major criminologist from Lombroso to Yochelson. Bundy is not an obvious born criminal, with degenerate physical characteristics; there is (as far as is known) no history of insanity in his family; he was not a social derelict or a failure. In her book *The Stranger Beside Me*, his friend Ann Rule describes him as "a man of unusual accomplishment." How could the most subtle "psychological profiling" target such a man as a serial killer?

The answer to the riddle emerged fairly late in the day, four years after Bundy had been sentenced to death. Before his conviction, Bundy had indicated his willingness to cooperate on a book about himself, and two journalists, Stephen G. Michaud and Hugh Aynesworth, went to interview him in prison. They discovered that Bundy had no wish to discuss guilt, except to deny it, and he actively discouraged them from investigating the case against him. He wanted them to produce a gossipy book focusing squarely on himself, like bestselling biographies of celebrities such as Frank Sinatra. Michaud and Aynesworth would have been happy to write a book demonstrating his innocence, but as they looked into the case, they found it impossible to accept this; instead, they concluded that he had killed at least twenty-one girls. When they began to probe, Bundy revealed the characteristics that

Yochelson and Samenow had found to be so typical of criminals: hedging, lying, pleas of faulty memory, and self-justification: "Intellectually, Ted seemed profoundly dissociative, a compartmentalizer, and thus a superb rationalizer." Emotionally, he struck them as a severe case of arrested development: "he might as well have been a 12-year-old, and a precocious and bratty one at that. So extreme was his childishness that his pleas of innocence were of a character very similar to that of the little boy who'll deny wrongdoing in the face of overwhelming evidence to the contrary." So Michaud had the ingenious idea of suggesting that Bundy should "speculate on the nature of a person capable of doing what Ted had been accused (and convicted) of doing." Bundy embraced this idea with enthusiasm, and talked for hours into a tape recorder. Soon Michaud became aware that there were, in effect, two "Teds"—the analytical human being, and an entity inside him that Michaud came to call the "hunchback." (We have encountered this "other person"—Mr. Hyde—syndrome in many killers, from William Heirens and Peter Sutcliffe to the Boston Strangler.)

After generalizing for some time about violence in modern society, the disintegration of the home, and so on, Bundy got down to specifics, and began to discuss his own development.

He had been an illegitimate child, born to a respectable young girl in Philadelphia. She moved to Seattle to escape the stigma, and married a cook in the Veterans' Hospital. Ted was an oversensitive and self-conscious child who had all the usual daydreams of fame and wealth. And at an early stage he became a thief and something of a habitual liar—as many imaginative children do. But he seems to have been deeply upset by the discovery of his illegitimacy.

Bundy was not, in fact, a brilliant student. Although he struck his fellow students as witty and cultivated, his grades were usually Bs. In his late teens he became heavily infatuated with a fellow student, Stephanie Brooks, who was beautiful, sophisticated, and came of a wealthy family. Oddly enough, she responded and they became "engaged." To impress her he went to Stanford University to study Chinese; but he felt lonely away from home, and his grades were poor. "I found myself thinking about standards of success that I just didn't seem to be living up to." Stephanie wearied of his immaturity, and threw him over—the severest blow so far. He became intensely moody. "Dogged by feelings of worthlessness and failure," he took a job as a busboy in a hotel dining room. And at this point, he began the drift that eventually turned him into a serial killer. He became friendly with a drug addict. One night, they entered a cliffside house that had been partly destroyed by a landslide, and stole whatever they could find. "It was really thrilling." He began shoplifting and stealing "for thrills," once walking openly into someone's greenhouse, taking an eight-foot tree in a pot, and putting it in his car with the top sticking out of the sunroof.

He also became a full-time volunteer worker for Art Fletcher, the black Republican candidate for Lieutenant-Governor. He enjoyed the sense of being a "somebody" and mixing with interesting people. But Fletcher lost, and Bundy became a salesman in a department store. He met Meg Anders in a college beer joint, and they became lovers—she had a gentle, easy-going nature, which brought out Bundy's protective side. But she was shocked by his kleptomania.

In fact, the criminal side—the "hunchback"—was now developing fast. He acquired a taste for violent pornography—easy to buy openly in American shops. Once, walking round the university district, he saw a girl undressing in a lighted room. This was the turning point in his life. He began to devote hours to walking around, hoping to see more girls undressing. He was back at the university, studying psychology, but his night prowling prevented him from making full use of his undoubted intellectual capacities. He obtained his degree in due course—this may tell us more about American university standards than about Bundy's abilities—and tried to find a law school that would take him. He failed all the aptitude tests and was repeatedly turned down. A year later, he was finally accepted—he worked for the Crime Commission for a month, as an assistant, and for the Office of Justice Planning. His self-confidence increased by leaps and bounds. When he flew to San Francisco to see Stephanie Brooks, the girl who had jilted him, she was deeply impressed, and willing to renew their affair. He was still having an affair with Meg Anders, and entered on this new career as a Don Juan with his usual enthusiasm. He and Stephanie spent Christmas together and became "engaged." Then he dumped her as she had dumped him.

By this time, he had committed his first murder. For years, he had been a pornography addict and a Peeping Tom. ("He approached it almost like a project, throwing himself into it, literally, for years.") Then the "hunchback" had started to demand "more active kinds of gratification." He tried disabling women's cars, but the girls always had help on hand. He felt the need to indulge in this kind of behavior after drinking had reduced his inhibitions. One evening, he stalked a girl from a bar, found a heavy piece of wood, and managed to get ahead of her and lie in wait. Before she reached the place, where he was hiding, she stopped at her front door and went in. But the experience was like "making a hole in a dam." A few evenings later, as a woman was fumbling for her keys at her front door, he struck her on the head with a piece of wood. She collapsed, screaming, and he ran away. He was filled with remorse, and swore he would never do such a thing again. But six months later, he followed a woman home and peeped in as she undressed. He began to do this again and again. One day, when he knew the door was unlocked, he sneaked in, entered her bedroom, and jumped on her. She screamed and he ran away. Once again, there was a period of self-disgust and revulsion.

This was in the autumn of 1973. On January 4, 1974, he found a door that admitted him to the basement room of 18-year-old Sharon Clarke. Now, for the first time, he employed the technique he later used repeatedly, attacking her with a crow-bar until she was unconscious. Then he thrust a bar torn from the bed inside her, causing internal injuries. But he left her alive.

On the morning of February 1, 1974, he found an unlocked front door in a students' rooming house and went in. He entered a bedroom at random; 21-year-old Lynda Healy was asleep in bed. He battered her unconscious, then carried the body out to his car. He drove to Taylor Mountain, 20 miles east of Seattle, made her remove her pajamas, and raped her. When Bundy was later "speculating" about this crime for Stephen Michaud's benefit, the interviewer asked: "Was there any conversation?" Bundy replied: "There'd be some. Since this girl in front of him represented not a person, but again the image of something desirable, the last thing we would expect him to want to do would be to personalize this person."

So Lynda Healy was bludgeoned to death; Bundy always insisted that he took no pleasure in violence, but that his chief desire was "possession" of another person.

Now the "hunchback" was in full control, and there were five more victims over the next five months. Three of the girls were taken to the same spot on Taylor Mountain and there raped and murdered—Bundy acknowledged that his sexual gratification would sometimes take hours. The four bodies were found together in the following year. On the day he abducted the two girls from Lake Sammanish, Bundy "speculated" that he had taken the first, Janice Ott, to a nearby house and raped her, then returned to abduct the second girl, Denise Naslund, who was taken back to the same house and raped in view of the other girl; both were then killed, and taken to a remote spot four miles northeast of the park, where the bodies were dumped.

By the time he had reached this point in his "confession," Bundy had no further secrets to reveal; everything was obvious. Rape had become a compulsion that dominated his life. When he moved to Salt Lake City and entered the law school there—he was a failure from the beginning as a law student—he must have known that if he began to rape and kill young girls there, he would be establishing himself as suspect number one. This made no difference; he had to continue. Even the unsuccessful kidnapping of Carol DaRonch, and the knowledge that someone could now identify him, made no difference. He merely switched his activities to Colorado. Following his arrest, conviction and escape, he moved to Florida, and the compulsive attacks continued, although by now he must have known that another series of murders in a town to which he had recently moved must reduce his habitual plea of "coincidence" to an absurdity. It seems obvious that by this time he had lost the power of choice. In his last weeks of freedom, Bundy showed all the signs of weariness and self-disgust that had driven Carl Panzram to contrive his own execution.

Time finally ran out for Bundy on January 24, 1989. Long before this, he had recognized that his fatal mistake was to decline to enter into plea bargaining at his trial; the result was a death sentence instead of life imprisonment. In January 1989, his final appeal was turned down and the date of execution fixed. Bundy then made a last-minute attempt to save his life by offering to bargain murder confessions for a reprieve—against the advice of his attorney James Coleman, who warned him that this attempt to "trade over the victims' bodies" would only create hostility that would militate against further stays of execution. In fact, Bundy went on to confess to eight Washington murders, and then to a dozen others. Detective Bob Keppel, who had led the investigation in Seattle, commented: "The game-playing stuff cost him his life." Instead of making a full confession, Bundy doled out information bit by bit. "The whole thing was orchestrated," said Keppel. "We were held hostage for three days." And finally, when it was clear that there was no chance of further delay, Bundy confessed to the Chi Omega Sorority killings, admitting that he had been peeping through the window at girls undressing until he was carried away by desire and entered the building. He also mentioned pornography as being one of the factors that led him to murder. Newspaper columnists showed an inclination to doubt this, but Bundy's earlier confessions to Michaud leave no doubt that he was telling the truth.

At 7 a.m., Bundy was led into the execution chamber at Starke State prison, Florida; behind Plexiglas, an invited audience of forty-eight people sat waiting. As two warders attached his hands to the arms of the electric chair, Bundy recognized his attorney among the crowd; he smiled and nodded. Then straps were placed around his chest and over his mouth; the metal cap with electrodes was fastened on to his head with screws and the face was covered with a black hood. At 7:07 a.m. the executioner threw the switch; Bundy's body went stiff and rose fractionally from the chair. One minute later, as the power was switched off, the body slammed back into the chair. A doctor felt his pulse and pronounced him dead. Outside the prison, a mob carrying "Fry Bundy!" banners cheered as the execution was announced.

The Bundy case makes it clear that, in one respect at least, the science of criminology needs updating.

It seems to be the general consensus among criminologists

that the criminal is a social inadequate, and that the few exceptions only underscore the rule. Faced with difficulties that require courage and patience, he is inclined to run away. He lacks self-esteem; he tends to see himself as a loser, a failure. Crime is a "shortcut" to achieve something he believes he cannot achieve through his own merit. But everyone who reads this description must be aware that, to some extent, it fits himself. Being undermined by self-doubt is part of the human condition. Which of us, faced with problems, has not at some time chosen a judicious retreat?

The Bundy case underlines the point. Even as a schoolboy he was witty and amusing, and in his early twenties he developed a poise and confidence that were the envy of other males. Michaud quotes a fellow office worker: "Frankly, he represented what it was that all young males ever wanted to be . . . I think half the people in the office were jealous of him . . . If there was any flaw in him it was that he was almost too *perfect*."

In their classic book *The Criminal Personality* (1976), Samuel Yochelson and Stanton E. Samenow argue that criminality is closely connected with inadequacy, laziness and self-pity; it is another name for defeat-proneness. By the time he was in his mid-twenties, Bundy had tasted enough success to stand outside this definition. Then what went wrong?

Ann Rule's book contains the vital clue. She comments that Bundy became violently upset if he telephoned Meg Anders from Salt Lake City—where his legal studies were foundering—and got no reply. "Strangely, while he was being continuously unfaithful himself, he expected—demanded—that she be totally loyal to him."

In 1954, the science fiction writer A. E. Van Vogt had encountered this same curious anomaly when he was studying male authoritarian behavior for a novel called *The Violent Man*. He was intrigued by the number of divorce cases in which habitually unfaithful husbands had expected total fidelity from their wives; such a husband might flaunt his own infidelities, while erupting into murderous violence if his wife so much as smiled at another man. Such men obviously regarded women with deep hostility, as if they expected to be deceived or betrayed—this is why they chose to marry gentle and unaggressive women. Their "conquests" were another form of aggression, the aim being to prove that they were masterful seducers who could have any woman they liked. Their whole unstable structure of self-esteem was founded upon this notion that women found them irresistible; so it was essential for the wife to behave like a slave in a harem. This also explained another characteristic of such men: that they could not bear to be contradicted or shown to be in the wrong; this also threatened their image of themselves as a kind of god or superman. If confronted with proof of their own fallibility, they would explode into violence rather than acknowledge that they had made a mistake. For this reason, Van Vogt labeled this type "the Right Man" or "the Violent Man." To his colleagues at work he might appear perfectly normal and balanced; but his family knew him as a kind of paranoid dictator.

Only one thing could undermine this structure of self-delusion. If his wife walked out on him, she had demonstrated beyond all doubt that she rejected him; his tower of self-delusion was undermined, and often the result was mental breakdown, or even suicide.

Expressed in this way, it seems clear that the Right Man syndrome is a form of mild insanity. Yet it is alarmingly common; most of us know a Right Man, and some have the misfortune to have a Right Man for a husband or father. The syndrome obviously arises from the sheer competitiveness of the world we are born into. Every normal male has an urge to be a "winner," yet he finds himself surrounded by people who seem better qualified for success. One common response is boasting to those who look as if they can be taken in—particularly women. Another is what the late Stephen Potter called "One-upmanship," the attempt to make the other person feel inferior by a kind of cheating—for example, by pretending to know far more than you actually know. Another is to bully people over whom one happens to have authority. Many "Right Men" are so successful in all these departments that they achieve a remarkably high level of self-esteem on remarkably slender talents. Once achieved, this self-esteem is like an addictive drug and any threat of withdrawal seems terrifying. Hence the violence with which he reacts to anything that challenges it.

It is obvious that the Right Man syndrome is a compensatory mechanism for profound self-doubt, and that its essence lies in convincing others of something he feels to be untrue; in other words, it is a form of confidence-trickery. It is, that is to say, a typically criminal form of "shortcut," like cheating in an exam, or stealing something instead of saving up to buy it.

Now the basic characteristic of the criminal, and also of the Right Man, is a certain lack of self-control. Van Vogt writes that the Right Man "makes the decision to be out of control"—that is, makes the decision to *lose* control at a certain point, exploding into violence rather than calling upon a more mature level of his personality. But he is adept at making excuses that place the blame for this lack of self-control on other people for provoking him. One British sex killer, Patrick Byrne, explained that he decided to terrorize women "to get my own back on them for causing my nervous tension through sex."

But the lack of self-control brings its own problems. Every time it happens he is, in effect, lowering his own bursting point. Carl Panzram told Henry Lesser never to turn his back on him: "You're the one man I don't want to kill. But I'm so erratic I'm liable to do anything." He is like a man who has trained an Alsatian dog to leap at people's throats, and finally realizes that the dog is stronger than he is. A 22-year-old sex killer named Stephen Judy begged the judge in Indianapolis to sentence him to death. He had been committing rapes and sex crimes since he was 12, and was on trial for killing a young mother and her three children. Aware that he would never be able to stop committing sex crimes, he told the jury: "You'd better put me to death. Because next time it might be one of you or your daughter." They agreed, and Judy was executed in 1981. Just before his death he told his stepmother that he had killed more women than he could remember, leaving a trail of bodies across the United States.

It should now be possible to see that the Right Man syndrome is the key to the serial killer, and that Bundy is a textbook case. From the beginning, he was obsessed by success: "I found myself thinking about standards of success that I just didn't seem to be living up to." The affair with Stephanie Brooks made it seem that success was within his grasp; he went to Stanford to study Chinese. But he lacked the application and self-confidence and she threw him over. This was the turning point; his brother commented: "Stephanie screwed him up . . . I'd never seen him like this before. He'd always been in charge of his emotions." It was after this rejection that Bundy became a kleptomaniac. This may seem a strange response to the end of a love affair. But stealing is a way of making a gesture of defiance at society. And this is what Bundy's thieving amounted to—as when he stole an eight-foot tree from a greenhouse and drove off with it sticking out of the roof of his car. It was essentially a symbolic gesture.

Seven years later, Bundy took his revenge on Stephanie Brooks. When she rang him to ask why he had not contacted her since their weekend together, he said coldly: "I have no idea what you're talking about," and hung up on her. "At length," says Ann Rule, "she concluded that Ted's high-power courtship in the latter part of 1973 had been deliberately planned, that he had waited all these years to be in a position where he could make her fall in love with him, just so he could drop her, reject her as she had rejected him." Stephanie Brooks wrote to a friend: "I escaped by the skin of my teeth. When I think of his cold and calculating manner, I shudder." The Right Man had escaped his feeling of vulnerability; he had established his dominance. Oddly enough, he committed his first violent sexual attack immediately after the weekend with Stephanie. He had proved that he was the conqueror; now, in this mood of exultation, he broke into the bedroom of a female student, battered her unconscious, and thrust an iron bar into her vagina. Three weeks later he committed his first murder. It was also completely typical of the Right Man that, when eventually caught, he should continue to deny his guilt, even in the face of overwhelming evidence.

But the remarks of Yochelson and Samenow about inadequacy certainly apply to the case of David Berkowitz, known as "Son of Sam."

On the night of July 29, 1976, two young girls sat talking in the front seats of a car on Buhre Avenue, New York City; they were Donna Lauria, a medical technician, and Jody Valenti, a student nurse. Donna's parents, on their way back from a night out, passed them at about 1 a.m., and said goodnight. A few moments after they reached their apartment, they heard the sounds of shots and screams. A man had walked up to the Oldsmobile, pulled a gun out of a brown paper bag, and fired five shots. Donna was killed, Jody wounded in the thigh.

Total lack of motive for the shooting convinced police they were dealing with a man who killed for pleasure, without knowing his victims.

Four months later, on November 26, two young girls were

sitting talking on the stoop in front of a house in the Floral Park section of Queens, New York; it was half an hour past midnight when a man walked towards them, started to ask if they could direct him, then, before he finished the sentence, pulled out a gun and began shooting. Donna DeMasi and Joanne Lomino were both wounded. A bullet lodged in Joanne's spine, paralyzing her. Bullets dug out of a front door and a mail box revealed that the two young women had been shot by the same .44 that had killed Donna Lauria and wounded Jody Valenti.

Although the police were unaware of it at this time, the same gun had already wounded yet another victim. Over a month earlier, on October 23, 1976, Carl Denaro and his girl-friend Rosemary Keenan were sitting in his sports car in front of a tavern in Flushing when there were several loud bangs; then a bullet tore through the rear window, and Denaro fell forward. He was rushed to the hospital, and in three weeks, had begun to recover, although his middle finger was perma-nently damaged. The .44 bullet was found on the floor of the car.

On January 30, 1977, a young couple were kissing good-night in a car in the Ridgewood area of New York; there was a deafening explosion, the windshield shattered, and Christine Freund slumped into the arms of her boyfriend John Diel. She died a few hours later in the hospital.

On March 8, 1977, Virginia Voskerichian, an Armenian stu-dent, was on her way home, and only a few hundred yards from her mother's house in Forest Hills, when a gunman walked up to her, and shot her in the face at a few yards range; the bullet went into her mouth, shattering her front teeth. She died immediately. Christine Freund had been shot only three hundred yards away.

By now police recognized that the bullets that had killed three and wounded four had all come from the same gun. And this indicated a homicidal psychopath who would probably go on until he was caught. The problem was that the police had no clues to his identity, no idea of where to begin searching. Unless he was caught during an attempted murder, the chance of arresting him seemed minimal. Mayor Beame of New York gave a press conference in which he announced: "We have a savage killer on the loose." He was able to say that the man was white, about five feet ten inches tall, well groomed, with hair combed straight back.

On the morning of April 17, 1977, there were two more deaths. Alexander Esau and Valentina Suriani were sitting in a parked car in the Bronx when the killer shot both of them. Valentina died instantly; Esau died later in the hospital, three bullets in his head. Only a few blocks away, Donna Lauria and Jody Valenti had been shot.

In the middle of the street, a policeman found an envelope. It contained a letter addressed to Captain Joseph Borrelli, and it was from the killer. "I am deeply hurt by your calling me a woman-hater. I am not. But I am a monster. I am the Son of Sam. I am a little brat . . ." It claimed that his father, Sam, was a brute who beat his family when he got drunk, and who ordered him to go out and kill. "I love to hunt. Prowling the streets looking for fair game—tasty meat. The wemen of Queens are prettyist of all . . ." It was reminiscent of the letters that Jack the Ripper and so many other "thrill killers" have written to the police, revealing an urge to "be" somebody, to make an impact on society. A further rambling, incoherent note, signed "Son of Sam," was sent to a New York columnist, James Breslin.

The next attack, on June 26, 1977, was like so many of the others: a young couple sitting in their car in the early hours of Sunday morning, saying goodnight after a date. They were Salvatore Lupo and Judy Placido, and the car was in front of a house on 211 Street, Bayside, Queens. The windshield shattered, as four shots were fired. The assailant ran away. Fortunately, his aim had been bad; both these victims were only wounded, and recovered.

It was now a year since Son of Sam had killed Donna Lauria; on the anniversary of her death, Queens and the Bronx were swarming with police. But Son of Sam had decided that these areas were dangerous, and that his next shootings would be as far away as possible. On July 31, Robert Violante and Stacy Moskowitz were sitting in a parking lot close to the Brooklyn shore; it was 1:30 on Sunday morning. The windshield exploded as four shots were fired. Both were hit in the head. Stacy Moskowitz died hours later in the hospital; Robert Violante recovered, but was blinded.

But this shooting brought the break in the case. A woman out walking her dog had noticed two policemen putting a ticket on a car parked near a fire hydrant on Bay 16th Street. Minutes later, a man ran up to the car, leapt in and drove off. Only four parking tickets had been issued in the Coney Island area that Sunday morning, and only one of those was for parking near a hydrant. The carbon of the ticket contained the car's registration number. And the vehicle licensing department was able to identify its owner as David Berkowitz, aged 24, of Pine Street, Yonkers.

On the Wednesday after the last killing, detectives found the Ford Galaxie parked in front of an apartment building in Pine Street. They peered in through its window, and saw the butt of a gun, and a note written in the same block capitals as the other Son of Sam letters. The car was staked out. When David Berkowitz approached it at 10:15 that evening, Deputy Inspector Tim Dowd, who had led the hunt, said, "Hello, David." Berkowitz looked at him in surprise, then said, "Inspector Dowd! You finally got me."

After the terror he had aroused, Son of Sam was something of an anticlimax, a pudgy little man with a beaming smile, and a tendency to look like a slightly moronic child who has been caught stealing sweets. He was a paranoid schizophrenic, a man who lived alone in a room lit by a naked bulb, sleeping on a bare mattress. The floor was covered with empty milk cartons and bottles. On the walls he had scrawled messages like "In this hole lives the wicked king," "Kill for my Master," "I turn children into killers." His father, who had run a hardware store in the Bronx, had retired to Florida after being robbed. Nat Berkowitz was not Son of Sam's real father. David Berkowitz, born June 1, 1953, was a bastard, and his mother offered him for adoption. He had felt rejected from the beginning.

He reacted to his poor self-image by boasting and lying—particularly about his sexual prowess. In fact, he was shy of women, and almost certainly a virgin when captured. He told the police that demons began telling him to kill in 1974—although one psychiatrist who interviewed him is convinced that this is untrue, and that Berkowitz's stories of "voices" was an attempt to establish a defense of insanity. Living alone in apartments that he allowed to become pig-sties, kept awake at night by the sound of trucks or barking dogs, he slipped into paranoia, telling his father in a letter that people hated him, and spat at him as he walked down the street. "The girls call me ugly, and they bother me the most." On Christmas Eve 1975, he began his attempt at revenge on women by taking a knife and attacking two of them. The first one screamed so loudly he ran away. The second, a 15-year-old schoolgirl, was badly cut, and had one lung punctured, but recovered. Seven months later, Berkowitz went out with a gun and committed his first murder.

The name Sam seems to have been taken from a neighbor called Sam Carr, whose black Labrador sometimes kept Berkowitz awake. He wrote Carr anonymous letters, and on April 27, 1977, shot the dog—which recovered. He also wrote anonymous letters to people he believed to be persecuting him. He had been reported to the police on a number of occasions as a "nut," but no one suspected that he might be Son of Sam.

Berkowitz was judged sane, and was arraigned on August 23, 1977. He pleaded guilty, saving New York the cost of a trial. He was sentenced to 365 years in prison.

The aftermath is worth describing. His Yonkers apartment block became a place of pilgrimage for sensation-seekers. They stole doorknobs, cut out pieces of carpet, even chipped pieces of paint from Berkowitz's door. In the middle of the night, people shouted "David, come out" from the street. Berkowitz's apartment remained empty, and a quarter of the building's tenants moved out, even though the landlord changed its number from 25 to 42 Pine Street to try to mislead the souvenir hunters.

Worth mentioning as an interesting parallel to the Son of Sam murders is the Zodiac case, which took place in San Francisco in the 1960s. Between December 1968 and October 1969, an unknown killer committed five "random" murders, and seriously wounded two more victims. On December 20, 1968, a man approached a car in a "lovers" lane" near Vallejo, California, and shot to death two teenagers. On July 5, 1969, he opened fire on another couple in a car near Vallejo, killing the woman and wounding the man. Letters sent to two San Francisco newspapers were signed "Zodiac," and claimed credit for the murders. Lines in code—decoded by a cipher expert—boasted that hunting humans was the most exciting of all sports.

On September 27, 1969, a plump, bespectacled man wearing a hood held two people at gunpoint in a picnic area beside Lake Berryessa and stabbed them both repeatedly, killing the woman. "Zodiac" reported his latest murder to the police by telephone. Two weeks later, on October 11, he shot to death a taxi driver in San Francisco, and sent a letter boasting of the crime to the San Francisco *Chronicle*, together with a bloody fragment of the driver's shirt. This was "Zodiac's" last known murder, although he continued to write letters threatening more killings. On October 22, 1969, a man claiming to be Zodiac took part in a Bay Area phone-in TV program—in which he identified himself as "Sam." The call was, in fact, traced to the Napa State Hospital, and the caller proved to be a mental patient there. It is interesting to speculate if David Berkowitz read about the program—which received nationwide publicity—and was influenced by it in choosing his *nom de guerre*.

Perhaps the most basic characteristic of the serial killer is one that he shares with most other criminals: a tendency to an irrational self-pity that can produce an explosion of violence. In that sense, Paul John Knowles may be regarded not merely as the archetypal serial killer but as the archetypal criminal.

Knowles, who was born in 1946, had spent an average of six months of every year in jail since he was 19, mostly for car thefts and burglaries. In Raiford Penitentiary in 1972, he began to study astrology, and started corresponding with a divorcee named Angela Covic, whom he had contacted through an astrology magazine. She flew down to Florida, was impressed by the gaunt good looks of the tall red-headed convict, and agreed to marry him. She hired a lawyer to work on his parole, and he was released on May 14, 1972. Knowles hastened to San Francisco to claim his bride, but she had had second thoughts; a psychic had told her that she was mixed up with a very dangerous man. Knowles stayed at her mother's apartment, but after four days Angela Covic told him she had decided to return to her husband, and gave him his air ticket back to Florida. Knowles exploded with rage and self-pity; he later claimed that he went out on to the streets of San Francisco and killed three people. This was never verified, but it is consistent with the behavior of the Right Man.

Back in his home town of Jacksonville, Florida, on July 26, 1974, Knowles got into a fight in a bar and was locked up for the night. He escaped, broke into the home of a 65-year-old teacher, Alice Curtis, and stole her money and her car. But he rammed a gag too far down her throat and she suffocated. A few days later, as he parked the stolen car, he noticed two children looking at him as if they recognized him—their mother was, in fact, a friend of his family. He forced them into the car and drove away. The bodies of 7-year-old Mylette Anderson and her 11-year-old sister Lillian were later found in a swamp.

What followed was a totally unmotivated murder rampage, as if Knowles had simply decided to kill as many people as he could before he was caught. The following day, August 2, in Atlantic Beach, Florida, he broke into the home of Marjorie Howie, 49, and strangled her with a stocking; he stole her television set. A few days later he strangled and raped a teenage runaway who hitched a lift with him. On August 23, he strangled Kathie Pierce in Musella, Georgia, while her 3-year-old son looked on; Knowles left the child unharmed. On September 23, near Lima, Ohio, he had several drinks with an accounts executive named William Bates, and later strangled him, driving off in the dead man's white Impala. After driving to California, Seattle and Utah (using Bates's credit cards) he forced his way into a trailer in Ely, Nevada, on September 18, 1974, and shot to death an elderly couple, Emmett and Lois Johnson. On September 21, he strangled and raped 42-year-old Mrs. Charlynn Hicks, who had stopped to admire the view beside the road near Sequin, Texas. On September 23, in Birmingham, Alabama, he met an attractive woman named Ann Dawson, who owned a beauty shop, and they traveled around together for the next six days, living on her money;

she was murdered on September 29. For the next sixteen days he drove around without apparently committing any further murders; but on October 16, he rang the doorbell of a house in Marlborough, Connecticut; it was answered by 16-year-old Dawn White, who was expecting a friend. Knowles forced her up to the bedroom and raped her; when her mother, Karen White, returned home, he raped her too, then strangled them both with silk stockings, leaving with a tape recorder and Dawn White's collection of rock records. Two days later, he knocked on the door of 53-year-old Doris Hovey in Woodford, Virginia, and told her he needed a gun and would not harm her; she gave him a rifle belonging to her husband, and he shot her through the head and left, leaving the rifle beside her body.

In Key West, Florida, he picked up two hitchhikers, intending to kill them, but was stopped by a policeman for pulling up on a curb; when the policeman asked to see his documents, he expected to be arrested; but the officer failed to check that Knowles was the owner of the car, and let him drive away.

On November 2, Knowles picked up two hitchhikers, Edward Hilliard and Debbie Griffin; Hilliard's body was later discovered in the woods near Macon, Georgia; the girl's body was never found.

On November 6, in a gay bar in Macon, he met a man named Carswell Carr and went home with him. Later that evening, Carr's 15-year-old daughter Mandy heard shouting and went downstairs, to find Knowles standing over the body of her father, who was tied up. It emerged later that Carr had died of a heart attack; Knowles had been torturing him by stabbing him all over with a pair of scissors. He then raped Mandy Carr—or attempted it (no sperm was found in the vagina)—and strangled her with a stocking. The bodies were found when Carr's wife, a night nurse, returned home.

The next day, in a Holiday Inn in downtown Atlanta, Knowles saw an attractive redhead in the bar—a British journalist named Sandy Fawkes; she went for a meal with him and they ended up in her bedroom. But he proved impotent, in spite of all her efforts. He had introduced himself to her as Daryl Golden, son of a New Mexico restaurant owner, and the two of them got on well enough for her to accept his offer to drive her to Miami. On the way there, he hinted that he was on the run for some serious crime—or crimes—and told her that he had a premonition that he was going to be killed some time soon. He also told her that he had tape-recorded his confession, and left it with his lawyer in Miami, Sheldon Yavitz. In another motel, he finally succeeded in entering her, after first practicing cunnilingus and masturbating himself into a state of excitement. But even so, he failed to achieve orgasm—she concluded that he was incapable of it.

Long before they separated—after a mere six days together—she was anxious to get rid of him. She had sensed the underlying violence, self-pity, lack of discipline. He pressed hard for another night together; she firmly refused, insisting that it would only make the parting more sad. He waited outside her Miami motel half the night, while she deliberately stayed away; finally, he gave up and left.

The following day, she was asked to go to the police station, and there for the first time realized what kind of a man she had been traveling with. On the morning after their separation, "Daryl Golden" had driven to the house of some journalists to whom he had been introduced four days earlier, and offered to drive Susan Mackenzie to the hairdresser. Instead, he took the wrong turn, and told her that he wanted to have sex with her, and would not hurt her if she complied. When he stopped the car and pointed a gun at her, she succeeded in jumping out and waved frantically at a passing car. Knowles drove off. Later, alerted to the attempted rape, a squad car tried to stop Knowles, but he pointed a shotgun at the policeman and drove off.

Knowles knew that he had to get rid of the stolen car. In West Palm Beach, he forced his way into a house, and took a girl named Barbara Tucker hostage, driving off in her Volkswagen, leaving her sister (in a wheelchair) and 6-year-old child unharmed. He held Barbara Tucker captive in a motel in Fort Pierce for a night and day, then finally left her tied up and drove off in her car.

Next day, Patrolman Charles F. Campbell flagged down the Volkswagen—now with altered license plates—and found himself looking down the barrel of a shotgun. He was taken captive and driven off, handcuffed, in his own patrol car. But the brakes were poor, and using the police siren, he forced another car—driven by businessman John Meyer—off the road, then drove off in Meyer's car, with Meyer and the patrolman in the back. In Pulaski County, Georgia, Knowles took them into a wood, handcuffed them to a tree, and shot both in the back of the head.

Soon after, he saw a police roadblock ahead, and drove on through it, losing control and crashing into a tree. He ran into the woods, and a vast manhunt now began, involving two hundred police, tracker dogs and helicopters. Knowles was arrested by a courageous civilian, who saw him from a house, and he gave himself up quietly.

The day after his appearance in court, as he was being transferred to a maximum security prison, Knowles unpicked his handcuffs and made a grab for the sheriff's gun; FBI agent Ron Angel shot him dead. Knowles had been responsible for at least eighteen murders, possibly as many as twenty-four.

Sandy Fawkes had seen Knowles in court, and was overwhelmed by a sense of his "evil power." But she had no doubt that he now had what he had always wanted: he was famous at last.

And enjoying his notoriety. The papers were filled with pictures of his appearance at Midgeville and accounts of his behavior. The street had been lined with people. Sightseers had hung over the sides of balconies to catch a glimpse of Knowles, manacled and in leg irons, dressed in a brilliant orange jumpsuit. He had loved it: the local coeds four-deep on the sidewalks, the courtroom packed with reporters, friends, Mandy's school chums and relatives of the Carr family. It was an event, he was the center of it and he smiled at everyone. No wonder he had laughed like a hyena at his capture; he was having his hour of glory, not in the hereafter as he had predicted, but in the here-and-now. The daily stories of the women in his life had turned him into a Casanova killer, a folk villain, Dillinger and Jesse James rolled into one. He was already being referred to as the most heinous killer in history.

So at last Knowles had achieved the aim of most serial killers: "to become known." He was quoted in a local newspaper as saying that he was "the only successful member of his family."

In the second half of the 1970s, another case of serial murder by a homosexual aroused uneasy memories of Dean Corll.

Between 1976 and his arrest in December 1978, John Wayne Gacy, a Chicago building contractor, killed thirty-two boys in the course of sexual attacks. Gacy's childhood—he was born in 1932—was in many ways similar to Corll's, with a harsh father and a protective mother. He was a lifelong petty thief. Like Corll, he also suffered from a heart condition. In childhood, he had been struck on the head by a swing, which caused a bloodclot on the brain, undetected for several years. He married a girl whose parents owned a fried-chicken business in Waterloo, Iowa, and—again like Corll—became a successful businessman. (Maslow would point out that this indicates that both belong to the "dominant five percent.") He was also known as a liar and a boaster. His marriage came to an end when Gacy was imprisoned for sexually molesting a teenager (although Gacy always claimed he had been framed). Out of jail, he married a second time and set up in business as a building contractor. He was successful (although notoriously mean), and was soon regarded as a pillar of the local community—he was even photographed shaking hands with First Lady Rosalynn Carter, the wife of President Jimmy Carter. His own wife found his violent temper a strain, and they divorced.

In 1975, while he was still married, one of his teenage employees vanished; it was after this that his wife noticed an unpleasant smell in the house. After their separation in the following year, Gacy made a habit of picking up teenage homosexuals, or luring teenagers to his house "on business," handcuffing them, and then committing sodomy. They were finally strangled, and the bodies disposed of, usually in the crawl space under the house.

In March 1978, a 27-year-old named Jeffrey Rignall accepted an invitation to smoke pot in Gacy's Oldsmobile. Gacy clapped a chloroform-soaked rag over his face, and when Rignall woke up he was being sodomized in Gacy's home. Gacy raped him repeatedly and flogged him with a whip; finally, he chloroformed him again and left him in a park. In the hospital, Rignall discovered that he had sustained permanent liver damage from the chloroform. Since the police were unable to help, he set about trying to track down the rapist himself, sitting near freeway entrances looking for black Oldsmobiles. Eventually he saw Gacy, followed him, and noted down his number. Although Gacy was arrested, the evidence against him seemed poor.

On December 11, 1978, Gacy invited a 15-year-old boy,

Robert Piest, to his house to talk about a summer job. When the youth failed to return, police tracked down the building contractor who had offered him the job, and questioned him at his home in Des Plaines. Alerted by the odor, they investigated the crawl space and found fifteen bodies and parts of others. When Gacy had run out of space, he had started dumping bodies in the river.

Gacy's story was that he was a "dissociated" personality, and that the murders were committed by an evil part of himself called Jack. In court, one youth described how Gacy had pulled him up, posing as a police officer, then handcuffed him at gunpoint. Back in Gacy's home, he was sodomized, after which Gacy made an attempt to drown him in the bath; but Gacy changed his mind and raped him again. Then, after holding his head under water until he became unconscious, Gacy urinated on him, then played Russian roulette with a gun which turned out to contain only a blank. Finally, Gacy released him, warning him that the police would not believe his story. Gacy proved to be right. The jury who tried him believed a psychiatrist who told them that Gacy was suffering from a narcissistic personality disorder that did not amount to insanity, and on March 13, 1980, John Wayne Gacy was sentenced to death.

But the case that, in retrospect, seems most typical of the late 1970s—in the way that Manson seems typical of the late 1960s—is that of the Hillside Stranglers, Kenneth Bianchi and Angelo Buono.

In fact, the first book on the case was called simply *The Hillside Strangler*,[1] because at that time the role of Bianchi's cousin was not fully grasped. Since then, it has become clear that this is one of these cases in which the interaction of two criminal personalities produces an explosive combination.

[1]Published by Doubleday, New York, 1981.

The crimes attributed to the Hillside Strangler took place in Los Angeles between October 1977 and February 1978. But it was another crime, which took place a year later, and almost a thousand miles to the north, that finally led the police to the killers.

The small town of Bellingham, in Washington State, looks out on one of the most beautiful views in the American northwest: the pine-covered slopes of San Juan and Vancouver islands, and the Strait of Juan de Fuca. With a population of only forty thousand, violent crime is a rarity. Which is why, when police chief Terry Mangan was told on a Friday morning that two girls were missing his first thought was that they had decided to go off on a long weekend. Their names were Karen Mandic and Diane Wilder, and both were students at Western Washington University. Karen's boyfriend was insistent that she would never go away without telling him. And when Police Chief Mangan learned that Karen had left her pet cat unfed, he had a sudden intuition that he was dealing with a double murder.

On the previous evening—January 11, 1979—Karen had told her boyfriend that she and Diane were going on a "housesitting" job. It was at the home of a couple who were travelling in Europe. Apparently its security alarm system had failed, and Karen merely had to sit there for two hours while the alarm was taken away and repaired; moreover she would be paid $100 for the inconvenience.

The man who had offered her this job was a security supervisor named Kenneth Bianchi. Mangan's first step was to check with Bianchi's boss Mark Lawrence, who owned the Coastal Security agency. Lawrence declared positively that it was impossible that Ken Bianchi had anything to do with the disappearance of the two girls. He was a young man of excellent reputation, and a conscientious worker. He lived with a local girl named Kelli Boyd; they had a baby son, and Bianchi was known to be a devoted father and breadwinner. In any case, he had no authority to offer Karen a "house-sitting" job. There had to be some kind of mistake . . .

This was soon confirmed by Bianchi himself. He told his boss that he had never heard of Karen Mandic, and had certainly offered no one a house-sitting job. He had spent Thursday evening at a Sheriff's Reserve meeting.

But by now, the police had learned some strange facts about the house-sitting job. Karen had told her boyfriend that the man who had offered it had sworn her to secrecy. He had also telephoned the woman who lived next door to the house, and who went in once a day to water the plants, to warn her not to go near it during the course of the evening. He explained that the security alarm was being repaired, and armed guards would be on patrol. It began to look as if someone had lured the missing students to the empty house.

Police were immediately dispatched to the empty house in the expensive Bayside area. A locksmith opened the front door, and the detectives entered cautiously. They were half-expecting to find two corpses, but everything seemed to be in order. The house was neat, and there was no sign of a struggle. But on the kitchen floor, the searchers found a single wet footprint. It was that of a man, and since it was still wet, must have been made within the last twelve hours or so.

At noon that day, the local radio began broadcasting descriptions of Karen's car—a green Mercury Bobcat—and asking the public to report any sightings. At 4:30 that afternoon, the description was heard by a woman who had just come home from work. She had seen such a car when she left home that morning, parked in a nearby cul-de-sac. She immediately rang the police.

As Detective Bill Geddes approached the car, he already knew what he was going to find. A glance through the rear window confirmed his fear. The corpses of the two girls lay huddled together, as if they had been thrown into the vehicle.

Both were fully clothed. Examination by the police doctor would reveal that both had been violently strangled and then subjected to some form of sexual assault.

Bianchi was obviously the chief suspect; he had to be arrested immediately. But at this point no one knew where he was; he was out somewhere driving his security truck. His boss, Mark Lawrence, agreed to set a trap. He contacted Bianchi by radio and asked him to go to a guard shack on the south side of town to receive instructions. Half an hour later, the police car arrived. The detectives approached cautiously; they had been warned that Bianchi was armed. But the good-looking young man who was waiting for them merely looked surprised to see them, and surrendered without protest. He seemed so totally free of guilt that Detective Terry Wright, who made the arrest, began to suspect that this was all a mistake. Either Ken Bianchi was innocent, or he was a superb actor.

Back at the police station, Bianchi denied knowing Karen Mandic. If someone calling himself Kenneth Bianchi had offered her a job, then it must be some imposter who had been using his name. The interrogators were inclined to believe him. They were even more convinced when Kelli Boyd, his common-law wife, arrived at the station. She was obviously horrified at the very idea that Ken Bianchi might be a murderer. He was a gentle lover and adoring father, totally incapable of violence. When the police asked permission to search their home, both gave it without hesitation.

The search revealed that, whether Bianchi was a murderer or not, he was certainly a thief. Hidden in the basement, the police found several expensive telephones and a new chain saw in its box; all these items had been reported stolen from places where Bianchi had worked as a security guard. Bianchi was charged with grand theft, and taken to the county jail.

A search of Bianchi's security truck revealed more evidence—the keys of the Bayside house, and a woman's scarf. Diane Wilder's friends reported that she had a passion for scarves.

But the most convincing evidence came from examination of the bodies. Both girls had been strangled by some kind of ligature applied from behind, and its angle also made it clear that the murderer had been standing above them at the time, as if walking downstairs. On the stairs leading to the basement of the Bayside home, detectives found a single pubic hair. Two more pubic hairs fell from Diane Wilder's body when it was lifted on to a sterile sheet. Semen stains were found on the underwear of both girls. Examination of Bianchi's underwear also revealed semen stains. Diane had been menstruating at the time of her death, and there was also menstrual blood on Bianchi's underpants. Carpet fibers found on the clothing of both girls, and on the soles of their shoes, matched the fibers in the empty house. For all his protestations of innocence, Bianchi had to be guilty.

Now, at last, it became possible tentatively to reconstruct the crime. Ken Bianchi had telephoned Karen Mandic and offered her the house-sitting job—he had made her acquaintance when he was a security guard in the department store where she worked. (This made it clear that he was lying when he said he had never heard of her.) He had sworn her to silence "for security reasons." But Karen had told her boyfriend where she was going. She had also telephoned a friend who was a security guard at the university and told him about the job. Her friend had been suspicious about the size of the remuneration, but he knew that the Bayside area contained many wealthy homes, full of valuables. If this was one of them, it *could* be worth it.

At seven o'clock that evening, Karen and Diane had driven to the Bayside house. Bianchi was already waiting for them in his security truck—local residents had noticed it. Karen parked her car in the drive, outside the front door. Bianchi had asked her to accompany him inside to turn on the lights, while Diane waited in the Mercury. When he reappeared a few minutes later, Diane had no suspicion that her friend was now lying dead in the basement. Like Karen, she walked down the stairs with Bianchi behind her, and the ligature was dropped over her neck and pulled tight with tremendous force. As far as could be determined, the killer had not raped either girl—or had been satisfied with only brief penetration, ejaculating on the underwear. Then he had carried both bodies out to Karen's car, and dumped them in the back. He drove to the cul-de-sac, carefully wiped the car clean of fingerprints, and walked back to the Bayside house where his own truck was parked, disposing of the ligature on the way. The baffling thing about the crime was that it seemed so oddly pointless.

Still, the case against Bianchi looked conclusive, even though he continued to insist—with the greatest apparent sincerity—that he had no memory of the murders. His bail was posted at $150,000. And now he was safely in jail, the police began checking on his background. He had been living in Glendale, a town (or suburb) eight miles north of downtown Los Angeles, before his move to Bellingham in the previous May. An investigating detective rang the Los Angeles County Sheriff's Department to see if they knew anything about Kenneth Bianchi. The call was taken by Detective Sergeant Frank Salerno, of the Homicide Division. And when Salerno was told that a former Glendale resident named Kenneth Bianchi had been booked on suspicion of a double sex murder, he was seized by immense excitement.

For the past fourteen months, Salerno had been looking for a sex killer who had committed a dozen similar murders in Los Angeles. The newspapers had christened him the Hillside Strangler. The last murder had taken place shortly before Bianchi left Los Angeles for Bellingham.

The first corpse had been found sprawled on a hillside near Forest Lawn cemetery, south of the Ventura freeway. The girl was tall and black, and had been stripped naked. It seemed clear that her body had been removed from a car and tossed down the slope.

It was the morning of October 17, 1977. The girl's body temperature indicated that she had been killed some time the previous evening. The first problem was to identify her, and this proved unexpectedly easy. Her prints were on file, and revealed her to be a prostitute named Yolanda Washington, who operated around Hollywood Boulevard. The autopsy showed that sexual relations had taken place and had involved two men. One of these was a "non-secretor," a man whose blood group cannot be determined from his bodily fluids. But the men could simply have been "johns," and had nothing to do with her murder. Cause of death was strangulation with a piece of cloth, and it had taken place when she was lying down, with the murderer above her, possible on the floor of a car.

The crime aroused little interest in the media; murders of prostitutes are too common to rate wide coverage.

The same was true of a second victim, discovered on the morning of November 1. She lay close to the curb in Alta Terrace Drive in La Crescenta, a town not far from Glendale, and it looked again as if she had been dumped from a car. As in the case of Yolanda Washington the body was naked, and death was due to strangulation with a ligature. She was little more than a child—15 at the most. Marks on her wrists and ankles, and in the area of her mouth, indicated that she had been bound with adhesive tape. Fibers on her eyelids also revealed that she had been blindfolded.

The autopsy disclosed a possible connection with the murder of Yolanda Washington. The girl had been subjected to anal and vaginal intercourse by two men, one of them a non-secretor. The position of the body also indicated that she had been carried by two men, one holding her under the armpits and the other by the knees. All this was an advance on the Yolanda Washington case. Now at least the police knew they were looking for two killers.

This time, unfortunately, her prints were not on file. Sergeant Frank Salerno, investigating her death, had no definite starting point. A hunch led him to ask questions in the area of Hollywood Boulevard, and to display the police artist's sketch of the dead girl to its floating population of drug addicts and prostitutes. Several of the "street people" had told him that she resembled a girl called Judy Miller, who had not been seen recently. It took Salerno another week to track down her parents. They lived in a cheap motel room, and one of their two remaining children slept in a cardboard box. With the curious lack of response of people who have received too many blows, they identified the morgue photographs as their daughter Judy, who had run away from home a month ago. Salerno already knew that she had made a living from prostitution—but in a half-hearted, amateurish way. She had given it away free to a casual boyfriend only an hour before she was last seen alive.

By the time Salerno located Judy's parents, there had already been another nude murder. On November 6, a jogger near the Chevy Chase Country Club in Glendale saw the body lying near the golf course. She had been strangled with a ligature and subjected to a sexual assault that had caused vaginal bleeding. This time identification was easy. Soon after a news broadcast describing the discovery of the body, a man telephoned the police to say that his daughter had been missing for two days. She was a 20-year-old dancer named Lissa Kastin, and she had recently been working as a waitress. The man's description made it likely that she was the unknown victim, and an hour later, Lissa Kastin's father identified her face on a television monitor screen.

Glendale was outside Salerno's jurisdiction, but he went to view the body nevertheless. The ligature marks around the neck, and lines around the wrists and ankles, suggested that the stranglers had been at work again. As Frank Salerno looked down at the body—the third in three weeks—it passed through his mind that this was beginning to look like an epidemic.

Even Salerno was unprepared for what actually happened in the last three weeks of November 1977—seven more strangled corpses, six of them naked. Eighteen-year-old Jill Barcomb, discovered on November 10, was a prostitute; her body was found at Franklin Cyn Drive and Mulholland. Kathleen Robinson, 17, differed from the other victims in being clothed when her body was found at Pico and Ocean boulevards on November 17, so it was possible that she was not another victim of the sex killer.

But the day that shocked the media into awareness of the "Hillside Strangler" was Sunday, November 20, when three nude corpses were found, two of them schoolgirls. These were Dollie Cepeda, 12, and Sonja Johnson, 14, and their bodies were discovered on a rubbish dump in an obscure street called Landa, near Stadium Way. The 9-year-old boy who found them thought they were discarded mannequins from a department store. Both girls had been missing since the previous Sunday evening, and the autopsy revealed that both had been raped and sodomized. Earlier that same day, another nude body had been discovered on a street corner in the hills that separate Glendale from Eagle Rock. The following morning, a missing person report helped to identify her as Kristina Weckler, a 20-year-old art student who lived in an apartment building in Glendale.

The next body was found on November 23, in some bushes

off the Golden State freeway. She was identified as a 28-year-old scientology student named Jane King, who had been missing since November 9. And the last victim of that November of spree killing was found in some bushes in Cliff Drive, Glendale, on the 29. Her parents identified her later in the day as Lauren Wagner, an 18-year-old student who had failed to return home the previous night. Lesions on her palms looked like burn marks, and suggested that she had been tortured before death.

Ten sex murders in six weeks was something of a record, even for Los Angeles, where there are several murders a day. The press reacted with a hysteria that was reminiscent of the coverage of the Son of Sam murders in New York earlier the same year. In fact, the "Hillside Strangler" featured in television reports all over the world. (The police took care not to advertise their certainty that they were looking for two men, for the less the killers knew about the progress of the investigation, the better.) Women became afraid to go out alone at night, and shops that sold tear gas and Mace quickly ran out of supplies. By the time Lauren Wagner's body was discovered, Los Angeles was in a state of panic. The reaction of the police department was to create a combined task force from members of the Los Angeles Police, the Glendale Police and the Los Angeles Sheriff's Office, for which Salerno worked.

In spite of the frustrating lack of clues, the investigation was making some progress. On the evening of the disappearance of the two schoolgirls, a boy had seen them go up to a car and speak to someone on the passenger side. Clearly, then, there had been a passenger. The girls had apparently been nervous of speaking to strangers, but one of them was known to admire policemen. It was therefore possible that the killers had posed as policemen. Under hypnosis, the boy was able to say that the car was a large two-color sedan.

There was also a promising lead in the Lauren Wagner

case. Her father had looked out of the window on the morning of November 29, and noticed her car across the street. Closer examination showed that the door was open and the interior light still on. In the house in front of which the car was parked, a woman named Beulah Stofer described how she had seen Lauren abducted. As Lauren's car had pulled up, another car—a big dark sedan with a white top—had halted alongside, and two men had got out. There was an argument, then Lauren had entered the other car and been driven away. Mrs. Stofer had heard her say: "You won't get away with this." She was even able to describe the men: the older one had bushy hair and was "Latin-looking," while the other, who was taller and younger, had acne scars on his neck. Beulah Stofer had been alerted to the incident when her dog had barked.

When a detective talked to Mrs. Stofer later, that day, she was in a state of near-collapse. The telephone had just rung, and a rough male voice with an East Coast accent asked her if she was the lady with the dog. When she said she was, the voice had told her that she had better keep quiet about what she saw last night, or she was as good as dead. It was a clear indication that the stranglers knew her evidence could be of central importance to the investigation.

If the police had grasped the significance of this phone call, they might have terminated the career of the Hillside Strangler within days. The only way a man could have obtained a telephone number without knowing the name of the subscriber was through some friend at the telephone exchange. A check on the girls with access to such information would almost certainly have revealed the Strangler's identity. But in the general confusion of the investigation, this was overlooked, and the Strangler was free to strike again.

This happened two weeks later, on December 14. The victim was a 17-year-old prostitute named Kimberly Diane Martin, and her naked body was found sprawled on a vacant lot on Alvorado Street, within sight of City Hall. This time there were more clues, for she had been sent by a call girl agency— appropriately named the Climax—to the Tamarind Apartment building in Hollywood. A man had called the agency, asking for a blonde in black underwear, for whom he would pay $150 in cash. The agency asked for the caller's telephone number and queried what sounded like a public telephone. The caller assured them he was at home (although a later check on the number revealed it to be that of the public library). The girl was dispatched to the Tamarind Apartments, and disappeared. The police interviewed everyone in the apartment building, and one tenant—a personable young man named Kenneth Bianchi—admitted that he had heard screams. And at the Hollywood public library, a woman described how a bushy-haired man had followed her around and glared at her ferociously. But there the investigation ran into its usual blank wall.

In mid-February, the police ignored what could have been another promising lead. A middle-aged schoolteacher described how she had seen two men trying to drag a girl into their car on Riverside Drive in Burbank; she had jumped out of her car and told the men to let the girl alone. One of them—a bushy-haired man—had snarled: "God will get you for this"; then they had driven off. The police decided that the woman was a crank and that her story was not worth investigating.

For the remaining weeks of 1977, there were no more murders, and the Los Angeles police hoped fervently that the Stranglers had moved elsewhere. On February 17, 1978, that hope was dashed when someone reported an orange Datsun halfway down a cliff below a lay-by on the Angeles Crest Highway north of Glendale. The trunk proved to contain another naked body. The girl was identified as Cindy Hudspeth, 20, a part-time waitress at the Robin Hood Inn, and ligature marks on the wrists left Frank Salerno in no doubt that she was another victim of the stranglers. The medical evidence indicated that two men had raped and sodomized her repeatedly.

Then, at last, the murders ceased.

That is why, when Sergeant Frank Salerno heard that Kenneth Bianchi had been arrested for a double sex killing, he lost no time in getting to Bellingham. And within hours of arriving, he was certain that he had found at least one of the Hillside Stranglers. A large cache of jewelry had been found in Bianchi's apartment, and at least two items matched jewelry taken from the victims.

Bianchi was apparently continuing to behave like an innocent man, and was being highly cooperative. He had told the police that his only close friend in Los Angeles was his cousin Angelo Buono, an automobile upholsterer who owned a house in Glendale. Salerno was excited. A German detective had flown from Berlin solely to tell the Strangler task force that he believed the stranglers were two brothers who were probably Italian. At the time no one had paid much attention. Now it sounded as if he might be very close.

A check on Angelo Buono—by an undercover agent— made it seem highly likely that he was the other strangler. He had bushy hair, and was 45 years-old—seventeen years older than his cousin Ken. Like Bianchi, Buono had been born in Rochester, New York, and Beulah Stofer, the woman who had received the threatening phone call, had thought the man had a New York accent. And when Bianchi's face appeared in the Los Angeles newspapers, the schoolteacher who had interrupted the abduction of the girl in Burbank came forward again and told her story to Homicide Sergeant Bob Grogan of the Strangler task force. Her description of the two men certainly sounded like Bianchi and Buono.

More interesting information about Buono came from a wealthy Hollywood lawyer. In August 1976, he had telephoned a call girl agency—the Foxy Ladies—and asked for a woman to be sent over to his Bel-Air home. The 15-year-old girl who arrived at his home looked so miserable that the lawyer asked her how she came to be working as a prostitute when she obviously hated it. The answer, it seemed, was that a girl named Sabra had lured her from her home in Phoenix—where she was unhappy—to work for a man named Angelo Buono. Buono and his cousin Ken had terrorized the girl and told her that she would be killed if she tried to run away. Buono had subjected her to sodomy so frequently that she had to wear a tampon in her rectum. He also made a habit of forcing his penis down her throat until she vomited.

The lawyer was horrified, and promptly bought the girl an air ticket back to Phoenix. Buono had then made threatening phone calls—until the lawyer had sent a well-muscled bouncer to see him. The bouncer had found Buono working in a car, and when he addressed him, Buono ignored him. The bouncer had reached in through the window and dragged Buono out by his shirtfront, demanding: "Do I have your attention, Mr. Buono?" After that, the lawyer heard no more from Buono or his Foxy Ladies agency.

The lawyer was able to give Grogan the Phoenix address of Becky Spears, as well as that of the other call girl, Sabra Hannan, who had now returned to Arizona. They were brought to Los Angeles, and verified that Buono and Bianchi had offered them jobs as "models," then forced them to work as prostitutes, beating them and threatening them with death.

As the detectives delved into his background, it became clear that Buono was a highly unsavory character. He had been married four times and fathered eight children; all the wives had left him because of his brutality. He was proud of his sexual stamina—he was virtually insatiable—and liked to refer to himself as the Italian Stallion. He had several girlfriends, some in their early teens, and had habituated them all to fellatio and sodomy.

Grogan and Salerno were feeling pleased with themselves. There seemed little doubt that Buono and Bianchi were the Hillside Stranglers—in that order. Buono was the dominant one; Bianchi, for all his charm, was something of a weakling and a drifter. Even his girlfriend, Kelli Boyd, was sick of his lack of maturity—she had left him in Los Angeles to rejoin her family in Bellingham, but Bianchi had followed her there.

The police also thought they were beginning to understand how Buono and Bianchi had developed into serial killers. Their activities as pimps had made them accustomed to dominating and beating women. (Becky and Sabra had not been their only call girls; there were several more.) For a man who prided himself on his macho image, the episode with the bouncer must have been a keen humiliation for Angelo Buono—the kind of thing that could fester. And there had been another irritating setback. From an experienced professional prostitute, they had purchased a list of men who liked to have girls sent over to their homes. The list had been duly delivered, but turned out to be of men who wanted to visit a prostitute in her room. Buono had been enraged at the trick that had been played on him. He had no idea where to find the prostitute who had sold him the useless list. But he *did* know where to find one of her friends, an expensively dressed black prostitute who had been with her when the list was delivered. The name of the friend was Yolanda Washington, the first victim of the Stranglers . . .

It began to look as if the case was virtually tied up. Bianchi would undoubtedly be found guilty of the Bellingham murders. In Washington State, that would probably mean the death sentence. With that hanging over him, he would be eager to return to Los Angeles, where he could expect a life sentence. It would therefore be in his interest to confess to the

Hillside murders, and to implicate his cousin. At present, evidence against Angelo Buono was slim; but with Bianchi's cooperation, it could be made impregnable. Buono had now been interviewed two or three times, and his attitude had an undertone of mockery; he seemed to be enjoying the thought that the police had no real evidence against him. All that, Salerno reflected with satisfaction, would change when his cousin returned to Los Angeles . . .

And then, with bewildering suddenness, the whole case threatened to collapse. What had happened was that Kenneth Bianchi had managed to get himself declared insane. Or, at all events, the next best thing: a "multiple personality." In layman's parlance, that means a Jekyll and Hyde character whose Jekyll is totally unaware of the existence of his evil alter ego.

Ever since his arrest, Bianchi had been insisting that he remembered absolutely nothing of the evening on which he killed Karen Mandic and Diane Wilder. The police, understandably, thought that was a feeble and not very inventive attempt to wriggle out of responsibility. But Bianchi's lawyer, Dean Brett, was impressed by his apparent sincerity, his protestations of horror at the thought of killing two women, and his hints that he was contemplating suicide. He called in a psychiatric social worker, John Johnston, who was equally impressed by Bianchi's charm, gentleness and intelligence. If his protestations of amnesia were genuine, then there was only one possible conclusion: he was a multiple personality.

The general public had become aware of the riddle of multiple personality as a result of the 1957 movie *The Three Faces of Eve*, based on the book by two psychiatrists. But doctors had known about the illness since the early nineteenth century. It seems to be caused by severe psychological traumas in childhood, experiences so bad (like sexual abuse or extreme cruelty) that the personality literally blots them out and hides them away in some remote corner of the mind. In later life, some violent shock can reactivate the trauma, and the "everyday self" blanks out, and a new personality takes over—for hours or sometimes days or months.

Whether Bianchi knew about multiple personalities at this stage is a matter for debate—the police were certainly unaware that he was an avid student of psychology, who hoped one day to become a professional psychoanalyst. What *is* clear is that Johnston's suggestion came to him as a revelation. So did a showing of the feature film *Sybil*—another study of multiple personality—on the prison television. From this, Bianchi learned that "multiples" often suffer from blinding headaches and weird dreams. He also learned that psychiatrists try to gain access to the "other self" through hypnosis. So when Professor John G. Watkins, a psychologist from the University of Montana, suggested hypnosis, Bianchi professed himself eager to cooperate. And within a few minutes of being placed in a trance, he was speaking in a strange, low voice and introducing himself as someone called Steve. "Steve" came over as a highly unpleasant character with a sneering laugh. He told Dr. Watkins that he hated "Ken," and that he had done his best to "fix him." Then, with a little more prompting, he went on to describe how Ken had walked in one evening when his cousin Angelo Buono was murdering a girl. At which point, Steve admitted, he had taken over Ken's personality, and made him into his cousin's willing accomplice.

Frank Salerno and his colleague Pete Finnigan were sitting quietly in a corner of the room, listening to all this. In his notebook Frank Salerno wrote down a single word: "Bullshit." But he knew that the investigation was in trouble. If Bianchi could convince a judge that he was a multiple personality, he would escape with a few years in a mental hospital. And since the testimony of a mental patient would be inadmissible in court, Angelo Buono would be beyond the reach of the law.

Back in Los Angeles, the investigation was looking slightly more promising. The boyfriend of Judy Miller—the second victim of the Stranglers—had identified a photograph of Angelo Buono as the "john" who had enticed Judy into his car on the evening she disappeared. And Beulah Stofer, the woman who had seen Lauren Wagner pushed into a car by two men, identified them from photographs as Buono and Bianchi. That would certainly help the case against Buono. But without Bianchi's testimony, it would still be a weak case.

The picture of Buono that had been built up through various interviews made it clear that he was brutal, violent and dangerous. He had hated his mother, and always referred to her as "that cunt"; later in life, it became his general term for all women. From the time he left school he had been in trouble with the police, and had spent his seventeenth birthday in a reform school. His hero was Caryl Chessman, the "Red Light bandit," who liked to hold up women at gunpoint and make them perform oral sex. At the age of 20 Buono had married a 17-year-old girl who was pregnant, but left her within weeks. After a short period in jail for theft, he married again, and quickly fathered four more sons. But he was always coarse and violent: one day when his wife declined to have sex, he threw her down and sodomized her in front of the children. She left him and filed for divorce. So did his third wife. The fourth one left him without bothering about divorce. After that, Angelo lived alone in his house at 703 Colorado Street, Glendale. A friend who had once shared an apartment with him described him as being obsessed by young girls. The friend had entered the room one day and found Angelo peering down at the girls' playground through a pair of binoculars and playing with himself. Angelo had boasted that he had seduced his 14-year-old stepdaughter. And one of Angelo's sons had confided that his father had seduced him too. Clearly, Angelo Buono was a man who spent his days thinking and dreaming about sex.

Back in the Whatcomb County Jail in Washington, Ken's sinister alter ago "Steve" was also telling stories of Buono's insatiable sexual appetite, and of his habit of killing girls after he had raped and sodomized them. These stories tended to contain certain anomalies—almost as if Steve wished to minimize his own part in the murders and throw most of the blame on Angelo—and the same applied to his later confessions to the police; but the general picture that emerged was clear enough. The first victim was the prostitute Yolanda Washington, who had been killed for revenge but raped by both men. They had found the experience so pleasant that two weeks later they had picked up 15-year-old Judy Miller, then—pretending that they were policemen and she was under arrest—taken her back to Buono's house, where both had raped her. The rape and kidnapping had been unnecessary, since she would have been glad to submit to sex for a payment of a few dollars. Then, with Bianchi kneeling on her legs, they had strangled her and suffocated her at the same time, placing a plastic supermarket bag over her head.

The next victim was the out-of-work dancer Lissa Kastin. They stopped her in her car and identified themselves as policemen, showing a police badge. Then they told her they were taking her to the station for questioning. Back in Buono's house, she was kept handcuffed while they cut off her clothes with scissors. But when they found she had hairy legs, both men felt repelled. Bianchi raped her with a root beer bottle, then strangled her, while Buono sat on her legs shouting "Die, cunt, die." Bianchi was in no hurry to kill her; he enjoyed tightening the cord until she lost consciousness, then loosening it to revive her; it gave him pleasure to feel that he had the absolute power of life and death. But they agreed afterwards that she had been a disappointment, a "dog." They dumped her near the Chevy Chase golf course.

Four days later, on November 9, they were out hunting again. Bianchi saw an attractive girl waiting alone at a bus stop and began a conversation; she told him she was a Scientology student, and Bianchi asked her to tell him all about it. In the midst of the conversation, Buono drove up, pretending he hadn't seen Bianchi for months, and offered him a lift home. Jane King made the mistake of agreeing to let them drive her home. Back in Buono's house, they were delighted to find that her pubis was shaven. She resisted Buono's rape, and struggled so hard as Bianchi sodomized her that they decided she needed a lesson. She was hog-tied, and a plastic bag placed over her head while Bianchi sodomized her; when Bianchi climaxed she was dead. They were surprised to read later in the newspaper that she was 28; she seemed younger.

The shaven pubis had excited them both; now Buono dreamed of raping a virgin. Only four days after their last killing, they saw two schoolgirls, Dollie Cepeda and Sonja Johnson, boarding a bus in Eagle Rock Plaza. The idea of raping two girls at once appealed to them. They followed the bus, and when the girls disembarked near their home, beckoned them over to the car. Bianchi identified himself as a policeman and told them that a dangerous burglar was loose in the neighborhood. The schoolgirls were vulnerable; they had just stolen a hundred dollars worth of costume jewelry from a department store, and were not disposed to argue with the police. Back in Buono's house, both had been subjected to violation, then Sonja was murdered in the bedroom. When they came to get Dollie, she asked: "Where's Sonja?" and Buono told her: "You'll be seeing her soon." Their corpses were dumped on a rubbish tip that Buono knew from his courting days. The police had reasoned, correctly, that whoever had dumped the bodies must have known the area intimately.

The next victim was a girl Bianchi had known when he lived in an apartment building on East Garfield, in Hollywood. Kristina Weckler was an art student, and she had spurned Bianchi when he had made advances. Now they knocked on her door, and Bianchi said: "Hi, remember me?" He told her that he was now a member of the police reserve, and that someone had crashed into Kristina's VW, parked outside the building. She went down with them to see, and was bundled into Buono's car and taken to his house. After the rape, they decided to try a new method of murder: injecting her with a cleaning fluid. It produced convulsions, but not death. At Buono's suggestion, they placed a bag over her head and piped coal gas into it, strangling her at the same time.

The Thanksgiving killing spree was almost over. On Monday, November 28, 1977, they saw a red-headed girl climbing into her car, and followed it. And when Lauren Wagner pulled up in front of her parents' home, Bianchi flourished his police badge and told her they were arresting her. While she protested—and a dog barked loudly in a nearby house—they bundled her into their car and drove her away. When she realized that their purpose was rape, she pretended to be cooperative, mentioning that she had spent the evening in bed with her boyfriend and was ready for more. While being raped, she behaved as if she enjoyed it. Nevertheless, she was strangled, after an unsuccessful attempt to electrocute her had only produced burns on her palms.

The realization that they had been seen by a neighbor made them decide to be more cautious. But three weeks later, both were dreaming of another rape. Kimberly Martin, a call girl, was summoned to the Tamarind Apartments, and taken back to Buono's. After raping her, both agreed she was no good in bed. Her body was dumped on a vacant lot.

The final Hillside killing was almost an accident. On February 16, Bianchi arrived at Buono's house to find an orange Datsun parked outside. A girl named Cindy Hudspeth had called to ask Buono to make new mats for her car. The opportunity was too good to miss. The girl was spreadeagled naked on the bed, her wrists and ankles tied to the legs, then they raped her for two hours. After that they strangled her. The Datsun was pushed off a cliff with her body in the trunk.

Bianchi had been twice questioned by the police in routine inquiries—he was one of thousands. But Buono was becoming nervous and irritable. He was getting sick of his cousin's lack of maturity, his naïvety and his carelessness. So when Bianchi told him that his girlfriend had left him and moved back to Bellingham, Buono strongly advised him to go and join her. At first Bianchi was unwilling—his admiration of his cousin amounted almost to worship. But Buono finally prevailed. On May 21, 1978, Kenneth Bianchi drove to Bellingham and rejoined Kelli Boyd and their newborn son. He obtained a job as a security guard, and was soon promoted to supervisor. But the small town bored him. He longed to prove to his cousin that he had the makings of a master criminal. And in the first week of January 1979, the craving for rape and murder became an intolerable itch. His mind went back to an attractive student called Karen Mandic, whom he had known when he worked in a department store.

A week later he was under arrest, and the Hillside stranglings were finally over.

The news that Kenneth Bianchi had accused his cousin of being his accomplice made Buono unpopular in the neighborhood, and he received several threatening letters.

But it began to look more and more likely that neither Bianchi nor Buono would ever appear in a Los Angeles courtroom. In the Whatcomb County Jail, Bianchi had not only convinced Professor Watkins that he was a multiple personality, but had aroused equal interest and enthusiasm in another expert on the subject: Dr. Ralph B. Allison, author of a remarkable work on multiple personality called *Minds in Many Pieces*. Allison's obvious sympathy made "Steve" even more confiding, and led him to make what would later prove to be a crucial mistake. At Allison's request he revealed his last name: Walker—although at the time, this interesting and important fragment of information went unnoticed. And in the May issue of *Time* magazine, America learned that Bianchi had been pronounced a multiple personality by two of America's most eminent psychiatrists. Ken was innocent; it was Steve who had killed a dozen or so girls.

At this point, the prosecution decided it was time to bring in their own expert. Dr. Martin T. Orne, of the University of Pennsylvania Hospital, was known as an authority on hypnosis. The sessions with "Steve" had been videotaped, and Orne was able to study them. They failed to answer the question that troubled him most: whether Bianchi was hypnotized or only pretending to be. But he *did* notice that the character of "Steve" seemed to develop during the course of the sessions. Steve was always coarse and foul-mouthed—his favorite term for the psychiatrists was "motherfuckers"—but he seemed to slip deeper into his role as the sessions progressed. To Dr. Orne, that suggested an actor rather than a true alter ego.

When the professor came to interview him, Bianchi was his usual cooperative self. Under hypnotic suggestion, he quickly slipped into a trance. Orne now decided to try a crucial experiment. Good hypnotic subjects can be made to hallucinate the presence of another person. Orne told Bianchi that his defense lawyer, Dean Brett, was sitting in an empty chair. And Bianchi immediately did something that Orne had never seen before in a similar situation: leapt to his feet and shook the hand of the imaginary lawyer. At that moment, Orne was certain that Bianchi was only feigning hypnosis. Genuinely hypnotized subjects are content to talk to their hallucinations; they never try to touch them.

Now Dr. Orne tried another interesting experiment. In the course of conversation, he casually dropped the information that most multiple personalities have more than one alter ego. And at the next session, Bianchi immediately produced another "personality," a frightened child named Billy. Asked if he knew Steve, Billy whispered miserably: "He's a bad egg." Now Orne knew beyond all doubt that Bianchi was malingering.

But it was Frank Salerno and his partner Pete Finnigan who made the discovery that finally exploded Bianchi's claim to be a multiple personality. Listening to the Allison tape, they heard "Steve" declare that his last name was Walker. Suddenly, both recalled that they had seen the name Steve Walker somewhere in Bianchi's papers. A careful search revealed a letter to the registrar at California State University signed "Thomas Steven Walker"—in Bianchi's handwriting—which requested a diploma without the name filled in. A little sleuthing revealed that the real Steve Walker *was* a graduate in psychology from California State University at Northridge, and he had answered an advertisement for a job by sending some of his academic papers. The advertisement had actually been placed by Bianchi, who had then used Walker's name— and his papers—to obtain for himself a fake diploma in psychology.

The defense psychiatrists declined to be convinced that Bianchi was shamming and should stand trial. (Dr. Allison was later to admit that he was mistaken; he had meanwhile become a prison psychiatrist, and professed himself shocked to discover that criminals were habitual liars.) Dr. Martin Orne and his colleague Dr. Saul Faerstein—who had also interviewed Bianchi, at the request of the prosecution—were insistent that Bianchi was a malingerer, and it was their opinion that carried the day at the sanity hearing on October 19, 1979. At that hearing, Bianchi pleaded guilty to the two Bellingham murders and to five murders in Los Angeles, sobbing and professing deep remorse. Under Washington law, the judge then sentenced him to life imprisonment without the formality of a trial. But there were still five more murder charges to answer in Los Angeles. And when the Los Angeles County DA's office offered Bianchi a deal—plead guilty and testify against his cousin, and he would get life with the possibility of parole—he quickly accepted. In interviews with Frank Salerno and Peter Finnigan, he described all the murders with a precision of detail that left no doubt that it was Ken, not Steve, who had committed them.

On October 22, 1979, Angelo Buono was finally arrested and charged with the Hillside stranglings. He was placed in the county jail, where Bianchi already occupied another cell. But Bianchi was already reneging on his plea-bargaining agreement, explaining that he had made it only to save his life, and that he was genuinely innocent. The reason for his change of heart was simple. The DA's office had made the incredible decision to drop the other five Los Angeles murder charges, for which Bianchi could have been sentenced to death. So now he had nothing to lose by refusing to be cooperative.

As far as Salerno and Grogan were concerned, it did not make a great deal of difference. The jewelry found in Bianchi's house linked him to some of the victims, while a wisp of fluff on the eyelid of Judy Miller, the second victim, was demonstrated by forensic scientists to be identical to a foamy polyester material found in Buono's house. Strand by strand, the case against the Hillside stranglers was becoming powerful enough virtually to ensure Buono's conviction.

For Bianchi, the case was by no means over. One of the characteristics of the psychopath is that he just never gives up.

And in June 1980, Bianchi glimpsed an incredible chance of proving his innocence. He received a letter signed "Veronica Lynn Compton, pen name Ver Lyn," asking for his cooperation on a play she was writing. The plot, she explained, was about a female mass murderer who injects male semen into the sex organs of her victims, thus making the police think that the killer is a male.

Bianchi was interested. He became even more interested when Veronica Compton came to visit him, and he realized that this glamorous brunette was obsessed by him. They fantasized about how nice it would be to go on a killing spree together, and Virginia suggested that they should cut off the private parts of the victims and keep them in embalming fluid. Soon after that they were exchanging love letters. Finally, Bianchi confided to her his brilliant scheme for getting out of jail. All she had to do was to go to Bellingham, and transform her play into reality: strangle a woman and inject semen into her vagina through a syringe. And Bianchi would then be able to point out that the Bellingham murderer was obviously still at large, and that he must therefore be innocent. But where would she get the semen? Simple, said Bianchi, he would provide it. And he did so by masturbating into the finger of a rubber glove, which he then smuggled to her in the spine of a book.

Veronica flew to Bellingham, and registered at a motel called the Shangri-la. In a nearby bar she made the acquaintance of a young woman named Kim Breed, and had several drinks with her. When she asked her to drive her back to her motel, her new friend agreed. At the Shangri-la, Veronica invited her into her room for a drink. Once inside, she excused herself to go to the toilet, armed herself with a piece of cord, then tiptoed out and sneaked up behind her unsuspecting victim, who was seated on the bed. Fortunately, Kim Breed was something of an athlete. She struggled frantically, and succeeded in throwing Veronica over her head and on to the floor.

Then she fled. When she returned to the motel with a male friend, Veronica had also fled. But the police had no difficulty in tracing her through her airline reservation. She was arrested and, in due course, the "copycat" slayer, as the newspapers labeled her, was sentenced to life. As soon as he learned of her failure, Bianchi lost interest in her, thereby fuelling deep resentment.

The case of Angelo Buono was due to come to court in September 1981. But pre-trial hearings, before Judge Ronald M. George, began long before that. The first matter on which Judge George had to make up his mind was a motion by the defense to allow bail to the accused. George turned it down. The next motion was to sever the ten murder charges from the non-murder charges such as pimping, rape and sodomy; this would ensure that the jury should know as little as possible about Buono's background. Because it might provide grounds for an appeal, the judge decided to grant this motion.

The next development staggered everybody, including the judge. In July, the assistant District Attorney, Roger Kelly, proposed that all ten murder counts against Buono should be dropped. The reason, he explained, was that Bianchi's testimony was so dubious and self-contradictory that it was virtually useless. Buono should be tried at a later date on the non-murder charges, and meanwhile be allowed free on a fifty-thousand-dollar bail . . . Grogan and Salerno could hardly believe their ears. It meant that even if Buono was convicted on the other charges, he would serve only about five years in jail.

The judge agreed to deliver his ruling on July 21, 1981. During the week preceding that date, morale among the police was at rock bottom; no one doubted that the judge would agree to drop the charges—after all, if the DA's office was so unsure of a conviction, they must know what they were talking about.

On the day of the ruling, Buono looked cheerful and his junior counsel, Katherine Mader, was beaming with confidence. But as the judge reviewed the evidence, it became clear that their confidence was misplaced. Whether Bianchi was reliable or not, said the judge, the evidence of various witnesses, and the Judy Miller fiber evidence, made it clear that there was a strong case against Buono. Therefore, concluded Judge George, he was denying the District Attorney's motion. And if, he added, the DA showed any lack of enthusiasm in prosecuting Buono, he would refer the case to the Attorney General.

Buono, who had expected to walk free from the courtroom, had to cancel his plans for a celebratory dinner with his lawyers.

At this point the DA's office decided to withdraw from the case. Thereupon, the Attorney General appointed two of his deputies, Roger Boren and Michael Nash, to prosecute Buono.

The trial, which lasted from November 1981 to November 1983, was the longest murder trial in American history. The prosecution called 251 witnesses and introduced over a thousand exhibits. But although the transcript was eventually to occupy hundreds of volumes, the trial itself held few surprises. It took until June 1982 to get to Bianchi's evidence—he was the two hundredth witness to testify—and he at first showed himself typically vague and ambiguous. But when the judge dropped a hint that he was violating his original plea-bargaining agreement, and that he would have to serve out his time in Washington's Walla Walla—a notoriously tough jail—he became altogether less vague. Bianchi spent five months on the stand, and the results were damning to his cousin.

The defense team raised many objections, and pursued a tactic of trying to discredit witnesses and evidence. On the submission that testimony obtained under hypnosis should be inadmissible, the judge ruled that Bianchi had been faking both hypnosis and multiple personality. More serious was a motion by the defense to dismiss the whole case because one of the prosecution witnesses—Judy Miller's boyfriend—had been in a mental home. This was also overruled: it was the defense's fault, the judge said, for failing to spot the material in the files. Finally, the defense called Veronica Compton, the "copycat slayer," to try to prove that she and Bianchi had planned to "frame" Angelo Buono. Veronica, still seething with resentment, gave her evidence with histrionic relish. But when she admitted that she had once planned to open a mortuary so she and her lover could have sex with the corpses, it was clear that the jury found it hard to treat her as a reliable witness.

In the final submissions in October 1983, Buono's defense lawyer Gerald Chaleff argued that Bianchi had committed the murders alone, and that his cousin was an innocent man. The judge had to rebuke him for implying that the whole case against his client was a conspiracy. The jury retired on October 21, 1983, and when they had spent a week in their deliberations, the defense began to feel gloomy and the prosecution correspondingly optimistic. It emerged later that one juror, who was resentful about not being chosen as foreman, had been consistently obstructive. But finally, on October 31 (Halloween), the jury announced that it had found Angelo Buono guilty of the murder of Lauren Wagner. During the following week they also found him guilty of murdering Dolores Cepeda, Sonja Johnson, Kristina Weckler, Jane King, Lissa Kastin and Cindy Hudspeth. But—possibly influenced by the fact that Bianchi had already escaped the death penalty—they decided that Buono should not receive a death sentence. On January 4, 1984, the judge ordered that, since he had done everything in his power to sabotage the case against his cousin, Kenneth Bianchi should be returned to serve his sentence in Washington. He then sentenced Angelo Buono to life imprisonment without possibility of parole, regretting that he could not sentence him to death. In his final remarks he told the defendants:

"I am sure, Mr. Buono and Mr. Bianchi, that you will both probably only get your thrills reliving over and over again the torturing and murdering of your victims, being incapable, as I believe you to be, of feeling any remorse."

Asked later whether such acts as Buono and Bianchi had committed did not prove them insane, he commented: "Why should we call someone insane simply because he or she chooses not to conform to our standards of civilized behavior?"

Perhaps more than any other case in this book, this one raises the question: what motivates people to do such things? This is not intended as an expression of moral indignation, which has no place in criminology, but as a question in practical psychology.

To grasp its significance, we need to look back over some of the ground we have covered in discussing the rise of pornography. There is a sense in which sex is not a "personal" relationship, particularly for the male (on whom we are focusing). A healthy male responds "automatically" to certain sights, such as a female undressing, just as a male stickleback will attack a piece of red cardboard because its aggression is aroused by another male's red underside. An inexperienced teenager may spend much of his time in a state of sexual arousal which is as impersonal as a dog's response to a bitch in heat. On the other hand, when a husband sees his wife removing her clothes on their honeymoon, his response is a mixture of "impersonal" desire and "personal" tenderness. And, since the purpose of sex is ultimately the raising of children, this is obviously closer to what sex is supposed to be. We all feel instinctively that sex without any "personal" dimension is rather crude and shameful, in that it leaves some basic human craving unsatisfied.

All human beings experience this desire for human contact and warmth, and this clearly applied to Buono and Bianchi, both of whom had close sexual relationships—albeit Buono preferred underage girls. How, then, could they continue to kidnap, rape and murder girl after girl, without any sense of compunction? Did they never feel sorry for some exhausted, violated victim as she was pleading for her life? If not, then how did they feel when they returned to their "normal" human relations—as Bianchi did with his common-law wife and child?

To say that they "divided their minds" is no answer. We can easily see that a man who began to develop a sadistic pleasure in beating dogs or children would find it difficult to return to being an affectionate master or father.

In this case, we observe—yet again—that rape becomes an addiction. The murder of Yolanda Washington removed their inhibitions about rape/murder, and from then on, the craving returned periodically. It was basically a desire to treat the woman *purely* as a sexual stimulant, with no personal relationship. Moreover, this also developed into a desire to torture the woman as well as rape her. It is as if treating women as "sexual throwaways" caused the development of some element that *may* be latent in all males, but about which "normal" males feel a deep inhibition.

What *is* it that can turn normal males into ruthless sexual predators? A sex-starved adolescent might suppose that it is simply the act of undressing a girl and penetrating her body, which strikes him as infinitely exciting. But a married couple know this is not true. "Normal" sex tends to stay normal, and not to develop into violence and rape.

Roy Hazelwood came close to an answer when he said that sex crime is not about sex but about power. We have seen that this statement needs to be qualified. *Some* sex crime springs purely out of sexual frustration, and is therefore "about sex." But in the majority of modern serial killers, it is true that sex crime is about power.

But why should that be addictive? In spite of the anarchist dictum that power corrupts, a man who achieves power in everyday life, say as colonel of a regiment or supervisor of an office, does not automatically want to become Commander in Chief or head of the corporation. He may have reached a level at which he feels comfortable. Then why is the kind of power involved in sex crime so addictive?

The answer clearly lies in the sense of revelation associated with sex—the sense of breaking through barriers, of overcoming obstacles, of asserting masculinity: in a word, the surge of *freedom*. The sex criminal would argue that the average man can never "drink his fill" of sex; he is only allowed to satisfy his desire within certain socially recognized limits. Sex murderer Leonard Lake—whom we shall encounter in the next chapter—expressed this attitude when he wrote: "The perfect woman is totally controlled . . . There is no sexual problem with a submissive woman. There are no frustrations—only pleasure and contentment." In drinking his fill of freedom, the sex killer imagines that he will experience total pleasure and contentment, and end with all his problems solved. A particularly articulate serial killer might argue that he regards rape as an instrument of spiritual evolution, just as a saint regards prayer, or a yogi meditation.

All this leads to the most interesting question of all: why, in fact, is there no case on record of a sex killer achieving "higher consciousness" through sex? Why, in fact, do so many of them—like Ian Brady and Ted Bundy—end with a curious sense of futility, of having "done it all"? After all, no saint or yogi or artist or philosopher ends with a sense of having "done it all."

The answer lies partly in the fact that man is essentially a social being, and that sex is an activity involving another person. (Even masturbation involves the image of another person.) Sade does his best to argue that the individual has no obligation to society, and can take his satisfaction as straightforwardly as a tiger eating its dinner. But if Sade really meant what he said, he would not bother to present it as an argument, for an argument is presented *to* other people, and involves the tacit assumption that they have the same rights that you have. No tiger argues with its dinner.

But there is another paradox. The "freedom feeling" involves a sense of expansion, of happiness and benevolence. In sex between lovers, this feeling finds its natural object in the other person. In violation, the act itself contradicts the sensation it arouses. Freedom is about the transcendence of the personality, the "godlike" sensation in which the personality seems to dissolve, to give way to immense vistas of "possibility." By contrast, crime involves entrapment in the personality, a sense of doing something that you prefer other people not to know about. The two sensations are in total opposition, pulling in opposite directions. The sex killer may dream about total fulfillment and higher consciousness, but when he has finished with his victim, he has to think about hiding the body, getting away without being seen, leaving no clues. The prison door has slammed again. Worse still, he feels trapped in a pattern of violence which has become his master. He is like a man who has become enslaved by a blackmailer.

In the 1970s, California became virtually the serial-killer center of the world. In addition to the Hillside Stranglers, there was John Linley Frazier, Herb Mullin, Ed Kemper and Richard Chase. With the possible exception of Kemper, it could be argued that all four were mentally disturbed to the point of psychosis, and therefore belong in a textbook of psychiatry rather than the present volume. Significantly, California at this time was pursuing a policy of turning out mental patients into the community.

When, in October 1970, Victor Ohta and his family were found murdered in their California home, a note on the doctor's Rolls-Royce read: "Today World War III will begin, as brought to you by the people of the free universe . . . I and my comrades from this day forth will fight until death or freedom against anyone who does not support natural life on this planet. Materialism must die or mankind will stop." The killer, the 24-year-old drop-out John Linley Frazier, had told witnesses that the Ohta family was "too materialistic" and deserved to die. In fact, Frazier was reacting with the self-centered narcissism of the children described by Becker. ("You gave him more juice." "Here's some more then." "Now *she's* got more juice than me . . .") He felt he had a long way to go to achieve "security," while Ohta had a swimming pool and a Rolls-Royce parked in the drive.

The irony is that Ohta himself would serve equally well as an example of Becker's "urge to heroism." He was the son of Japanese immigrants who had been interned in 1941; but Ohta had finally been allowed to join the American army; his elder brother was killed in the fighting in Europe. Ohta had worked as a railway track-layer and a cab driver to get through medical school, and his success as an eye surgeon came late in life. Ohta achieved his sense of "belongingness" through community work; he was one of the founders of the Dominican Hospital in Santa Cruz—a non-profit-making hospital—and often gave free treatment to patients who could not afford his fees. Frazier was completely unaware of all this. But it would probably have made no difference anyway. He was completely wrapped up in his own little world of narcissism.

In April 1973, 25-year-old Ed Kemper—six foot nine

inches tall—crept into his mother's bedroom and killed her with a hammer; the following day he killer her friend Sara Hallett. Then he drove to Pueblo, Colorado, and rang the Santa Cruz police department to confess. In custody, Kemper confessed to six horrific sex murders, all with a strong necrophiliac element. In 1963, at the age of 14, Kemper had murdered his grandfather and grandmother, with whom he was living, and spent five years in mental hospitals. In 1972, he picked up two female hitchhikers, threatened them with a gun, and murdered them both; he later dissected the bodies, cutting off the heads. Kemper's usual method was to take the bodies back to his mother's house—she worked in a hospital—and rape and dissect them there; he particularly enjoyed having sex with a headless body. The bodies were later dumped over cliffs or left in remote mountain areas. Kemper was sentenced to life imprisonment.

Another psychopathic mass killer, Herb Mullin, was operating in California at the same time as Kemper. As a teenager, Mullin had been voted by his class "most likely to succeed," but by the time he was 21—in 1969—he was showing signs of mental abnormality. In October 1972, driving along a mountain highway, Mullin passed an old tramp, and stopped to ask the man to take a look at the engine; as the man bent over, Mullin killed him with a baseball bat, leaving the corpse by the roadside. Two weeks later he picked up a pretty college student, stabbed her with a hunting knife, and tore out her intestines. In November 1972 he went into a church and stabbed the priest to death. On January 25, 1973, he committed five murders in one night, killing a friend and his wife, then murdering a woman and her two children who lived in a nearby log cabin. In the Santa Cruz State Park he killed four teenage boys in a tent with a revolver. On February 13, 1973, he was driving to his parents' home when a voice in his head told him to stop and kill an old man who was working in his front garden. A neighbor heard the shot, and rang the police, who picked up Mullin within a few blocks. At his trial, Mullin explained that he was convinced that murders averted natural disasters—such as another San Francisco earthquake. But he was found to be sane and sentenced to life imprisonment.

Richard Chase—who earned himself the soubriquet "the Dracula Killer"—was first arrested in August 1977, near Pyramid Lake, Nevada, when police found a raw liver—apparently human—in a plastic bucket in his car. Nearby, Chase—aged 27—was sitting on a rock, half naked and covered in blood. But when tests revealed that the liver was from a cow, Chase was released. If the police had decided to question his sanity, several lives would have been spared.

Four months later, on December 29, 1977, a Sacramento engineer named Ambrose Griffin was shot as he walked between his car and his house—apparently by a random sniper. He died some days later in the hospital. The following day, a man sitting in a car fired a handgun at a boy on a bicycle, fortunately missing him. The bullet was found and proved to be fired from the gun that had killed Ambrose Griffin.

On January 23, an intruder walked into the house of newly married Teresa Wallin, 22, in the Watt Avenue area of Sacramento, and shot her three times, then mutilated the body with a knife. There was no sign of rape, but evidence that the killer had drained some of her blood into a yogurt cup and drunk it.

Around that time, many people in the area reported seeing a dirty, disheveled man in an orange jacket, who sometimes knocked on doors and made incomprehensible demands.

Four days later, 38-year-old Evelyn Miroth, the mother of two small sons, was found shot and mutilated on her bed, and a boyfriend, Danny Meredith, was found shot dead in the next room. One of her children, 6-year-old Jason, had also been shot. A 22-month-old baby, David Ferreira, whom the victim had been baby-sitting, was missing. Evelyn Miroth's other two sons were away from home at the time. The post mortem showed that she had been sodomized. Again, there was evidence that the killer had drunk some of her blood.

The following day, a woman named Nancy Holden contacted the police, and told them about an encounter she had had with a man named Richard Chase, on the day of the Wallin murder. Chase, who had been at school with her, had accosted her in a store and tried to persuade her to give him a lift. Worried by his wild appearance, she had made some excuse.

The police checked on Chase and discovered that he had a record of mental illness. When they called at his apartment to interview him, Chase tried to run away; he was finally handcuffed before he could draw a gun.

The body of David Ferreira was found—decapitated—in a box near a church.

On January 2, 1979, Richard Chase was tried on six counts of murder. It became clear from the evidence that one of his peculiarities was to dabble his fingers in the intestines of his victims—hence the nickname "the Dracula Killer." Chase was sentenced to death, but on December 26, 1980, he committed suicide with an overdose of his anti-depression pills, which he had been saving up for weeks.

Oddly enough, it was in England that the most widely publicized case of serial murder of the 1970s occurred. As the years passed without any clue to his identity, "the Yorkshire Ripper" achieved the same notoriety as Jack the Ripper in the late nineteenth century. Typically, much of this evaporated with the arrest of the murderer.

On an evening in late August 1969, a prostitute walking down St. Paul's Road, in the red-light area of Bradford, Yorkshire, was struck violently on the head by a brick in a sock. She followed her assailant, and noted the number of the van

in which he drove away. The police soon traced the owner of
the van, who told them that he had been in the red-light area
with a friend, who had vanished down St. Paul's Road late at
night. The police went to see the friend, whose name was
Peter Sutcliffe. He was a shy, rather inarticulate young man,
who insisted that he had only struck the woman with the flat
of his hand. Since he had no criminal record, he was let off
with a caution. The attack was the first crime of the man who
would become known as the Yorkshire Ripper.

This attack was not quite "motiveless." Two months earlier,
Sutcliffe had become intensely jealous of his girlfriend,
Sonia, who was seeing another man and—he believed—being
unfaithful to him. To "get even," he picked up a prostitute—
the first time he had ever done such a thing—but the encounter was not a success. The woman took his £10, then got
her pimp to chase him away. Three weeks later, he saw the
woman in a pub, and demanded his money back; instead, she
jeered at him and made him a laughing-stock. Sutcliffe was a
shy, sensitive man, and the experience filled him with rage
and embarrassment. It festered until he became a sadistic
killer of women—innocent housewives and schoolgirls as
well as prostitutes.

Five years later, on July 4, 1975, Sutcliffe walked up behind a pretty divorcee named Anna Rogulskyj, and struck her
three times on the head with the ball end of a ball-pein hammer. Then, as she collapsed, he raised her blouse and made
several slashes with a knife. He was about to plunge it into her
stomach when a man's voice called out to ask what was happening. Sutcliffe fled. Anna Rogulskyj recovered after a brain
operation. Six weeks later, on August 15, 1975, he crept behind a 46-year-old office cleaner named Olive Smelt, and
struck her to the ground with the hammer. Then he raised her
clothes and made some slashes on her buttocks with a hacksaw blade before going to rejoin a friend who was waiting for

him in a car. When the friend asked him what he had been doing, he explained in a mumble that he had been "talking to that woman." Olive Smelt also recovered after an operation to remove bone splinters from her brain.

On October 29, 1975, Sutcliffe picked up a 28-year-old prostitute named Wilma McCann, and went with her to a playing field near her home. But he found it impossible to achieve an erection at short notice. When the woman told him he was "fuckin' useless," he asked her to wait a moment, got the hammer from the toolbox of his car, and struck her on the head. Then he tugged down her white slacks and stabbed her nine times in the abdomen and five in the chest.

Wilma McCann was the first of thirteen murder victims over the course of five years. Some of the victims were "amateur prostitutes," mothers of single-parent families trying to earn money. Some, like 16-year-old Jayne MacDonald, were schoolgirls who happened to be returning home late at night. Some were working women, like 47-year-old Marguerite Walls, a Department of Health official who had been working overtime. Although Sutcliffe was later to insist that he was interested only in killing prostitutes, his craving to kill and mutilate extended to all women.

By the late 1970s, the murder hunt for the Yorkshire Ripper (as the press christened him) was the biggest in British criminal history. Thousands of people were interviewed—including Peter Sutcliffe—but all this information was not computerized, and so overwhelmed the investigators. Sutcliffe was interviewed in connection with the murder of a prostitute named Jean Jordan, a 20-year-old Scot, whom he had killed in the Southern Cemetery in Manchester, stripping her naked and stabbing her in a frenzy. After the murder, Sutcliffe looked for her handbag, which contained the £5 note he had given her—a new one he had been paid in his wage packet. In due course, this was found by the police, and all the employees of twenty-five firms in Bradford were interviewed, including Sutcliffe. His wife confirmed his alibi, and the police filed a report saying they had found nothing to arouse their suspicions.

In 1978 and 1979 the police had received three letters signed "Jack the Ripper," which had led them to mount an extensive investigation in the Wearside area, 100 miles to the north of Bradford. And on June 26, 1979, the police received a recorded tape beginning with the words "I'm Jack," and taunting them for failing to catch him; the accent was "Geordie"—again, from the Wearside area. After Sutcliffe's arrest, the letters and the tape were recognized as hoaxes, but at the time, most police officers on the case assumed that the Ripper was from somewhere around Durham.

In December 1980, after the thirteenth murder, the police decided to set up an advisory team consisting of four police officers and a forensic expert, Stuart Kind. There had been seventeen attacks in all—including the ones of Anna Rogulskyj and Olive Smelt, and two more in the autumn of 1979 when the victims survived. The main clues were three sets of tire tracks at three scenes of crime, three sets of footprints also found near three of the victims, and finally the new £5 note found in Jean Jordan's handbag. It will be recalled that this had been found far from the sites of the earlier Ripper murders, across the Pennines in Manchester, so it seemed highly likely that the "Ripper" had taken it with him from Bradford—Sutcliffe had received it in his pay packet two days before the murder. But if the Ripper lived in the Bradford area, then the search of Wearside was a waste of time. In that case, the tape was probably also a hoax, for although the "Geordie" Ripper might live in Bradford, the extensive police investigations had failed to pinpoint such a suspect. This is why, at the beginning of the investigation, the five-man team decided that the tape and letters should be dismissed as irrelevancies.

There was another reason. The team had gone to examine all the murder sites, including that of a Bradford University student, Barbara Leach, who was killed returning to her flat in the early hours of the morning. As they were looking at the site, one of the police officers, Commander Ronald Harvey, had one of these sudden hunches that come from years of experience, and he remarked: "Chummy lives in Bradford and he did it going home." What he was suggesting was that the Ripper lived in this area, and that he killed Barbara Leach on his way home, perhaps after an unsuccessful search for a victim.

The comment impressed Stuart Kind, for surely here was an important point: that a murder committed in the early hours of the morning indicated that the killer was not far from home, whereas a murder committed earlier in the evening suggested that he had driven far from home in search of a victim and had to get back. Anna Rogulskyj had been attacked in Keighley, close to Bradford, at 1:10 in the morning. But Olive Smelt, attacked at 11 p.m., had been in Halifax. Josephine Walker had been murdered in Halifax at 11:30 p.m. Helen Rytka had been attacked in Huddersfield—even farther from Bradford—at nine in the evening. Vera Millward had been murdered in Manchester at nine in the evening. Admittedly, this pattern did not hold for all the seventeen attacks—Emily Jackson had been murdered in nearby Leeds at seven in the evening—but it held for most of them.

So it looked as if the Ripper was probably a local man living in Bradford or Leeds, where ten out of seventeen attacks took place. Next, the team took a map of the area, and computed the "center of gravity" of the attacks. The basic principle was to stick a pin in the seventeen sites, then to take an eighteenth pin, and join it to the other seventeen by lengths of thread, minimizing the amount of thread required. The eighteenth pin proved to be squarely in Bradford. (In fact, the "pin test" was carried out on the forensic laboratory computer.)

The team suggested that a special squad of detectives should concentrate their energies on Bradford. That would involve rechecking all the men in Bradford who had been interviewed. And since the £5 note was the most vital clue so far, the men who had been interviewed in this connection would have been top of the list. Since the police possessed samples of the tire tracks of the Ripper's car, it would have been a simple matter to check the tire tracks of each of these men.

It can be seen that this method should have led infallibly to Peter Sutcliffe, who was by then living with his wife Sonia at 6 Garden Lane, in the Heaton district of Bradford. That it did not do so was due to the simple circumstance that the Yorkshire Ripper was finally arrested within two weeks of the interim report being completed. On January 2, 1981, in the early evening, Peter Sutcliffe drove the 30 or so miles from Bradford to Sheffield, and in the red-light district there, picked up a black prostitute named Olive Reivers, and backed into a drive. She removed her knickers and handed him a condom; he unbuttoned his trousers and struggled uncomfortably across her in the passenger seat. But he was unable to obtain an erection. As he sat beside her again, telling her about his wife's frigidity, they were dazzled by the lights of a police car which pulled up with its nose to the hood of Sutcliffe's old Rover. Sutcliffe told Olive Reivers to back up his story that she was his girlfriend, and gave his name as Peter Williams. One of the policemen went to the nearest telephone and checked the car's number plates with the national police computer at Hendon; within two minutes, he had learned that the plates on the Rover actually belonged to a Skoda. Sutcliffe had stolen them from a car scrap-yard and fixed them on with Sellotape, because he knew the police were noting the number plates of cars in red-light areas.

As both policemen escorted Olive Reivers to the police car, Sutcliffe hurried behind a nearby oil storage tank, explaining that he was "busting for a pee," and there managed to dispose of the ball-pein hammer and knife that had been concealed under his seat. The police then took him to Hammerton Road police station. There he revealed that his name was Sutcliffe, and explained that he was using false number plates because his insurance had lapsed and he was due to. appear on a drunken driving charge. He was placed in a cell for the night. And at eight o'clock the next morning—Saturday—he was taken to the Ripper Incident Room at Leeds. Here it was immediately noted that the size of his shoe was the same as that of the footprint found at three of the murder sites. When he volunteered the information that he had been among those questioned about the new £5 note, and had also been questioned routinely as a regular visitor to red-light areas, the investigators suddenly became aware that this man could well be the Ripper. When they learned that his car had also been logged in Manchester, it began to look even more likely. Yet there was still no real evidence against Sutcliffe, and after a long day of questioning, during which he had been pleasantly cooperative, the police recognized this lack of evidence. But five and a half years of fruitless search for the Ripper had made them persistent; they decided to hold him for another night. And, back in Sheffield, the policeman who had arrested him heard that he was still being questioned by the Ripper squad. On an impulse, he went back to the oil storage tank where Sutcliffe had urinated. There he found the hammer and knife on a pile of leaves.

When Sutcliffe was told about the find, he admitted that he was the Yorkshire Ripper, then went on to dictate a statement describing his murders in detail.

"I imagined him to be an ugly hunchback wi' boils all over his face, somebody who couldn't get women and resented 'em for that." This was the comment of Carl Sutcliffe when he learned that his eldest brother Peter had been charged with being the Yorkshire Ripper. Peter Sutcliffe was not an ugly hunchback; he was strikingly handsome, in a brooding, Elvis Presley sort of way, with black hair and a beard and a superb physique. And he had no difficulty getting girls; although a considerate and attentive husband, he seized any opportunity afforded by his wife's absence to sleep with local girls, and found them more than willing to oblige.

Then why did Peter Sutcliffe commit thirteen particularly sadistic murders? A book on the case which appeared within weeks of his conviction—and which claimed to be an "in-depth study of a mass killer"—shed surprisingly little light on the problem. The portrait of the Ripper that emerged seemed to be entirely in terms of negatives. He was not a brutal or resentful or violent person; on the contrary, he was gentle, meditative, courteous and good-tempered. It was practically impossible to provoke him into anger or self-assertion; and this was not due to an iron self-control, but to a genuine sweetness of disposition. He was the sort of person you would have trusted implicitly as a baby-sitter or an escort for your teenage daughter; what is more, you would have been perfectly right to do so. Under normal circumstances, Peter Sutcliffe would not have harmed a fly.

The mystery, of course, is what peculiar pressures turned this quiet man into a maniac who stole up behind women in the dark, smashed in their skulls with blows from a ball-headed hammer, then pulled up their skirts and blouses and carefully inflicted dozens of wounds with a specially sharpened screwdriver. This is a problem that came to obsess the journalist Gordon Burn, and he sought his answers in the Ripper's home territory—Bingley, near Bradford. The result is a book that will undoubtedly become a classic in the field of investigative criminology.

It was Aldous Huxley, talking about D. H. Lawrence, who commented on the stifling intimacy of working-class family life, an intimacy the middle classes find almost unimaginable. What Huxley could not understand was the curiously *stagnant* mentality created by this kind of environment. When people live that close together, they come to share one another's values, one another's states of mind, just as they would share one another's germs if they all used the same toothbrush. This is why so many people, born into such an environment, end their lives living just around the corner from the place where they were born. They take it utterly for granted that there is no escape. This also explains the oddly resentful attitude towards people who have "made it"; Gordon Burn mentions the hostility that local people seem to feel about John Braine, who was an assistant librarian in Bingley when he wrote *Room at the Top*.

This is, of course, hard luck on the people who *are* slightly different, but who lack the energy or passion to heave themselves out of the swamp by brute force. Burn's book makes it very clear that this was one of the major factors in the Ripper's inauspicious development.

Peter Sutcliffe was his mother's first child: a shy, scrawny, miserable little boy who spent hours staring blankly into space. He clung—quite literally—to his mother's skirts for years after he had learned to walk. At school he was so withdrawn and passive that after his arrest, most of his schoolteachers could not even remember who he was.

The Sutcliffe home was no background for this kind of child. The father, John Sutcliffe, was a dominant extrovert, a bully who was detested by his family—one daughter admits she had dreams of murdering him. The younger brothers shared some of his characteristics; one of them once floored the local boxing champion by punching him in the testicles. The house was always jammed with people, and John Sutcliffe enjoyed "feeling up" any young girls who strayed too close. The atmosphere was heavy with sexuality; even Sutcliffe's mother, a quiet doormat of a woman, had a love affair with a local police sergeant; the father retaliated by moving in with the deaf and dumb woman a few doors away. Various kinds of illegality were also taken for granted; Sutcliffe senior was arrested for breaking and entering; the second brother was always in and out of jail; some of Peter's best friends were burglars.

So the pathologically shy boy began to try to develop the characteristics that would make him less of a misfit. He did body-building exercises, learned to walk on his hands, drove at eighty miles an hour in built-up areas, boasted of sleeping with prostitutes. The latter was fantasy; but Sutcliffe *was* morbidly fascinated by the local red-light districts, and liked to cruise around them, just eyeing the prostitutes. All the same, when he finally found himself a girl, it was a Czech emigrée, who was even shyer than he was, and so plain that even Sutcliffe senior never tried to feel her up.

It was this girl—Sonia—who started the train of events that turned Peter Sutcliffe into a sadistic killer. She began having an affair with an Italian who owned a sports car; Sutcliffe was plunged into an agony of jealousy. To revenge himself, he went off to the red-light district to find a woman. Even this turned out to be a flop. He was unable to raise an erection, and the girl swindled him out of five pounds. Worse still, when he saw her later in a pub and asked for his money, she jeered at him and told the story at the top of her voice, so he became a laughing stock.

'Life being what it is," said Gauguin, "one dreams of revenge." Sutcliffe was caught in a peculiar emotional whirlpool, dreaming of sex, of violence, of getting his own back. One day, eating fish and chips in a friend's mini-van, he thought he saw the prostitute who had swindled him, and slipped out of the van. He was carrying in his pocket a brick inside a sock for precisely this purpose. He hit the woman on the back of the head, then ran back to the van. She succeeded in taking his number, and the next day he was questioned by the police. He convinced them it had been a straightforward quarrel, and the woman decided not to press charges.

For the next five years he kept out of trouble; to begin with, he was working nights. Sonia had gone to London and had a schizophrenic breakdown, and Sutcliffe nursed her back to health; in 1974 they were married. But hatred of prostitutes continued to obsess him. He would stop the car and ask a woman how much she charged, then persuade her to take less. The bargain concluded, he would shout "Is that all you're worth?" and drive off. If a woman looked like a prostitute he would ask her roughly if she was on the game. It was totally uncharacteristic of the gentle, courteous Peter; but he was turning into a dual personality.

In July 1975 he approached a woman in the red-light district and, when she turned him down, followed her and hit her with a hammer. Then he raised her clothes and took out a knife. A man saw them and called out; Sutcliffe fled. A month later, he was sitting in a pub with a friend when a 45-year-old office cleaner went past; Sutcliffe said "I bet you're on the game," and received an abusive answer. Later, he saw her in the street, and slipped out of the car. Again he battered her to the ground with the hammer, again he was disturbed and fled.

Two months later, he picked up a drunken prostitute who was thumbing a lift. They went on to a playing field, where he again failed to raise an erection. Then, as she cursed him, he hit her with the hammer, and stabbed her repeatedly in the breast and stomach.

How does a man acquire a taste for disemboweling women? I suspect the answer may be: all too easily. I read Burns's book on the Ripper on a train journey to London, en route to do a breakfast TV show. On my way back to Paddington, I began to discuss the case with the hire-car driver, Andrew Fowler, who provided me with a hair-raising insight. Fowler told me that he had worked for two years in a slaughterhouse, because it paid so well. He had always been an animal lover, but found that killing cattle could be treated merely as a job. Then, one day, he found that he was beginning to look at horses and dogs with the thought: "I wonder what it would be like to kill it . . ." He decided that it was time to change his job. Fowler also described to me a slaughterman who was not happy until he was covered from head to foot in blood; once he was in this state, his eyes began to bulge in an odd way . . .

What seems clear is that Sutcliffe's obsession, which began as a hatred of prostitutes, soon became a desire to obtain sexual satisfaction by killing any woman. When he murdered Jean Jordan in Manchester in October 1977, he left the body hidden in bushes. Realizing that the five-pound note he had given her might provide a clue to his identity, he went back a week later to look for her handbag. He stripped her, stabbed her repeatedly, then used a piece of glass to open the body from the knee to the shoulder. The stench made him vomit, but he still went on to try to cut off her head with a hacksaw blade. The worm of death and violence had made its home in his sexual nerve. When he killed 16-year-old Jane MacDonald in the middle of a park, he must have known she was not a prostitute. It made no difference; he had conditioned himself to need this ultimate form of rape, and it was impossible to stop. And when, after thirteen murders, he was caught by a random police check, he had even lost count of the number he had committed—he thought it was eleven.

Perhaps the most important point to emerge from Gordon Burn's book, *Somebody's Husband, Somebody's Son*, is that mass killers like Sutcliffe, Dennis Nilsen, Ian Brady, even

Jack the Ripper himself, are not necessarily human monsters, creatures of nightmare, driven by a craving for violence. Sutcliffe was a basically normal person, who slipped into murder as gently and gradually as a child slips into a swimming pool at the shallow end. The morbid craving that drove him to wander round red-light areas, and to spend hours in a waxworks displaying horrible diseases and accidents, can be found in most children, and in far more adults than we would like to believe. Sutcliffe's problem was that he was more shy, more imaginative, more intelligent, than the people around him, and that in his environment, these qualities were worse than useless. In self-defense, he had to develop opposite qualities. And it was this discordant jumble of primary and secondary qualities, stitched together like a Frankenstein monster, that turned him into the most dangerous man in England. Gordon Burn reveals his insight into the problem when he describes Sutcliffe at his trial as looking like "a seaside cabinet doll that has known better days." But that description has one slight inaccuracy: this particular doll had never known better days.

THE 1980S AND 1990S

ON SEPTEMBER 8, 1888, MRS. MARY BURRIDGE, OF 132 BLACK-friars Road, South London, bought the Late Final edition of the evening newspaper *The Star*, and when she read the headline about the "latest horrible murder in Whitechapel," she collapsed and died of "a fit." There was much the same profound sense of shock and horror in America in the 1970s as news of the murders of Dean Corll, John Gacy, and the Hillside Stranglers was brought home with nauseating immediacy on the television screen. The general feeling was that the world was going downhill like a toboggan on a ski slope and that nothing could stop it. I recall the impact as being very like that of the revelation of the Nazi death camps in the last days of the Second World War, with the piles of skeletal corpses. But in a sense it was worse; because when Hitler died in the Berlin bunker, the world could at least heave a sigh of relief, and feel that the powers of evil had now been defeated. Corll, Gacy and Bundy revealed that they were as active as ever, and that our welfare society was actually nurturing such monsters.

As already noted, the term "serial killer" was coined in the late 1970s by FBI agent Robert Ressler, who worked at the new

FBI Academy at Quantico, Virginia. The Academy—founded by J. Edgar Hoover—had virtually created a new science called "psychological profiling." The study of dozens of murderers had revealed that they left their "personality fingerprints" behind at the scene of the crime—for example, evidence of panic and confusion usually indicated a young offender. For instance, on September 2, 1977, a 14-year-old schoolgirl named Julie Wittmeyer disappeared on the way home from school in Platte City, Kansas. Her clothing—minus her panties—was found in a field a few days later, and her naked and mutilated body the next day. The local police decided to try the new Behavioral Science Unit at Quanitco. After studying the evidence, the Unit sent back a "profile" of the offender: that he knew the victim, that he was a sexually frustrated "loner," probably below average intelligence and of more than average physical development, and that his contemporaries probably regarded him as "strange." Police Chief Marion Beeler exclaimed: "Sure as shootin', that's him"—for the description fitted a youth named Mark Sager. In fact, Sager was found guilty and sentenced to ten years.

Again, in the early 1980s, police in Anchorage, Alaska, were investigating the murder of a number of "exotic dancers" who worked in bars and strip joints. Most had been buried—naked—in shallow graves, and had been shot in the head. One 17-year-old prostitute escaped from a "john" who had chained her up and tortured her, and her description sounded like a wealthy and respected businessman named Robert Hansen, who owned a bakery business. But Hansen seemed to have an excellent alibi. The investigators decided to contact the Behavioral Science Unit at Quantico, and offer them the evidence on the crimes without going into detail about their suspect. The resulting "profile" convinced them that Hansen could indeed be their man. The friends who had given him an alibi were interviewed, and told that it might cost them two years in jail if they were perjuring themselves. They broke and admitted they were. Hansen was arrested, and a search of his home revealed "trophies" from his victims, and a map dotted with asterisks. This led them to more naked bodies—twenty in all. Hansen then confessed that he drove women out into the woods and asked them for oral sex; if they failed to satisfy him, he made them run naked through the snow, stalking them with a hunting rifle and finally killing them. He was sentenced to life imprisonment.

One interesting point emerges from Hansen's confession. He described how he had killed his first victim when she had asked him for money—he was obsessively mean—and that after murder he was physically sick. Soon afterwards he stabbed to death a prostitute who failed to fellate him satisfactorily. This time he no longer felt sick, but found he was looking back on the murder with pleasure. After that—as with so many serial killers—it became an addiction.

Robert Ressler was consulted in the case of the Sacramento murderer Richard Chase—described in the last chapter. He constructed a "profile" describing the killer as thin and undernourished, slovenly and unkempt, with a history of mental illness, and between 25 and 27 years of age. Chase was caught soon after, and proved to fit Ressler's profile with astonishing precision.

When Ressler attended various international seminars on crime in the late 1970s, murders like those of "Son of Sam" were described as "Stranger Killings." At a session at the Bramhill police academy, near London, Ressler heard discussions of crimes that came in "series"—like rapes, burglaries, arsons and so on. It was after this that Ressler began to refer to "serial killers" (unaware that crime writer John Brophy had used the term "serial murderer" in his book *The*

Meaning of Murder, in 1966.[1] The label stuck. And by the early 1980s the general public suddenly became aware of its existence when journalists began writing articles about "serial murder."

What was being discussed in these early articles was not primarily the type of serial murder committed by Corll and Gacy, in which the killer lured victims into his own home, but the notion of killers who wandered around from place to place, killing casually and at random. It was this that made it all so frightening. One policeman was quoted as saying: "There may be as many as five hundred of them out there." This meant ten to every state in America, or about one to every major city. This was the figure accepted by psychiatrist Joel Norris in his book *Serial Killers: The Growing Menace* (1988), although another authority, Elliott Leyton, estimated the number at a hundred.

When writing my own book *The Serial Killers* (with Donald Seaman, 1990), I found myself questioning these figures. It's true that a few serial killers—like Corll and Gacy—had killed thirty people. But even allowing a conservative ten victims per killer, Norris's figure would make about five thousand victims a year—roughly a quarter of the total American murder rate. That seemed impossible. Even Leyton's figure seemed high. So I wrote to FBI agent Gregg McCrary, one of the Quantico team who had given us such generous help with our book, and asked for his own estimate. It was less than fifty, accounting for, at most, a few hundred serial murders per year. So the usual estimate *was* well over the top, reflecting the journalist's desire for a bloodcurdling story rather than the true figures.

In the early 1980s the British police were learning the same lessons as their American counterparts. The Yorkshire

[1] I owe this observation to the criminologist Candice Skrapec.

Ripper case had taught them an important lesson. If suspects, like car number plates, had been fed into a computer, Sutcliffe would probably have been taken in for questioning when he was wearing the boots whose imprint was found beside Jo Whitaker—and three lives would have been saved. A computer would have had no problem storing 150,000 suspects and 22,000 statements. Yet even with the aid of a computer, the task of tracking down a random serial killer like Sutcliffe would have been enormous. It could only display such details as the methods of known sex offenders, and the names of suspects who had been interviewed more than once. In their next major investigation of a serial killer, the Surrey police began with a list of 4,900 sex offenders— which, as it happened, contained the name of the man they were seeking.

The "Railway Rapist" began to operate in 1982; at this stage, two men were involved in sexual attacks on five women on or near railway stations. By 1984, one of the men had begun to operate alone. He threatened his victims with a knife, tied their hands, and raped them with a great deal of violence. Twenty-seven such attacks occurred in 1984 and 1985. In January 1986, the body of 19-year-old Alison Day was found in the River Lea; she had vanished seventeen days earlier on the way to meet her boyfriend. She had been raped and strangled. In April 1986, 15-year-old Maartje Tamboezer, daughter of a Dutch oil executive, was accosted as she took a short cut through woods near Horsley, and dragged off the footpath; she was also raped and strangled. Her attacker was evidently aware of the most recent advance in forensic detection, "genetic fingerprinting," by which a suspect can be identified from the distinctive pattern in the DNA of his body cells. The killer had stuffed a burning paper handkerchief into her genitals. A man who had been seen running for a train soon after the murder was believed to be the rapist, and two million train tickets were examined in an attempt to find one with his fingerprints.

A month later, a 29-year-old secretary named Ann Lock disappeared on her way home from work; her body was found ten weeks later. Again, an attempt to destroy sperm traces by burning was found.

It was at this point that the police forces involved in the investigation decided to link computers; the result was the list of 4,900 sex offenders, soon reduced to 1,999. At number 1,594 was a man called John Duffy, charged with raping his ex-wife and attacking her lover with a knife. The computers showed that he had also been arrested on suspicion of loitering near a railway station. (Since the blood group of the Ann Lock strangler had been the same as that of the "Railway Rapist," police had been keeping a watch on railway stations.) Duffy was called in for questioning, and his similarity to the "Railway Rapist" noted. (Duffy was small, ginger-haired and pock-marked.) But when the police tried to conduct a second interview, Duffy was in the hospital suffering from amnesia, alleging that he had been beaten up by muggers. The hospital authorities declined to allow him to be interviewed. And since he was only one of two thousand suspects, the police did not persist.

Faced with these problems, the investigation team decided that an "expert" might be able to help. They asked Dr. David Canter, a professor of psychology at the University of Surrey, to review all the evidence. Using techniques similar to those used by the Yorkshire Ripper team—studying the locations of the attacks—he concluded that the "center of gravity" lay in the North London area, and that the rapist probably lived within three miles of Finchley Road. He also concluded that he had been a semi-skilled worker, and that his relationship with his wife had been a stormy one. When Canter's analysis was matched up against the remaining suspects, the computer immediately threw up the name of John Duffy, who lived in Kilburn. Police kept him under surveillance until they decided that they could no longer take the risk of leaving him at liberty—another schoolgirl had been raped with typical violence since Duffy was committed to the hospital—and arrested him. When a fellow martial arts enthusiast admitted that Duffy had persuaded him to beat him up so he could claim loss of memory, the police were certain that he was the man they were seeking. Five of the rape victims picked him out at an identity parade, and string found in the home of his parents proved to be identical with that which had been used to tie Maartje Tamboezer's wrists. When forensic scientists matched fibers from Alison Day's sheepskin coat to fibers found on one of Duffy's sweaters, the final link in the chain of evidence was established; although he continued to refuse to admit or deny his guilt, John Duffy was sentenced to life imprisonment.

Dr. David Canter has described the techniques he used to pinpoint where the railway rapist lived:

Many environmental psychology studies have demonstrated that people form particular mental maps of the places they use. Each person creates a unique representation of the place in which he lives, with its own particular distortions. In the case of John Duffy, journalists recognized his preference for committing crimes near railway lines to the extent that they dubbed him the "railway rapist." What neither they nor the police appreciated was that this characteristic was likely to be part of his way of thinking about the layout of London, and so was a clue to his own particular mental map. It could therefore be used to see where the psychological focus of this map was and so specify the area in which he lived.[1]

[1]*New Society*, March 4, 1988.

By the time John Duffy was arrested in 1985, the techniques of "psychological profiling" had already—as we have seen—been in use in America for a decade. And the use of the computer had also been recognized as a vital part of the method. A retired Los Angeles detective named Pierce Brooks had pointed out that many serial killers remained unapprehended because they moved from state to state, and that before the state police realized they had a multiple killer on their hands, he had moved on. The answer obviously lay in linking up the computers of individual states, and feeding the information into a central computer. Brooks's program was labeled VICAP—the violent criminal apprehension program—and the FBI Academy at Quantico, Virginia, was chosen as the center for the new crimefighting team. VICAP proved to be the first major step towards the solution of the problem of the random sex killer.

In France, unfortunately, the technical resources of the police remained relatively primitive well into the 1980s, which explains why a serial killer who created in Paris the same atmosphere of terror as the Yorkshire Ripper in the north of England was able to remain undetected for so many years.

On October 5, 1984, 91-year-old Germaine Petitot was attacked in her home in the Clichy area by two robbers, and left bound and gagged. She had also been beaten, an unnecessary act of violence that puzzled the police, since she was obviously too old to put up any resistance. Unfortunately, she was too shocked to be able to describe her attackers.

Later the same day, 83-year-old Anna Barbier-Ponthus was inserting her key in her door in the rue Saulnier when she was attacked, pushed inside, and suffocated with a pillow. Her body, gagged and bound, was found soon afterwards. Like the previous victim she had also been beaten. In neither case was there any sign of sexual assault. The motive had been robbery—in this case, to take about £40 from her purse.

Four days later, on October 9, firemen called to a blaze in the rue Nicolet found the body of Suzanne Foucault, 89, who had been suffocated with a plastic bag. Her watch and some money were missing.

Four weeks passed without further attacks; then, in five days, five more old ladies were murdered. On November 3, 1984, a retired schoolteacher, Iona Seigaresco, 71, was found brutally battered; this time the killers had escaped with 10,000 francs (over £1,000) in bonds. She was found two days later. Alice Benaim, found by her son on November 7, had been forced to drink caustic soda and strangled. The next day, 80-year-old Marie Choy was found tied up with wire, her skull fractured. The next day again, 75-year-old Maria Mico-Diaz was killed and robbed. Five days later, on November 12, two bodies were found—those of Jean Laurent, 82, and Paule Victoire, 77; medical evidence showed that these had died about a week earlier.

There had been eight murders in a month, and in every case, the violence had been disproportionate; this was obviously a killer—or killers—who hated old women. The press soon labeled him "the phantom." There was a public outcry; riot squads patrolled the XVIIIth *arrondissement*, and all pensioners in the area were asked to attend a meeting at the Town Hall, where politicians made speeches and tried to sound reassuring.

The meeting seemed effective in frightening the "phantom." The murders ceased. The police worked as hard as ever, but they had no clues. The fingerprints they had found at the crime scenes matched those of no known offender.

Thirteen months later, the murders began again, although not in the same *arrondissement*. On December 20, 1985, the body of 91-year-old Estelle Donjoux was found in the Observatoire area. On January 4, 1986, Andrée Ladam, 77, was strangled and robbed; on January 9, Yvonne Couronne, 83, was killed in her home. For their relatives, the only consolation was that the marks of sadistic beatings were absent.

Between January 12 and 15, three more women—Marjem Jurblum, 81, Françoise Vendôme, 83, and Yvonne Schaible, 77—were killed, bringing the total up to fourteen. Virginie Labrette, 76, found on January 31, made fifteen.

There was a five-month break until June 14 1986, when Ludmiller Lierman, an American widow, was killed in her home in Passy. Then, once more, another long break until late November 1987, when Rachel Cohen, 79, was killed in Entrepot; on the same day, 87-year-old Madame Finalteri was found close by in the rue D'Alsace. But now, at last, the police seemed to have a break; Madame Finalteri was just alive. The killer had suffocated her with a mattress and left her for dead.

While police waited by her bed, Genevieve Germont, 73, was suffocated in a room in nearby rue Cail. Although no one knew it, this was the last murder by the "phantom." A few days later, Madame Finalteri was able to give a description of her attacker: a tall half-caste with dyed blond hair and earring. On December 1, 1987, Police Superintendent Francis Jacob saw a young man answering this description in the Entrepot area. He asked to see his identity papers, and the man—who seemed untroubled at being questioned—gave his name as Thierry Paulin, 24. As soon as he was taken in for questioning, Paulin's career as a killer of old women was over; his fingerprints matched those of the "phantom." Paulin quickly confessed to twenty murders, and implicated his lover, Jean-Thierry Mathurin.

Paulin had been born in 1963 on the Caribbean island of Martinique, child of a white father, Gaby Paulin, and a West

Indian mother, who was only 17 at the time. She soon farmed him out to his white grandmother, but she was too busy running a restaurant to give the child much attention. When he was 9, he returned to his mother's home in the capital, Fort-de-France—she had now remarried—but his stepfather found the child violent and difficult. He was sent to live with his father in Toulouse. But Gaby Paulin found him just as difficult, as well as disappointingly effeminate. When he was 18 Paulin began his military service; home on leave two years later, he threatened an old woman who ran a grocer's shop with a butcher's knife and got away with nearly £200. Arrested soon after, he explained that he had wanted to buy some expensive clothes with the money; he was placed on probation.

After military service he want to Paris and joined the gay community. He worked at the Paradis Latin, which specialized in transvestite revues, and met Jean-Thierry Mathurin, also 21, who came from Guyana; the two became lovers. Paulin's mother came to see the revue and was so shocked at the sight of her son in women's clothes that she left before the end.

After a violent scene in a restaurant with his lover, Paulin lost his job. Short of money, the two men attacked their first victim, Germaine Petitot, following her into her apartment. She survived, and if she had been able to give the police a description of her attackers, the crimes might have ceased there and then. But she was traumatized, and four days later, the "phantom" murders began.

Paulin's hatred of elderly white women was almost certainly based on dislike of his grandmother, and in the course of the first eight murders, this hatred was given full reign. Then, after the eighth murder in November 1984, Paulin and Mathurin decided that Paris had become too hot to hold them, and moved south to Toulouse, moving in with Paulin's father. But the old antagonism remained, and soon Mathurin moved back to Paris. Paulin, using the money he had acquired from the robberies, set out to try and launch a business as an agency for transvestite revues. He had considerable charm, dressed well, and was a persuasive talker. But the following November, he was tired of provincial Toulouse, and moved back to Paris and his lover. Now the new series of murders began. Meanwhile, Paulin found himself a job in a theatrical agency called Frulatti, and handled contracts for photographers and models. He became something of a young businessman-about-town, and no one suspected that a large part of his income came from murder. But a huge transvestite party he organized—called "A Look into Hell"—bankrupted Frulatti.

In August 1986, Paulin was jailed for beating up a cocaine dealer—by now he was himself dealing in drugs—and spent a year behind bars. But the French computer system was too inefficient to identify his fingerprints with that of the "phantom." And so he emerged in 1987 to kill more. He celebrated his 24th birthday with an enormous party, sending out printed invitations and providing champagne; it gave him great satisfaction that it took place in a restaurant in Les Halles where he had worked as a waiter during thin times in 1985. Four days later he was arrested.

Paulin's coldness about his victims baffled psychiatrists; he obviously felt no more compunction about slaughtering elderly ladies than a butcher does about killing sheep.

Paulin was charged with eighteen of his twenty murders, but he never came to trial. An X-ray revealed that he was suffering from lesions on the brain (like so many serial killers), and it soon became clear that he was also suffering from AIDS. In March 1989 he was rushed to the hospital, where he fell into a coma; on the 16th of the following month, he died. At the time of writing, Mathurin is still awaiting trial.

England's equivalent of the Paulin case was solved rather more quickly. In April 1986, it became clear that a killer of old people was operating in South London. (The police even considered the possibility that the "phantom" had moved across the Channel.) The first victim, 78-year-old Eileen Emms, was an ex-schoolteacher who lived alone in her basement flat in Wandsworth. When she was found dead in bed on April 9, 1986, it was at first assumed that she had died of natural causes; then someone noticed that her television set was missing. Closer examination revealed that she had been strangled and raped. On June 9, 67-year-old Janet Crockett was strangled in her flat in Overton Road, Stockwell. On June 27, the killer entered an old people's home in Stockwell and tried to strangle 73-year-old Frederick Prentice. After three unsuccessful attempts to subdue the struggling man, the intruder fled when Prentice pressed the alarm buzzer. But the following night, he returned and strangled two residents at the same home: 94-year-old Zbigniew Stabrawa, and 84-year-old Valentine Gleim, who was also sodomized.

The "Stockwell Strangler"—as the press now called him—moved to Islington, North London, to kill 82-year-old William Carmen on July 8, 1986, whom he also sodomized. He also stole £500. On July 12, the strangler killed 75-year-old Trevor Thomas in Clapham. Then he returned to the scene of his second murder, and strangled and sodomized William Downes, 74, in Overton Road, Stockwell. Finally, in 1986, he strangled and raped half-blind and disabled Florence Tisdall, 80, in her flat in Fulham.

The breakthrough came when a palm print found at the scene of the Downes murder was identified in the files as that of 23-year-old Kenneth Erskine, who had a lengthy record of burglaries. He proved to be registered with a Department of Health and Social Security office in Southwark, and was arrested on July 28, when he went to collect his benefit. He proved to have a building society account with £350 in it. Erskine was a half-caste—with a white mother and Antiguan father—who seemed to share with Paulin a pathological hatred of old people. He had a mental age of only 11, and a history of violence, attempting to drown fellow pupils in the school swimming pool and attacking a nurse with a pair of scissors. For the past eleven years he had been a drifter who slept rough, lived by petty crime, and took drugs. Erskine—who is believed to have committed at least two more murders—received seven life sentences, and twelve years for the attempted murder of Frederick Prentice.

It was in 1963 that the American pubic became aware of the "wandering serial killer," through the arrest of a murderer who seemed to embody everybody's worst nightmares. Over a period of months, a drifter named Henry Lee Lucas confessed to committing over three hundred and sixty murders. Pedro Lopez, the "Monster of the Andes," had confessed to killing and raping about three hundred and fifty under-age girls in Eucador and Columbia. And in 1986, while the newspapers were still full of stories about Lucas, another South American killer, Daniel Camargo Barbosa, confessed to killing seventy-two women and girls in Eucador in the course of that year. But with his "more than three hundred and sixty," Lucas seemed to be far and away the worst serial killer in American history—in fact, in world history.

The story that was to make world headlines began in the early hours of June 15, 1983, when Joe Don Weaver, the jailer on duty in the Montague County Jail, Texas, was startled by loud shouts coming from one of the cells. Weaver rushed down the hallway.

"What do you want?"

"There's a light in here," said Henry Lee Lucas in a quavering voice.

"No there's not." In fact, the cell was in pitch darkness.

"There's a light. And it's talking to me."

"You're seeing things," said Weaver, "Shut up and get some sleep." He made his way back to the office.

Lucas was a little man—five feet eight inches tall and of slight build—who was in jail for a minor weapons offense; he was also suspected of two murders. Only three nights before, Weaver had found him hanging in his cell, with blood dripping from slashed wrists. After a couple of days in a prison hospital, Lucas had been moved to a special cell in the women's section, where he could be kept under closer observation. But he had looked sick and miserable, and Weaver was not surprised that he was having hallucinations.

Another yell echoed down the hall.

"Jailer! Come here, quick!"

Weaver peered in through the aperture in the food-service door known as the "bean hole."

"What the hell is it this time?"

There was a long pause, and then Lucas spoke in a sad, quiet voice.

"Joe Don, I done some pretty bad things."

Weaver said sternly: "If it's what I think it is, Henry, you better get on your knees and pray."

There was another long pause, then Lucas said: "Joe Don, can I have some paper and a pencil?"

Half an hour later, Lucas handed the letter out through the bean hole. It was addressed to Sheriff Bill F. Conway, and began:

"I have tried to get help for so long, and no one will believe me. I have killed for the past ten years and no one will believe me. I cannot go own [sic] doing this. I also killed The only Girl I ever loved . . ."

Weaver hurried to the telephone. He had no hesitation about waking Sheriff Conway in the middle of the night. This, he knew, was the break Conway had been waiting for.

The unshaven, smelly little vagrant who now waited in his dark cell had been a hard nut to crack. Since the previous September, he had been suspected of killing an 80-year-old widow named Kate Rich, who had vanished from her home; Sheriff Conway had learned that she had been employing an odd-job man called Henry Lee Lucas, together with his common-law wife, 15-year-old Becky Powell. Lucas had left Mrs. Rich's employment under a cloud, and gone to live in a local religious commune. Not long after that, Becky had also disappeared.

Sheriff "Hound Dog" Conway had arrested Lucas in the previous October, and questioned him for days. Lucas was a coffee addict and a chain smoker; but even when deprived of these drugs, he refused to crack. He insisted that he knew nothing about the disappearance of Kate Rich. As to Becky Powell, he claimed that she had run off with a truck driver when they were trying to hitch-hike back to her home in Florida. He had passed several lie-detector tests, and the sheriff had finally been forced to let him go.

A week ago, the situation had changed. The Rev. Reuben Moore, the man who ran the House of Prayer where Lucas lived, had mentioned that Lucas had given his wife a gun for safe keeping. That was against Texas law, for Henry Lee Lucas was an ex-convict, and therefore not entitled to own a gun. The excuse was good enough, and Sheriff Conway had arrested the little tramp again. Once again Conway tried the effect of depriving him of coffee and cigarettes. The first result had been the suicide attempt. But now, it seemed, the technique had worked; Lucas was confessing to the murder of Becky Powell.

A few hours later, Henry Lee Lucas sat in Sheriff Conway's office, a large pot of black coffee and a pack of Lucky Strikes in front of him. He was a strange-looking man, with a glass eye, a thin, haggard face, and a loose, downturned mouth like a shark. When he smiled, he showed a row of rotten, tobacco-stained teeth. In the small office, his body odor was overpowering.

"Henry," said the sheriff kindly, "You say in this note you want to tell me about some murders."

"That's right. The light told me I had to confess my sins."

"The light?" Conway knew Lucas had smashed the bulb in his cell.

"There was a light in my cell, and it said: 'I will forgive you, but you must confess your sins.' So that's what I aim to do."

Lucas *looked* sane enough; after the coffee and cigarettes, he sounded calm and lucid. Conway hid his doubts and said:

"Tell me what you did to Kate Rich."

"All right. I drove to her house . . ."

"Do you mind if I tape record this?"

"Go ahead. I left the House of Prayer around six in the evening, and drove to her house in Ringgold . . ."

What followed was a chillingly detailed confession—Lucas seemed to have total recall—of the murder of the 80-year-old woman and the violation of her dead body. Lucas described how he had gone to Kate Rich's house and offered to take her to church. She had asked him questions about the disappearance of his "wife" Becky Powell, and at some point, Lucas had decided to kill her. He had taken the butcher's knife that lay between them on the bench seat of the old car, and suddenly jammed it into her left side. The knife entered her heart and she had collapsed immediately. Then, speaking as calmly as if he was narrating some everyday occurrence, Lucas described how he had dragged her down an embankment, then undressed and raped her. After that, he dragged her to a wide section of drainpipe that ran under the road, and stuffed the body into it. Later, he had returned with two plastic garbage bags, and used them as a kind of makeshift shroud. He buried her clothes nearby. Then he drove back to his room in the House of Prayer, made a huge fire in the stove, and burned the body. The few bones that were left he buried in the compost heap outside.

Sheriff Conway showed no emotion as he listened to this lengthy and detailed recital. By the time it was over, they were both tired. And now that he had confessed, Lucas had ceased to look pale and harassed. Whether or not he had been telling the truth about the "light," he was obviously relieved to be talking frankly.

Later that day, together with another colleague—Texas Ranger Phil Ryan, who had also been working on the case—they again sat in Conway's office, with the tape recorder running. Conway asked him what had happened to Becky Powell. This time the story was longer, and Lucas's single eye often overflowed with tears. By the time it was over, both Conway and Ryan were trying to hide their feeling of nausea.

Lucas had met Becky Powell in 1978, when she was 11 years old; she was the niece of his friend Ottis Toole, and Lucas was staying at the home of her great aunt in Jacksonville, Florida. Becky's full name was Frieda Lorraine Powell, and she was slightly mentally retarded. Even at 11 she was not a virgin. The family situation was something of a sexual hothouse. Ottis Toole had been seduced by his eldest sister Drusilla when he was a child. He grew up bisexual, and liked picking up lovers of both sexes—including Henry Lee Lucas. And he liked watching his pick-ups make love to Becky or her elder sister Sarah.

Ottis had another peculiarity; he liked burning down houses because it stimulated him sexually.

In December 1981, Becky's mother Drusilla committed suicide, and she and her younger brother Frank were placed in juvenile care. Lucas decided to "rescue" her, and in January 1982, he and Ottis fled with Becky and Frank; they lived on the proceeds of robbery—mostly small grocery stores. Lucas felt heavily protective about Becky, he explained, and she called him "Daddy." But one night, as he was saying goodnight to her, and he was making her shriek with laughter by tickling her, they began to kiss. Becky had raised no objection as he undressed her, then himself. After that, the father-daughter relation changed into something more like husband and wife. At 12, Becky looked as if she was 19.

But in the House of Prayer, in 1982, Becky had suddenly become homesick, and begged him to take her back to Florida. Reluctantly, Henry agreed; they set out hitch-hiking. Later, in the warm June night, they settled down with blankets in a field. But when they began arguing about her decision to go home, Becky had lost her temper and struck him in the face. Instantly, like a striking snake, Lucas grabbed a carving knife that lay nearby, and stabbed her through the heart. After that he had violated her body. And then, since the ground was too hard to dig a grave, he cut her into nine pieces with the carving knife, then scattered the pieces in the thick undergrowth. The next day, he hitch-hiked back to the House of Prayer, and told them that Becky had run away with a truck driver. His sorrow was obviously so genuine that everyone sympathized. In fact, Lucas told the law men, he felt as if he had killed a part of himself.

The two policemen felt exhausted, and the night was half over. Ryan asked wearily:

"Is that all?"

Lucas shook his head. "Not by a long way. I reckon I killed more'n a hundred people."

Conway and Ryan were experienced policemen, who had heard many confessions. But this one left them shaken and incredulous. If Lucas was telling the truth, he was far and away the worst mass murderer in American criminal history. But was he telling the truth? Or was he merely suffering from hallucinations?

The first step was to check his story about Kate Rich. Lucas had pointed out the spot on a map. Still dazed from lack of sleep, Conway and Ryan drove there in the darkness. They quickly located the wide drainage pipe than ran under the road. Lying close to its entrance was a pair of knickers, of the type that would be worn by an old lady. There was also a length of wood; Lucas had told them he had used a similar piece to shove the body deeper into the culvert. On the other side of the road, they also found broken lenses from a lady's glasses.

In the House of Prayer, near Stoneburg, they looked into the unutterably filthy room that Lucas had occupied in a converted chicken barn, and in the stove, found fragments of burnt flesh, and some pieces of bone. On the rubbish heap they found more bone fragments.

Later that day, they drove to Denton, a college town north of Dallas, where Lucas said he had killed Becky Powell. This time, Lucas accompanied them. In a field fifty yards off the main highway, in a grove of trees, they found a human skull, a pelvis, and various body parts in an advanced stage of decomposition. Becky's orange suitcase still lay nearby, and articles of female clothing and make-up were strewn around.

So far, it was obvious that Lucas had been telling the truth; he had killed Becky and Kate Rich just as he had described. But what about all the other victims he had mentioned?

Even after killing Becky, Lucas told them, he had murdered another woman. Telling the Rev. Reuben Moore that he was going off to look for Becky, Lucas had drifted to California, then down to New Mexico, then north again to Decatur, Illinois, where he had tried to find work as a laborer. Since he had no identification, he was turned down. A truck gave him a lift to a truck-driver's eatery in Missouri, and there he saw a young woman waiting by the pumps for gas. He went up to her, pushing a knife into her ribs, and told her he needed a lift, and would not harm her. Without speaking, she allowed him to climb into the driver's seat. All that night he drove south towards Texas, until the woman finally fell into a doze. Lucas had no intention of keeping his promise. He wanted money—and sex. Just before dawn he pulled off the road, and as the woman woke up, plunged the knife into her throat. Then he pushed her out on to the ground, cut off her clothes and violated the body. After that, he dragged it into a grove of trees, took the money from her handbag, and drove the car to Fredericksburg, Texas, where he abandoned it.

Lucas was unable to tell them the woman's name, but his description of the place where he abandoned the car offered a lead. In fact, the Texas Rangers near Fredericksburg were able to confirm the finding of an abandoned station wagon in the previous October. And a little further checking revealed that the police at Magnolia, Texas, had found the naked body of a woman with her throat cut, at about the same time. Again, it was clear that Lucas was telling the truth.

On June 17, 1983, two days after he had started to confess, Henry Lee Lucas appeared in the Montague County Courthouse, accused of murder and of possessing an illegal firearm. A Grand Jury indicted him on both counts.

The following day, in the press room of the Austin Police Department, a bored reporter named Mike Cox was talking casually to a police lieutenant when the lieutenant mentioned that he had heard rumors of a man in north Texas who had been murdering women for sex. Cox did some telephoning, and learned that the man, Henry Lee Lucas, was about to be arraigned in the Montague County Courthouse. It sounded unpromising, but since there was nothing else to do . . .

The following day, Tuesday June 21, 1983, Mike Cox was in the courtroom when the unimpressive little man who looked like an out-of-work roadsweeper was led in between two deputies. The only other reporters in the court were from the nearby Wichita Falls television station, who intended to put out an item on their local news. From all appearances, it looked as if the arraignment would take only a matter of minutes.

When Judge Frank Douthitt had heard the indictment concerning Kate Rich, he asked the prisoner if he understood the seriousness of the indictment against him. Lucas replied quietly:

"Yes, sir. I have about a hundred of them."

It was said so casually that for a moment Cox failed to grasp its significance. Was this man really saying he had killed a hundred people? Yes, apparently he was, for the judge was now asking him if he had ever had a psychiatric examination. The little man replied in the affirmative. "I tell them my problems and they didn't want to do anything about it . . . I know it ain't normal for a person to go out and kill girls just to have sex with them."

Moments later, as Lucas was led out of court, Cox rushed over to District Attorney McGaughey. How many murders was Lucas suspected of? The DA was cautious. He had told the police about seven of far. "But there's still a lot of work to be done. He may be spinning yarns."

The following morning, the Austin newspaper carried headlines which were a variant on: DRIFTER CONFESSES TO A HUNDRED MURDERS. The wire services immediately picked up the story, and by evening it was on front pages all over the country.

For the past ten years, the American public had been kept in a state of shock at the revelations about mass murderers who had killed an unprecedented number of victims. Cases like that of Ted Bundy made it clear that one of the major problems was simply how to detect a "wandering" killer, who might not be recognized for what he was because of lack of police cooperation between various states. In November 1982, while Henry Lee Lucas was still at large, a meeting of police from all over the country decided to establish a national crime computer, into which details of every homicide would be automatically fed. This became known as the NCAVC, the National Center for the Analysis of Violent Crime.

And now, just over six months later, the confessions of Henry Lee Lucas made it clear that the NCAVC had been formed not a moment too soon. The "wandering killer" was obviously a new type of menace. Suddenly, every newspaper in America was talking about serial killers.

Meanwhile, the cause of all this excitement was sitting in his jail cell in Montague County, describing murder after murder to a "task force" headed by Sheriff Jim Boutwell and Texas Ranger Bob Prince. It soon became clear that a larger number of these murders had not been committed on his own, but in company with his lover Ottis Elswood Toole.

Toole, who had a gap in his front teeth and a permanent stubble on his chin, looked even more like a tramp than Lucas. And even before Lucas was arrested in Montague County, Toole was in prison in his home town, Jacksonville. He was charged with setting fires in Springfield, the area where he lived. On August 5, 1983, he was sentenced to fifteen years for arson.

One week later, in a courtroom in Denton County—where he had killed Becky Powell—Lucas staggered everybody by pleading not guilty to Becky's murder. He was, in fact, beginning to play a game that would become wearisomely familiar to the police: withdrawing confessions. It looked as if, now he was in prison, the old Henry Lee Lucas, the Enemy of Society, was reappearing. He could no longer kill at random when he felt the urge, but he could still satisfy his craving for control over victims by playing with his captors like a cat with mice.

It did him no good. On October 1, 1983, in the courtroom where he had been arraigned, Lucas was sentenced to seventy-five years for the murder of Kate Rich. And on November 8, 1983, he was sentenced to life imprisonment for the murder of Becky Powell. Before the courts had finished with him, he would be sentenced to another seventy-five years, four more life sentences, and a further sixty-six years, all for murder. For good measure, he was also sentenced to death.

When Henry Lee Lucas began confessing to murders, it seemed to be a genuine case of religious conversion. Later, when he was moved to the Georgetown Jail in Williamson County, he was allowed regular visits from a Catholic laywoman who called herself Sister Clementine, and they spent hours kneeling in prayer. He was visited by many lawmen from all over the country, hoping that he could clear up unsolved killings. Sometimes—if he felt the policeman failed to treat him with due respect—he refused to utter a word. At other times, he confessed freely. The problem was that he sometimes confessed to two murders on the same day, in areas so wide apart that he could not possibly have committed both. This tendency to lie at random led many journalists to conclude that Lucas's tales of mass murder were mostly invention.

None of the officers who knew him closely believed that for a moment. Too many of his confessions turned out to be accurate.

For example, on August 2, 1983, when he was being arraigned for the murder of a hitch-hiker known simply as "Orange Socks," Lucas was taken to Austin to be questioned about another murder. On the way there, seated between two deputies, Lucas pointed to a building they passed and asked if it had been a liquor store at one time. The detectives looked at one another. It had, and it had been run by a couple called Harry and Molly Schlesinger, who had been robbed and murdered on October 23, 1989. Lucas admitted that he had been responsible, and described the killings with a wealth of detail that only the killer could have known. He then led the deputies to a field where, on October 8, 1979, the mutilated body of a girl called Sandra Dubbs had been found. He was also able to point out where her car had been left. There could be no possible doubt that Lucas had killed three people in Travis County in two weeks.

When asked if Ottis Toole had committed any murders on his own, Lucas mentioned a man in his fifties who had died in a fire set by Toole in Jacksonville. Toole had poured gas on the man's mattress and set it alight. Then they had hidden and watched the fire engines; a 65-year-old man was finally carried out, badly burned. He had died a week later. Police assumed he had accidentally set the mattress on fire with a cigarette.

Lucas's description led the police to identify the victim as George Sonenberg, who had been fatally burned in a fire on January 4, 1982. Police drove out to Raiford Penitentiary to interview Toole. He admitted it cheerfully. When asked why he did it, he grinned broadly. "I love fires. Reckon I started a hundred of them over the past several years."

There could be no possible doubt about it. Toole and Lucas had committed a number of murders between them. At one point, Lucas insisted that the total was about 360—he went on to detail 175 committed alone, and 65 by himself and Ottis Toole.

In prison after his original convictions, Lucas seemed a well satisfied man. Now much plumper, with his rotten teeth replaced or filled, he had ceased to look so sinister. He had a special cell all to himself in Sheriff Boutwell's jail—other prisoners had treated him very roughly during the brief period he had been among them, and he had to be moved for his own safety. But he was now a national celebrity. Magazines and newspapers begged for interview, television cameras recorded every public appearance. Police officers turned up by the dozen to ask about unsolved murder cases, and were all warned beforehand to treat Lucas with respect, in case he ceased to co-operate. Now, at least, he was receiving the attention he had always craved, and he reveled in it. And some visitors, like the psychiatrist Joel Norris, the journalist Mike Cox—who had filed the original story on Lucas—and the crime writer Max Call, came to interview him in order to learn about his life, and to write books about it. Lucas co-operated fully with Call, who was the first to reach print—as early as 1985—with a strange work called *Hand of Death*.

Here, for the first time, the American public had an opportunity to satisfy its morbid curiosity about Lucas's rampage of crime. The story that emerged lacked the detail of later studies, but it was horrific enough.

Lucas, Call revealed, had spent most of his life from 1960 to 1975 in jail. After his release he had an unsuccessful marriage—which broke up when his wife realized he was having sex with her two small girls—and lived for a while with his sister Wanda, leaving when she accused him of sexually abusing her young daughter. He seems to have met Ottis Toole in a soup kitchen in Jacksonville, Florida, in 1978. Ottis had a long prison record for car stealing and petty theft, and he invited Lucas back home, where he was soon regarded as a member of the family.

According to Lucas, he had already committed a number of casual murders as he wandered around. These were mostly crimes of opportunity—as when he offered a lift to a girl called Tina Williams, near Oklahoma City, after her car had broken down. He shot her twice and had intercourse with the body. Police later confirmed Lucas's confession.

Even so, the meeting with Toole seems to have been a turning point. Now, according to both of them, they began killing "for fun." According to Toole's confession, they saw a teenage couple walking along the road in November 1978, their car having run out of fuel. Lucas forced the girl into the car, while Toole shot the boy in the head and chest. Then, as Toole drove, Lucas raped the girl repeatedly in the back of the car. Finally, Toole began to feel jealous, and when they pulled up, shot the girl six times, and left her body by the road. The police were also able to confirm this case: the youth was called Kevin Key, the girl Rita Salazar. The man in charge of the murder investigation was Sheriff Jim Boutwell, and the case was the first of more than a score of similar murders along the Interstate 35 Highway that kept him busy for the next five years. The victims included teenage hitch-hikers, elderly women abducted from their homes, tramps and men who were killed for robbery. Lucas was later to confess to most of these crimes.

Lucas and Toole began robbing "convenience stores," forcing the proprietor or store clerk into the back. Lucas described how, on one occasion, they tied up the young girl, but she continued to try to get free. So he shot her through the head, and then Toole had intercourse with her body.

On October 31, 1979, the naked body of a young girl was found in a culvert on the Interstate 35; her clothes were missing, except for a pair of orange socks by the body. After his arrest, Lucas described how he and Toole had picked up "Orange Socks," who was hitch-hiking, and when she had refused to let Lucas have sex, he strangled her. Lucas eventually received the death sentence for the murder of the unidentified girl.

When Lucas and Toole abducted Becky and Frank Powell

in January 1982, they took them with them when they robbed convenience stores; Becky looked so innocent that the proprietor took little notice of the two smelly vagrants who accompanied her—until one of them produced a gun and demanded the money from the till. And, according to Lucas, Becky and Frank often became witnesses to murder—in fact, in one confession he even claimed they had taken part in the killings.

Eventually, Frank and Ottis Toole returned home to Florida, while Becky and Lucas continued "on the road." In January 1982, a couple named Smart, who ran an antique store in Hemet, California, picked them up, and for five months Lucas worked for them. Then the Smarts asked Lucas if he would like to go back to Texas to look after Mrs. Smart's mother, Kate Rich. He accepted. But after only a few weeks, the Smarts received a telephone call from another sister in Texas, telling them that the new handyman was spending Mrs. Rich's money on large quantities of beer and cigarettes in the local grocery store. Another daughter who went to investigate found Mrs. Rich's house filthy, and Lucas and Becky Powell drunk in bed. Lucas was politely fired. But his luck held. Only a few miles away, he was offered a lift by the Rev. Reuben Moore, who had started his own religious community in nearby Stoneburg. Moore also took pity on the young couple, and they moved in to the House of Prayer. There everyone liked Becky, and she seemed happy. She badly needed a home and security. Both she and Henry became "converts".

But Becky began to feel homesick, and begged Henry to take her back to Florida. A few days later, pieces of her dismembered body were scattered around a field near Denton. And Lucas's nightmare odyssey of murder was beginning to draw to a close . . .

The American public, which at first followed Lucas's confessions with horrified attention, soon began to lose interest. After all, he was already sentenced. So was Ottis Toole (who would also be later condemned to death for the arson murder of George Sonenburg). And as newspapers ran stories declaring that Lucas had withdrawn his confessions yet again, or that some police officer had proved he was lying, there was a growing feeling that Lucas was not, after all, the worst mass murderer in American history.

It was a couple named Bob and Joyce Lemons who first placed this conviction on a solid foundation. Their daughter, Barbara Sue Williamson, had been murdered in Lubbock, Texas, in August 1975 by an intruder in her home. Lucas confessed to this murder when asked about it by Lubbock lawmen. When the Lemons heard the confession they felt it was a hoax. Lucas said he recalled the house as being white, that he had entered by the screen door, and killed the newly married woman in her bedroom. It was a green house, the screen door had been sealed shut at the time, and Barbara had been killed outside.

The Lemons went and talked to Lucas's relatives, and soon came up with a list of the periods when he had stayed in Florida which contradicted dozens of his "confessions." But when they confronted Texas Ranger Bob Prince with these discoveries, he became hostile and ordered them out of his office.

Another investigator was also having doubts. Vic Feazell, District Attorney of Waco, Texas, was supposed to be prosecuting Lucas for three murders to which he had confessed, and for which there was not a shred of evidence apart from Lucas's own words—no fingerprints, no forensic evidence, no witnesses. Feazell joined forces with the Lemons, and was soon convinced that many of Lucas's confessions were lies. He learned that during one period in 1979, when Lucas had cashed forty-three pay checks at the local store in Florida—and was therefore presumably resident there—he was on record as confessing to forty-six murders in sixteen states. It was just possible if he rushed around the country by airplane, otherwise highly unlikely. (Feazell began to refer to him jokingly as "Rocket Man.")

Confronted by Feazell, and shown the evidence that disproved his confessions, Lucas smiled and said: "I was wonderin' when somebody was goin' to get wise to this."

When Feazell announced these conclusions to the press, the roof fell in. Within three days he was under investigation by the FBI for corruption, and his house was searched. He was accused of murder, burglary, bribery and racketeering—charges that could have led to a sentence of eighty years in jail. In fact, Feazell defended himself, and was found not guilty on all counts. He sued the Dallas TV station that had repeated the allegations, and was awarded record damages of $58,000,000.

Feazell is convinced that the Texas Ranger Task Force was behind the persecution. Whether true or not, this acquittal and the enormous damages had the effect of discrediting the Task Force—and, of course, Lucas's confessions. Lucas had been convicted of ten murders. Feazell is on record as saying that he may be innocent of all of them.

But if Lucas's own accounts of the murders convinced local police officers that he was guilty—because of the intimate knowledge he showed—then how could he be innocent? According to Feazell (who has become Lucas's attorney), because the Task Force demanded details of the crimes *before* local police forces were allowed to interview him about them, and they allowed Lucas to read the reports. Yet this raises the question of why, in that case, he got the Barbara Sue Williamson murder so wrong.

Equally intriguing is the question of why, if Lucas's confessions to serial murder were all lies, his partner Ottis Toole did not vigorously protest his own innocence to avoid a death sentence. Loyalty to a friend hardly demands accepting a multiple "murder rap."

In the resulting confusion, it looks as if Lucas may escape the death sentence—which is clearly what he wants. Yet this in turn raises the further question of whether his new claims of innocence may not be as unreliable as his earlier claims of guilt.

Looking back over the case, from the moment Lucas decided to confess because he saw a "light" in his cell, it seems virtually impossible to believe that he is totally innocent. At the very least he killed Becky, Kate Rich and "Orange Socks."

At the time of writing (1993), it begins to look as if the likeliest scenario was as follows. Lucas's original confessions, whether prompted by hallucinations or by genuine religious conversion, were true: he killed Kate Rich and Becky Powell. It is hard to believe that he made these confessions with his tongue in his cheek. It seems likely that many of his subsequent confessions were also true, including murders committed in partnership with Toole. But as the confessions brought notoriety and comfort—he became aware of the benefits of being a "star," and began to wonder how he could maintain this status without the inevitable penalty of the electric chair. The answer was to continue confessing to more murders, and to hope that, sooner or later, these confessions would be recognized as lies, and that this would throw doubt on the murders for which he had been convicted. So when Vic Feazell turned up in his cell with proof that at least forty-six murders were inventions, he must have heaved a sigh of relief. "I was wonderin' when somebody was goin' to get wise to this."

And what of Boutwell and Prince? Were they dupes, conmen, or simply good policemen who were doing their best? One thing seems obvious: that their present feelings towards

Lucas must be highly uncharitable. He brought them celebrity, then derision. Whatever now happens—even if Lucas is executed—their reputations are irreparably damaged. Yet Boutwell knows that Lucas killed Kate Rich, Becky Powell, and probably a number of others. He also knows that, because of Lucas's policy of lying, withdrawing the lie and then repeating it, no one will ever be certain whether Lucas and Toole are America's worst serial killers, or two undistinguished hold-up men. It now seems clear that, whether his claim to be America's most prolific serial killer is true or not, the mild little man with the glass eye has achieved what he always wanted: a place in American history.

Lucas made the world aware of the "wandering killer," yet in fact, this type of serial murder has remained relatively rare—no doubt because serial killers, like other human beings, prefer the security of a home. So most serial murders have been associated with a specific place—Whitechapel, Hanover, Düsseldorf, Boston. The "wandering killers"— from Vacher and Earle Nelson to Knowles and Lucas—can be counted on the fingers of both hands. And the cases of serial murder that always create the greatest stir are those in which the murders occur in the same place, and remain unsolved over a period—the classic Jack the Ripper pattern. In this sense, the first "classic" case of the 1980s was the Atlanta child murders.

By the beginning of July 1980, seven black children in Atlanta had been murdered, and three had vanished without leaving a trace. The series had started a year earlier, when two black teenagers had been found dead near Niskey Lake. In October 1979, two 9-year-old boys vanished; one was found in the crawl-space of an abandoned elementary school. In March 1980, a 12-year-old girl was found tied to a tree and suffocated with her own briefs; she had been raped. But since by now it was assumed that the killer was homosexual (even though there had been no sexual assault), this was not generally counted as one of the "series."

The suspicion that white racists were responsible caused civil unrest in Atlanta, but the police were inclined to believe that the killer was a black, since the children had been picked up mostly in black neighborhoods, where a white would stand out.

By mid-May 1981, the number of victims had risen to twenty-seven, and black groups had formed to demand action and to raise a reward.

The break in the case came on May 22, when police close to a bridge on the Chattahoochee River heard a splash, and saw a man climb into a station wagon. It proved to be a plump young black named Wayne Williams, 23, who said he was a music promoter. He was allowed to go after being questioned, but when, two days later, the body of 27-year-old Nathaniel Cater was found in the river, attention switched back to Williams. Dog hairs found on the victim's body matched those found in Williams's station wagon, and a witness testified to seeing Williams leaving a theater hand in hand with Cater just before his disappearance. Another witness testified to seeing Williams with Jimmy Payne, also found in the river. Forensic examination established that carpet fibers and dog hairs found on ten more victims matched those in the home where Williams lived with his schoolteacher parents. A brilliant young man who studied astronomy and ran his own local radio station, Williams was known to be obsessed by police work. Obsessed also by a desire for quick success, he was also known as a pathological liar.

Although the evidence was circumstantial, Williams was found guilty of the murders of Cater and Payne. Many felt misgivings about the guilty verdict (the black writer James Baldwin regarded the case against Williams as a conspiracy, and saw the rejection of his own book about the case as further evidence of the conspiracy), but the murders stopped after Williams's arrest.

At the time the Henry Lee Lucas case was causing shock waves in America, a British serial killer was causing much the same sensation across the Atlantic. The British have always felt a certain complacency about their murder record, which has remained relatively constant and relatively low for decades. (Per unit of population, the British rate is less than a sixth that of America.) Besides, England is too small for wandering serial killers. But the case of Dennis Nilsen demonstrated that, even in non-violent Britain, it is still appallingly easy to get away with mass murder in a large city.

On the evening of February 8, 1983, a drains maintenance engineer named Michael Cattran was asked to call at 23 Cranley Gardens, in Muswell Hill, north London, to find out why tenants had been unable to flush their toilets since the previous Saturday. Although Muswell Hill is known as a highly respectable area of London—it was once too expensive for anyone but the upper middle classes—No. 23 proved to be a rather shabby house, divided into flats. A tenant showed Cattran the manhole cover that led to the drainage system. When he removed it, he staggered back and came close to vomiting: the smell was unmistakably decaying flesh. And when he had climbed down the rungs into the cistern, Cattran discovered what was blocking the drain: masses of rotting meat, much of it white, like chicken flesh. Convinced this was human flesh, Cattran rang his supervisor, who decided to come and inspect it in the morning. When they arrived the following day, the drain had been cleared. And a female tenant told them she had heard footsteps going up and down the stairs for much of the night. The footsteps seemed to go up to the top flat, which was rented by a 37-year-old civil servant named Dennis Nilsen.

Closer search revealed that the drain was still not quite clear; there was a piece of flesh, six inches square, and some bones that resembled fingers. Detective Chief Inspector Peter Jay, of Hornsey CID, was waiting in the hallway of the house that evening when Dennis Nilsen walked in from his day at the office—a Jobcenter in Kentish Town. He told Nilsen he wanted to talk to him about the drains. Nilsen invited the policeman into his flat, and Jay's face wrinkled as he smelt the odor of decaying flesh. He told Nilsen that they had found human remains in the drain, and asked what had happened to the rest of the body.

"It's in there, in two plastic bags," said Nilsen, pointing to a wardrobe.

In the police car, the Chief Inspector asked Nilsen whether the remains came from one body or two. Calmly, without emotion, Nilsen said: "There have been fifteen or sixteen altogether."

At the police station, Nilsen—a tall man with metal-rimmed glasses—seemed eager to talk. (In fact, he proved to be something of a compulsive talker, and his talk overflowed into a series of school exercise books in which he later wrote his story for the use of Brian Masters, a young writer who contacted him in prison.) He told police that he had murdered three men in the Cranley Gardens house—into which he moved in the autumn of 1981—and twelve or thirteen at his previous address, 195 Melrose Avenue, Cricklewood.

The plastic bags from the Muswell Hill flat contained two severed heads, and a skull from which the flesh had been stripped—forensic examination revealed that it had been boiled. The bathroom contained the whole lower half of a torso, from the waist down, intact. The rest was in bags in the wardrobe and in the tea chest. At Melrose Avenue, thirteen days and nights of digging revealed many human bones, as well as a check book and pieces of clothing.

The self-confessed mass murderer—he seemed to take a certain pride in being "Britain's biggest mass murderer"—was a Scot, born at Fraserburgh on November 23, 1945. His mother, born Betty Whyte, married a Norwegian soldier named Olav Nilsen in 1942. It was not a happy marriage; Olav was seldom at home, and was drunk a great deal; they were divorced seven years after their marriage. In 1954, Mrs. Nilsen married again and became Betty Scott. Dennis grew up in the house of his grandmother and grandfather, and was immensely attached to his grandfather, Andrew Whyte, who became a father substitute. When Nilsen was seven, his grandfather died and his mother took Dennis in to see the corpse. This seems to have been a traumatic experience; in his prison notes he declares "My troubles started there." The death of his grandfather was such a blow that it caused his own emotional death, according to Nilsen. Not long after this, someone killed the two pigeons he kept in an air raid shelter, another severe shock. His mother's remarriage when he was nine had the effect of making him even more of a loner.

In 1961, Nilsen enlisted in the army, and became a cook. It was during this period that he began to get drunk regularly, although he remained a loner, avoiding close relationships. In 1972 he changed the life of a soldier for that of a London policeman, but disliked the relative lack of freedom—compared to the army—and resigned after only eleven months. He became a security guard for a brief period, then a job-interviewer for the Manpower Services Commission.

In November 1975, Nilsen began to share a north London flat—in Melrose Avenue—with a young man named David Gallichan, ten years his junior. Gallichan was later to insist that there was no homosexual relationship, and this is believable. Many heterosexual young men would later accept Nilsen's offer of a bed for the night, and he would make no advances, or accept a simple "No" without resentment. But in May 1977, Gallichan decided he could bear London no longer, and accepted a job in the country. Nilsen was furious; he felt rejected and deserted. The break-up of the relationship with Gallichan—whom he had always dominated—seems to have triggered the homicidal violence that would claim fifteen lives.

The killings began more than a year later, in December 1978. Around Christmas, Nilsen picked up a young Irish laborer in the Cricklewood Arms, and they went back to his flat to continue drinking. Nilsen wanted him to stay over the New Year but the Irishman had other plans. In a note he later wrote for his biographer Brian Masters, Nilsen gives as his motive for this first killing that he was lonely and wanted to spare himself the pain of separation. In another confession he also implies that he has no memory of the actual killing. Nilsen strangled the unnamed Irishman in his sleep with a tie. Then he undressed the body and carefully washed it, a ritual he observed in all his killings. After that he placed the body under the floorboards where—as incredible as it seems—he kept it until the following August. He eventually burned it on a bonfire at the bottom of the garden, burning some rubber at the same time to cover the smell.

In November 1979, Nilsen attempted to strangle a young Chinaman who had accepted his offer to return to the flat; the Chinaman escaped and reported the attack to the police. But the police believed Nilsen's explanation that the Chinaman was trying to "rip him off" and decided not to pursue the matter.

The next murder victim was a 23 year-old Canadian called Kenneth James Ockendon, who had completed a technical training course and was taking a holiday before starting his career. He had been staying with an uncle and aunt in Carshalton after touring the Lake District. He was not a homosexual, and it was pure bad luck that he got into conversation with Nilsen in the Princess Louise in High Holborn around December 3, 1979. They went back to Nilsen's flat, ate ham, eggs and chips, and bought £20 worth of alcohol. Ockendon watched television, then listened to rock music on Nilsen's hi-fi system. Then he sat listening to music wearing earphones, watching television at the same time. This may have been what cost him his life; Nilsen liked to talk, and probably felt "rejected". "I thought bloody good guest this . . ." And sometime after midnight, while Ockendon was still wearing the headphones, he strangled him with a flex. Ockendon was so drunk that he put up no struggle. And Nilsen was also so drunk that after the murder, he sat down, put on the headphones, and went on playing music for hours. When he tried to put the body under the floorboards the next day, rigor mortis had set in and it was impossible. He had to wait until the rigor had passed. Later, he dissected the body. Ockendon had large quantities of Canadian money in his moneybelt, but Nilsen tore this up. The rigorous Scottish upbringing would not have allowed him to steal.

Nilsen's accounts of the murders are repetitive, and make them sound mechanical and almost identical. The third victim in May 1980, was a 16-year-old butcher named Martyn Duffey, who was also strangled and placed under the floorboards. Number four was a 16-year-old Scot named Billy Sutherland—again strangled in his sleep with a tie and placed under the floorboards. Number five was an unnamed Mexican or Philipino, killed a few months later. Number six was an Irish building worker. Number seven was an undernourished down-and-out picked up in a doorway. (He was burned on the bonfire all in one piece.) The next five victims, all unnamed, were killed equally casually between late 1980 and late 1981. Nilsen later insisted that all the murders had been without sexual motivation—a plea that led Brian Masters to entitle his book on the case *Killing for Company*. There are moments in Nilsen's confessions when it sounds as if, like so many serial killers, he felt as if he was being taken over by a Mr. Hyde personality or possessed by some demonic force.

In October 1981, Nilsen moved into an upstairs flat in Cranley Gardens, Muswell Hill. On November 25, he took a homosexual student named Paul Nobbs back with him, and they got drunk. The next day, Nobbs went into University College Hospital for a check-up, and was told that bruises on his throat indicated that someone had tried to strangle him. Nilsen apparently changed his mind at the last moment.

The next victim, John Howlett, was less lucky. He woke up as Nilsen tried to strangle him and fought back hard; Nilsen had to bang his head against the headrest of the bed to subdue him. When he realized Howlett was still breathing, Nilsen drowned him in the bath. He hacked up the body in the bath, then boiled chunks in a large pot to make them easier to dispose of. (He also left parts of the body out in plastic bags for the dustbin men to take away.)

In May 1982, another intended victim escaped—a drag-artiste called Carl Stottor. After trying to strangle him, Nilsen placed him in a bath of water, but changed his mind and allowed him to live. When he left the flat, Stottor even agreed to meet Nilsen again—but decided not to keep the appointment. He decided not to go to the police.

The last two victims were both unnamed, one a drunk and one a drug-addict. In both cases, Nilsen claims to be unable to remember the actual killing. Both were dissected, boiled and flushed down the toilet. It was after this second murder—the fifteenth in all—that the tenants complained about blocked drains, and Nilsen was arrested.

The trial began on October 24, 1983, in the same court where Peter Sutcliffe had been tried two years earlier. Nilsen was charged with six murders and two attempted murders, although he had confessed to fifteen murders and seven attempted murders. He gave the impression that he was enjoying his moment of glory. The defense pleaded diminished responsibility, and argued that the charge should be reduced to manslaughter. The jury declined to accept this, and on November 4, 1983, Nilsen was found guilty by a vote of 10 to 2, and sentenced to life imprisonment.

Perhaps the most horrific serial murder case of the 1980s was one that came to light in California in June 1985.

On Sunday, June 2, a shop assistant at the South City Lumber Store in San Francisco noticed when a young man walked out without paying for a $75 vice. The assistant hurried outside to speak to Police Officer Daniel Wright, and by the time the young man—who looked Asiatic—was putting the vice in the trunk of a car, the officer was right behind him. When he realized he was being followed, the young man fled. Wright gave chase, but the skinny youth was too fast for him, and vanished across a main road.

When Wright returned to the car—a Honda Prelude—a bearded, bald-headed man was standing by it. "It was a mistake," he explained. "He thought I'd paid already. But I *have* paid now." He held out a sales receipt.

That should have ended the incident—except for the fact that the young Asian had fled, ruling out the possibility that it *was* merely an honest mistake. Wright wondered if anything else in the car might be stolen. "What's in there?" he asked, pointing at a green holdall.

"I don't know. It belongs to him."

Wright unzipped it and found that it contained a .22 pistol, with a silencer on the barrel. Americans have a right to own handguns, but not with silencers—such attachments being unlikely to have an innocent purpose.

"I'm afraid I'll have to ask you to come down to headquarters to explain this."

At the police station, the bearded man handed over a driver's license to establish his identity; it indicated that he was Robin Scott Stapley. He explained that he hardly knew the youth who had run away—he had just been about to hire him to do some work.

"We'll have to do a computer check on the car. But you'll probably have to post bond before you can be released."

"Stapley" asked if he could have some paper and a pencil, and a glass of water. When the policemen returned with these items, he scribbled a few words on the sheet of paper, tossed a capsule into his mouth and swallowed it down with water. Moments later, he slumped forward on the tabletop.

Assuming it was a heart attack, the police called an ambulance. The hospital rang them later to say that the man had been brain-dead on arrival, but had been placed on a life support system.

The medic added that he was fairly certain the man had not suffered a heart attack; it was more likely that he had swallowed some form of poison. In fact, the poison was soon identified as cyanide. The note "Stapley" had scribbled had been an apology to his wife for what he was about to do. Four days later, removed from the life support system, the man died without recovering consciousness.

By this time, the police had realized that he was not Robin Stapley. The real Robin Stapley had been reported missing in February. But soon after this there had been a curious incident involving his camper, which had been in a collision with a pickup truck. The young Chinaman who had been driving the camper had accepted responsibility and asked the other driver not to report it. But since it was a company vehicle, the driver was obliged to report the accident.

The Honda the two had been driving proved to be registered in the name of Paul Cosner. And Cosner had also been reported missing. He had told his girlfriend that he had sold the car to a "weird-looking man" who would pay cash, and driven off to deliver it; no one had seen him since.

The Honda was handed over to the forensic experts for examination; they discovered two bullet holes in the front seat, two spent slugs, and some human bloodstains.

If the bearded man was not Robin Stapley, who was he? Some papers found in the Honda bore the name Charles Gunnar, with an address near Wilseyville, in Calaveras County, 150 miles north-east of San Francisco. Inspector Tom Eisenmann was assigned to go and check on Gunnar. In Wilseyville he spoke to Sheriff Claude Ballard, and learned that Ballard already had his suspicions about Gunnar, and about the slightly built Chinese youth, Charles Ng (pronounced Ing) with whom he lived. They had been advertising various things for sale, such as television sets, videos and articles of furniture, and Ballard had suspected they might be stolen. However, checks on serial numbers had come to nothing. What was more ominous was that Gunnar had offered for sale furniture belonging to a young couple, Lonnie Bond and Brenda O'Connor, explaining that they had moved to Los Angeles with their baby and had given him the furniture to pay a debt. No one had heard from them since. And at a nearby camp site at Schaad Lake, another couple had simply vanished, leaving behind their tent and a coffee pot on the stove.

By now, a check on the dead man's fingerprints had revealed that he had a criminal record—for burglary and grand larceny in Mendocino County—and had jumped bail there. His real name was Leonard Lake.

Eisenmann's investigation into Lake's background convinced the detective that this man seemed to be associated with many disappearances. His younger brother Donald had been reported missing in July 1983 after setting out to visit Lake in a "survivalist commune" in Humboldt County. Charles Gunnar, whose identity Lake had borrowed, had been best man at Lake's wedding, but had also vanished in 1985. Together with Stapley and Costner and the Bond couple and their baby, that made seven unexplained disappearances.

The next step, obviously, was to search the small ranch in Blue Mountain Road, where Lake and Ng had lived. Sheriff Ballard obtained the search warrant, and he and Eisenmann drove out with a team of deputies. The "ranch" proved to be a two-bedroom bungalow set in three acres of land. It looked ordinary enough from the outside, but the sight of the master bedroom caused the detectives a sense of foreboding. Hooks in the ceiling and walls suggested that it might be some kind of torture chamber, while a box full of chains and shackles could have only one use: to immobilize someone on the bed. A wardrobe proved to contain many women's undergarments and some filmy nightgowns.

There was also some expensive video equipment. This led Eisenmann's assistant, Sergeant Irene Brunn, to speculate whether it might be connected with a case she had investigated in San Francisco. A couple called Harvey and Deborah Dubs had vanished from their apartment, together with their 16-month-old baby son, and neighbors had seen a young Chinese man removing the contents of their apartment—including an expensive video. She had the serial numbers in her notebook. Her check confirmed her suspicion: this was the missing equipment.

Deputies came in to report that they had been scouring the hillside at the back of the house, and had found burnt bones that looked ominously human. Ballard and Eisenmann went out to see. Among the bones were teeth that looked human. Ballard also noted a trench that seemed to have been intended for a telephone cable; he ordered the deputies to dig it up.

Close to the trench there was a cinderblock bunker that had been cut into the hillside and covered over with earth. Ballard had heard that "Gunnar" was a "survival freak," one who expected a nuclear war to break out, and who was determined to outlive it; this looked like his air raid shelter. He ordered the deputies to break in.

The room on the other side of the door was a storeroom containing food, water, candles and guns. A trap door in the floor led into a kind of cellar, from whose ceiling were suspended more hooks and chains. The walls were covered with pictures of girls posing in their lingerie. What was disturbing about this was that the backdrop of many of these showed a forest scene mural that covered one of the walls; they had obviously been taken in the same room. And the expression on some of the faces suggested that the girls were not enjoying it.

A filing cabinet in the basement proved to be full of videotapes. Eisenmann read the inscription on one of these—"M. Ladies, Kathy/Brenda"—and slipped it into the recorder. A moment later, they were looking at a recording of a frightened girl handcuffed to a chair, with a young Chinaman—obviously Charles Ng—holding a knife beside her. A large, balding man with a beard enters the frame and proceeds to remove the girl's handcuffs, then shackles her ankles, and orders her to undress. Her reluctance is obvious, particularly when she comes to her knickers. The bearded man tells her: "You'll wash for us, clean for us, fuck for us." After this, she is made to go into the shower with the Chinaman. A later scene showed her strapped naked to a bed, while the bearded man tells her that her boyfriend Mike is dead.

After "Kathy" the video showed "Brenda"—identified by Sheriff Ballard as the missing Brenda O'Connor—handcuffed to a chair, while Ng cut off her clothes. She asks after her baby, and Lakes tells her that it has been placed with a family in Fresno. She asks: "Why do you guys do this?", and he tells her: "We don't like you. Do you want me to put it in writing?" "Don't cut my bra off." "Nothing is yours now." "Give my baby back to me. I'll do anything you want." "You're going to do anything we want anyway."

Other videos showed more women being shackled, raped and tortured with a knife. Sergeant Brunn recognized one of these as Deborah Dubs, who had vanished from her San Francisco apartment with her husband and baby. Leonard Lake had spent his last two years making home-made "snuff movies." The prefix "M. Ladies" obviously stood for "murdered ladies."

When the deputies digging in the trench outside reported finding two bodies, the shaken police officers became aware that this could be one of the worst cases of serial murder in California's history—or, indeed, in the history of America.

Lake's accomplice Charles Ng was now one of the most wanted men in America, but had not been seen since his disappearance. Police had discovered that he had fled back to his apartment, traveled out to San Francisco Airport on the BART, and there bought himself a ticket to Chicago under the name "Mike Kimoto." Four days later, a San Francisco gun dealer notified the police that Ng had telephoned him from Chicago. The man had been repairing Ng's automatic pistol, and Ng wanted to know if he could send him the gun by post, addressing it to him at the Chateau Hotel under the name Mike Kimoto. When the gun dealer had explained that it would be illegal to send handguns across state lines, Ng had cursed and threatened him with violence if he went to the police.

By the time Chicago police arrived at the Chateau Hotel, the fugitive had already left. From there on, the trail went dead.

Meanwhile, the team led by Eisenmann and Ballard were continuing to explore Leonard Lake's chamber of horrors. The position of the first two badly decomposed bodies near the top of the trench led to the recognition that there would almost certainly be more lower down. The Coroner Terry Parker was sent for, and Chief Inspector Joseph Lordan in San Francisco notified that additional men would be needed. The next two bodies to be unearthed were black men. Ng, who was known for his hatred of blacks, had once taken two blacks to the ranch as laborers.

Some of the burnt bones dumped on the hillside were in small, neat segments. (Lake had used two fifty-gallon drums as incinerators.) This was explained when the police found a bloodstained power saw, which had obviously been used to cut up the bodies. Coroner Parker supervised the collection of the bones, which were taken away in plastic sacks.

Tracker dogs were brought in to sniff for other bodies. They soon located a grave that proved to contain the remains of a man, woman and baby. These could be either the Dubs family or the Lonnie Bond family—they were too decomposed for immediate recognition. A bulldozer removed the top layer of earth to make digging easier.

As work proceeded in the hundred-degree heat, crowds of reporters lost no opportunity to ask questions. Magazines like *Time* and *Newsweek* had reported the finds, so this latest story of American serial murder soon achieved international notoriety. Earlier cases—like the Dean Corll murders in Texas in the early 1970s, or the John Gacy murders in Chicago in the early 1980s—had caused much the same shock effect. But in this case, even the sensational press seemed oddly subdued in its approach to the story, and gave it less space-inches than might be expected. It was as if the sheer horror of the details was too much even for the most news-hungry editor.

The discovery of the cabinet of snuff videos was followed by one that was in some ways even more disturbing: Lake's detailed diaries covering the same two-year period. The first one, for 1984, began: "Leonard Lake, a name not seen or used much these days in my second year as a fugitive. Mostly dull day-to-day routine—still with death in my pocket and fantasy my goal."

The diaries made it clear that his career of murder had started before he moved into the ranch on Blue Mountain Road. He had been a member of many communes, and in one at a place called Mother Lode, in Humboldt County, he had murdered his younger brother Donald. A crude map of northern California, with crosses labeled "buried treasure," suggested the possibility that these were the sites of more murders; but the map was too inaccurate to guide searchers to the actual locations.

Who was Leonard Lake? Investigation of his background revealed that he had been born in 1946 in San Francisco, and that he had a highly disturbed childhood. Rejected by both parents at an early age, he was raised by his grandmother, a strict disciplinarian. Both his father and mother came from a family of alcoholics. The grandfather, also an alcoholic, was a violent individual who subjected the child to a kind of military discipline. Lake's younger brother Donald, his mother's favorite, was an epileptic who had experienced a serious head injury; he practiced sadistic cruelty to animals and tried to rape both his sisters. Lake protected the sisters "in return for sexual favors." From an early age he had displayed the sexual obsession that seems to characterize the serial killer. He took nude photographs of his sisters and cousins, and later became a maker of pornographic movies starring his wife.

Lake shared another characteristic of so many serial killers—he lived in a world of fantasy—boasting, for example, of daring exploits in Vietnam when, in fact, he had never seen combat. On the other hand, it seems clear that his experiences in Vietnam caused some fundamental change that made him antisocial and capable of violence. Yet he was skillful in hiding his abnormality, teaching grade school, working as a volunteer firefighter, and donating time to a company that provided free insulation in old people's homes. He seemed an exemplary citizen. But his outlook was deeply pessimistic, convinced that World War Three would break out at any moment. Like other "survivalists," he often dressed in combat fatigues, and talked of living off the land. Once out of the marines, his behavior became increasingly odd. After being forced to flee from the earlier compound because of the burglary charge, he had moved to the ranch near Wilseyville. Marriage to a girl called Cricket Balazs had broken up, but she had continued to act as a fence for stolen credit cards and other items. Lake seems to have loved her—at least he said so in a last note scrawled as he was dying—but he nevertheless held on to the paranoid idea that women were responsible for all his problems.

It was while living in an isolated village called Miranda in the hills of Northern California that Lake thought out the plan he called Operation Miranda: the plan he went on to put into effect in the ranch on Blue Mountain Road. It was to stockpile food, clothing and weapons against the coming nuclear holocaust, and also to kidnap women who would be kept imprisoned and used as sex slaves. "The perfect woman," he explained in his diary, "is totally controlled." (He meant that he, Lake, would have total control over her.) "A woman who does exactly what she is told to and nothing else. There is no sexual problem with a submissive woman. There are no frustrations—only pleasure and contentment."

The journal left no doubt about Lake's method for collecting his sex slaves. Leonard Lake had made a habit of luring people to the house, often inviting them—like the Bond family—to dinner. Then the man and the baby were murdered, probably almost immediately. The woman was stripped of her clothes, shackled, and sexually abused until her tormentors grew bored with her. Then she was killed and buried or burned. The thought of the mental torment inflicted on girls like Brenda O'Connor, Deborah Dubs and Kathy Allen sickened everyone on the case.

But one other thing also emerged clearly from these journals, and was noted by the psychiatrist Joel Norris, who published a study of Lake in his book *The Menace of the Serial Killer*: that when Lake killed himself, he was in a state of depression and moral bankruptcy.

His dreams of success had eluded him, he admitted to himself that his boasts about heroic deeds in Vietnam were all delusions, and the increasing number of victims he was burying in the trench behind his bunker only added to his unhappiness. By the time he was arrested in San Francisco, Lake had reached the final stage of the serial murderer syndrome: he realized that he had come to a dead end with nothing but his own misery to show for it.

Two weeks after the digging began, the police had unearthed nine bodies and forty pounds of human bones, some burnt, some even boiled. The driving licenses of Robin Stapley and of Ng's friend Mike Carroll (the boyfriend of Kathy Allen), and papers relating to Paul Cosner's car, confirmed that they had been among the victims.

When the "survival bunker" itself was finally dismantled and taken away on trucks, it seemed clear that the site had yielded most of its evidence. This suggested that Lake had murdered and buried twenty-five people there. The identity of many of the victims remained unknown. The only person who might be able to shed some light on it was the missing Charles Ng. It was believed that he had crossed the border into Canada—a man answering to Ng's description had been seen in the men's room at a bus station shaving off his sideburns and trimming his eyebrows.

Then, on Saturday July 6, 1985, nearly five weeks after Ng's flight, a security guard in a department store in Calgary, Alberta, saw a young Chinaman pushing food under his jacket; when he challenged him, the youth drew a pistol; as they grappled, he fired, wounding the guard in the hand. He ran away at top speed, but was intercepted by other guards. The youth obviously had some training in Japanese martial arts, but was eventually overpowered and handcuffed. Identification documents revealed that he was Charles Ng.

FBI agents hurried to Calgary, and were allowed a long interview. Ng admitted that he knew about the murders, but put the blame entirely on Lake. And before the agents could see him again, Ng's lawyers—appointed by the court—advised him against another interview. And after a psychiatric examination, Ng was tried on a charge of armed robbery and sentenced to four and a half years. But efforts by the California Attorney-General John Van de Kamp to make sure he was extradited after his sentence, met with frustration. California, unlike Canada, still had the death penalty, and the extradition treaty stipulates that a man cannot be extradited if he might face the death penalty.

In November 1989, after serving three and a half years of his sentence, Ng was ordered back to California to face the murder charges against him. Amnesty International protested against the extradition on the grounds that it might result in Ng's execution. A government lawyer replied that if Canada became known as a "safe haven" for killers, other U.S. murderers could flee there. Amnesty International's action caused widespread indignation, and calls for Ng to be sent back immediately. In due course, Ng was returned to California.

At the time of writing, Ng has still not been brought to trial. If and when that happens, the full extent of the horrors that occurred at the Blue Mountain Road ranch may finally emerge in court. But it is hard to see how public disclosure of Lake's depravity can serve any useful purpose.

The case of Leonard Lake and Charles Ng is an example of what we have described as *folie à deux*—cases in which crimes would almost certainly not have taken place unless two participants had egged each other on. An earlier case, while it created a sense of shocked incredulity in California, has received far less publicity. Yet it may be seen as the American equivalent of the Moors murder case.

Soon after midnight on Sunday November 2, 1980, a young couple emerged from the Carousel restaurant in Sacramento, California, where they had been attending a dance. As they crossed the car parking lot they were accosted by a pretty blonde whose swollen stomach indicated pregnancy. They stopped politely—then realized she was holding a gun. "Get in," she said, pointing to an Oldsmobile van parked a few feet away. The sullen-looking man in the passenger seat was also holding a gun. They decided it would be best to obey and climbed into the back.

Before the blonde could enter the driver's door, a passing student with a freakish sense of humor was ahead of her, slipping into the driver's seat. Andy Beal had invited the young couple back to his room for a late night drink. But a single glance at the face of his friends told him there was something wrong. This was confirmed when the pretty blonde flew at him with a stream of obscenities: "Get out of my fucking car!" and slapped his face. As he watched the car drive away, with a screech of tires, Andy Beal had the presence of mind to memorize its number plate, then write it down. Minutes later, he was telephoning the police to report the abduction of Craig Miller and his fiancée Beth Sowers.

The Oldsmobile proved to be registered to a girl called Charlene Williams, daughter of a wealthy Sacramento businessman. The police found her at her parents' home the following morning. Charlene insisted that she had spent the previous evening alone, and had no idea who had used her car. Soon after the police had left, they heard that Craig Miller's body had been found; he had been shot three times in the back of the head. When they returned to ask Charlene further questions, she had left. So had her "husband," an ex-convict called Gerald Gallego.

Five days later, the body of Beth Sowers was also found —dumped, like Craig Miller, in a field. She had been raped and shot. It looked as if the motive for the abduction and murder of the young couple had been simply the rape of Beth Sowers.

The manhunt for Gerald Gallego and Charlene Williams ended two weeks later, as Charlene emerged from a Western Union office in Omaha, Nebraska, with $500 her parents had wired her. The Williamses had also tipped off the police. By now, the Sacramento police had been doing a great deal of research into the background of Gerald Armand Gallego. It seemed to indicate that he and Charlene made a habit of abduction and murder, and that the motive was Gallego's uncontrollable sexual appetite. On July 17, 1980, a pretty waitress named Virginia Mochel had vanished after leaving the tavern where she worked; her naked body had been found not long before the latest murders. And two years earlier, two teenage girls, Rhonda Scheffler and Kippi Vaught, had vanished from a Sacramento shopping mall. Forty-eight hours later, their bodies were found in a meadow; both had been raped, then knocked out with a tire iron and shot. In July 1980, the decomposing bodies of two more teenage girls, Stacy Ann Redican and Karen Chipman-Twiggs, were found in Nevada; they had also vanished from a Sacramento shopping center four months earlier.

When it became clear to Charlene Williams that she and her "husband" faced the death penalty for the murders of Craig Miller and Beth Sowers, she decided to enter into plea bargaining, and agreed to tell the whole story. They had, she admitted, been responsible for the deaths of the four teenagers abducted from Sacramento shopping malls, and for that of the waitress Virginia Mochel. These, together with Craig Miller and Beth Sowers, made seven. And there were another three, of which the Sacramento police knew nothing. The motive, she explained, was Gerald Gallego's peculiar obsession. He wanted to find "the perfect sex slave," a girl who would be anything he asked. And she, Charlene, was so besotted with him that she had agreed meekly to help him kidnap the "slaves."

Gallego, the police discovered, was already wanted on a different charge in Butte County. In 1978, two weeks after he had killed Rhonda Scheffler and Kippi Vaught, his 14-year-old daughter, Sally Jo, had gone to the police and told them that her father had been committing incest with her since she was 8. And to celebrate his thirty-second birthday, he had spent the afternoon with his daughter and her teenage girlfriend in Charlene's Oldsmobile, committing rape and sodomy. And Sally Jo, already full of resentment at her father's new ladylove, had decided this was the last straw. Gallego fled to avoid arrest.

Charlene described how she had met Gallego on a blind date in 1977. At 21 she had already been married and divorced twice; most of the men she had been sleeping with since her early teens had been inadequate. This strutting little ex-con—he was only five feet seven tall—had a gruff dominance that enchanted her. According to Charlene, his sexual appetite was immense, and she was expected to help him satisfy it without receiving any pleasure in return. Being something of a masochist, she explained, she accepted this as part of her duty. When he excited himself sexually by confiding in her his violent fantasies of rape and violence, she also accepted this as one of the peculiarities of her macho lover. And when Gallego told her that he dreamed of the "perfect sex slave," and asked her to help him find one, she felt she had no alternative; he was her master . . .

Gallego was undoubtedly a highly disturbed man, and his life cannot be understood without knowing that his father was also a killer. Gerald Albert Gallego had first been arrested for stealing his stepfather's car; it took seven policemen to get the cuffs on him and he swore revenge. Released from youth custody at the age of 18 in 1946, Gallego senior met an 18-year-old girl who had already been married twice, and married her five hours later; when she gave birth to Gerald Gallego, her husband was doing a stint in San Quentin. He committed his first murder soon after, killing a man in a rage by beating him to death with his fists. But it was in May 1954, when in a town jail on suspicion of murder that Gallego Sr. attacked the guard, grabbed his gun, then made him drive out of town before killing him. "It made me feel real good inside." Recaptured, he escaped again four months later, with another convicted killer; they overpowered a guard by throwing acid in his eyes, then kicked him to death. Hunted down with bloodhounds, he was executed in the death chamber at San Quentin in March 1955, at the age of 28. His 9-year-old son knew nothing of this—until he was 17 he believed that his father had died in an accident.

But by that time it was obvious that Gerald Armand Gallego was following in his father's footsteps. He had started getting into trouble at the age of 10; at 13 he was found guilty of having sex with a 7-year-old girl, and sentenced to juvenile detention—in the same reformatory where his father had served time.

From now on, his life was dominated by a craving for sex and by hatred of authority. He once told a prison visitor: "The only thing I want is to kill God." By the time he was 32 he had been married six times—the sixth wife being Charlene Williams, whom he liked to call Ding-a-Ling.

Charlene's father Chuck Williams had started in business as a supermarket butcher, moved to Sacramento as a supermarket manager, and eventually became vice-president of a nationwide supermarket chain. When his wife Mercedes had an accident to her back that made her less mobile, the teenage Charlene took over the job of hostess to her father's business associates.

In her mid-teens, Charlene became a rebel and tried drugs, alcohol and sex. She came close to being expelled from school; but her father was usually able to smooth over her problems. But two marriages quickly collapsed—perhaps because her husbands were unable to live up to her father-image of the dominant male.

In September 1977 she went—unwillingly—on a blind date with a friend; her partner was Gerald Gallego. He had the kind of dominance she admired. But long before they had collaborated on ten murders, Charlene insisted, she had realized her mistake, and longed to escape from the brutal, insensitive little egoist . . .

This, at all events, was Charlene's story. It was flatly contradicted by Gallego, and Eric van Hoffmann, the author of a book on the case called *Venom in the Blood*, agrees with Gallego. According to Hoffmann, Charlene Williams was a bisexual nymphomaniac. Her sex life with Gallego was satisfactory enough until, in 1978, Gallego brought home a

16-year-old go-go dancer, who shared their bed for a night and was sodomized by Gallego. The next day Gallego returned unexpectedly from work to find Charlene and the girl engaged in sex with a dildo. He threw the girl out and beat Charlene; from then on, he lost his appetite for Charlene. But when, on his daughter's fourteenth birthday, Gallego had sex with both her and her girlfriend, it was clear to Charlene (who was present) that he was not impotent. At this point, according to Hoffmann, Charlene suggested the idea of kidnapping and murder. In each case, the victims were forced to have sex with Charlene as well as Gallego. Charlene liked to bite one of the girls—in one case virtually biting off a nipple—as the other brought her to a climax with oral sex. Hoffmann's account suggests that Charlene was the driving force behind the murders. As absurd as it sounds, Gallego emerges at the end of the book as *her* victim.

This certainly makes more sense than the other book on the case, *All His Father's Sins* by Biondi and Hecox, in which Charlene is presented as the pliable victim. And once again we become aware that one of the basic keys to the mind of the serial killer is a kind of "spoiltness" that leads to a total inability to identify with other human beings. In this case, it seems clear that it was the spoiled rich girl who was trapped in total self-centeredness, while the working-class Gallego, for all his faults, was more normal and realistic.

According to Charlene's confession, it was because she was completely enslaved to Gallego that she had approached the two pretty teenagers, Rhonda Scheffler and Kippi Vaught, in the shopping mall and asked them if they would like to smoke some pot. Unsuspectingly, the girls had accompanied her back to the Oldsmobile van. Then Gallego had confronted them with a gun, and Charlene had to drive to a remote spot, where the girls were ordered out. They were taken into some pine trees; Gallego was carrying a sleeping bag. Hours later, Gallego returned with the girls, who looked disheveled and tear-stained. Charlene was told to drive to another remote place; then he took the girls, one by one, and shot them. As they were about to drive away, he noticed that one of them—Kippi Vaught—was still moving; he got out of the van and shot her in the back of the head. The coroner later discovered that the first shot had only grazed her skull. If she had not moved, she would have been alive when the police reached her, and been able to describe her assailant . . .

It was two weeks later that Gallego's daughter told the police about the long-term incest, and Gallego was on the run.

The next two victims, again teenage girls, were picked up at the annual county fair in Reno on July 24, 1978. Charlene approached Kaye Colley and Brenda Judd, and asked if they would like a job distributing leaflets. In the back of the van, they were confronted by Gallego with a pistol. This time there was a mattress and blankets on the floor. Charlene drove; Gallego ordered the girls to strip—one of them had vomited. Then Gallego raped them both. A long time later, Charlene was ordered to drive on. The girls were taken out one by one and killed with hammer blows to the skull.

Ten months later, on April 24, 1980, Stacy Ann Redican and Karen Chipman-Twiggs were accosted by the pretty blonde girl in the Sunrise Mall in Sacramento; they were totally unsuspicious until confronted by the little man with a gun. This time, in remote Nevada woods, Charlene left the van while Gallego raped the girls and made them perform the various services that might qualify them as "perfect sex slaves." Then, as before, he took them off one by one and killed them with a hammer. Not long after that murder, Gallego and Charlene were married. But since Gallego had omitted to get a divorce from a previous wife, it was not legal anyway.

Scarcely a month later, on June 6, 1980, they passed an attractive hippie walking along the road between Port Orford, Oregon, and Gold Beach; her name was Linda Teresa Aguilar, and she was five months pregnant. The man and woman in the van looked safe enough, so she accepted a lift. As Charlene drove, Gallego climbed over into the back with the hippie and ordered her to undress. Then Charlene stopped the van and went for a walk. When she finally returned, Gallego was complaining that the girl had been unable to "do anything for him." He took her away and knocked her unconscious with a hammer; an autopsy would later reveal that she was still alive when he buried her in the sand.

The next victim had been the waitress, Virginia Mochel, a pretty blonde girl not unlike Charlene. On July 17, 1980, after the tavern had closed, Gallego accosted the waitress as she climbed into her own car. It was a dangerous thing to do—there were still many customers around, and Gallego had been talking to the girl all evening. Virginia, who had left her two children with a baby-sitter, begged to be allowed to call and explain that she was delayed. Gallego told her to shut up. They drove back to the apartment Charlene shared with him, and Charlene went inside while Gallego raped Virginia in the van, then strangled her. It was dawn when they finally dumped her on a levee road.

As already noted, Gallego's account, which is accepted by van Hoffmann, has Charlene taking a far more active part in the murders.

Whatever the truth, the rampage was now almost over. After Craig Miller and Beth Sowers had been abducted from outside the Carousel restaurant on November 2, 1980, Charlene drove to a remote field; Miller was made to get out and lie on the ground, then killed with three bullets in the back of the head. Beth Sowers was taken back to the Gallego apartment and raped, while—Charlene declares—she waited in the next room. Then Beth was also taken to a remote place and shot. But this time, Gallego's carelessness—in abducting his latest victims in a parking lot with other customers around—led to his downfall.

At the arraignment proceedings, Gallego leapt to his feet and screamed at reporters: "Get the hell out of here! We're not funny people! We're not animals." He fought violently, over-turning tables and chairs before he was subdued.

Because of the sheer horror caused by the case, the Gallego trial was moved from Sacramento to Martinez, near San Francisco. It became clear that Gallego was an almost insane egoist. But his attempts to exclude Charlene's testimony—on the grounds that they were married—failed when it was proved that he had still not divorced his second wife. On June 21, 1983, he was sentenced to die by lethal injection in San Quentin. Since that time, he has proved to be a consistently difficult prisoner, whose violence and abusiveness have meant that he has spent most of his time separated from other prisoners. Charlene Williams received sixteen years.

Does not Charlene's involvement contradict the view, suggested elsewhere in this book, that all serial killers are working-class? In fact, as far as I can see, there is no psychological law that dictates that a middle- or upper-class person would be incapable of being a serial killer. The fact that all serial killers have had working-class backgrounds only proves that childhood misery and poverty can produce the kind of resentment that leads to serial murder. But the fifteenth-century child murderer Gilles de Rais was spoilt and wealthy, and there seems to be no reason why a modern Gilles should be an impossibility.

Fortunately, at the time of writing, no such person has emerged. When I came across the case of the New Jersey "torso killer" Richard Cottingham, I was at first inclined to believe that he was an exception. Cottingham, a computer operator who worked for an insurance company, was arrested in May 1980 after screams from a motel room alerted the manager that something was wrong. Cottingham had been torturing a prostitute for several hours, and fairly certainly intended to kill her, as he had killed half a dozen other women. Cottingham's method was to pick up a woman, take her to a bar and slip a drug into her drink, then take her to a motel and rape and torture her. Some victims were allowed to go; others were strangled and mutilated.

Cottingham was the son of an insurance salesman who was brought up in a suburban home, and had attended high school before he married and became a computer programmer. But Ron Leith's book *The Prostitute Murders* reveals that he was born in the Bronx—which might be regarded as New York's equivalent of London's East End—and spoke with a Bronx accent. He spent the first ten years of his life in the Bronx, before the family moved to New Jersey. His father was absent from home most of the time, and Cottingham—an only child—found it difficult to make friends at school. Nothing is known of the psychological causes of his passion to humiliate and torture women. But it seems clear that Cottingham is another example of the working class serial killer.

Cottingham's most obvious characteristic was a high degree of conceit. Like so many serial killers, he seems to have had no doubt that he was the cleverest person in the courtroom. Ron Leith, who was in court, comments that it was Cottingham himself who cemented the state's case, giving an implausibly intricate alibi, and lecturing the judge on the strange world of prostitution. "His arrogance seemed limitless."

This, then, seems to be the common denominator of serial killers—egoism combined with a kind of tunnel vision. But then, we have all known people like that—people who obviously believe that they are the most fascinating person in the world, and who regard it as natural to begin every sentence with "I." There must always have been such people. Then why is it that, in our own time, a percentage of them have turned into serial killers?

We have noted already the distinction Robert Ressler made between a serial killer—one who continues killing over a long period, usually at regular intervals—and the "spree killer," such as Charles Starkweather, Richard Speck or Paul John Knowles, who commits a number of murders in a sudden rampage over a brief period of time. Perhaps the best-known spree killer of the 1980s was Bernard Christopher Wilder, a young and wealthy Australian businessman and racing driver, who lived in luxury in Miami, Florida, from the mid-1970s. In 1980 he was charged with raping two teenage girls after drugging them with a doctored pizza, but was only bound over. Back in Australia he was charged with abducting and raping two 15-year-old girls, but allowed to return to America on bail. In the seven weeks between February 26, 1984 and April 12, 1984, Wilder drove from Florida to Georgia, then Texas, Oklahoma, Kansas, Colorado, Nevada and California, then returned east to Indiana, New York, Massachusetts and New Hampshire. During this time he abducted eleven women, posing as a magazine photographer looking for models, and raped and killed nine of them. On March 20, 1984, guests in a motel in Bainbridge, south Georgia, broke into a room when they heard a girl screaming, and found a 19-year-old girl who had locked herself in the bathroom. She described how she had been picked up in Tallahassee, Florida, by Wilder, who said he wanted her to model for him, and was knocked unconscious as she posed in a public garden. Wilder had then smuggled her into a motel room in a sleeping bag, glued her eyelids with superglue, bound her hands, then raped and tortured her. She had managed to persuade him to allow her to go to the bathroom, then locked herself in and screamed until she was released; Wilder fled.

Most of his other pickups were less fortunate. Only two girls, who were forced to spend a night with him in a motel in Akron, Ohio, escaped with their lives—one of them stabbed several times. In Boston, Wilder put the other on a plane for Los Angeles, handing her five hundred dollars, then abducted another girl whose car had broken down. She succeeded in jumping out of his car at a traffic light. The next day, Friday April 13, two policemen approached Wilder's car, and as one of them grappled with him, Wilder was fatally shot; the policeman was only wounded.

The nationwide chase after Wilder was one of the major factors that led to the formation of a nationwide crime center, the National Center for the Analysis of Violent Crime (NCAVC) in Quantico in June 1984. Here, as we have seen, the crime computer records crimes that take place all over America—which would formerly have been recorded only in the state in which they took place—and searches for similarities that might reveal a traveling criminal. Although difficulties have arisen in recent years—as individual states complain that the NCAVC takes the credit that is often due to them, and sometimes decline to co-operate—the NCAVC has remained the most important advance in crime detection in the late twentieth century.

The importance of these technological advances is emphasized again by the solution of another widely publicized case of the 1980s, that of the man who became known as "the Night Stalker."

Throughout 1985 handgun sales in Los Angeles soared. Many suburbanites slept with a loaded pistol by their beds. A series of violent attacks upon citizens in their own homes had shattered the comfortably normality of middle-class life. Formerly safe neighborhoods seemed to be the killer's favorite targets. The whole city was terrified.

The attacks were unprecedented in many ways. Neither murder nor robbery seemed to be the obvious motive, although both frequently took place. The killer would break into a house, creep into the main bedroom and shoot the male partner through the head with a .22. He would then rape and beat the wife or girlfriend, suppressing resistance with threats of violence to her or her children. Male children were sometimes sodomized, the rape victims sometimes shot. On occasion he would ransack the house looking for valuables while at other times he would leave empty-handed without searching. During the attacks he would force victims to declare their love for Satan. Survivors described a tall, slim Hispanic male with black, greasy hair and severely decayed teeth. The pattern of crimes seemed to be based less upon a need to murder or rape but a desire to terrify and render helpless. More than most serial killers the motive seemed to be exercising power.

The killer also had unusual methods of victim selection. He seemed to be murdering outside his own racial group, preferring Caucasians and specifically Asians. He also seemed to prefer to break into yellow houses.

In the spring and summer of 1985 there were more than twenty attacks, most of which involved both rape and murder. By the end of March the press had picked up the pattern and splashed stories connecting the series of crimes. After several abortive nicknames, such as "The Walk-In Killer" or "The Valley Invader," the *Herald Examiner* came up with "The Night Stalker," a name sensational enough to stick.

Thus all through the hot summer of 1985 Californians slept with their windows closed. One policeman commented to a reporter: "People are armed and staying up late. Burglars want this guy caught like everyone else. He's making it bad for their business." The police themselves circulated sketches and stopped anyone who looked remotely like The Night Stalker. One innocent man was stopped five times.

Despite these efforts and thorough forensic analysis of crime scenes there was little progress in the search for the killer's identity.

Things were obviously getting difficult for The Night Stalker as well. The next murder that fitted the pattern occurred in San Francisco, showing perhaps that public awareness in Los Angeles had made it too taxing a location. This shift also gave police a chance to search San Francisco hotels for records of a man of The Night Stalker's description. Sure enough, while checking the downmarket Tenderloin district police learned that a thin Hispanic with bad teeth had been staying at a cheap hotel there periodically over the past year. On the last occasion he had checked out the night of the San Francisco attack. The manager commented that his room "smelled like a skunk" each time he vacated it and it took three days for the smell to clear.

Though this evidence merely confirmed the police's earlier description, The Night Stalker's next shift of location was to prove more revealing. A young couple in Mission Viejo were attacked in their home. The Night Stalker shot the man through the head while he slept, then raped his partner on the bed next to the body. He then tied her up while he ransacked the house for money and jewelry. Before leaving he raped her a second time and forced her to fellate him with a gun pressed against her head. Unfortunately for the killer, however, his victim caught a glimpse of him escaping in a battered orange Toyota and memorized the license plate. She immediately alerted the police. LAPD files showed that the car had been stolen in Los Angeles' Chinatown district while the owner was eating in a restaurant. An all-points bulletin was put out for the vehicle, and officers were instructed not to try and arrest the driver, merely to observe him. However, the car was not found. In fact, The Night Stalker had dumped the car soon after the attack, and it was located two days later in a car parking lot in Los Angeles' Rampart district. After plain clothes officers had kept the car under surveillance for twenty-four hours, the police moved in and took the car away for forensic testing. A set of fingerprints was successfully lifted.

Searching police fingerprint files for a match manually can take many days and even then it is possible to miss correlations. However, the Los Angeles police had recently installed a fingerprint database computer system, designed by the FBI, and it was through this that they checked the set of fingerprints from the orange Toyota. The system works by storing information about the relative distance between different features of a print, and comparing them with a digitized image of the suspect's fingerprint. The search provided a positive match and a photograph. The Night Stalker was a petty thief and burglar. His name was Ricardo Leyva Ramirez.

The positive identification was described by the forensic division as "a near miracle." The computer system had only just been installed, this was one of its first trials. Furthermore, the system only contained the fingerprints of criminals born after January 1, 1960. Richard Ramirez was born in February 1960.

The police circulated the photograph to newspapers, and it was shown on the late evening news. At the time, Ramirez was in Phoenix, buying cocaine with the money he had stolen in Mission Viejo. On the morning that the papers splashed his name and photograph all over their front pages, he was on a bus on the way back to Los Angeles, unaware that he had been identified.

He arrived safely and went into the bus station toilet to finish off the cocaine he had bought. No one seemed to be overly interested in him as he left the station and walked through Los Angeles. Ramirez was a Satanist, and had developed a belief that Satan himself watched over him, preventing his capture.

At 8:15 a.m. Ramirez entered Tito's Liquor Store at 819 Towne Avenue. He selected some Pepsi and a pack of sugared doughnuts; he had a sweet tooth that, coupled with a lack of personal hygiene, had left his mouth with only a few blackened teeth. At the counter other customers looked at him strangely as he produced three dollar bills and awaited his change. Suddenly he noticed the papers' front pages, and his faith in Satan's power must have been shaken. He dodged out of the shop and ran, accompanied by shouts of, "It is him! Call the cops!" He pounded off down the street at a surprising speed for one so ostensibly unhealthy. Within twelve minutes he had covered two miles. He had headed east. He was in the Hispanic district of Los Angeles.

Ever since the police had confirmed that The Night Stalker was Hispanic there had been a great deal of anger among the Hispanic community of Los Angeles. They felt that racial stereotypes were already against them enough without their being associated with psychopaths. Thus more than most groups, Hispanics wanted The Night Stalker out of action.

Ramirez, by now, was desperate to get a vehicle. He attempted to pull a woman from her car in a supermarket lot until he was chased away by some customers of the barber's shop opposite. He carried on running, though exhausted, into the more residential areas of east Los Angeles. There, he tried to steal a 1966 red Mustang having failed to notice that the owner, Faustino Pinon, was lying underneath repairing it. As Ramirez attempted to start the car Pinon grabbed him by the collar and tried to pull him from the driver's seat. Ramirez shouted that he had a gun, but Pinon carried on pulling at him even after the car had started, causing it to careen into the gatepost. Ramirez slammed it into reverse and accelerated into the side of Pinon's garage, and the vehicle stalled. Pinon succeeded in wrenching Ramirez out of his car, but in the following struggle Ramirez escaped, leaping the fence and running off across the road. There he tried to wrestle Angelina De La Torres from her Ford Granada. "Te voy a matar!" (I'm going to kill you!) screamed Ramirez, "Give me the keys!", but again he was thwarted and he ran away, now pursued by a growing crowd of neighbors. Manuel De La Torres, Angelina's husband, succeeded in smashing Ramirez on the head with a gate bar and he fell, but he managed to struggle up and set off running again before he could be restrained. Incredibly, when Ramirez had developed a lead, he stopped, turned around and stuck his tongue out at his pursuers, then sped off once more. His stamina could not hold indefinitely however, and it was De La Torres who again tackled him and held him down. It is possible that Ramirez would have been lynched right there and then had not a patrolman called to the scene arrived: Coincidentally the patrolman was the same age as the killer, and he too was called Ramirez. He reached the scene just as The Night Stalker disappeared under the mob. He drove his patrol car to within a few feet of where Ramirez was restrained, got out and prepared to handcuff the captive.

"Save me. Please. Thank God you're here. It's me, I'm the one you want. Save me before they kill me," babbled Ramirez. The patrolman handcuffed him and pushed him into the back of the car. The crowd was becoming restless, and the car was kicked as it pulled away. Sixteen-year-old Felipe Castaneda, part of the mob that captured Ramirez remarked, "He should never, *never* have come to East LA. He might have been a tough guy, but he came to a tough neighborhood. He was Hispanic. He should have known better."

"The Night Stalker" was in custody, at first in a police holding cell and then in Los Angeles county jail. While in police care he repeatedly admitted to being "The Night Stalker" and begged to be killed.

The case against Ramirez was strong. The murder weapon, a .22 semi-automatic pistol, was found in the possession of a woman in Tijuana, who had been given it by a friend of Ramirez. Police also tried to track down some of the jewelry that Ramirez had stolen and fenced, by sending investigators to his birth-place El Paso, a spiraling town on the Texas–Mexico border. Questioning of his family and neighbors revealed that Ramirez' early life had been spent in petty theft and smoking a lot of marijuana. He had never joined any of the rival teenage gangs that fight over territory throughout El Paso, preferring drugs and listening to heavy metal. It had been common knowledge that Ramirez was a Satanist; a boyhood friend, Tom Ramos said he believed that it was Bible-study classes that had turned the killer that way.

The investigators also found a great deal of jewelry, stashed at the house of Ramirez' sister Rosa Flores. The police were also hoping to find a pair of eyes that Ramirez had gouged from one of his victims that had not been found in any previous searches. Unfortunately they were not recovered.

The evidence against Ramirez now seemed unequivocal. In a controversial move, the Mayor of Los Angeles said that whatever went on in court, he was convinced of Ramirez' guilt. This was later to prove a mainstay in a defense argument that Ramirez could not receive a fair trial in Los Angeles.

The appointed chief prosecutor in the case was deputy District Attorney P. Philip Halpin, who had prosecuted the "Onion Field" cop-killing case twenty years earlier. Halpin hoped to end the trial and have Ramirez in the gas chamber in a relatively short period of time. The prosecutor drew up a set of initial charges and submitted them as quickly as possible. A public defender was appointed to represent Ramirez. However Ramirez' family had engaged an El Paso lawyer, Manuel Barraza, and Ramirez eventually rejected his appointed public defender in favor of the El Paso attorney. Barraza did not even have a license to practice law in California.

Ramirez accepted, then rejected three more lawyers, finally settling upon two defenders, Dan and Arturo Hernandez. The two were not related, although they often worked together. The judge advised Ramirez that his lawyers did not even meet the minimum requirements for trying a death-penalty case in California, but Ramirez insisted, and more than seven weeks after the initial charges were filed, pleas of "not guilty" were entered on all counts.

The Hernandez' and Ramirez seemed to be trying to force Halpin into making a mistake out of sheer frustration, and thus to create a mis-trial. After each hearing the Hernandez' made pleas for, and obtained, more time to prepare their case. Meanwhile one prosecution witness had died of natural causes, and Ramirez' appearance was gradually changing. He had had his hair permed, and his rotten teeth replaced. This naturally introduced more uncertainty into the minds of prosecution witnesses as to Ramirez' identity. The racial make-up of the jury was contested by the defense, which caused delays. The defense also argued, with some justification, that Ramirez could not receive a fair trial in Los Angeles, and moved for a change of location. Although the motion was refused it caused yet more delays. It actually took three and a half years for Ramirez' trial finally to get underway.

Halpin's case was, in practical terms, unbeatable. The defense's only real possibility of success was in infinite delay. For the first three weeks of the trial events progressed rela-

tively smoothly. Then Daniel Hernandez announced that the
trial would have to be postponed as he was suffering from
nervous exhaustion. He had a doctor's report that advised
six weeks' rest with psychological counseling. It seemed
likely that a mis-trial would be declared. Halpin tried to
argue that Arturo Hernandez could maintain the defense,
even though he had failed to turn up at the hearings and trial
for the first seven months. However this proved unnecessary
as the judge made a surprise decision and denied Daniel
Hernandez his time off, arguing that he had failed to prove
a genuine need.

Halpin, by this stage, was actually providing the Hernandez' with all the information that they required to mount an
adequate defense, in order to move things along and prevent
mis-trial. For the same reasons the judge eventually appointed
a defense co-counsel, Ray Clark. Clark immediately put the
defense on a new track: Ramirez was the victim of a mistaken
identity. He even developed an acronym for this defense—
SODDI or Some Other Dude Did It. When the defense case
opened Clark produced testimony from Ramirez' father that
he had been in El Paso at the time of one of the murders of
which he was accused. He also criticized the prosecution for
managing to prove that footprints at one of the crime scenes
were made by a size eleven-and-a-half Avia trainer without
ever proving that Ramirez actually owned such a shoe. When
the jury finally left to deliberate however, it seemed clear that
they would find Ramirez guilty.

Things were not quite that easy however. After thirteen
days of deliberation juror Robert Lee was dismissed for inat-
tention and replaced by an alternative who had also witnessed
the case. Two days later, juror Phyllis Singletary was murdered in a domestic dispute. Her live-in lover had beaten her,
then shot her several times. She was also replaced.

At last on September 20, 1989 after twenty-two days of

deliberation the jury returned a verdict of guilty on all thirteen counts of murder, twelve of those in the first degree. The jury also found Ramirez guilty of thirty other felonies, including burglary, rape, sodomy and attempted murder. Asked by reporters how he felt after the verdict, Ramirez replied, "Evil."

There remained only the selection of sentence. At the hearing Clark argued that Ramirez might actually have been possessed by the devil, or that alternatively he had been driven to murder by over-active hormones. He begged the jury to imprison Ramirez for life rather than put him on death row. If the jury agreed, Clark pointed out, "he will never see Disneyland again," surely punishment enough. After five further days of deliberation, the jury voted for the death penalty. Again, reporters asked Ramirez how he felt about the outcome as he was being taken away, "Big deal. Death always went with the territory. I'll see you in Disneyland."

Any attempt to trace the source of Ramirez' violent behavior runs up against an insurmountable problem. No external traumas or difficulties seem to have brutalized him. He had a poor upbringing, he was part of a racial minority, but these things alone cannot explain such an incredibly sociopathic personality. Ramirez seems to have created himself. He was an intelligent and deeply religious child and early teenager. Having decided at some stage that counter-culture and drug-taking provided a more appealing lifestyle, he developed pride in his separateness. In the El Paso of his early manhood, people would lock their doors, if they saw him coming down the street. He was known as "Ricky Rabon" Ricky the thief, a nickname he enjoyed as he felt it made him "someone." By the time he moved to Los Angeles, he was injecting cocaine and probably committing burglaries to support himself. He let his teeth rot away, eating only childish sugary foods. He refused to wash. He listened to loud heavy metal music.

It has been argued that it was his taste in music that drove him to murder and Satanism, but this would seem to be more part of the mood of censorship sweeping America than a genuine explanation. Anyone who takes the trouble to listen to the music in question, particularly the AC/DC album cited by American newspapers at the time of the murders, will find that there is little in it to incite violence.

Ramirez' obvious attempts to repel others in his personal behavior, and his heavy drug use, seem more likely sources of violence than early poverty or music. His assumed "otherness" seems in retrospect sadly underdeveloped, having never progressed beyond a teenager's need to appal staid grown-up society.

This is not to say that Ramirez was unintelligent. His delaying of his trial and his choice of the Hernandez' to continue the delays shows that he had worked out the most effective method of staying alive for the longest period either before or soon after he was captured. His remarks in court upon being sentenced were not particularly original, yet they are clearly expressed:

"It's nothing you'd understand but I do have something to say . . . I don't believe in the hypocritical, moralistic dogma of this so-called civilized society. I need not look beyond this room to see all the liars, haters, the killers, the crooks, the paranoid cowards—truly *trematodes* of the Earth, each one in his own legal profession. You maggots make me sick—hypocrites one and all . . . I am beyond your experience. I am beyond good and evil, legions of the night, night breed, repeat not the errors of the Night Prowler [a name from an AC/DC song] and show no mercy. I will be avenged., Lucifer dwells within us all. That's it.

Ramirez remains on Death Row. It is unlikely that he will be executed before the year 2000.

The kind of good fortune that led to the arrest of Ramirez—the single fingerprint that identified the killer—failed to favor the team who spent most of the 1980s trying to trap the sadist who became known as the Green River Killer.

On August 12, 1982, a slaughterman gazing into the slow-flowing Green River, near Seattle, was intrigued by the mass of bubbles surrounding a log—they suggested a decomposing animal. He strolled down a fisherman's track to the riverbank for a closer look. What he saw was a bloated female corpse that had come to rest against a broken tree trunk. The shoulder-length auburn hair floated on the surface.

The police pathologist succeeded in lifting an excellent set of prints from the swollen flesh. These enabled the criminal identification department to name the victim as 23-year-old Debra Lynn Bonner, known as "Dub"; she was a stripper with a list of convictions as a prostitute.

The man in charge of the case, Detective Dave Reichert, recalled that a month earlier, another tattooed corpse had been found in the Green River, half a mile downstream, strangled with her own slacks. The girl had been identified as 16-year-old Wendy Coffield. In spite of her age, Wendy had a record as a prostitute—in fact, as a "trick roll," someone who set up her clients ("johns") for robbery. It was a dangerous game, and Reichert was not surprised that the investigation had failed to turn up a likely suspect. On the whole, he decided, it was unlikely that the two murders were connected.

This view was reinforced by a visit to Dub Bonner's parents in nearby Tacoma. It produced the information that Dub had vanished on July 25, 1982, three weeks earlier, after being bailed from the local jail, together with her drug-dealing pimp. There was, it seemed a possible suspect—another dealer who had threatened Dub Bonner's life unless her pimp paid a drug-debt.

But before he had time to follow this lead, Reichert heard the news that two more bodies had been found in the Green River. The call came just after he had returned from church— it was Sunday, August 15, 1982—and when Reichert arrived at the scene, they had still not been taken out of the water. Both women were black, both were naked, and they had been weighted down to the river bottom with large rocks. But what made Reichert swear under his breath was that they were only a few hundred yards upstream from the spot where Dub Bonner had been found three days earlier, and that they had almost certainly been there at the time. Reichert had searched up and downstream for clues—but not, apparently, far enough.

Determined not to repeat his error, Reichert tramped along the bank towards the place where Dub Bonner had been found. He was hoping to find the route that the killer had used to transport the bodies. What he found, in fact, was another body. This one lay face downward, and the cause of death was clearly the pair of slacks knotted around her neck. Her upper half was clothed, although her bra had been pulled up to release her breasts. Like the other two, she was black. The outthrust tongue and the shocked expression on her face showed that death had not come easily.

Reichert's Superior, Major Richard Kraske of the Kings County CID, came to view the bodies, and Reichert described what he had learned about Dub Bonner. This led them to toy with the idea that these women might be victims of a gang war among pimps; then Kraske discounted it. Pimps were unlikely to destroy their means of livelihood. It seemed far more likely that they were dealing with a psychopath—a "sick trick"—whose perverted needs involved the total domination of his sex-partner, and her final destruction. Reichert recalled gloomily that he had investigated the murder of another prostitute, Leann Wilcox, in March of that same year. Her body had been found miles from the river, but cause of death— strangulation—seemed to fit the pattern.

The medical report on the latest victims deepened his depression. Of the two bodies in the river, one had been immersed for a week, the other for only two or three days. That meant that the killer had returned to the river *since* Dub Bonner had been found. Moreover, the body found on the bank still showed signs of rigor mortis, the stiffening of the muscles which usually disappears within two days. So the killer *had* returned—as many killers do to the sites where they have dumped bodies. He *must* have heard the news of the discovery of Dub Bonner's body, yet he had still returned. And if the police had kept a watch on the riverbank, he would now be in custody . . .

It was the first of a series of mischances that would make this one of the most frustrating criminal cases in Seattle's history. The next—and perhaps the worst—occurred two days later, when a local TV station announced that the riverbank was now under round-the-clock surveillance, and dashed the last hope of catching the killer on a return visit . . .

During the course of the next few days, the three black victims were identified. The first was Marcia Faye Chapman, a 31-year-old prostitute and mother of three children. She was known to work "the Strip," the motel-studded highway that ran south from Seattle to the airport and on to Tacoma. The method was to stand by the roadside, apparently "hitching." If a car pulled up, and the driver indicated his willingness to go to a "party," he was taken to a cheap motel, or to an area of condemned houses north of the airport, where his needs could be satisfied in the car. With the expansion of the "Sea-Tac" Airport's traffic in the 1970s, the Strip had also seen a spectacular expansion in prostitution, and the crimes that go with it. Marcia Chapman had been missing since August 1, 1982, when she told her children she was going to the store, and had failed to return.

The second body found in the river was that of 17-year-old Cynthia Hinds, another prostitute who worked the Strip; she had last been seen on August 11, not far from where Marcia Chapman had disappeared. The third body—the one found on the bank—was that of 16-year-old Opal Mills, a half-caste girl with no record of prostitution, but with a background of quarrels at home and minor brushes with the police. After viewing her daughter's body, Kathy Mills was haunted by the "silent scream" on her face. She was to campaign for more police activity, and to intensify the frustration that turned this case into a nightmare for investigating officers.

But it was the medical findings on Marcia Chapman and Cynthia Hinds that confirmed the suspicion that the Green River Killer was a "sick trick"; both women had pointed rocks jammed into their vaginas. There was speculation that they had been dumped in clear water, with their feet weighted by stones, so that the killer could go back and look at their faces magnified by the water. Intact sperm was found in the vaginas of all three victims. Opal Mills's body was scraped and scratched—probably from being dragged over the ground; it looked as if the killer had been interrupted before he could throw her in the river.

In cases involving the murder of prostitutes, investigators are faced with the baffling problem of where to begin. Approximately eighty thousand cars a day drive along the Strip, making eighty thousand possible suspects. Since the contact that led to the murder is made by chance, there is no logical starting point. Vice squad detectives tried questioning prostitutes about "johns" who had acted suspiciously, and undercover agents hung around bars frequented by pimps, hoping to pick up rumors of "sick tricks." They heard many stories of women who had been half-strangled in motel rooms, or who had been driven to remote spots and then raped at gunpoint. Dozens of suspects were questioned, including the drug-dealing pimp who had threatened to kill Dub Bonner; all had to be released.

Meanwhile, more girls were disappearing. Two days after Wendy Coffield's body had been found in the Green River, a 17-year-old prostitute named Giselle Lavvorn vanished on her beat along the Strip. On Saturday August 28, 1982, a prostitute named Kase Lee left her pimp's apartment to "turn a trick," and vanished. The next day it was Terri Milligan, who took an hour off from soliciting to go for a meal; apparently a car pulled up for her as she walked to the fast-food joint, and, unwilling to reject business, she climbed in.

The following day, 15-year-old Debra Estes—known to the police as Betty Jones—was picked up by a john in a blue and white pickup truck; he drove her to a remote spot, made her undress at gun point, then ordered her to give him a "blow job." After that he robbed her of $75 and left her in some woods with her hands tied. This man was pulled in by police who recognized the description of his pickup truck, and identified as the attacker. But a lie-detector test established his innocence of the Green River murders. In fact, while he was still in custody, 18-year-old Mary Meehan, who was eight months pregnant, disappeared, and became victim No. 9.

Ironically, within three weeks of her unpleasant encounter, Debra Estes would become the tenth victim of the real Green River Killer. Six more victims in August, October, November and December would bring his total up to at least sixteen—the largest annual total for any American serial killer up to that time.

Yet, as strange as it sounds, the American public was already beginning to lose interest in the Green River Killer.

This was partly because the killer's standard method—strangling or suffocation—failed to produce the same shock effect as the mutilations of Jack the Ripper or the Cleveland Torso Killer. But it was also because this apparently endless disappearance of prostitutes led to a certain attention-fatigue—in March 1983, Alma Smith and Delores Williams; in April, Gail Mathews, Andrea Childers, Sandra Gabbert and Kimi-Kai Pitsor.

Moreover, there was a monotonous similarity about the cases. It was on April 17 that 17-year-old Sandy Gabbert picked up a "trick" and vanished. Only an hour later, 17-year-old Kimi Kai Pitsor was walking with her pimp when a pock-marked man driving a green pickup truck caught her eye; she climbed in and vanished. Presumably the same man abducted and killed both girls on the same evening. Yet they were not even reported missing to the police for several weeks.

This attention-fatigue could also explain one of the oddest episodes in the case. On April 30, 18-year-old Marie Malvar and her "boyfriend" were walking along the Strip when a man in a pickup truck signaled for her to get in. The boyfriend, Bobby Woods, followed in his own car, but lost them; Marie vanished. A few days later, accompanied by Marie's father and brother, Bobby Woods, spent hours driving around the area where he had last seen her. In a driveway in a cul-de-sac, he saw a pickup truck that he was certain was the one in which she had last been seen. The police were notified, and called at the house. But when the man who answered the door told them there was no woman in the house, they simply went away. To Bobby Woods it looked as if the police, like the general public, were losing interest in the case: a conclusion that seems to be supported by a subsequent development. On May 17, Marie Malvar's driving license was found by a cleaner at the airport. It could well have contained the killer's fingerprints. Yet although the police were notified, nobody bothered to collect the license, and it was routinely destroyed six months later.

And the disappearances continued: in May, Carol Christensen, Martina Authorlee, Cheryl Wims and Yvonne Antosh; in June, Keli McGinness, Constance Naon, Tammy Lies and Carrie Roice; in July, Kelly Ware and Tina Thompson. Now the killer seemed to have abandoned the river as a dumping ground, preferring remote areas. Sometimes the girl vanished for ever. Sometimes bodies were found that corresponded to none of the known victims.

Photographs of the women often show sullen and defeated faces, and eyes that seem glazed with drugs. Kathy Mills, mother of Opal Mills, paraded with a placard that pointed out that the killer of a policeman's daughter was arrested the next day, while the attitude of the police towards the Green River victims was: "Too bad." It was not entirely fair comment, but she had a point. By the end of 1983, the number of the killer's known victims had reached forty, with another seven unaccounted for.

In fact, the police were about to step up the pace of the investigation. In mid-January 1984 they announced the formation of a Green River Task Force that would be devoted entirely to catching the killer. It was led by an experienced detective, Captain Frank Adamson, and its chief consultant was special investigator Bob Keppel, of the Attorney-General's office, the man who had played a major role in tracking down serial killer Ted Bundy. The team included undercover officers who watched prostitutes on the Strip and followed them as they drove off with johns. Dozens of sheepish or angry men were interviewed and asked for identification, and the suspect file continued to swell. And prostitutes who had taken customers to a dead-end road not far from where three skeletons had been discovered continued to be defiant, and to insist that they could look after themselves.

In April 1984, three more skeletons were found near Star Lake, south of Sea-Tac Airport, and another in woods about a mile away. One of these finds presented a new puzzle to the investigators. It was identified as that of Amina Agisheff, who had been missing since July 7, 1982, and was therefore one of the earliest—perhaps the first—of the Green River victims. But Amina did not fit the pattern. She was 35 years old, had two children, worked as waitress, and had no record of prostitution. She had vanished towards midnight as she left her mother to catch a bus. Had she been kidnapped? Or had she been given a lift by someone she knew—someone who turned out to be the Green River killer? It now struck the police as a real possibility that there were two Green River killers, one who dumped his victims in the river, and one who left them on land.

The first step was to investigate Amina Agisheff's background to find a potential killer. The next was to get the crime analysis unit to look back over the past ten years or so, to try to find earlier murders that might be linked to the series. Few mass murderers begin in full spate, so to speak; many have records for lesser sex crimes. The Green River killer might be caught by some earlier crime that had not been recognized as his handiwork . . . But, like so many other promising approaches, these led nowhere.

March 21, 1984, is a highly significant date in the Green River case. On that day, a man working on a sports field north of the airport recognized a bone in his dog's mouth as a human leg bone. A female skeleton was found in nearby bushes. Close by, a police bloodhound found a second skeleton. On that same day, 17-year-old Cindy Ann Smith, a topless dancer and prostitute, vanished, like so many other girls, while hitch-hiking along the Strip. There was one significant difference. As far as we know, Cindy Smith was the last victim of the Green River Killer.

In mid-March of the following year, 1985, the head of the Green River Task Force announced what the general public had guessed for many months: that the murders seemed to have ceased.

But the investigation continued in top gear. By midsummer, Seattle police suspected that the Green River killer had moved south to Portland, Oregon, just over the state border from Washington. Four young prostitutes had vanished; their bodies were found in remote and lonely areas. Then, on July 14, 1985, a young prostitute named Lottie was held at knifepoint by a pudgy customer who bound and blindfolded her, and drove her in his van down the freeway. Desperation gave her the strength to gnaw through her bonds; she tried to grab the knife and the van went into a ditch. Passing drivers seized the abductor. He proved to be Richard Terry Horton, a navy veteran. Triumphant detectives were convinced they had the Green River killer; but Horton's record showed he had been at sea during many of the Green River murders. He was sentenced to two years for kidnapping.

In January 1985, following the discovery of two skeletons near the Mountain View Cemetery, Captain Adamson allowed himself the optimistic prediction that the killer would be caught in 1986. He clearly had a suspect in mind. On February 6, a trapper named Ernest McLean was arrested. He had a record for burglary, and police survey teams had followed him to many spots where human bones had been found. But McLean insisted that he had been in these places merely to trap animals for their fur. When a lie-detector test indicated his innocence, he was released. In May 1986, the resources of the Green River Task Force were severely cut.

In September 1987, Seattle newspapers asked: "Is the Green River Killer Back?" Sixteen-year-old Rosie Kurran, a "mixed-up youngster" who had been given up by her parents as uncontrollable, left home on August 26, and vanished. Her body was found in a plastic bag in a ditch a week later. In November and December, two more girls, 14-year-old Debbie Gonsales and 24-year-old Dorothea Prestleigh, also vanished. The police declined to put these women on the list of Green River victims. And, to their relief, time seemed to prove them correct.

December 7, 1988, was another crucial date in the Green River case. On that evening, a two-hour TV documentary on the killings was broadcast: *Murder Live: A Chance to End the Nightmare*. The public was asked to ring in with information; within minutes of the start of the program, the switchboard was deluged; in two days, a hundred thousand people had called. It looked as if, once again, the investigation was going to be swamped with too many suspects.

One of these tips stood out above the rest. In 1981, a man named William Jay Stevens II, serving a sentence for burglary, had walked out of an open prison, and vanished. It seemed that he had spent much of that time in Spokane, Washington. He had a degree in psychology, had been in the Military Police, and was known to have an obsession about police insignia and uniforms. (It had been suggested many times that the Green River killer may have enticed his victims away by posing as a police officer.)

A check by the Spokane police on Stevens' whereabouts during the period of the Green River murders seemed to confirm that he *could* be the killer. On January 9, 1989, Stevens was arrested at his parents' home in Spokane. Police seized a large number of firearms, a box full of photographs of nude women, several driving licenses and credit cards under false names, as well as stolen credit cards. Former friends of Stevens testified that he had frequented the red-light areas of Seattle and shown a deep interest in the Green River case. When stolen items of police equipment were also found, neither the police nor the media had any doubt that Stevens was the Green River Killer. He had even bought a house in Tigard—with stolen money—near which remains of two dead women were found.

The euphoria began to collapse when a study of Stevens' credit cards revealed that he was undoubtedly elsewhere at the time of some of the murders. It was still, of course, possible that he might have been guilty of the others. But in October 1989, Captain Bob Evans, the new commander of the Task Force, announced that he had cleared Stevens of involvement in the Green River murders.

Seven and a half years after the murders began, the police had admitted that the expenditure of $12 million, interviews with 15,000 suspects, and the use of a $200,000 computer had left them virtually where they had been at the beginning— when a careless news broadcast had destroyed the main hope of catching the killer in the act.

The anticlimax pleased nobody; but there was at least one consolation: the activities of this sexual predator had turned the Seattle police department into one of the most efficient and up-to-date in the United States.

After Corll, Gacy, Lake and the Green River Killer, it seemed unlikely that any American sex killer would ever again produce quite the same effect of shock on the American psyche. But in 1991, a 31-year-old white male disproved that notion with a series of murders that revived disturbing memories of the Wisconsin necrophile Ed Gein.

On the evening of July 22, as a police patrol car was cruising along 25th Street, Milwaukee, a cry of "Help!" made the driver brake to an abrupt halt. A slim black man was running towards them, and a handcuff was dangling from his left wrist. His relief when he saw the police car was almost hysterical, and the tale he babbled out sounded so extraordinary that the officers had difficulty in following it. All they could gather was that a madman had been trying to kill him. The policemen climbed out of the car and accompanied the man—who gave his name as Tracy Edwards—to the white low-rise building called Oxford Apartments, a rooming house occupied almost exclusively by blacks.

The tall, good-looking young man who answered the door of room 213 had sandy hair and was white. As he stood aside politely to let them in, he seemed perfectly calm, and looked at Edwards as if he had never seen him before. Both policemen had a feeling that this was a false alarm—until they smelt the unpleasant odor of decay, not unlike bad fish, that pervaded the apartment.

When they asked the man—who gave his name as Jeffrey Dahmer—why he had threatened Tracy Edwards, he looked contrite, and explained that he had just lost his job, and had been drinking. They asked him for the key to the handcuff, and Dahmer suddenly looked nervous and tried to stall. When they insisted, his calm vanished, and he suddenly became hysterical. There was a brief struggle, and another resident heard one of the policemen say: "The son of a bitch scratched me." Moments later, Dahmer was face down on the floor in handcuffs, and his rights were being read to him.

The policeman called headquarters on his portable radio, and asked them to run a check on the prisoner; the answer came back quickly: Dahmer had a felony conviction for sexual assault and for enticing a 13-year-old boy.

That supported the story that Edwards—now able to speak calmly—went on to tell them. The 32-year-old Edwards, a recent arrival from Mississippi, had met Dahmer about four hours ago in a shopping mall in Grand Avenue. He had accepted Dahmer's invitation to go back to his apartment for a party.

Edwards did not like the smell of Dahmer's small apartment, nor the male pin-ups on the walls—his own preference was for women. But he was fascinated by a fish tank containing Siamese fighting fish. Dahmer told him he liked to watch them fighting, and that the combat invariably ended with one of them dead. They sat on the settee and drank beer, then rum and coke. Edwards found himself feeling oddly sleepy. But when Dahmer tried to embrace him, Edwards suddenly came awake and announced that he was going.

Seconds later, a handcuff had snapped around one of his wrists. He began to struggle, and Dahmer's attempt to handcuff the other cuff was unsuccessful. And for the next hour, Edwards sat on Dahmer's bed and watched a video of *The Exorcist*, while Dahmer held a large butcher's knife against his chest.

Finally Dahmer grew tired of the video and told Edwards that he intended to cut his heart out and eat it. But first he was going to strip Edwards and take some photographs . . . As Dahmer stood up to get the camera, the prisoner seized his opportunity; he swung his right fist in a punch that knocked Dahmer sideways; then he kicked him in the stomach and ran for the door. Dahmer caught him up there, and offered to unlock the handcuff; Edwards ignored him, wrenched open the door, and fled for his life . . .

When Edwards had finished telling his story, he was told to wait outside in the hallway, which was crowded with curious neighbors. As they tried to peer into the room, one of them saw a policeman open the door of the refrigerator, and gasp: "There's a goddamn head in here."

That was the moment Dahmer began to scream—a horrible, unearthly scream like an animal. One of the policemen rushed downstairs for shackles. When the writhing body was secure, the two policemen began their search of the apartment.

Within minutes, they realized that they had discovered a mixture of a slaughterhouse and torture chamber. The freezer compartment of the refrigerator contained meat in plastic bags, one of which looked ominously like a human heart. Another freezer contained three plastic bags, each one with a severed head inside. A filing cabinet contained three skulls—some painted grey—and some bones; a box contained two more skulls, and an album full of more gruesome photographs. Two more skulls were found in a kettle, while another contained some severed hands and a male genital organ. The blue plastic barrel proved to contain three male torsos. An electric saw stained with blood made it clear how Dahmer had dismembered his victims. There was also a large vat of acid.

Journalists and TV crews were soon outside the apartment, and before midday, the people of America had learned that Milwaukee was the scene of the latest outbreak of homosexual serial murder. According to Dahmer, who confessed freely soon after his arrest, he had killed less than Dean Corll or John Gacy—only seventeen. But then, there was a major difference; Dahmer was a cannibal. The plastic bags of meat in the freezer were intended to be eaten. He described how he had fried the biceps of one victim in vegetable oil. The threat to eat Tracy Edwards' heart had been no bluff. Dahmer had little food in the apartment but potato chips, human meat and a jar of mustard.

Back at police headquarters, Dahmer was obviously relieved to be co-operating; he seemed glad that his career of murder was over. The police learned how, as a child, he had been fascinated by dissecting animals. Then, when he was 18 years old, in 1978, he had killed his first male victim, a hitch-hiker, then masturbated over the body. It had been almost ten years before he committed his next murder. But recently, the rate of killing had accelerated—as it often does with serial killers—and there had been no fewer than three murders in the last two weeks. He had attempted to kill Tracy Edwards only three days after his last murder.

Dahmer was also able to help the police towards establishing the identities of the victims—which included twelve blacks, one Laotian, one Hispanic and three whites. Some of their names he remembered; the police had to work out the identities of others from identity cards found in Dahmer's reeking apartment, and from photographs shown to parents of missing youths.

All Dahmer's confessions were sensational; but the story of one teenage victim was so appalling that it created outrage around the world. Fourteen-year-old Laotian Konerak Sinthasomphone had met Dahmer in front of the same shopping mall where the killer was later to pick up Tracy Edwards; the boy agreed to return to Dahmer's apartment to allow him to take a couple of photographs.

Unknown to Konerak, Dahmer was the man who had enticed and sexually assaulted his elder brother three years earlier. Dahmer had asked the 13-year-old boy back to his apartment in September 1988, and had slipped a powerful sleeping draught into his coffee then fondled him sexually. Somehow, the boy succeeded in staggering out into the street and back home. The police were notified, and Dahmer was charged with second-degree sexual assault and sentenced to a year in a correction program, which allowed him to continue to work in a chocolate factory.

Now the younger brother Konerak found himself in the same apartment. He was also given drugged coffee, and then, when he was unconscious, stripped and raped. After that, Dahmer went out to buy some beer—he had been a heavy drinker since schooldays. On his way back to the apartment, Dahmer saw, to his horror, that his naked victim was talking to two black teenage girls, obviously begging for help. Dahmer hurried up and tried to grab the boy; the girls clung to him. One of them succeeded in ringing the police, and two squad cars arrived within minutes. Three irritable police officers wanted to know what the trouble was about.

When Dahmer told them that the young man was his lover, that they lived together in the nearby apartments, and that they had merely had a quarrel, the policemen were inclined to believe him—he looked sober and Konerak looked drunk. So they left the youth in Dahmer's apartment, to be strangled, violated and dismembered.

Back at District Three station house, the three policemen made their second mistake of the evening—they joked about the homosexual quarrel they had just broken up. But a tape recorder happened to be switched on, and when Dahmer was arrested two months later, and admitted to killing the Laotian boy, the tape was located and played on radio and television.

The public outcry that followed was not due simply to the tragic mistake made by three policemen. It was also because they had apparently preferred to believe Dahmer because he was white, and ignored Konerak because he was colored—at least, that is how Milwaukee's non-whites saw it. It had also been remarked that when Dahmer had been arrested, TV cameramen had been requested not to take pictures; someone in the crowd had shouted that if he had been black, they would have allowed the cameras down his throat. Again, when Dahmer appeared in court for the first time on July 25, he was dressed in his own clothes, not in the orange prison uniform; this again was seen as deliberately favoring a white. The Dahmer case caused an unpleasant build-up of racial tension in Milwaukee, and police crossed their fingers that nothing would ignite race riots. Fortunately, nothing did.

The twelve charges read out in court all concerned men who had been murdered since Dahmer had moved into the Oxford Apartments in March 1988. But according to Dahmer, his first murder had taken place thirteen years earlier, at the home in Bath Township, in north-eastern Ohio, where he had grown up and gone to school. At the time, his parents were in the process of a bitter and messy divorce, both alleging cruelty and neglect. Jeffrey had already learned to take refuge in alcohol.

According to Dahmer's confession, he had found himself alone in the family house at 4480 West Bath Road; his father had already left, and his mother and younger brother David were away visiting relatives. He had been left with no money, and very little food in the broken refrigerator. That evening, he explained, he decided to go out and look for some company.

It was not hard to find. A 19-year-old white youth, who had spent the day at a rock concert, was hitch-hiking home to attend his father's birthday party. When an ancient Oldsmobile driven by someone who looked about his own age pulled up, the boy climbed in. They went back to Dahmer's house and drank some beer, and talked about their lives. Dahmer found he liked his new friend immensely. But when the boy looked at the clock and said he had to go, Dahmer begged him to stay. The boy refused. So Dahmer picked up a dumbbell, struck him on the head, then strangled him. He then dragged the body to the crawl space under the house, and dismembered it with a carving knife. It sounds an impossible task for an 18-year-old, but Dahmer was not without experience—he had always had a morbid interest in dismembering animals.

He had wrapped up the body parts in plastic bags. But after a few days, the smell began to escape. Dahmer's mother was due back soon, and was sure to notice the stench. He took the plastic bags out to the wood under cover of darkness and managed to dig a shallow grave—the soil was rock-hard. But even with the bags now underground, he still worried—children might notice the grave. So he dug them up again, stripped the flesh from the bones, and smashed up bones with a sledgehammer. He scattered them around the garden, and the property next door. When his mother returned a few days later, there was nothing to reveal that her son was now a killer.

Unfortunately, Dahmer was unable to recall the name of his victim. The Milwaukee police telephoned the police of Bath Township and asked them if they had a missing person case that dated from mid-1978. They had. On June 18, a youth named Stephen Mark Hicks had left his home in Coventry Township to go to a rock concert. Friends had driven him there, and they agreed to rendezvous with him that evening to take him home. Hicks failed to turn up at the meeting place, and no trace of him was ever found. The family had offered a reward for information, hired a private detective, and even consulted a psychic.

The Bath Township police had two photographs of Stephen Hicks on file. When shown these, Dahmer said casually: "Yes, that's him."

In the crawl space under the house, a blood-detecting chemical called Luminol caused certain spots to glow in the dark; these proved to be human blood. Luminol sprayed on a concrete block caused a bloody handprint to appear. The following day, more bones and three human teeth were found. Dental records eventually revealed that they had belonged to Stephen Hicks.

Dahmer's first murder was the most difficult to confirm. The remaining sixteen were much easier.

For nine years after killing Stephen Hicks, Dahmer kept his homicidal impulses under control. A period of three years in the army had ended with a discharge for drunkenness. After a short stay in Florida, he had moved in with his grandmother Catherine, in West Allis, south of Milwaukee. But he was still drinking heavily, and was in trouble with the police for causing a disturbance in a bar. His family was relieved when he at last found himself a job—in the Ambrosia Chocolate Company in Milwaukee.

Dahmer soon discovered Milwaukee's gay bars, where he became known as a monosyllabic loner. But it was soon observed that he had a more sinister habit. He would sometimes engage a fellow customer in conversation, and offer him a drink. These drinking companions often ended up in a drugged coma. Yet Dahmer's intention was clearly not to commit rape. He seemed to want to try out his drugs as a kind of experiment, to see how much he had to administer, and how fast they worked. But other patrons noticed, and when one of Dahmer's drinking companions ended up unconscious in the hospital, the owner of Club Bath Milwaukee told him that he was barred.

On September 8, 1986, two 12-year-old boys reported to the police that Dahmer had exposed himself to them and masturbated. Dahmer alleged that he had merely been urinating. He was sentenced to a year on probation, and told his probation officers, with apparent sincerity: "I'll never do it again." (Judges and probation officers were later to note that Dahmer had a highly convincing manner of donning the sackcloth and ashes.) This period ended on September 9, 1987.

A year of good behavior had done nothing to alleviate Dahmer's psychological problems; on the contrary, they had built up resentment and frustration. Six days after his probation ended, the frustration again exploded into murder. On September 15, Dahmer was drinking at a gay hang-out called Club 219, and met a 24-year-old man called Stephen Tuomi. They decided to go to bed, and adjourned to the Ambassador Hotel, where they took a room that cost $43.88 for the night. Dahmer claims that he cannot recall much of that night, admitting that they drank themselves into a stupor. When Dahmer woke up, he says Tuomi was dead, with blood coming from his mouth, and strangulation marks on his throat.

Alone in the hotel room with a corpse, and the desk clerk likely to investigate whether the room had been vacated at any moment, Dahmer solved the problem by going out and buying a large suitcase, into which he stuffed the body. Then he got a taxi to take him to his grandmother's house in West Allis, where he had his own basement flat. There he dismembered it, and stuffed the parts into plastic bags which, like Dennis Nilsen, he put out for garbage collection.

As a result of the murder of Stephen Tuomi, Dahmer seems to have acknowledged that murder was, in fact, what he needed to satisfy his deviant sexual impulse. The fifteen murders that followed leave no possible doubt about it.

These took place between January 16, 1988, and July 19, 1991. The method was usually much the same: Dahmer picked up a male—usually black—and invited him back to his apartment. There the victim was offered a drugged drink, after which he was violated and killed—mostly by strangulation, although Dahmer later began using a knife. The body was dismembered; parts of it were stored for eating, and the rest left out for the garbageman.

In September 1988, Catherine Dahmer had finally decided she could no longer put up with the smells and her grandson's drunkenness. On September 25, Dahmer moved into an apartment at 808 N. 24th Street.

There can be no doubt that Dahmer intended to use his new-found freedom to give full reign to his morbid sexual urges. But an unforeseen hitch occurred. Within twenty-four hours, the four-time murderer was in trouble with the police. On September 26, 1988, he met a 13-year-old Laotian boy named Sinthasomphone, lured him back to his apartment, and drugged him. But the elder brother of later victim Konerak somehow managed to escape, and Dahmer was charged with sexual assault and enticing a child for immoral purposes. He spent a week in prison, then was released on bail. On January

30, 1990, he was found guilty; the sentence would be handed out four months later.

But even the possibility of a long prison sentence could not cure Dahmer of his obsessive need to kill and dismember. When he appeared in court to be sentenced on May 23, 1989, he had already claimed his fifth victim. But Dahmer's lawyer Gerald Boyle argued that the assault on the Laotian boy was a one-off offense, and would never happen again. Dahmer himself revealed considerable skill as an actor in representing himself as contrite and self-condemned. "I am an alcoholic and a homosexual with sexual problems." He described his appearance in court as a "nightmare come true," declared that he was now a changed man, and ended by begging the judge: "Please don't destroy my life." Judge William Gardner was touched by the appeal. This clean-cut boy obviously needed help, and there was no psychiatric help available in prison. So he sentenced Dahmer to five years on probation, and a year in a House of Correction, where he could continue to work at the chocolate factory during the day.

From the Community Correctional Center in Milwaukee, Dahmer addressed a letter to Judge Gardner, stating: "I have always believed a man should be willing to assume responsibility for the mistakes he makes in life. The world has enough misery in it without my adding more to it. Sir, I assure you that it will never happen again. That is why, Judge Gardner, I am requesting a sentence modification."

Dahmer was released from the Correctional Center two months early—on March 2, 1990. Eleven days later, he moved into the Oxford Apartments, and began the murder spree that ended with his arrest eighteen months later. In that time he killed twelve more young men.

Dahmer's career of slaughter almost came to an abrupt end on July 8, 1990; it was on that day that he made the mistake of varying his method. He approached a 15-year-old Hispanic boy outside a gay bar, and offered him $200 to pose for nude photographs. The boy returned to room 213 and removed his clothes. But instead of offering him the usual drugged drink, Dahmer picked up a rubber mallet and hit him on the head. It failed to knock him unconscious, and the boy fought back as Dahmer tried to strangle him. Somehow, the boy succeeded in calming his attacker. And, incredibly, Dahmer allowed him to go, even calling a taxi.

The boy had promised not to notify the police. But when he was taken to the hospital for treatment, he broke his promise. For a few moments, Dahmer's future hung in the balance. But when the boy begged them not to allow his foster parents to find out that he was homosexual, the police decided to do nothing about it.

When he saw his probation officer, Donna Chester, the next day, Dahmer looked depressed and unshaven. He said he had money problems and was thinking of suicide. She wanted to know how he could have money problems when he was earning $1,5000 a month, and his apartment cost less than $300 a month. He muttered something about hospital bills. And during the whole of the next month, Dahmer continued to complain of depression and stomach pains, and to talk about jumping off a high building. Donna Chester suggested that he ought to find himself another apartment in a less run-down area. She was unaware that Dahmer was an addict who now urgently needed a fix of his favorite drug: murder.

It happened a few weeks later, on September 3, 1990. In front of a bookstore on Twenty-seventh, Dahmer picked up a young black dancer named Ernest Miller, who was home from Chicago, where he intended to start training at a dance school in the autumn. They had sex in Apartment 213, then Dahmer offered him a drugged drink, and watched him sink into oblivion. Perhaps because he had not killed for three months, Dahmer's craving for violence and its nauseating aftermath was stronger than usual. Instead of strangling his victim, Dahmer cut his throat. He decided that he wanted to keep the skeleton, so after cutting the flesh from the bones, and dissolving most of it in acid, he bleached the skeleton with acid. He also kept the biceps, which he put in the freezer.

Neighbors were beginning to notice the smell of decaying flesh; some of them knocked on Dahmer's door to ask about it. Dahmer would explain politely that his fridge was broken and that he was waiting to get it fixed.

On March 25, there occurred an event that psychiatrists believe may be responsible for the final spate of multiple murder. It was on that day that Dahmer's mother Joyce contacted him for the first time in five years. Joyce Dahmer—now Flint—was working as an AIDS counselor in Freso, California, and it may have been her contact with homosexuals that led her to telephone her son. She spoke openly about his homosexuality—for the first time—and told him she loved him. The call was a good idea—or would have been if she had made it a few years earlier.

But Dahmer was nearing the end of his tether, and even drink could not anesthetize him for long. Neighbors kept complaining about the smell, and he solved this by buying a 57-gallon drum of concentrated hydrochloric acid, and disposing of some of the body parts that were causing the trouble. All this meant he was frequently late for work, or even absent. On July 15, 1991, the Ambrosia Chocolate Company finally grew tired of his erratic behavior and fired him.

His reaction was typical. The same day he picked up a 24-year-old black named Oliver Lacy, took him back to his apartment, and gave him a drugged drink. After strangling him, he sodomized the body.

But the murder spree was almost over. Four days later, the head of the final victim joined the others in the freezer. He was 25-year-old Joseph Brandeholt, an out-of-work black who was hoping to move from Minnesota to Milwaukee with his wife and two children. But he accepted Dahmer's offer of money for photographs, and willingly joined in oral sex in Room 213. After that, he was drugged, strangled and dismembered. His body was placed in the barrel of acid, which was swiftly turning into a black, sticky mess.

That Dahmer's luck finally ran out may have been due to the carelessness that leads to the downfall of so many multiple murderers. The last intended victim, Tracy Edwards, was a slightly built man, and should have succumbed to the drug like all the others. For some reason, he failed to do so; it seems most likely that Dahmer failed to administer a large enough dose. Equally puzzling is the fact that, having seen that the drug had failed to work, he allowed Edwards to live, and spent two hours watching a video with him. Was the homicidal impulse finally burning itself out? Dahmer knew that if he failed to kill Tracy Edwards, he would be caught; yet, with a large knife in his hand, he allowed him to escape from the apartment.

It sounds as if he recognized that the time had come to try to throw off the burden of guilt and rejoin the human race.

On January 27, 1992, Wisconsin's worst mass murderer came to trial in Milwaukee before Judge Lawrence Gram, entering a plea of guilty but insane. On February 15, the jury rejected this plea and found Dahmer guilty of the fifteen murders with which he had been charged. He was sentenced to fifteen terms of life imprisonment.

On April 14, 1992, just two months after Dahmer was sentenced, another trial—this time in Russia—drew the attention of the world's press. The accused was a 48-year-old grandfather named Andrei Chikatilo, and he was charged with the murders of fifty-three women and children.

On December 24, 1978, the mutilated body of 9-year-old

Lena Zakotnova was found in the Grushevka River where it flows through the Soviet mining city of Shakhti. It had been tied in a sack and dumped in the water some forty-eight hours before its discovery. She had been sexually assaulted and partially throttled, and her lower torso had been ripped open by multiple knife wounds.

Lena was last seen after leaving school on the afternoon of her death. A woman named Burenkova reported seeing a girl of Lena's description talking to a middle-aged man at a nearby tram stop, and they walked away together.

The Shakhti police soon arrested a suspect. Aleksandr Kravchenko had been in prison for a similar murder in the Crimea. He had been too young to be executed, so served six years of a ten-year sentence. He had been a prime suspect from the beginning of the investigation and when he was caught attempting a burglary the police decided to charge him with the murder.

Unconcerned at the fact that Kravchenko was only twenty-five, not "middle-aged," the Shakhti police soon extracted a confession. In the dock Kravchenko insisted that it had been beaten out of him, but this carried little weight with the judge (Soviet trials had no juries; a judge both decided guilt and passed sentence). Kravchenko was found guilty and sentenced to fifteen years in a labor camp.

There was a public outcry at the leniency of the sentence, and the prosecution, as allowed in Soviet law, appealed to increase it to death. A new judge agreed and Kravchenko was executed by a single shot in the back of the head in 1984. By that time the real killer of Lena Zakotnova had murdered at least sixteen other women and children.

Born in the Ukrainian farm village of Yablochnoye on October 6, 1936, Andrei Romanovich Chikatilo was soon well acquainted with death. Stalin, in his drive to communize the peasantry, had reduced the Ukraine to a chaos of starvation and fear. In his first ten years, Chikatilo witnessed as much state-condoned brutality and killing as any soldier.

When he was 5 years old, Chikatilo's mother told him about the disappearance of one of his cousins, seven years previously, and that she believed he had been kidnapped and eaten. The gruesome story made a deep impression on Chikatilo. For years afterwards, he later admitted, he would brood on the story and recreate his cousin's sufferings in his imagination. There can be no doubt that this strongly influenced his sexual development.

Chikatilo's father was called up early in the Second World War and did not return until after the Nazi defeat. But his father's return brought little comfort for the family. Roman Chikatilo had been captured by the Germans and the paranoid Stalin considered returning prisoners of war as virtual traitors to communism. Roman Chikatilo found that he had to tread carefully to avoid the suspicions of the secret police—very little stood between him and a firing squad.

Oddly enough, 10-year-old Andrei Chikatilo agreed with Joseph Stalin and was deeply ashamed of his father. He was a devout communist and his father's survival was a constant source of humiliation. He found relief by escaping into the world of literature.

He was fascinated by a novel called *Molodaya Gvardiya* or *The Young Guard* which concerned the heroic exploits of a group of young Russian partisans fighting the Germans in the vast Soviet forests and eventually dying to a man, proclaiming loyalty to Stalin. A predictably bloody tale, it also contained several scenes in which prisoners were tortured for information. This positive, even heroic depiction of torture in isolated woodland made a deep impression on the child.

At school Chikatilo had few friends and was painfully shy. He was nicknamed *Baba*—meaning woman—because he had chubby breasts and lived in terror that his chronic bed-wetting and short-sightedness would be discovered by his classmates. His weak sight was something of an obsession with him and it was not until he was 30 that he eventually obtained a pair of glasses, so keen was he to conceal the defect.

As he grew into his teens, his chubbiness turned to size and strength—his new nickname was "Andrei Sila" meaning Andrew the Strong. Classmates remembered him as a voracious reader with a prodigious memory. At 16 he became editor of the school newspaper and was appointed as student agitator for political information; a post which required him to read out and explain the articles in *Pravda* and other Party news organs. Even so, his fervor was restricted to politics. He found it almost impossible to communicate socially, especially with the opposite sex.

At 18, he applied for a place in Moscow University to study Law. He was humiliated when he failed the entrance exams and blamed his father's war record. This was typical of Chikatilo; all his life he would blame his failures on others.

Overcoming his shyness with women he attempted several relationships, but they all failed. His major problem was a conviction that he was impotent. Like a lot of teenage boys, he was so scared during his first attempts at sex that he failed to achieve an erection. As the years went on he became convinced that he was incapable of a normal sex life. Addicted to solitary masturbation, he despaired of ever having a happy sex life.

It was during his national service that he first experienced orgasm with a girl, and that was because she suddenly decided that things were going too far and tried to break his hold on her. She had no chance against his abnormal strength and he was surprised at the sexual passion her struggles aroused in him. He held her for only a few moments before releasing her unharmed, but had already ejaculated into his trousers. Thinking about it afterwards he realized that it was her fear and his power over her that had excited him so much. He had started to find sex and violence a stimulating concoction.

In the years following his national service he moved out of the Ukraine, east to Russia, where job prospects and the standard of living were better. He found work as a telephone engineer and a room in Rodionovo-Nesvetayevsky, a small town just north of the large industrial city of Rostov. A short while afterwards his mother, father and sister came to live with him in this comparative luxury. His younger sister, Tatyana, was worried that he was not married at 27 and after several failed matchmaking attempts, introduced him to a 24-year-old girl called Fayina. Chikatilo was as shy as usual, but Fayina found this attractive. Things went well with the courtship and they were married in 1963.

He still thought of himself as impotent and made embarrassed excuses on their wedding night. A week later Fayina persuaded him to try again and, with some coaxing, the marriage was consummated. Even so, Chikatilo showed no enthusiasm for sex. His dammed sexual drives were by then pushing him in other, more unwholesome directions.

In 1971, he passed a correspondence degree course in Russian philology and literature from the Rostov university. With the new qualification, the 35-year-old Chikatilo embarked upon a fresh career as a teacher. He found that he lacked all aptitude for the work. His shyness encouraged the pupils either to ignore his presence or openly to mock him. Other members of staff disliked his odd manner and his tendency to self-pity, so he was virtually shunned by all. Yet he soon found himself enjoying the work as his sexual fantasies began to center around children.

Over the next seven years Chikatilo committed numerous indecent assaults on his pupils. Apart from voyeurism, these included surreptitious gropings, excessive beatings and, on one occasion, mouthing the genitals of a sleeping boy in a school dormitory. His sexual drive to dominate and control had centered on children as the easiest target and, as time went on, he developed a taste for fantasizing about sadism.

The oddest part of the situation was the inaction of the authorities. Chikatilo was forced to resign from several teaching jobs for his behavior, but his record remained spotless each time. In the Soviet teaching system the failure of one teacher reflected on his colleagues and superiors as well, so they simply passed him on and pretended that nothing had happened.

In 1978, the Chikatilos and their two children moved to the town of Shakhti. Fayina had heard the rumors of his sexual misdemeanors, but had chosen to ignore them. He behaved quite normally towards their own son and daughter, aged 9 and 11, and she was unable to believe that a man who could barely produce one erection a month could marshal the sexual energy to be a pervert.

Chikatilo now bought an old shack in the slum end of town and began to invite down-and-out young women back with offers of food and vodka. There he would request them to perform sexual acts—notably fellatio—that he would never have requested from his strait-laced wife. He would often be unable to achieve erection, but this seemed to matter less with the kind of derelicts who accepted his invitation. Yet his real interest remained pre-pubescent children, and on December 22, 1978, he persuaded one to follow him to his shack.

Lena Zakotnova had caught his eyes as soon as he saw her waiting at the tram stop. He had sidled up to her and started chatting. She soon revealed to the grandfatherly stranger that she desperately needed to go to the toilet and he persuaded her to follow him to his shack.

Once through the door he dropped his kindly facade and started to tear at her clothes. Muffling her screams by choking her with his forearm he blindfolded her with her scarf and tried to rape her. Once again he failed to achieve an erection, but ejaculated anyway. In an ecstasy he pushed his semen into her with his fingers and ruptured her hymen. The sight of the blood caused him to orgasm again and filled him with sexual excitement. Pulling out a pocket knife he stabbed at her repeatedly, tearing open her whole lower torso. When he returned to his senses he felt terrified—he knew he would face the death sentence if caught. Wrapping the corpse in a few sacks he crept outside, crossed the street and a stretch of wasteland and dropped Lena in the fast-flowing Grushevka River. The autopsy later showed that she was still alive when she hit the water.

After watching the bundle float away, Chikatilo went home. But in his agitation he forgot to turn off the light in the shack. His neighbors on the slum street had not seen the pair arrive or heard Lena's muffled screams. However, one of them did note that Chikatilo's light had been left on all night and mentioned it to a policeman asking questions from door to door. Chikatilo was called in for questioning.

The police soon guessed that the sullen teacher was using the shack for assignations, but this was not incriminating in itself. What interested them was the fact that some very young girls had been seen entering and leaving with Chikatilo, and a few enquiries at his old schools had revealed his taste for pedophilia.

He was called in for questioning nine times in all. Then the police transferred their attention to Kravchenko. They did not even examine the shack for traces of blood.

Chikatilo continued teaching until 1981, when staff cuts made him redundant. On September 3, 1981, six months after losing his job, he killed again.

He was now working as a supply clerk for a local industrial conglomerate. This involved traveling around, often to the other side of the country, to obtain the necessary parts and supplies to run the Shakhti factory.

It would undoubtedly have been better if Chikatilo had remained a schoolteacher. In a restricted environment his opportunities would have been confined. The new job allowed him to travel, and spend as much time as he liked doing it. Now he was free to hunt as he willed.

He met Larisa Tkachenko at a bus stop outside the Rostov public library. She was a 17-year-old absentee from boarding school who was used to exchanging the odd fling for a nice meal and a drink or two. Her usual dates were young soldiers, but when the middle-aged man asked if she wanted to go to a local recreation area she agreed without much hesitation.

After a short walk they found themselves on a gravel path leading through a deserted stretch of woodland. Away from possible onlookers Chikatilo could not keep his hands off her any longer. He threw her down and started to tear at her trousers. Although she almost certainly expected to have sex with him, this was too frightening for her and she started to fight back. His already overstretched self-control snapped and he bludgeoned her with his heavy fists in an ecstasy of sadosexual release. To stifle her cries he rammed earth into her mouth then choked her to death. He bit off one of her nipples as he ejaculated over the corpse.

This time he did not come back to earth with a jolt as he had after killing Lena Zakotnova. He ran around the corpse waving her clothes and howling with joy. He later said, "I felt like a partisan," a reference to his childhood favorite *The Young Guard*. After half an hour he calmed down, covered Larisa's corpse with some branches and hid her clothes. She was found the next day, but no clues to the identity of the killer were discovered.

The murder of Lena Zakotnova had made Chikatilo aware of the basic nature of his desires; the murder of Larisa

Tkachenko made him aware that he was destined to go on killing.

All serial killers seem to cross this mental Rubicon. The initial horror and guilt gives way to an addiction to hunting that transcends all social and moral boundaries. They never seem to break the habit; once hooked, they continue until they are caught or die.

Ten months later, on June 12, 1982, Chikatilo killed again. Thirteen-year-old Lyuba Biryuk left her home in the little settlement of Zaplavskaya to get some shopping from the nearby village of Donskoi Posyulok. She was last seen alive waiting at a local bus stop, but apparently decided to walk home in the warm sunshine. Chikatilo fell in step with her and started a conversation. Children always found his manner reassuring, but as soon as they came to a secluded stretch of path he attacked and tried to rape her. Failing as usual, he pulled a knife from his pocket and stabbed wildly at her until her struggles and screams ceased. He covered her body, hid her clothes and shopping in the undergrowth and escaped unobserved. She was found two weeks later. In the heat of the southern Russian summer she had decayed to no more than a skeleton.

Chikatilo killed six more times that year: once in July, twice in August, twice in September and once in December. Four of these were girls ranging in age from 10 to 19 but the other two were boys, aged 15 and 9. This bisexual choice of victims would confuse the police investigation later on. Indeed, in the early stages of linking the murders some of the boys were officially classified as girls (despite their male names) because officers could not believe the killer could be attracted to both sexes.

In fact, as any criminal psychologist could have told them, the sex of the victims was almost immaterial. Chikatilo wanted to be in total control of his victims. Boys served his purpose as well as girls. His need to revenge himself on a world he hated and resented pushed him further from the norm, and killing boys was a way of being even more wicked.

Most of these victims were killed in the Rostov region, but two he killed on his business trips to other republics. Even when the majority of his victims had been linked into one investigation, these, and others killed outside the Rostov district, were not connected until Chikatilo himself confessed to them. A police force with more experience of serial crime would have quickly noted a linking pattern in the murders. All the victims were children or teenagers who had somehow been lured to secluded, usually wooded areas. They had been savagely attacked, sexually assaulted and usually butchered with a long bladed knife. Most strikingly, in almost every case, wounds were found around the eyes of the victim.

After killing a 10-year-old girl called Olya Stalmachenok on December 11, 1982, Chikatilo lay low once again. His next murder did not take place until mid-June 1983: a 15-year-old Armenian girl called Laura Sarkisyan. Her body was never found and the murder only came to light when Chikatilo confessed years later.

The next month he met a 13-year-old girl in the Rostov train station. He recognized her as Ira Dunenkova, the little sister of one of his casual girlfriends from teaching days. It was obviously a risk to approach somebody who could—even tenuously—be linked to himself, but from her ragged clothes he quickly realized that she had become one of the innumerable vagrants that haunted every Soviet city, despite their official non-existence. Taking a chance that she might not be missed for some time, if ever, he persuaded her to go for a walk with him in the nearby stretch of heath called Aviators' Park. Reaching a quiet spot he tried to have sex with her and, failing to get an erection, he used a more reliable instrument; a kitchen knife.

Chikatilo killed three more times that summer. On uncertain dates he killed Lyuda Kutsyuba, aged 24, and a woman aged between 18 and 25 whose identity has not been discovered. On August 8 he persuaded 7-year-old Igor Gudkov to follow him to Aviators' Park and then butchered him.

This brought his number of victims to fourteen, of which about half had been discovered by the police. Even for an area with a high—if unofficial—crime rate like Rostov, over half-a-dozen murdered children was enough to catch the attention of the central police authority in Moscow. A team of investigators was sent to assess the situation in September 1983. Their report was highly critical of the inept handling of the murders by the local police and concluded that six victims were definitely the work of one sexual deviant. The report was accepted and its suggestions quickly implemented, but, as was typical of the Soviet system, the public were not warned of the danger.

Shielded by public ignorance, Chikatilo killed three more people before the turn of the year: a 22-year-old woman called Valya Chuchulina and Vera Shevkun, a prostitute aged 19; and finally, on December 27, a 14-year-old boy called Sergei Markov, his seventeenth victim.

Nineteen-eighty-four was to prove the most terrible year in Chikatilo's murderous career. Between January and September he murdered fifteen women and children.

Shortly after the New Year, he was accused of stealing two rolls of linoleum from his factory and was sacked, but he soon found another supply clerk job in the middle of the teeming city of Rostov.

Chikatilo's method of hunting victims was time-consuming and, fortunately, rarely successful. He would hang around train stations, bus stops, airports and other public places, and would approach potential victims and strike up an innocuous conversation.

If they warmed to him he would offer them the bait. To children he would propose going to his home to watch videos (then and now a rare luxury in Russia). He might also make the same suggestion to young adults, or he might offer to take them, via a little-known short-cut, to some place they wanted to go. To vagrants or prostitutes he would simply offer vodka, food or money for sex in the woods.

Living near Rostov it had proved difficult to spend so much time hunting. Now, as he traveled, it was suddenly easier.

On January 9, he killed 17-year-old Natalya Shalapinina in Aviators' Park. Then on February 21, he killed a 44-year-old tramp called Marta Ryabyenko in almost exactly the same spot. On March 24, Chikatilo killed a 10-year-old girl, Dima Ptashnikov, just outside the town of Novoshakhtinsk. Nearby, police found a footprint in a patch of mud which they were convinced belonged to the murderer. It was little enough, but it was their first solid piece of forensic evidence, and it improved the flagging morale of the investigators.

In May 1984, Chikatilo took his greatest risk ever. Haunting the Rostov train station he bumped into an ex-girlfriend, Tanya Petrosyan, a 32-year-old divorcee whom he had not seen for six years. He invited her for a picnic, but she replied that she had no time then. Common sense dictated that he should have left it at that. If he made a date for a later time she might tell other people about it. Even so, he took her address.

A few days later he arrived at Tanya's house carrying a new doll for her 11-year-old daughter. He was also carrying a knife and a hammer. He later insisted that he had only wanted sex from Tanya, but he now carried his killing tools as a matter of habit. He found himself being introduced to Tanya's elderly mother, and was told that Sveta, the daughter, would have to go with them on the picnic.

They took a train to a nearby stretch of woodland. As Sveta played with her doll a little way off, Chikatilo and

Tanya undressed and started to have oral sex. After a while Chikatilo tried to enter Tanya, but failed. It was then that she made the greatest mistake of her life; she jeered at his inability. Seeing red, he grabbed the knife from his pocket and drove it into the side of her head. Then he beat her to a pulp with the hammer.

Hearing her mother's dying screams, Sveta tried to run away, but Chikatilo soon caught her. He knocked her down and then killed her with dozens of blows from the knife and hammer. The attack was so furious that he completely beheaded the little girl. Afterwards he dressed himself and caught the train home.

Tanya's mother was old and mentally subnormal. She waited for three days before contacting the police, and even then could not remember what the stranger had looked like. Once again, his luck had held.

He had now killed twenty-two, and over the next four months this rose to thirty-two. Most were in the Rostov area, but three he killed on business trips; two in Tashkent and one in Moscow. As usual his targets were of both sexes, aged between 11 and 24. He would have doubtless killed more that year, but at last his luck seemed to run out. He was arrested on suspicion of being the Rostov serial killer on September 14, 1984.

Inspector Aleksandr Zanasovski had questioned Chikatilo for acting suspiciously at the Rostov train station two weeks previously. On the evening of September 13, he spotted him again, this time across the square at the Rostov bus station. Again he noted that Chikatilo was trying to strike up conversations with young people with almost manic persistence.

Zanasovski followed Chikatilo until four the next morning. In that time they traveled backwards and forwards on various forms of public transport with no destination ever becoming apparent. Eventually, when Chikatilo appeared to receive oral sex from a young lady on a public bench, the inspector arrested him. In the briefcase that the suspect had carried all night the police found a jar of vaseline, a length of rope and a kitchen knife with an eight-inch blade.

Yet still Chikatilo's incredible luck held. When the forensic department tested his blood, the case fell apart.

The semen found on and around the victims proved to belong to a "secreter"; that is, a man who secretes minute amounts of blood into his spittle and semen. The tests had shown the killer to have "AB" blood—Chikatilo was type "A."

Despite this major setback, the investigators found it hard to believe that he was innocent. Under Soviet law they could only hold a suspect for a maximum of ten days without preferring charges, but they needed more time to build a case against him. They checked his previous record, learned about the theft of the two rolls of linoleum and booked him on that.

On December 12, 1984, Chikatilo was found guilty by the people's Court of the crime of Theft of State Property, and sentenced to a year of correctional labor. However, since he had already spent three months in jail, the judge waived the sentence.

On August 1, 1985, Chikatilo went back to killing. The victim was 18-year-old Natalya Pokhlistova, a mentally subnormal transient he met during a business trip to Moscow. They went off to a deserted spot and tried to have sex. When he failed he mutilated her with a knife then strangled her.

Chikatilo killed again that month. On August 27, 1986, he murdered Irina Gulyayeva. Like his last victim, she was an 18-year-old, mentally subnormal vagrant. He met her in Shakhti—the place where he killed for the very first time—and butchered her in the nearby woods. She was his thirty-fourth victim, and the last for a year and nine months.

On May 16, 1987, Chikatilo killed a 13-year-old boy called Oleg Makarenkov in Siberia.

He killed twice more in 1987, both in areas far from Rostov. The thirty-sixth victim was a 12-year-old boy called Ivan Bilovetski, killed in Chikatilo's native Ukraine on July 29. The thirty-seventh was Yura Tereshonok, aged 16, outside Leningrad on September 15.

Once again, he ceased killing for the winter months, perhaps because it was harder to get people to accompany him into snowbound woods. Some time in April 1988, he killed an unidentified woman in the Krasny region. Then, on May 14, he butchered 9-year-old Lyosha Voronko near the Ilovaisk train station in the Ukraine. His last victim that year, bringing the sum total to forty, was 15-year-old Zhenya Muratov, on July 14.

The following year, on March 1, 1989, he killed indoors for the second time. Tatyana Ryzhova, a 15-year-old runaway, was induced to follow Chikatilo to an apartment that belonged to his daughter, Ludmila. The place had been empty since Ludmila had divorced her husband and moved in with her parents. Chikatilo had the job of swapping it for two smaller apartments ("*swapping*" was the typical method of property dealing in the Soviet Union). It was a task he was in no hurry to complete since it provided the perfect place to bring prostitutes.

He gave the girl food and vodka, and tried to have sex with her. Soon she became restless and started to shout. Chikatilo tried to quiet her, but when she started to scream, he silenced her by stabbing her in the mouth. Some of the neighbors heard Tatyana's screams, but did nothing; wife-beating is a common occurrence in Russia.

When Chikatilo had ceased to mutilate Tatyana he realized his danger. Somehow he had to get her body out of the apartment without being seen. He was in a populated area and for all he knew the police might already be on their way.

He solved the problem by cutting off her head and legs and wrapping them in her clothes. Then he mopped the bloody floor and went out to steal a sled to remove the body. Finding one nearby, he set off into the night with Tatyana's remains firmly tied down.

All seemed to be going well until he tried to pull the sled over a rail-crossing and it stuck due to the thin snow cover. To his horror he saw a stranger walking toward him and wondered if he should either run or try to kill the witness. The man pulled level with him and, without a word, helped Chikatilo lift the burdened sled across the tracks, then went on his way. Tatayna's mutilated body was found stuffed into some nearby pines on March 9.

Chikatilo killed four more times that year. On May 11, he murdered 8-year-old Sasha Dyakonov in Rostov. Traveling to the Vladimir region to the northeast he killed 10-year-old Lyosha Moiseyev on May 11. In mid-August he killed Yelena Varga, aged 19, on another business trip, this time to the Rodionovo-Nesvetayevski region. Finally, he murdered Alyosha Khobotov on August 28.

He met 10-year-old Khobotov outside a video salon (a modern-day Russian equivalent of a movie house) in the town of Shakhti. The boy happily told him that he preferred horror movies above all others. Chikatilo replied that he owned a video machine and a large collection of horror videos. Alyosha jumped at his offer to view them.

Chikatilo led his victim through the local graveyard to a quiet spot where a shovel stood by an open grave. He had dug the trench himself some time earlier in a fit of suidical depression. Now, in a different mood, he bit out Alyosha's tongue, cut off his genitals and threw him into the pit. Then he filled in the grave.

On January 14, 1990, he murdered 11-year-old Andrei Kravchenko. As with the last victim, he picked up Andrei outside the Shakhti video salon by offering to show him horror movies. The following March 7, he persuaded a 10-year-old boy called Yaroslav Makarovto to follow him to a party. He led him into the Rostov Botanical Gardens, then molested and butchered him. His next victim was Lyubov Zuyeva, a 31-year-old mentally handicapped woman whom he met on a train to Shakhti sometime in April. He persuaded her to have sex with him in the woods, then stabbed her.

On July 28, he persuaded 13-year-old Vitya Petrov, waiting for a late train with his family at Rostov Station, to follow him to the Botanical Gardens. Once out of the sight of others, he stabbed the boy to death. Strangely enough, Chikatilo had tried to pick up Vitya's younger brother, Sasha, only a few hours earlier, but had been scolded away by the boys' mother. Chikatilo's fiftieth victim was 11-year-old Ivan Fomin, killed on a river beach in Novcherkassk on August 14. The corpse was found three days later.

Chikatilo temporarily now decided to make a journey to Moscow. For some months he had been involved in a petty dispute with some Assyrian builders over garages that had been built next to his son's house, blocking the light. Since his son was away doing his national service, Chikatilo had made strenuous complaints via official channels, but nothing had happened.

Growing increasingly paranoid, Chikatilo decided that some sort of illegal conspiracy was being directed against him, and in Moscow demanded audiences with both President Gorbachev and parliamentary head Anatoly Lukyanov. Needless to say he was granted neither, but stayed on for a few days in the "tent city" of protesters that had steadily grown outside the Kremlin since the introduction of glasnost. After that he had to return to work, so he packed up his tent and protest sign and went back to Rostov.

On October 17, 1990, he met a mentally handicapped 16-year-old called Vadim Gromov in the Novocherkassk train. He persuaded the young man to get off the train with him at the wooded station of Donleskhoz by offering to take him to a party. Gromov's body was found just over two weeks later, by which time Chikatilo had murdered again. This time the victim was 16-year-old Vitya Tishchenko, who disappeared after buying train tickets from the Shakhti station on the last day of October. He was found, mutilated, three days later.

Oddly enough, the investigators were beginning to feel more optimistic. For most of the inquiry, morale had been abysmal. They had always been undermanned and badly organized, and it had been easy for Chikatilo to play games with them. He would kill in Rostov, and when the police concentrated their manpower in that area, he would kill in Shakhti or Novocherkassk, throwing them into confusion.

Now, the killer was becoming careless. The woman in the Shakhti ticket office reported seeing a tall middle-aged man in dark glasses hanging around when Tishchenko bought the tickets. Her teenage daughter added that she had seen the same man trying to pick up a boy several days before. With this rough description and increased manpower, the investigation at last seemed to have a chance. If only the killer would return to one of his known murder locations they might get him before he murdered again.

This was exactly what Chikatilo did, but, once again, the police missed him. His fifty-third victim was a 22-year-old girl called Sveta Korostik, whom he killed in the woods outside Donleskhoz train station. Trying to double-guess the killer, only one policeman was posted there to check the identities of any suspicious persons alighting on the platform.

Sveta's body was found a week later. But when Sergeant Igor Rybakov, the officer on duty at the station on the day of

Sveta's murder, was questioned, an amazing fact emerged. He had interviewed a suspicious-looking man that day and had sent a report in, but, for some reason, it had not been processed.

Rybakov reported that at 4 p.m. on October 6, he had observed a large, mud-spattered, middle-aged man emerge from the forest and wash his hands in the dribble of water flowing from the platform fire hydrant. The sergeant would probably have ignored him, taking him for one of the many mushroom pickers that frequented the station, but noticed that he was wearing a grey suit, an odd attire for rain-soaked woods. He asked for identification, and was handed a passport that bore the name Andrei Romanovich Chikatilo. The man explained that he had been visiting a friend. The officer studied Chikatilo and noticed that his hand was bandaged and there was a streak of red liquid on his cheek. Nevertheless, he allowed him to board a train and leave.

Chikatilo's name was checked and the investigators learned of the Lena Zakotnova questioning, the pedophilia and the 1984 arrest. But for the fact that his blood group was wrong he would have been a prime suspect. It was at this point that somebody remembered a circular that had been sent around to all Soviet police departments. Japanese scientists had found that in one case in a million, the blood type secreted into the semen and the actual blood type can be different. It was just possible that Chikatilo might be such a person.

Chikatilo was placed under 24-hour surveillance, but the fear that he might commit another murder or commit suicide led the investigators to arrest him on November 20, 1990. He offered no resistance and came quietly. His semen type was tested and proved to be "AB"; the same as that found on the bodies of the victims.

Now certain they had the right man, the police wanted a confession. After days of relentless questioning, Chikatilo slowly began to admit the truth. He started by confessing to molesting children while he had been a schoolteacher, but eventually described fifty-five sex murders, including that of Lena Zakotnova. The stunned police, who had only linked thirty-six victims to the Rostov murderer, had now to recognize that they had executed an innocent man.

Chikatilo was finally charged with the brutal murder of fifty-three women and children. Shortly before he confessed he said to the interviewing officer, "Everything I have done makes me tremble . . . I feel only gratitude to the investigating bodies that they captured me."

Over the next year and a half, Chikatilo was studied by doctors and criminologists. During that time he led officers to undiscovered bodies and, with a shop dummy and a stage knife, acted out how he had killed each victim.

His habits had become fixed over the years. For example, he would usually bite off the victim's tongue and nipples. Wounds on or around the eyes were almost invariable. He would cut or bite off the boys' penises and scrotums and throw them away like so much rubbish. With the girls and women he would cut out the uterus and chew it manically as he stabbed at them. The psychiatrists ruled that this was not technically cannibalism, since he did not swallow human material, but was in fact motivated by the same impulse that makes people give love bites in the height of sexual passion. Chikatilo simply commented, "I did not want to bite them so much as chew them. They were so beautiful and elastic."

Chikatilo's wife was stunned when she was told of the reason for his arrest. She had thought he was being persecuted for protesting about the Assyrian garages and, at first, refused to believe that the man she had been married to for twenty-five years was a monster. He had always been a loving, if weak-willed father to their children and doted on their grandchildren. How could he have concealed over a decade of slaughter from her? Yet, when Chikatilo himself admitted the crimes to her face she was forced to accept the terrible truth. She cursed him and left, never to contact him again. For their part, the police believed that she had known nothing of her husband's activities and provided her with a change of identity and a home in another party of the country.

The trial opened on April 14, 1992. The shaven-headed Chikatilo raved and shouted from the cage that held and protected him from the angry public. At one point he even stripped off his clothes and waved his penis at the court shouting, "Look at this useless thing! What do you think I could do with that?" His extreme behavior might well have been motivated by the fact that his only hope of escaping execution was a successful insanity plea.

The defense tried to prove that Chikatilo was driven by an insane and undeniable need to kill and was not in control of his actions during the murders. They had little chance of convincing the judge, since Chikatilo clearly planned many of the killings, and had long dormant periods.

An attempt was made on Chikatilo's life during the trial. One day, as the court was being cleared, a young man whose 17-year-old sister had been killed by the defendant took a heavy metal ball from his pocket and hurled it through the bars of the cage. It just missed Chikatilo, smashing into the wall behind his head. The guard commander, seeing that the judge had not witnessed the incident, let the would-be assassin go.

On October 14, 1992, Judge Akubzhanov found Chikatilo guilty of all fifty-three murders. On the following day, he sentenced him to be executed; as of this writing—May 1993—he remains on Death Row.

In yet another ironic twist to the case, Japanese psychiatrists have recently offered an undisclosed sum to the Russian authorities to study Chikatilo's brain when he dies. Thus the traditional Soviet method of execution—a single shot to the back of the head—is unlikely to be used on him.

By comparison with Chikatilo's highly publicized homicides and confessions, the case of Arthur Shawcross, the "Genesee River killer," received very little publicity. The reason may lie in his appearance; unlike Chikatilo—whose staring eyes made him *look* like a monster—Shawcross was a commonplace little man with a large paunch and balding head who looked much older than his forty-four years. Yet, with his penchant for sadism and necrophilia, he was at least as dangerous as either Chikatilo or Dahmer.

The Genesee River flows through the small city of Rochester, in New York State. But it was 15 miles outside Rochester, at a bridge over Salmon Creek, that the body of the first victim, "Dotsie" Blackburn, a known prostitute, was found on March 24, 1988. She had been strangled, and the killer had bitten a piece out of her genitals. The last time she had been seen alive was a month earlier, in the Rochester red-light district on Lake Avenue.

The second victim, Anna Steffen, vanished in late May. When her body was found, at the edge of the river, it was badly decomposed, but water in the lungs indicated that she had died of drowning.

It was more than a year later, in June 1989, that Dorotny Kneller, a homeless waitress in her late thirties, disappeared. When her body was found it was little more than a skeleton, and the skull was missing. Between then and the end of the year, seven more women vanished from the Rochester area. Only one of these, a retarded girl called June Stotts, was not a prostitute. Her body had been cut open and eviscerated, and her sexual organs were missing.

The murder caused a panic in the red-light district, and prostitutes began to study potential customers with more care

than ever before. Yet the killing continued. Agent Gregg Mc-
Crary, of the FBI team at Quantico, correctly deduced that the
killer looked so ordinary and harmless that he was almost in-
visible. When the local police told him they had arrested a
transvestite who was driving a car, he told them: "No, that's
not the man you're looking for." The killer, it seemed clear,
was a driver, but the car would also be nondescript. Since
most of the victims were in their late twenties, McCrary deduced that the killer was probably slightly older, in his early
thirties. He would probably work in a menial job, and might
well be a sportsman—this was deduced from the fact that so
many victims had been found in or near the river, which the
killer probably knew as a fisherman, and that June Stotts had
been eviscerated as a hunter eviscerates game.

Most important, McCrary also suggested that the killer
might be the kind of person who liked to return to the body,
possibly even to have sex with it. This is why, in January
1990, a police helicopter began to fly over the Genesee River,
looking for more victims from the air. At Salmon Creek
bridge—where the first victim's body had been found—they
spotted a body, almost under the bridge, encased in ice. And
on the bridge just above it there was a parked car—a Chevrolet—and a man sitting with his legs out of the passenger door,
where he could see the body, apparently masturbating. As the
helicopter swooped down, the car drove away down Route
31—towards the town of Spencerport. The helicopter followed, and saw the car turn into a municipal parking lot. A
heavily built man got out and walked across to the Wedge-
wood Nursing Home on the other side of the street. The police radioed a police patrol car to go and park behind the
Chevrolet.

The driver of the patrol car had no difficulty finding the
person who had just entered the home. The grey-haired,
paunchy man, who seemed completely unperturbed, offered

his identity papers, which gave his name as Arthur J. Shaw-cross, with an address in nearby Rochester. He explained that his girlfriend Clara Neal—the owner of the car—worked in the home as a cook. He seemed to think he was being questioned because—according to his own account—he had been urinating into a bottle on the Salmon Creek Bridge.

Inspector Dennis Blythe found the prisoner co-operative. Shawcross raised no objections when Blythe had him photographed. But when the photograph was taken to a prostitute who had reported a curious encounter with a "john" who could only obtain an erection when she "played dead," she immediately picked out Shawcross from a group of other photographs.

A check on police records showed that Shawcross had been arrested for burglary as a teenager, later for arson, and had spent fifteen years in jail for child murder. He had killed—and mutilated—an 11-year-old boy, Jackie Blake, and raped and suffocated an 8-year-old girl, Karen Ann Hill. He had been tried only on the second count, and in 1972 sentenced to twenty-five years. He had been paroled after fifteen, and lived for a while in Binghamton, NY. But when neighbors there had learned of his conviction for child murder, they had virtually "run him out of town."

Shawcross was married to a girl named Rose Walley, but he also had a mistress, Clara Neal, whose hired car he was driving.

For the next two days, Shawcross showed himself highly co-operative with the police, but denied knowing anything about the murders. When shown a photograph of the ninth victim, Elizabeth Gibson, and told that he had been seen with her before her disappearance, he was silent. Finally Blythe asked quietly: "I hope Clara wasn't involved in this?" Shawcross hung his head. "No, I was the only one involved."

Shawcross then talked in detail about the murders. He was also to talk about them to psychiatrist—and expert on serial murder—Joel Norris. But although Norris quotes these accounts without comment—in *The Genesee River Killer*—it is very obvious that Shawcross is constantly lying. He explained that he had killed Dotsie Blackburn after she began to give him a "blow job," and bit his penis until the blood came.

Anna Steffen, the second victim, had been frolicking with Shawcross in the river when he gave her a playful shove and she fell on her side. She began screaming, saying she was pregnant and that she was going to call the police. He held her head under the water until she drowned.

The third victim, Dorothy Keller, was a friend of Shawcross and his wife. They had been spending the morning on an island in the river when—he explained—she threatened to tell his wife Rose that they were lovers. He had hit her with a piece of wood and broken her neck.

Patty Ives, the fourth victim, was removing his wallet from his back pocket when he caught her. They quarreled, and he strangled her while having anal intercourse.

The fifth victim, Frances Brown, died accidentally, according to Shawcross. He was "deep throating her" while he performed cunnilingus, and his penis choked her to death.

June Stotts, the retarded girl, was also a friend of Shawcross and his wife. They went together to a spot beside the river, and she took off her pants and his trousers—after explaining that she was a virgin. After having sex, she began screaming: "I'm going to tell," until he silenced her by strangling her. Then he had more sex with the body, and "cut her wide open in a straight line . . . from her neck to her asshole. Cut out her pussy and ate it. I was one sick person . . ."

Maria Welsh, the seventh victim, also tried to steal his wallet while they were having sex. "I asked for my money back. She told me to go fuck myself." So he strangled her.

Darlene Trippi, the eighth victim, declined to return his thirty dollars when he was unable to get an erection, and laughed unsympathetically, so he strangled her.

Elizabeth Gibson also tried to steal his wallet, then scratched his face with her fingernails.

June Cicero, victim number ten, made fun of him when he failed to get an erection, called him a faggot, and threatened to tell the cops (Shawcross did not specify what about). He strangled her, and three days later, returned to the body and cut out the vagina, which he "ate."

The eleventh victim was a black prostitute named Felicia Stephens. She put her head in the rear window of his car, and he closed it on her throat, suffocating her. This, he explained, was because black inmates had raped him in jail, and the murder was an act of self-preservation.

Jackie Blake, the first child victim, had also—according to Shawcross—provoked his own murder. The boy, he said, was following him, and when he told him to go home, started cursing and said he would go wherever he wanted to. So Shawcross, in a rage, hit him with his fist. Later, he agreed, he had returned to the corpse and cut off the genitals, which he ate. Medical examination suggested that the boy had been forced to undress and to run some distance before he had been sexually assaulted and killed.

In the case of the 8-year-old Karen Hill, Shawcross explained that he was "mad at her for going down to the river alone." He raped her, then, when she began to cry, suffocated her by stuffing grass and leaves into her mouth and up her nose.

What becomes very clear from Norris's book is that Shawcross lacked Chikatilo's honesty in describing his crimes and their motivation. This motivation—which was entirely sexual—sprang out of his low self-esteem. He had a highly dominant mother and a weak father, who allowed her to browbeat him; therefore he lacked a masculine "role model"—in that sense, Shawcross's situation resembled that of Henry Lee Lucas.

Also—like Lucas—Shawcross suffered a number of head injuries as a child and young adult. Struck on the head with a stone in a local gang fight, he was knocked unconscious and needed several stitches. After that, he began to experience paralysis below the waist. At school he was knocked out on the sports field by a discus, which caused amnesia about the whole incident. As a member of a construction crew he was accidentally struck on the head with a sledgehammer, and was again unconscious for hours. And during infantry training in the army he fell off a ladder and landed on the back of his head, which resulted in concussion.

Dr. Dorothy Lewis, a psychiatrist who examined Shawcross, also carried out a study of fourteen juveniles sentenced to death in America, and found that all fourteen had suffered severe head injuries during childhood. Once again—as in so many other cases—we note how often serial killers have suffered brain abnormalities due to head injuries.

Like so many other serial killers, Shawcross was also driven by powerful sexual urges from an early age—he claims he was introduced to oral sex before he was 9 by an aunt who was staying with them, and that he also practiced oral sex on his sister, four years his junior. When his mother caught him masturbating—which was more than once—she threatened to cut off his penis with a butcher's knife. At fourteen, when he was leading a fairly active (oral) sex life with his sister, a cousin and a girl at school, he was offered a lift by a man who then raped him, suddenly introducing disturbing traumas into a sex life that had been relatively uninhibited.

According to Shawcross, it was Vietnam that turned him into a serial killer. There, in the jungle, he murdered two Vietnamese girls, raping and disemboweling one and roasting and partly eating the other's severed leg. On another occasion he opened fire on a group of Vietnamese who were sitting around a camp fire, killing (he estimates) twenty-six.

Once back in America, there were more humiliations from his overbearing mother, complex marital problems—and finally, the sex murders of Jackie Blake and Karen Hill. It is clear that Shawcross chose children because his ability to control them brought a sense of power accompanied by sexual potency. And later, when he began murdering prostitutes, he killed them before having sex with the bodies. He also returned to many of them to have sex later. He was considering having sex with the corpse of June Cicero—even though he had cut out her genitals—when the police helicopter saw him on the bridge.

Shawcross's defense was of insanity, but the jury were unconvinced; after a five-week trial they took only a few hours to find him guilty, and he was sentenced to a total of two hundred and fifty years in prison.

Looking back on the case, and on his "profile" of Shawcross, Gregg McCrary was intrigued to realize that he had been wrong about only one detail. He had estimated Shawcross's age at around 30, when in face he was in his midforties. Then the explanation dawned on him: Shawcross had spent fifteen years in prison. It was exactly as if his life was "on pause" for that period.

With Dahmer and Shawcross behind bars, America quickly registered another "first" in serial murder: the first female serial killer. This, of course, has to be immediately qualified by admitting that Anna Zwanziger and Gesina Gottfried were serial poisoners, and that Belle Gunness has a strong claim to be America's first female serial killer. But these three women all had specific motives for getting rid of individual victims: usually profit, sometimes revenge, occasionally a mere passing grudge. If by serial killer we mean someone who experiences a psychopathic need to kill, devoid of apparent motive, then Aileen Wuornos certainly qualifies as America's first female serial killer.

Twelve days before Christmas, 1989, two friends, scrap-metal hunting in the woods outside Ormond Beach, Florida, found a male corpse wrapped in an old carpet. The body had been there for about two weeks and was badly decomposed due to Florida's almost perpetually hot weather. However, the forensics lab managed to identify the victim as Richard Mallory, 51-year-old electrician from the town of Clearwater. The autopsy showed that he had been shot three times in the chest and once in the neck with a .22 caliber handgun.

Because of the proximity of Daytona Beach—a notorious crime black spot—and the overall lack of evidence, the in-vestigating officers made only routine efforts to find the per-petrator. In all likelihood Mallory had been shot in a fight or a mugging, then hidden in the woods to avoid detection. Such crimes took place all the time around Daytona, and the chances of catching the killer were minimal.

The police were soon forced to reappraise the situation. Over the next twelve months, five more victims were discov-ered in almost identical circumstances. A 43-year-old con-struction worker, David Spears, was found on June 1, 1990, shot six times with a .22 handgun. Five days later the corpse of rodeo worker Charles Carskaddon, aged 40, was found covered with an electric blanket with nine bullet holes in him. A 50-year-old truck driver called Troy Burress was found on August 4, killed by two .22 caliber bullets. On September 12, a 56-year-old child abuse investigator, Charles Humphreys, was found shot six times in the torso and once in the head. Fi-nally, on November 19, the body of Walter Gino Antonio was found, shot dead by four .22 caliber bullets.

In each case the victim was a middle-aged, heterosexual male. They all appeared to have been killed in or near their cars, just off one of the state highways, and hidden in nearby scrub or woodland. Some were partially stripped, but no evidence of sexual or physical abuse could be found. Used prophylactics found near some of the bodies suggested that they had been involved in a sexual encounter before they were murdered.

In every case, money, valuables and the victim's vehicle had been stolen. The cars were generally found dumped shortly after the murder with the driver's seat pulled well forward, as if to allow a comparatively short person to reach the drive pedals.

When it was found that the same handgun was being used in each of the killings the police were forced to accept that they might have a serial killer on their hands; yet, disturbingly, the murders did not fit any known pattern. Why would a heterosexual serial murderer kill middle-aged men? On the other hand, if the killer was homosexual, why was there no evidence of sexual abuse?

It was the FBI's profiling unit that provided the startling answer: the killer was probably a woman. Predictably, media attention, which had been minimal, grew exponentially when this was revealed.

At least the Florida police started the investigation with a solid lead. Many serial killers steal from their victims, but usually for souvenir purposes only. The Florida Highway Killer was clearly stealing for profit. The money or valuables might be traced when she used or sold them.

As it turned out, the killer made an even more serious blunder. On July 4, 1990, she and her girlfriend skidded off the road in a car she had stolen from Peter Seims, a 65-year-old part-time missionary she had killed in early June, somewhere in southern Georgia. Witnesses told the police that they had seen the two women—one tall and blonde, the other a short, heavy-set brunette—abandon the damaged Pontiac Sunbird after removing the license plates.

Police took detailed descriptions of the pair, but did not initially connect them with the highway killings. When it became clear that they were looking for a female killer they reviewed the Seims case and, since he was still missing, added him to the list. They also issued artist's impressions of the two women with the request for further information. It seemed the case was taking a new turn; they might have a *pair* of female murderers on their hands.

By December 1990, the police had two names to attach to the artist's sketches, thanks to tips from members of the public. The brunette was possibly one Tyria J. Moore, a 28-year-old occasional hotel maid, and the blonde could be her live-in lover, a 34-year-old prostitute who went under several names, one of them being Lee Wuornos.

Shortly afterwards, a check on a Daytona pawn shop revealed several items that had belonged to Richard Mallory. The pawn ticket that went with the belongings was made out to a Cammie Green, but the statutory thumbprint—that all Florida pawn tickets must carry—proved to be that of Wuornos.

The police arrested her outside the Last Resort bikers' bar on January 9, 1991. Shortly afterwards Tyria Moore was located at her sister's house in Pennsylvania. Strangely enough, the officers who went to pick her up did not arrest her. Instead they took her to a nearby hotel. What took place there has yet to be made clear, but it has been alleged that a deal was struck and, possibly, a contract signed.

To understand these claims fully it is necessary to look at the influence of the media on the case, and vice versa. Movies like *The Silence of the Lambs, Thelma and Louise* and *Basic Instinct* had recently made serial killers and women outlaws two of the major money-spinners in the US entertainment industries. Even before Wuornos' arrest, up to fifteen movie companies were rumored to be offering film contracts for the story. An obvious target for such money would be the investigating officers.

By the time of her apprehension the police had ascertained that Tyria Moore could not have been directly involved in at least some of the murders. There were various witnesses who could swear that she was working as a motel maid at the time of these killings. If she was not charged with any criminal offense, the movie contract lawyers could bid for her story without infringing the "Son of Sam" law. This ruling made it illegal for convicted felons to profit directly from their crimes. Any money from movies, books, press interviews and so forth went to the victims, or their families if the victim were dead.

It has been alleged that in return for immunity from prosecution—and a cut of the profits—Moore signed a contract with officers Binegar, Henry and Munster to sell her story, in conjunction with theirs, to a movie company.

Tyria Moore—who admitted that "Lee" Wuornos had told her about at least one of the murders—agreed to help the prosecution in return for immunity from the charge of "accessory after the fact." She led officers to the creek where Wuornos had thrown the .22 revolver used in the murders and, under police supervision, made eleven bugged phone calls to Lee in prison. In them she claimed that she was still undiscovered by the police and urged Lee to confess. Wuornos, who was plainly still in love with Moore, tried to soothe her and agreed to make a statement.

On January 16, 1991, Wuornos gave a three-hour videotaped confession in Volusia County Jail. In it she admitted to killing Mallory, Spears, Carskaddon, Seims, Burress, Humphreys and Antonio. She also gave details that only a witness to the murders could have known, apparently confirming her testimony. Defending her actions, she insisted that she had only gone to the woods with them to trade sex for money. Each of the seven men had tried to attack or rape her, she said, forcing her to kill them in self-defense. When asked why she was confessing, she replied that she wanted to clear Tyria Moore's name.

It was decided that Wuornos was to be tried for each murder separately. Her defense counsels contended that it would be prejudicial to the trial if the jury heard evidence connected with the other murders, but at the first trial, for the killing of Richard Mallory, Judge Uriel Blount Jr. ruled otherwise. Florida's Williams Rule allowed evidence of similar offenses to be revealed to a jury when the judge considered it important to the case. Of course, this seriously undermined Wuornos's claim that she had fired in self-defense. To believe that even a hard-working street prostitute had to kill seven men in the space of a single year stretched the jury's credulity to breaking-point.

For some reason the defense lawyers declined to call character witnesses for the defendant and, incredibly, did not inform the court that Richard Mallory had previously served a prison sentence for rape. It is possible that this was done deliberately to increase the chances for a claim of mis-trial at any ensuing appeal, but it left Lee Wuornos with hardly a leg to stand on in court. The jury found her guilty and Judge Blount sentenced her to the electric chair.

At a subsequent arraignment for three of the other murders, Wuornos pleaded unconditionally guilty and requested the death sentence without trial on the grounds that she wanted to "be with Jesus" as soon as possible. It seems likely that this was an all-or-nothing gamble to win the judge's sympathy and receive life imprisonment instead of further death sentences. Wuornos became outraged when the judge complied with her request, shouting that she was being executed for being a rape victim. As she left the courtroom she loudly wished similar experiences on the judge's wife and children.

Lee Wuornos remains on Death Row as of this writing

(May 1993). Before the Mallory trial, the "Son of Sam" ruling remained in force; but, bizarrely enough, the US Supreme court has recently overturned this law. It is now theoretically possible for a person to become a murderer with the ultimate goal of making money. Lee Wuornos, who has regularly complained that others were making a profit from her suffering, is now allegedly charging $25,000 for interviews and may sign as many movie contracts as she wishes.

Of course, it is arguable that the money will do her little good if she is on her way to the electric chair, but recent revelations concerning the officers who apprehended Tyria Moore may change even that. Following a bugged telephone call, in which he spoke of a movie deal, Major Dan Henry has resigned. The other officers, Sergeant Bruce Munster and Captain Steve Binegar, have been transferred from the Criminal Investigation Division. If it is found that the detectives *had* received money during the investigation, it is possible that all Lee Wuornos' death sentences might be overturned.

In conclusion, there is one important question to be considered: is Aileen Wuornos really a serial killer? If we discount her own defense, that she was a victim of circumstance, we are left with a tantalizing lack of motive for the murders.

Some have argued that she killed simply for financial profit: robbing a client, then shooting him to silence the only witness. To support this view it has been pointed out that she was clearly desperate not to lose her lover, Tyria Moore. On her own part, Moore appears to have been unwilling to work during the period of their relationship, but insisted on living in expensive motels. It seems clear that she knew how Wuornos was getting her money, but never objected to it—even after Lee had told her about the murder of Richard Mallory.

There may indeed be some truth in this theory, but it does

not seem enough to explain the murder of seven men, none of whom would have appeared particularly well-off. A more likely theory is that Wuornos killed to revenge herself on men.

She was brought up by her grandparents when her real parents abandoned her as a baby. She has claimed that she was regularly beaten and occasionally sexually abused by her grandfather throughout her childhood. When she was 13, she was driven into the woods and raped by a middle-aged friend of her grandparents. From her early teens on it appears that she made money through prostitution and claims to have been beaten up and raped by clients quite often. She had several affairs and was married to a man fifty years her senior, but they all ended acrimoniously. It was only with Tyria Moore that she seemed to be reasonably happy.

On the available evidence, it seems likely that the first victim, Richard Mallory, may well have raped Wuornos. Did this push her into serial crime?

Over 1990 she admits to having had hundreds of clients, all but seven of whom she apparently had no trouble with. On the other hand, the similarities between the murder victims and the circumstances of the rape when she was 13 are unmistakable.

Perhaps, like Arthur Shawcross, the "Genesee River Killer," her trigger was resistance or threat. She may indeed be telling the truth when she insists that the men she killed threatened her and refused to pay after sex. This may have thrown her into a rage in which she—justifiably, in her view— shot them dead.

Whatever the reasons, she has caused a major stir in law enforcement circles. The possibility that she may be the start of a new trend in serial murder has disturbing ramifications. As Robert Ressler—former FBI agent and originator of the term "serial killer"—said of the case: "If Wuornos is said to be a serial killer we have to rewrite the rules."

*   *   *

Since the conviction of Aileen Wuornos, Britain has also convicted its first female serial killer, 23-year-old children's nurse Beverley Allitt. She was arrested in May 1991, after tests on a blood sample from a five-month-old child suggested that someone had injected a large dose of the drug insulin, used in cases of diabetes. And since Paul Crampton was not diabetic, this had brought him very close to death.

Beverley Allitt had been hired as a nurse in mid-February 1991. She was lucky; she had failed many job interviews, and her records—if anyone had bothered to consult them—showed that she suffered from a personality disorder that involved a constant craving for attention. But the small Grantham and Kesteven General Hospital was short-staffed, and no one had replied to their advertisements for nurses. So Beverley Allitt was taken on a six-month contract. In the next fifty-eight days she was responsible for four murders, and attacks on nine other children that left several of them permanently disabled.

On February 23, seven-week-old Liam Taylor was admitted to Ward 4 with a heavy chest cold. He became suddenly exhausted and listless; thirty-six hours later, his heart stopped, and he died in his parents' arms. A post mortem revealed serious heart damage—of the kind that might be sustained by a middle-aged man who smoked and drank to excess.

After Beverley Allitt's arrest, it was asked: why did this not instantly alert the authorities to the possibility that something suspicious was going on? After all, the death of a baby from something that should only happen to middle-aged men ought to raise urgent questions that are pursued until they are answered. But all this is being wise after the event. No one in that cottage hospital—in a peaceful midland town with a low crime rate—had the least reason to believe that they had a killer in their midst.

Ten days later, 11-year-old Tim Hardwick was admitted

after a bout of epilepsy, and died of a massive heart attack. Doctors said that he had died of continual epileptic fits—although, in fact, he had had the last fit four hours before his death. But since the child had been an epileptic, this explanation was accepted.

The next baby to suffer a mysterious collapse was fifteen-month-old Cayley Desmond, whose heart stopped twice. She was transferred to the Queens Medical Centre in Nottingham, where she recovered. No one noticed the black bruise under her armpit where air had been injected into her.

The fourth victim was five-month-old Paul Crampton. Three times in a week his blood sugar sank so low that he fell into a coma. The child became cold, clammy and listless. It was clear that he was suffering from hypoglycemia—caused by low blood sugar—yet there was no obvious reason for this. A sample of Paul's blood was sent off for analysis to the University of Wales. Unfortunately, it was not marked urgent, and the intervention of Easter delayed the analysis further. It was fifteen days before the laboratory discovered that the insulin level in Paul's blood was abnormally high—enough to suggest that someone had injected it . . .

On the day the blood sample was sent off, five-year-old Bradley Gibson was found to have stopped breathing. His parents rushed to the hospital and watched as doctors tried to revive him, using a manual pump to make him breathe. Transferred to the Queens Medical Center, he recovered. But at home a few days later, he was unable to walk, or to control his bowels or his bladder.

Doctors at the Medical Center decided that he must have been given the wrong drug by mistake, yet failed to pass on this disquieting information to the Grantham hospital. In fact, the "wrong drug" was potassium, injected by Beverley Allitt.

The same week, three-month-old Becky Philips, one of a pair of twins, was admitted with breathing problems. After treatment she was allowed home. In the middle of that night she went into a coma. Her parents rushed her to the hospital, but it was too late, and she died during attempts at resuscitation. It was diagnosed as a cot death. In fact, it was due to an overdose of insulin.

Concerned about their other twin, Kate, the parents decided to allow her to go into the hospital for observation. Tests showed her to be completely normal and healthy. Yet before the day was over, she had had three attacks in which she stopped breathing. After the third, doctors failed in their attempt to start the heart, and her parents were told she was dead. After forty-two minutes, Kate suddenly began breathing again, and recovered. But the attack had caused permanent brain damage which meant that she would always be retarded.

Now, at last, on April 12, 1991, the tests on Paul Crampton's blood—sent fifteen days earlier—revealed that he appeared to have been injected with insulin. The Grantham Hospital was immediately informed. Yet the information only caused bewilderment. How was it possible that such a thing could happen? The only explanation that suggested itself was that some member of the public was getting into the ward, and so one set of doors was locked. It would be another eighteen days before the police were finally informed. And in that time, three more children were attacked, and another one murdered. Christopher King had four attacks of "breathing difficulty," and his parents were certain he was going to die; but when transferred to the Queens Medical Center, he unexpectedly recovered. Patrick Elstone—again a twin—came close to death on two occasions, but recovered. Back at home, it was clear that he also had something wrong with his legs which prevented him from keeping up with his twin Anthony. But when two-month-old Christopher Peasgood stopped breathing twice, there was finally a clamor for something to be done.

Medical staff requested that video cameras be installed, but were refused.

There would be one more victim, the thirteenth. On Monday, April 22, fifteen-month-old Clare Peck was admitted to Ward 4. Two hours later she was dead. Her blood showed an unusually high level of potassium, but her death was diagnosed as being due to asthma.

Incredibly, it was another eight days before the police were finally called in. The first thing they did was to examine the "ward notebook" kept by nurses. They immediately noticed that some pages had been cut out—for example, pages relating to Paul Crampton, whose "insulin attack" had led to suspicion. It took very little time for them to realize that the common factor in all the attacks—twenty-six of them—was the presence of the new nurse Beverley Allitt. When she left the ward, children who had suffered convulsions or breathing difficulties recovered; when she returned, the problems began again.

A search of Beverley Allitt's bedroom revealed some of the missing medical records. Twenty days after the police had been called in, she was arrested. In November 1991 she was finally charged with four murders, eight attacks and ten cases of grievous bodily harm with intent. She had injected insulin and potassium—in one case putting it into the child's drip—and when she had neither available, fell back on suffocation.

At first, parents found it unbelievable. The Philips,who had lost their daughter Becky, then almost lost her sister Kate, were particularly shattered; Beverley Allitt had been holding Becky when she died, and they were convinced that, far from attacking Kate, Beverley Allitt had saved her life. "Bev" had become a family friend, who often called around after work to take Kate for walks; she was even asked to be her godmother.

Now a study of her medical record quickly revealed that

Beverley Allitt should never have been let anywhere near a children's ward. During her two years' nurse's training, she had had no fewer than a hundred and thirty days off with various ailments. She had repeatedly wasted doctors' time with ailments varying from pregnancy to a brain tumor—all false alarms. This disorder is known as Munchausen's Syndrome, in which patients present themselves at hospitals with an endless series of imaginary ailments; it seems to be due to a craving for attention.

None of the doctors who studied her record was able to discover why Beverley Allitt had developed this peculiar illness. Until the age of 13 she had been a perfectly normal child. Then she began to lie, and to behave with cruelty towards friends. (Other cases in this book suggest that such personality change is often the result of a blow on the head, but nothing of the sort seems to be recorded of Beverley Allitt.) Her ex-boyfriend, Steve Biggs, told how he had broken off the affair as a result of her outbursts of violence. "She'd get mad and kick me in the balls." When she criticized his driving—on the day she passed her test—and he told her to shut up, she hit him in the face when they were traveling at sixty miles an hour. This was the last straw; but when he told her that he intended to break off the engagement, she grabbed him by the hair and forced him to his knees—he had to be rescued by her sister.

After her arrest, when her destructive urges could no longer be directed at children, they turned inward, and she was often unable to appear in court as a result of anorexia nervosa—the "slimmer's disease."

On May 28, 1993, she was found guilty on all counts, and given thirteen life sentences. Mr. Justice Latham told her; "There is no real prospect that a time will ever come when you will be safely released."

On the day of her sentence, a prison psychiatrist, Dr. James

Higgins, revealed an interesting sidelight on her motivation. Commenting on her low self-esteem, and her failure to win a place on a nursing course, Higgins quoted her as saying: "I had to prove I was better than what people thought."

At first this sounds baffling. Surely murdering helpless children and betraying the trust of their parents proves you are worse, not better, than "people thought"? But then it becomes clear that she was not speaking about being morally better. She was speaking of feeling superior. "You may regard me as a nobody, but there's far more to me than you think. In fact, I'm highly dangerous."

Suddenly we can see that this is one of the basic motivations of the serial killer. Why did Jack the Ripper and Neil Cream write letters to the police? Why did Peter Kürten like to return to the scene of his murders, and listen to the horrified comments of sightseers? Why did John Collins go to a funeral home and ask if he could photograph the corpse of his latest victim? We can see that it is a craving to feel "different," to feel superior. But is not the act of murder itself enough to convince someone that they are not like other people? Obviously not. We may as well ask why an actor wants to read his reviews, or why a beautiful woman wants to look in a mirror. Human consciousness is feeble; our memory is short. We want to have our sense of "difference" confirmed by other people.

In other words, you could say that serial murder is the underachiever's way of of feeling a "somebody." And to recognize this is suddenly to understand why there have been so many serial killers since the Second World War. For more than two centuries now, western society has insisted on the equality of man. But when there exists an enormous social gulf between rich and poor, this makes little practical difference. The "gentleman" seems to be a gentleman by inborn right; the poor man may be his equal before the law, but he doesn't *feel* it. Even if he happens to belong to the "dominant 5 per cent," he is still inclined to accept a sense of social inferiority.

Two world wars and the "caring society" have changed all that. As social differences are erased by education—and television—everyone feels that he has some right to a share of the prizes. The pop star may be more responsible for this change in attitude than anyone else; he demonstrates that it is possible to be working-class, an educational dropout, and still become an international icon and a multi-millionaire. (It is significant that Charles Manson wanted to become a pop star, and that the first murders took place in a house that had recently been vacated by a recording agent against whom he had a grudge.)

But on our overcrowded planet, there is still as little "room at the top" as ever. The result is an ever-increasing number of dominant personalities who feel alienated, frustrated and resentful. A large percentage of these become petty crooks— muggers, burglars, car thieves. A very tiny percentage become serial killers.

Yet even this insight leaves a major question unanswered. In the years since the term "serial murder" was invented, cases have succeeded one another with such frequency—usually overlapping—that they produce the impression of an epidemic. The increasingly gruesome nature of the crimes lends urgency to the question: what is there about our society that incubates this atavistic urge to *kill*?

At least part of the answer has emerged during the course of this book. Most serial killers have deep emotional problems; seldom overpowering enough to allow us to regard them as insane, but sufficient to make them totally self-absorbed, so that they regard other people as abstractions. This also produces a sensation of meainglessness—what psychologists call "lack of affect," inability to feel. Jeffrey Dahmer spoke for most serial killers when he said in a prison interview: "I couldn't find any meaning in my life when I was out there. I'm sure as hell not going to find it in here." When the mind is becalmed, negative impulses multiply like algae in a stagnant pond.

Dahmer's biographer Brian Masters has argued that we need to stretch the definition of insanity to cover murderers like Dahmer and Chikatilo. Psychiatrist Dorothy Lewis, who studied Shawcross, is inclined to agree. "I think it does very bad things to our society if we become a mindless group of people that doesn't care why someone did what he did, and thinks only in terms of punishing the individual or doing away with him."

John Douglas, head of the Quantico profiling unit, takes a more pragmatic view.

> We have to put ourselves in the shoes of the victims. So what I flash back to is victims who are screaming, begging for their lives. I have tapes here of victims who are being murdered, who are regressing in their behavior, calling out for their mammies, calling out for their daddies, and begging "Please God don't kill me." But they kill them. So when I see the day of execution, and the little vigil outside the penitentiary, I may feel sorry for a second, but then I want to pull out the file jacket of these guys, I want to look at those crime scene photographs, I want to look at that autopsy protocol, and look at those autopsy photographs. I want to see the interviews of the victims and the families. I want to put myself back into that victim. So I have no sympathy at all for these people.

But surely the two points of view are reconcilable? Those who lack Douglas's experience—or lack the imagination to understand what he is saying—may feel sympathy for killers like Dahmer, Chikatilo and Shawcross. But the sympathy is irrelevant. What is needed is real understanding. Dorothy Lewis expressed it as well as anyone when she said: "If we're going to be a humane society, we have to protect ourselves, but we also have to understand what made these people the way they are, and then work very hard to try to prevent society creating more people like that."

What this book makes clear is that at the present stage, our understanding is so crude as to be almost non-existent.

1995: THE CASE OF FRED AND ROSE WEST

THE CASE OF FRED AND ROSEMARY WEST IS UNIQUE IN BRITISH criminal history, for the chances of a sex maniac and a nymphomaniac forming a murderous alliance must be a million to one.

In August 1991, the Gloucester builder Frederick West was charged with sexual offenses against one of his seven children, a thirteen-year-old. But the case came to nothing when the child changed her mind about testifying. A year later, in August 1992, the case against West (which involved his wife Rosemary) was dropped.

Detective Constable Hazel Savage had become friendly with the daughter who refused to testify, and was worried in case her life might be in danger. In May 1987, sixteen-year-old Heather West had disappeared—the Wests claimed she had run off with a lesbian. Heather had told friends she intended leaving home and taking a job in a holiday camp. Yet she had failed to collect her social benefit. Would a girl about to start a new life leave her benefit behind?

Hazel Savage pressed the reluctant girl to tell her everything. The girl shook her head. "If I say anything, my dad says I'd end up in the back garden like my sister Heather."

When Hazel Savage took this story to her superiors, they were reluctant to take her seriously. If they began another investigation, and failed to back it up with evidence, West would have grounds for suing them for harassment. And now Hazel Savage was suggesting that they should dig up his back garden.

Eventually, her persistence triumphed. On February 23, 1994, Detective Superintendent John Bennett obtained a search warrant; the following day, policemen disguised as council workmen began digging up the back garden.

The Wests' home, 25 Cromwell Street, Gloucester, was a three-story semi-detached house; the Wests had been there since 1972. Rosemary West, a small, plump, bespectacled woman of forty-one, was interviewed that evening in her sitting room by a detective sergeant. Asked about Heather, she claimed that she had left home while she, Rose, was out shopping. The problem, Rose West explained, was that Heather was a lesbian. Asked what made her think so, she explained: "She knew exactly what kind of knickers the woman teacher had on."

The following day, Fred and Rosemary West were arrested, both protesting loudly. Newspaper photographs of Fred West showed a swarthy-looking man with long sideburns, piercing blue eyes, and a gap between his front teeth. The features were slightly simian—for a man who, according to workmates, boasted of having forty-two illegitimate children, he hardly looked the Casanova type.

That night, in police custody, Fred West confessed to the murder of his daughter Heather, and described exactly where the police would find her body.

When digging began again the next day, the police soon found a skull, identified as that of a teenage girl, in a corner of the garden. Three feet farther down they found the rest of the body, cut into pieces. Dental records identified her as Heather West. During the next two days, they found another dismembered female body, this time under the patio. A few feet away, there was a decomposed fetus. The girl was identified as eighteen-year-old Shirley Ann Robinson, who had lived in the Wests' house as a lodger in the late 1970s. Other lodgers declared that she had been the lover of both Fred and Rosemary West, and that West was the father of the baby. She had last been seen in May 1978.

A few days later, on February 28, another body was found under the patio. This was identified as sixteen-year-old Alison Chambers, who had vanished in 1979, and who had been a regular visitor at 25 Cromwell Street. Like the others, she had been dismembered, and rope and masking tape found with the body indicated that she had been bound and gagged. She had been naked at the time of her death.

Suddenly, the "House of Horror" was on the front page of every newspaper in England, and the road outside was permanently crowded with sightseers, supplied with refreshment by hamburger stalls and ice cream vans. Local landladies made a fortune letting their front rooms at top rates to reporters and pararazzi—one television team paid £1,000 for a room facing the Wests' home

The Wests had let out three bedsits for as little as £5 a week—"the cheapest rooms in Gloucester"—and the press theorized that their victims had all been lodgers or girls who visited the house regularly. This was disproved when a body found under the floor of the basement proved to be a twenty-one-year-old Swiss student, Therese Siegenthaler, who had vanished on April 15, 1974, when she was hitchhiking her way to Ireland. The next body—the fifth—was that of fifteen-year-old Shirley Hubbard, who had been training as a shop assistant in Debenhams, Worcester; she had last been seen as she left the shop at 5:30 in the evening. It looked as if she had been abducted. But would it be possible to drag a girl into a car in the midst of the rush hour? And was it likely that she would accept a lift from a lone man? The police began to formulate the theory that both Fred and Rose West had been in the car, and that this was why Therese Siegenthaler and Shirley Hubbard had accepted lifts.

Three more dismembered bodies were found in the basement and identified as Lucy Partington, twenty-one, a student at Exeter University, who had vanished after she left the home of a girlfriend to catch a late night bus; Juanita Mott, eighteen, who had vanished on her way from Newent to Gloucester on April 11, 1985; and fifteen-year-old Carole Anne Cooper, who had spent the afternoon with her grandmother before she vanished in Gloucester on November 10, 1973. Under the bathroom floor, the searchers found a body identified as Lynda Carol Gough, who had been a regular visitor to the Wests' home when she vanished in April 1973.

Fred West was charged with the nine murders. Rose West had been released on bail, and was living in a "safe house," where she had been placed by the police. Her son Stephen said that she spent much of her time in tears. She insisted that she had no idea that the bodies were buried in her house.

Fred West had been married twice; his first wife, Catherine (known as Rena) was a Scot, who had not been seen since late 1968. Her daughter Charmaine was also missing. So was a friend of Rena's called Anne McFall, who had lived with Fred and Rena in a caravan. The search now moved to Letterbox Field, not far from the Herefordshire village of Much Marcle, where West had spent his early years. Rena West's body was found buried in Letterbox Field on April 10, 1994. The body of the child Charmaine was found underneath the kitchen floor in the Wests' previous home at 25 Midland Road, Gloucester. Finally, the body of Anne McFall in nearby Fingerpost Field on June 7, bringing the bodycount up to twelve.

It seemed that Fred West was not only one of Britain's most prolific murderers; he had also been killing for longer than any of them.

On April 20, 1994, Rosemary West was also charged with five of the murders; later, this charge was increased to ten, including baby Charmaine. She was also charged with two cases of rape of an eleven-year-old girl, in association with two men, William Smith and Whitley Purcell.

By this time, Fred West, who had been charged with twelve murders, had confessed to them, but insisted that his wife was innocent. Looking at photographs of the small house in Cromwell Street, newspaper readers wondered how it was possible that a man could murder nine women, while his wife remained unaware of what was going on.

What looked like the answer began to emerge when reporters located Caroline Raine (later Owens), a girl who, in 1972, had lived with the Wests as an *au pair*—when she was sixteen (and Rose herself was only nineteen). Caroline had met the Wests when they gave her a lift from Tewkesbury, and soon after she went to work for them at £4 a week. She had left in November 1972 because she alleged that Rose had made lesbian advances, and Fred talked endlessly of group sex (although she later admitted that she herself had had sex with two of the male lodgers, one immediately after the other).

Four weeks later, on December 6, 1972, Caroline went to Tewkesbury to meet her boyfriend, and was later offered a lift home in a car by Fred and Rose. She felt she was perfectly safe, so she accepted. Rose West climbed into the back with her. As they drove along, Fred asked her if she had had sex with her boyfriend that afternoon—it was obvious that the idea excited him. She blushed and said no. Then Rose began trying to kiss her on the mouth, and fondling her breasts. She tried to push her away, and Fred stopped the car and punched her until she was unconscious. When she came round her hands were tied behind her back; the Wests then put adhesive tape around her mouth.

At 25 Cromwell Street, West dragged her upstairs, "laughing and mauling me." West cut the tape from around her mouth, and untied her hands; Rose West then sat beside her on the settee, and began kissing her and fondling her. After that, they all drank tea—Caroline later suspected hers had been drugged. Then the Wests undressed her, tied her hands behind her again, and gagged her with cotton wool. She was placed on a mattress on the floor, her legs spreadeagled, and West then beat her between the legs with a belt, using the buckle end.

After about a dozen blows, Rose lay between her undressed and had sex with her.

Ten minutes later, when it was over, Rose West went to the bathroom, and Fred took advantage of her absence to move on to Caroline and briefly have sex. Apparently he was anxious for Rose not to see.

Finally, the Wests fell asleep, and Caroline tried to escape out of the window, but her hands were tied and she was unable to raise it. In the early morning, someone came to the door, and Caroline did her best to make a noise; Rose was furious, and held a pillow over her head. When West returned, he was also angry, and told her that he would keep her in the cellar for his black friends to use, then bury her under the paving stones of Gloucester—where, he said, there were already several girls buried.

Rose West went off to see the children, and West again took advantage of her absence to rape Caroline. Then, astonishingly, he apologized to her, explaining that "it was all her (Rose's) idea." Rose came back, and both of the Wests asked her to return again as a nanny. Seeing her opportunity to escape, she quickly agreed. She even hoovered the room, as she used to, to indicate that she was again a member of the family. She was then made to take three baths in an attempt to get the gum of the sticking tape off her skin and hair. Finally, Fred West dropped off his wife and Caroline at a laundrette. After a few minutes, Caroline walked out and was given a lift by a friend to her home in Cinderford.

She felt too ashamed to tell her mother what had happened, feeling that she was somehow to blame; instead, she went to bed. But when she got up, her mother saw the bruises, and got the story out of her. She rang the police, and Fred and Rose West were arrested and charged with assault. But Caroline felt unable to face the ordeal of telling her story in court. So when the Wests appeared, on January 12, 1973, they were charged only with indecent assault and actual bodily harm. The magistrates obviously felt that since a man and wife had been involved, it could not be too serious. They fined the couple £25 each, and Fred and Rose West walked free.

Their near escape seems to have made them recognize that it was dangerous to allow their victims to remain alive to testify against them. From now on, if they felt there was any danger of the victim going to the police, they killed her. Later, at the trial of Rose West, Caroline Owens sobbed in court "I feel like it was my fault." This is obviously untrue; but some blame must attach to the magistrate John Smith, who failed to send them to prison.

Who was Fred West, and how did he turn into a serial killer?

He was born on September 29, 1941, in a farm laborers' cottage in Much Marcle, a small Herefordshire village that even today has a population of only 700. His father, Walter West, was a twenty-four-year-old widower when he met Daisy Hill, a sixteen-year-old maidservant, at the Ledbury Flower Show, where she was displaying her needlework. She was three months pregnant when they married in January 1940—but the child lived only one day. Later, after Fred's birth, the Wests would have five more children, two sons and three daughters.

In the West household, sexual abuse was commonplace; the father often told his daughters: "I made you—I'm entitled to touch you" (words Fred West would later repeat to his own daughters). His wife retaliated by seducing Fred when he was only twelve years old. The two of them were always very close; West's brother Douglas said: "In her eyes Fred could do no wrong."

In this intense atmosphere of incest and seduction, Fred's interest in sex became a non-stop obsession. He was later to tell his daughter Mae's boyfriend that he used to play a game with his sisters and other young girls in which "they all used to dive in the hay so just the back end was showing, and I just used take pot luck."

As a child and teenager, West was mild and unaggressive. His sister-in-law remarked: "He was soft as hell. . . . He would sooner get a bloody nose than fight."

But when Fred was sixteen, there occurred what may well have been the most fateful event of his life. Walking up a fire escape behind a village girl, he reached up her skirt. The girl turned and gave him a violent push; he struck his head, and was unconscious for twenty-four hours. After this, the family noticed a change in his character. Two years later, when he was eighteen, he had a motorcycle accident which again injured his head.

Many sex murderers have sustained head injuries as a child, causing brain damage. Injury to the brain's frontal lobes—one of whose functions is to control feeling—can decrease their ability to inhibit violent emotion. This is almost certainly what happened to Fred West. Normally quiet and good tempered, he could be thrown into a violent rage by frustration or opposition. In effect, West became a Jekyll and Hyde—a comment actually made by a woman who knew him well.

When West was nineteen, he impregnated his thirteen-year-old sister and had to leave home. His brother Douglas later commented that they were so shocked by this that they refused to speak to Fred.

West was prosecuted for having sex with an under-age girl. But Detective Geoff Painter was not allowed to give evidence, and Fred himself declined to say anything. The result was that he walked free.

When he left home, he took a job as a lorry driver, and eighteen months later met a pretty Scottish teenager with dyed blonde hair, Rena Costello, who was working as a waitress in the New Inn at Ledbury. Rena had been born in Coatsbridge, Glasgow, in April 1944, and when she became pregnant by an Asian bus driver when she was eighteen, she decided to move south. Fred appeared not to mind about her pregnancy, and they were married in the Gloucester Registry Office on November 17, 1962. In early 1964, they moved into a slum council house in Glasgow. Fred was working on an ice cream van, and the marriage was already under strain because of his overpowering impulse to sleep with every woman he saw—while other drivers returned their vans at midnight, Fred was usually out until four in the morning.

In spite of the marital problems, Rena became pregnant again, and another daughter, Anne Marie, was born on July 6, 1963.

Where his wife was concerned, Fred's Mr. Hyde aspect was dominant; he often dragged her out of bed in the early hours of the morning to beat her. She seems to have taken these thrashings with working-class resignation. But she finally retaliated for the infidelities by starting an affair with a neighbor called John McLachlan. One night when West caught them kissing in the park, he hurled himself on her, punching and slapping her, and McLachlan defended her and ended by giving Fred a beating. The next day, Rena was badly bruised and had a broken tooth. Yet Fred and McLachlan remained on speaking terms, and McLachlan later recorded that he once lent Fred his gardening shed for one of his assignations.

Rena became friendly with a girl called Anne McFall, who was five years her junior. Anne also came from a slum home, and was accustomed to seeing her mother beaten up in domestic quarrels. Oddly enough, Anne became increasingly interested in Fred West, and was soon convinced that she was in love with him. And when Fred and Rena announced they were returning to the Gloucester area, Anne decided she may as well go too.

Fred returned south, and when he came back, announced that he had rented a house large enough for all of them—including a friend of Anne's called Isa McNeill. The four Wests and their passengers set out in a van that stank of butchered meat—for Fred's latest job was in an abattoir—a place where he learned the skills that were to serve him so well later. When they arrived at the village of Kempley, near Much Marcle, the women were disgusted to find that the "large house" was, in fact, a small caravan on a caravan site. West was a pathological liar, who always said what he thought other people wanted to hear.

But they moved in—Fred and Rena in a tiny room at the end of a draw-across shutter, the two children in beds that pulled down from the wall, and Anne and Isa at the other end.

The two young girls found it boring. They had hoped to get jobs and earn some money, but they were four miles from Gloucester, and could not afford bus fares. They had to be content with occasional baby-sitting jobs on the site, for which they were often paid in cigarettes.

Fred became more violent; Anne and Isa found it all so traumatic that they would take the children to a neighbor's caravan until he stopped beating Rena. It was Isa who was to describe Fred as a Jekyll and Hyde.

Finally, Isa managed to telephone John McLachlan, and begged him to come and collect them all. He agreed to drive down with a friend at the weekend, while Fred was at work. But Anne McFall was unable to keep her mouth shut; she told Fred, and when John McLachlan arrived, Fred was waiting. There was a screaming row; Fred refused to let the children go. Finally, Rena and Isa drove off. Anne declared that she would remain behind because she had a job in Gloucester. It was undoubtedly a lie; she looked forward to having Fred to herself.

A few months later, in September 1966, Anne McFall was pregnant. But in April 1967, a month before the baby was due, she disappeared. Fred later told his son Stephen that he had stabbed her, but was vague about the reason; she may have decided that she also wanted to return to Glasgow.

West also told Stephen that he had killed a fifteen-year-old Gloucester waitress named Mary Bastholm, who vanished on January 6, 1968. A man named Vincent Oakes went to the police soon after her disappearance, and reported that he had seen her "four or five times" in the autumn of 1967 with the same man, often sitting in a car a few hundred yards from her home. When, in 1994, he saw a picture of Fred West as a young man, Oakes identified him as the man he had seen with Mary. If this is true, then it is possible that the murder of Mary Bastholm was not a sex crime, but that West became romantically involved with her, then killed her in one of his Jekyll and Hyde rages.

By 1967, Rena was missing her children, and in July, she asked Isa to return with her to Gloucester to try to get them back. But Isa was about to get married, and wanted to stay where she was. So Rena returned alone. She seems to have moved in with Fred again. But on New Year's Day, 1969, she was also murdered. West later said that she had decided to take the children back to Scotland; he had got her drunk—Rena enjoyed her alcohol—and strangled her. He told acquaintances that she had run away with an engineer. Rena, like Anne McFall, had never been close to her family, and no one asked her whereabouts.

Fred was again working as a lorry driver; he was now living in another caravan, this one at Bishops Cleeve, near Cheltenham.

A friend named Fred Crick shared the caravan for a while. He later described how Fred had become an abortionist, picking up pregnant girls in pubs. He performed the abortions in a garage next door, and kept Polaroid photographs of the bloodstained women—he obviously derived satisfaction from the sight of blood. (This could explain why—as the judge hinted in the summing up—he later seemed to enjoy dismembering victims.)

It was some time in 1968, at a bus stop on the Stoke Road between Tewkesbury and Cheltenham, that Fred West—now a baker's roundsman—met a fourteen-year-old schoolgirl, Rose Letts, and engaged her in conversation. Rose was to declare later that he was scruffy and dirty, and that she was disinclined to talk to him. But he proved to have "the gift of gab," and had soon persuaded her to meet him in a local pub. She proved remarkably easy to seduce.

Rosemary Pauline Letts was one of a family of seven children. She had been born November 29, 1953, in Barnstaple, Devon. Her father, Bill Letts, was an electrical engineer in the Royal Navy. He was also what psychologists describe as a "Right Man"—a man driven by some deep psychological insecurity to behave like a dictator towards his family, and who will on no account ever admit that he might be in the wrong.

Such men have an almost pathological desire to be a "somebody," and if the world fails to bolster their craving for self-esteem, they try to satisfy it by entering into a domination fantasy with their wives and children.

Bills Letts would order his children to clean the house, and if he found a speck of dust, would make them do it all over again. When they dug the garden, he would inspect it like a sergeant major. He would beat the children brutally on the slightest pretext, and his mild-mannered wife Daisy was treated just as badly. One daughter took an overdose after he had beaten her black and blue. Neighbors complained to the police so often about the screams and shouts that he had to move home twice.

Yet Rose was never beaten. The reason was simple. From an early stage, Bill Letts had been committing incest with her. In some ways, the situation was weirdly similar to that in the West family home in Much Marcle. Even when Daisy Letts, driven to desperation by her husband's violence, walked out with her children and moved to a derelict farmhouse, Rose stayed on with her father. Some relatives had no doubt about the reason: she was enjoying the sexual attention she received from him.

At her trial, Rose West was to try to gain sympathy by describing in some detail how she had been twice raped in her teens, then "seduced" by Fred West. The truth, as her younger brother Graham revealed, was that Rose had never needed any encouragement to have sex. In spite of the puritanism of her home—that meant that no one was allowed to walk around the house even partly undressed—Rose always left the bathroom door open, and paraded naked along the landing.

While her parents—now back together—were out working in the evening, Rose had to bath the younger children and prepare them for bed. One evening she climbed into bed with her brother Graham and introduced him to sex.

By the time she was fifteen, her preference for older men was unmistakable; she would return home late at night in cars driven by boyfriends twice her age. She began working for her brother-in-law Jim Tiler, in his roadside snack bar. On a number of occasions, Tiler arrived there at four in the afternoon to find its shutter down, and Rose in a lorry with a driver.

So Rose Letts met Fred West—as far as we know—some time in that summer of 1968, met him later in a local pub, and had soon accepted his suggestion of returning to his trailer for sex. Soon, he had persuaded her to give up her job, and become the nanny of his children. Rose continued to take home her wages every week, but Fred was giving it to her.

Finally, Rose decided to take Fred West home to introduce him to her father. The result was predictable: Bill Letts exploded in jealous rage, and ordered her never to see "that gypsy" again. He divined, correctly, that Fred was a pathological liar when the unhygienic laborer told him that he owned a caravan and a hotel in Scotland. And when Rose ignored her father's orders, and continued to spend most of her free time in West's caravan, Bill Letts had her taken into care.

As soon as she turned sixteen, the local authorities were unable to hold her, and she moved into West's caravan. Her father never spoke to her again.

Living with West removed the last of her inhibitions; her brother Graham was later to say that Rose had always been a quiet girl, but that after moving in with West she became obsessed by sex, talking of nothing else. She even began to adopt West's rough, coarse manner of speaking.

It seems clear that there was some incredibly powerful chemistry between them. For West, the original attraction was undoubtedly that she was a teenage girl who looked still younger than her age, and that, by contrast with his own, her background seemed almost middle class. Socially, she was "above" him.

For Rose, West represented freedom from a life of repression, and she found him as exciting a contrast as he found her. She had always enjoyed sex; now it became the center of her life. West's first wife Rena had told a friend that Fred had some "kinky" demands. Rose apparently had no objection to these, and the sequel makes it clear that her sexual appetite developed until she was virtually insatiable. It is a curious thought that she was probably not even aware that Fred was a sex maniac; years of intimacy with her perverted father would have made it seem normal.

It never emerged during the trial why Fred murdered his wife Rena. Earlier newspaper reports had stated that Fred met Rose Letts after he murdered Rena on New Year's Day 1969. The knowledge that he met Rose many months earlier—and that Rose needed so little persuasion to move into his trailer—throws new light on the murder. He was having an affair with an underage girl, and he wanted to bring her back to the caravan. While Rena was there that was impossible. That is almost certainly the reason that he strangled Rena when she was drunk and buried her in a field.

Fred had been morbidly jealous with Rena, but when he realized that Rose was a nymphomaniac, it excited him, and he began to dream of watching her having sex with other men—and women. Rose (who soon realized that she liked women as much as men) found her husband's fantasies as exciting as he did. Life became a non-stop sexual orgy. They experimented with "kinky" variants—later evidence points to leather gear, rubber face masks that covered the head, whips and handcuffs. At this point Fred asked the social services if they would take the children into care while he tried to "sort out" his marriage; it seems more likely that he wanted to be able to have uninhibited orgies in the caravan.

In October 1970, less than a year later, Fred and Rose West moved into 10, then 25 Midland Road, Gloucester (Fred seemed to have an odd preference for 25—the trailer had also been No. 25). Here they launched themselves into trying to involve others in their sex life. Their next door neighbor was a nineteen-year-old girl named Liz Agius, who had two children; her Maltese husband worked abroad. Fred made her acquaintance when he helped her downstairs with a pram, and invited her to tea. Oddly enough, Fred introduced Rose—whom Liz Agius describes as looking about fourteen years old, and heavily pregnant—as his girlfriend, which suggests that he already had designs on their new acquaintance, and that she might be more willing to betray a girlfriend than a wife. On two occasions Liz Agius baby-sat for them, and on the second, they told her that they had been driving around looking for young girls, preferably homeless. They explained they would offer them a home, then get them to work as prostitutes. Liz Agius was not unduly shocked when Fred told her that Rose was a prostitute.

Fred also made no secret of the fact that he wanted to sleep with Liz Agius; he went into detail about what he would like to do to her in bed, including tying her up; in return, "I could tie him up and do all sorts of things to him." Liz Agius said she refused. One day, Fred even snapped handcuffs on her and said: "Now I've f—ing got you." It was Rose who ordered him to remove the handcuffs; Fred obeyed instantly.

Liz Agius also described how Rose West had called on her, and tried to persuade her to join in three-in-a-bed sex; Liz Agius told her indignantly that if she wanted to keep her friendship, she should not mention it again.

But finally, Fred had his way. After being given a cup of tea, Liz Agius felt strangely drowsy; when she woke up, it was morning, and she was naked in bed between the Wests. Fred told her that he had had sex with her while she was unconscious. Throughout the rest of that day, she felt drowsy and sick. But apparently she held no grudge against the Wests, for she later visited them at Cromwell Street, and was shown around their new home.

When Liz Agius's husband turned up, West was violently jealous, particularly when her husband put his arm round her shoulders—West later told her that her husband ought to be under ground, and threatened to whip him before he killed and buried him.

In 1971 and 1972, Fred West spent two terms in prison for dishonesty, on one occasion for stealing tires and a car tax disc from his landlord—he had been in trouble for petty theft since his teens. (He stole all the materials used in improving his house, and took the children on thieving expeditions to building sites.) He and Rose exchanged letters that reveal the intense romantic chemistry between them; he signs himself "your ever worshipping husband," while she begins her letter: "To my dearest lover," and writes across the top: "From now until forever." She tells him: "I know you love me darling, but it just seems queer that anyone should think so much of me."

According to the prosecution, it was during West's first period in jail in 1971 that the child Charmaine—then eight—disappeared. On May 22, 1971, Rose had written: "Darling, about Charm. I think she likes to be handled rough. But darling, why do I have to be the one to do it? I would keep her for her sake if it wasn't for the rest of the children." It seems clear that she had already decided that Charmaine had to go.

Rose seems to have made a habit of handling Charmaine "rough." A neighbor named Shirley Giles told how she had sent her daughter downstairs to borrow some milk; the child had walked into the kitchen without knocking, and found Charmaine standing on a chair, her hands tied behind her with a leather strap, while Rose West was menacing her with a wooden spoon. Fred was also capable of treating Charmaine brutally. A neighbor in Glasgow recalls how, when Charmaine reached for an ice cream in West's van, he slapped her face.

Rose West was to insist that Fred was out of jail when Charmaine vanished, but the evidence suggests otherwise. Fred West was sent to jail for the first time on December 4, 1970, on several charges involving theft. The total sentence was ten months, and he was given a four-month remission, coming out of prison in mid-1971. But Charmaine was seen for the last time in the spring of 1971, while West was in jail. Questioned later by the police, Rose West said that Charmaine had been taken away by her mother Rena. Asked when was the last time she saw Rena, Rose West answered: "When she took Charmaine." By this time, Rena West had been dead for more than two years.

Rose West would continue to deny that she killed Charmaine, insisting that the child vanished after Fred West came out of prison. But the police believe that what happened is that Rose strangled Charmaine and hid her body in the coal cellar until Fred came out of prison and buried her under the floor at 25 Midland Road. The evidence seems to show that Charmaine was already dead when Rose West wrote the letter about "treating Charmaine rough."

In December, 1972, the Wests picked up Caroline Owens in Tewkesbury and raped her. The following January they were fined £25 each by Gloucester magistrate John Smith. Three months later, they committed what seems to have been their first joint murder. One of their male lodgers, Ben Stanniland, had met a nineteen-year-old girl named Lynda Gough in a Gloucester cafe, and brought her back to Cromwell Street, where the couple had sex. Lynda Gough also had sex with another lodger, David Evans. Both males were also Rose West's lovers—Stanniland described how Rose West had climbed into bed with himself and another male lodger the very first evening they moved into Cromwell Street.

Lynda Gough was on bad terms with her parents, and had had a number of quarrels. In early April, 1973, she had been collected from her home by a man and woman, who took her out for the evening. Two weeks later, on April 19, 1973, she left home, leaving a note telling her parents that she had found herself a flat. Her mother, June Gough, made inquiries at the Co-op, where Lynda had worked as a seamstress, but she had not been back there since she left home. Finally— two weeks later—June Gough found her way to 25 Cromwell Street. The woman who came to the door—Rose West—was the same one who had called for Lynda to take her out, and Mrs. Gough realized that she was wearing Lynda's slippers and her cardigan. She also noticed some of Lynda's clothes on the washing line. Rose West explained that Lynda had left them behind when she left for Weston-super-Mare to look for work.

It was Lynda's body that was found under the bathroom at 25 Cromwell Street. It had once been the garage, and Lynda had been buried in the inspection pit. She had evidently been bound and gagged, and two-inch sticky tape had been wrapped lightly around the head to form a mask.

What had happened can be inferred. Lynda had originally been brought back to Cromwell Street by a male lodger with whom she had had intercourse. She had later had sex with another lodger. We know that Fred West would become feverishly excited at the thought of a girl giving herself to men, for his nature was basically voyeuristic; we also know that both lodgers were also Rose's lovers, and would certainly have told her about it. And when the Wests learned that Lynda was on bad terms with her parents and looking for a flat, they knew that it should not be too difficult to lure her into their home. They probably discussed the move when they took her out for the evening. They also undoubtedly warned her to tell no one where she was going.

Caroline Raine had also been gagged with masking tape six months earlier, but its only purpose was to keep her silent. To bind the whole face and forehead in tape, so that the victim would have looked like a mummy, was obviously unnecessary if the only purpose was to keep her silent. The purpose of the tape was to make Lynda Gough *look* like a mummy, to satisfy the Wests' enthusiasm for bondage. Unlike Caroline Raine, Lynda was almost certainly intended to die. They even had a place ready to bury the body—the inspection pit of the garage, which was going to be turned into a bathroom. . . .

It was also at about this time that West began to have sex with his nine-year-old daughter, Anne Marie. At the preliminary hearing, she would describe how, at the age of eight or nine (in 1971 or 1972), her father had tied her to a U-shaped metal bar, with her legs apart, and then inserted a vibrator into her vagina. When she screamed, Rose West sat on her head. After West withdrew the vibrator, she remembered him "taking red things like frogspawn out of my vagina. He put it in the bowl. There was quite a lot of it. Rose was laughing and smirking at me."

Later, West made a device rather like a chastity belt, which would hold the vibrator inside her. Rose West used to strap it on, "then I had to walk around the house with it inside me. I could hear the buzzing noise. I was left like that for a few hours."

When she was nine, West began having regular intercourse with her, and she soon began menstruating. The incest continued until her late teens, when she married and left home. When she was twelve, she also had been made to go to bed with Rose West's lovers—about five of them, mostly black. While this happened, she was aware that her father was spying on her through a hole in the wall—a plaque with the word

"Rose," which could be unscrewed for a spyhole. She was aware that this excited him. "I never wanted to be with those men. I often told her that, but she never answered. Rose is a very strong character."

When she was thirteen, Rose made her perform oral sex on her, while Rose squeezed her breasts. After Rose reached orgasm, Anne Marie rushed to the bathroom to wash out her mouth with gargle. "I made sure Rose did not see me."

West obviously found the idea that he had turned his daughter into a kind of prostitute intensely stimulating—on one occasion, he inserted a condom tied at the end and full of sperm, inside her vagina, and made her wear it inside her as she watched television. The sperm came from Rose's lovers.

But Rose was jealous of her stepdaughter, whose relationship with her father had always been exceptionally close. (As a child, Anne Marie had wanted to marry him.) So West had to have sex with Anne Marie without Rose's knowledge. This would happen when he took her out in the van, or when she was helping him on decorating jobs in empty flats. For some unexplained reason, there was a purple light on the dashboard, and West would switch this on when they stopped. "I would have a funny feeling in my tummy then. I knew that we would have intercourse."

At fifteen, Anne Marie became pregnant by her father. It was a fallopian pregnancy, and ended in a miscarriage. At this point, Anne Marie left home, to live on the streets.

The next of the Wests' murder victims was fifteen-year-old Carol Anne Cooper, known as Caz. She had been born in 1958, and her parents had separated when she was a child. She went to live with her mother, but her mother died when she was eight. Her father married again, and she returned to live with him; but when this marriage broke up, she was placed in a children's home, The Pines, in Worcester. She settled down well, and her social worker described her as "a lovely, intelligent girl who never gave any trouble."

On November 10, 1973, Carol and a group of friends went to the Odeon cinema, and afterwards Carol's boyfriend, Andrew Jones, saw her to the bus. They had been quarreling, but had made it up before she climbed on the bus. She waved to him as it pulled away. That was the last he saw of her.

Fred and Rose West probably picked her up as she walked the short distance from the bus stop to The Pines. Her body was one of the five found in the cellar at Cromwell Street. The Wests must have intended to kill her when they picked her up, since she was unknown to them, and was unlikely to remain silent about being kidnapped and raped.

The next victim was Exeter University student Lucy Partington, twenty-one, niece of the novelist Kingsley Amis. She spent the Christmas of 1973 at home with her family, and on December 27, went into Cheltenham to see a disabled friend, Helen Render. Lucy was a quiet, serious girl who was intending to become a Catholic. That evening, she wrote a letter applying for a place in the Cortauld Institute, and when she left at 10:15 to catch her bus, was carrying the letter to drop in a nearby post box. If she missed the last bus, she intended to return to Helen Render's, whose father would drive her home. That night, the bus was late, and she may have assumed she had missed it—which is why she almost certainly accepted a lift from the Wests. Her body was also found in the cellar.

By the end of that year, 1973, when the Wests had been fined £25 each for assaulting Caroline Raine, they had gone on to murder three girls.

Almost exactly a year after their first murder, the Wests picked up another hitchhiker—a twenty-one-year-old Swiss girl named Therese Siegenthaler, who lived in a flat in Lewisham, and studied sociology at the Woolwich College of further education. On April 15, 1974, she set out to hitchhike to Ireland to see a priest she had become friendly with. Friends had advised against it, but Therese was skilled in judo, and was convinced that she could cope with any emergency. She intended to travel via Holyhead, in North Wales, and her most direct route would have taken her via Gloucester. Her body was also found in the cellar at Cromwell Street.

Once again, as if following a pattern, the Wests waited until November before searching for another victim. It was another fifteen-year-old girl, Shirley Ann Hubbard, who, like Carol Cooper, had been in care since her parents split up. She was working as a trainee shop assistant in Debenhams in Worcester, and on November 5, 1974, she went to have tea at the home of a youth, Daniel Davies, who also worked in the shop, and they went to a cinema. She arranged to go out with him again the next day, but never returned to Debenhams. She was on her way home to her foster parents in Droitwich when she disappeared. When her body was found in the Wests' cellar, her skull was completely covered with a mask of adhesive tape, and plastic tubes had been inserted up her nose to allow her to breathe.

Juanita Mott, 18, the last of the women found buried in the basement, was another of the Wests' lodgers. Like so many of the victims, she had found herself without a home when her parents split up. She had lived in a flat with a boyfriend for a while, then moved into Cromwell Street, but soon left there, for reasons that are not clear, and moved in with a friend of her mother's at Newent. She was due to baby-sit a large group of children on April 12, 1975, when the woman she was staying with got married, but on the previous day she left Newent for an evening out. It seems fairly certain that she either returned to see someone at Cromwell Street, or was offered a lift by the Wests. When her body was found, there was also a clothes line that had been used to tie her—it came from Mrs. West's back garden. When asked later whether she had not noticed that one of her clothes lines had gone missing, Rose West replied that there were clothes lines all over the place—Fred West had an odd habit of picking up bits and pieces of rope and bringing them home. Juanita's sister Belinda continued to frequent the Cromwell Street house, unaware of the part played in her sister's disappearance by the Wests.

After the death of Juanita Mott, there is a three-year gap before that of the next victim, Shirley Ann Robinson. It is unusual for serial killers to stop killing for that long, and it may be that Fred West, having filled his basement with as many bodies as it would hold, began burying victims elsewhere—he later told his son Stephen that there *had* been many other victims. He was later to tell a social worker that there were as many as twenty, and that they had been buried on a farm.

What we *do* know is that in 1975, a thirteen-year-old girl called Sharon Williams was taken to 25 Cromwell Street by a friend who lived in the same children's home, Russet House. Like so many of the Wests' victims, she came from a broken home. She was also to allege that her father and brother had sexually abused her.

Rose West treated her kindly, and she often called at Cromwell Street. In 1976, she moved to the Jordan's Brook Children's Home. On Fridays she was allowed to go to spend the weekend in Tewkesbury with her mother, and on her way to the bus, often called in at the Wests. They had sent her a birthday card on her fifteenth birthday.

One night in the summer of 1977, she ran away from the children's home, and spent the night walking the streets. The following evening she called at 25 Cromwell Street. It was 11 o'clock at night, and the door was answered by Rose West, dressed only in a bra and panties. Sharon was taken into the lounge, and sat beside Rose on the sofa. As she was crying and explaining her problems, Rose began kissing her and caressing her breasts through her blouse. But when Sharon showed obvious signs of discomfort, Rose stood up and got her a blanket; the girl slept on the settee.

The next day she was found wandering the streets and taken back to the home. She lost her privileges, and it was six weeks before she again called on the Wests.

Again it was Rose who let her in. Sharon had to hurry to the toilet—a bladder cyst had made her incontinent, and she left her wet knickers in the lavatory.

When she came out, Rose told her there were two girls of her own age in the next room and took her in. It proved to be a bedroom, and Sharon was startled to discover that the two girls were naked, and that Fred was wearing only his shorts. One girl was black, one white, both about fourteen.

Rose West put her arms around Sharon and said that it was all right to feel and touch and enjoy affection. Then she unbuttoned Sharon's dress and went on to undress her until she was naked.

After this, Rose went over to Fred and did a kind of strip tease, wriggling seductively as she undressed.

The white girl was then laid on her back, and Fred West bound her wrists together across her chest. Then she was turned over and her legs spread apart and taped down to the bed. ("Her legs were so far apart it almost split her.") After this, Rose West inserted a vibrator into the girl's vagina, and she groaned in pain. Rose helped Fred remove his shorts, and Fred pulled the girl's buttocks apart and kissed the cleavage. Then he climbed on her and had intercourse—Sharon could not see whether it was vaginal or anal. When he climaxed, he left the room, and Rose untied the girl.

Now it was Sharon's turn. Rose approached her and began kissing and caressing her. Then, as Sharon sat on the bed, her wrists were also taped across her chest. While Fred stood by the bed masturbating, Rose turned Sharon on her face, and taped her ankles apart. Rose then teased her by allowing the vibrator to approach close to her genitals, then taking it away.

After that, Rose pushed two fingers into her vagina, caressing her breast with the other hand, and twisting the nipple hard, repeating "Enjoy." Then Sharon felt something hard and cold enter her anus—she thought it was a candle. It was very painful, and she heard a popping sound. After this, Fred climbed on her, and entered her vagina. Rose held his penis as he moved it in and out. Finally, when Fred shouted that he was coming, Rose told him to withdraw, and Sharon felt the sperm on her back, and Rose rubbing it in. After this she was released and the tape was cut off.

Sharon went into the bathroom with her dress, and saw that her anus was bleeding. She put the dress on and crept out of the house, leaving her underwear behind.

She was too ashamed to tell anyone what had happened, but felt angry and betrayed. Two weeks later she returned to Cromwell Street with a can of petrol and a box of matches; she intended to pour the petrol through the letter box and throw in a match. But at the last minute, she could not go through with it. When she told the story seventeen years later, her identity was shielded under the pseudonym of Miss A. By this time she had been married and divorced twice, been in a home for battered wives, and attempted suicide.

The next murder victim, eighteen-year-old Shirley Ann Robinson, was again a lodger in the Wests' home. But she seems to have enjoyed it there (her best friend later said that the years she spent in Cromwell Street were the happiest of her life), and became the lover of both Fred and Rose West. She also worked as a prostitute for the Wests, sleeping with Rose's "clients."

Shirley Robinson seems to have been in love with Fred, who occasionally teased his wife by telling her that Shirley was going to be his next wife. Another witness, Janet Leach, claimed that Shirley had tried to persuade Fred to leave Rose and set up home with her.

In the autumn of 1977, Shirley Robinson became pregnant, and applied for supplementary benefit on April 10, 1978. She later moved into the room of another friend who lived in the house, Liz Brewer, who was also pregnant by her boyfriend—she told Liz that she was afraid of the Wests. Her baby was due in June. On May 9, she and Liz Brewer went into Woolworths together to get their photographs taken in a booth. The next day, Shirley vanished. Her body was discovered under the patio, with the eight-month-old fetus nearby. Janet Leach reported that West had told her that Rose had killed Shirley while he was out at work.

There was—as far as we know—only one more victim to be murdered at 25 Cromwell Street for purely sexual reasons. Again, sixteen-year-old Alison Chambers had found herself in a children's home after her parents split up. She and another girl had been taken to Cromwell Street by a girl whose middle name was Ann—probably Shirley Ann Robinson. In September 1979, Alison's mother received a letter in which Alison said she was living with a "really nice homely family,"and that one of the girls treated her like a big sister. This was not entirely true, for Alison was still living in the Jordan's Brook home, and working in a solicitor's office. One day she packed her clothes in a rucksack and left the home. Her body was one of the three found under West's patio.

Did the Wests then give up killing for sex? It is just conceivable (although unlikely). West was forty-eight, Rose thirty-six. Most sex killers are young—between eighteen and twenty-eight. Even sex killers who go on longer than that gradually "burn out" as they approach middle age. Fred and Rose West had been conducting a more-or-less continuous orgy for more than twenty years; even they must have begun to lose their frantic desire for "forbidden" pleasures. Rose had her regular male visitors, and Fred often accompanied them upstairs and filmed the sex. On one occasion, Rose had walked into the street in a negligee and accousted a Jamaican named Andrew Angus, asking him if he knew anything about televisions. Angus went into the house and looked at the set; when he turned round, Rose West was wearing only some revealing underwear. Minutes later, they were in bed, in a room whose ceiling was a huge mirror. Angus found her insatiable. She told him that she was "turned on" by black men, and that several of her children were half-castes. When Fred West came home from work, Angus was astonished that he appeared to have no objection to his wife seducing a stranger.

Angus remained Rose's lover, and described how they often made love for three hours at a time. "She was totally sex mad. She always knew exactly what she wanted and how to get it."

A housewife named Kathryn Mary Halliday, who had just separated from her husband, and was depressed and vulnerable, told a *Sunday Mirror* reporter how she had met Fred when he came to repair a leak at her home in Cromwell Street. She said he talked non-stop, "a real Jack-the-lad." He told her his wife liked "a bit of both" and invited her home. They sat at a bar, and as Rose—in a miniskirt—wiggled against her, the skirt rose revealing that she was wearing no underwear. After several large drinks, Rose led her upstairs by the hand, followed by Fred. "She literally ripped my blouse off." Then they undressed and had sex, watched by Fred. After that, Fred joined in, obviously excited by the spectacle.

From then on, Rose would call for her after the West children had gone to school, and they returned to drink coffee, then retire to bed. "She was absolutely insatiable. She used to say that no man or woman could ever satisfy her. I don't think she got much sexual pleasure from Fred—he wasn't very well endowed."

The Wests often urged her to move in, but Mary felt an odd sense of unease. "Something stopped me."

The only day Mary was never allowed to call was on Thursday. This was the day when Rose had a string of clients. They paid £40 each, although some long-term lovers were not charged. She often had as many as eight men in an afternoon.

When Fred came home he enjoyed watching, and often video-ing the sex. He also constructed a hole in the wall through which he could watch Rose without the client knowing. There were also intercoms, so he could listen to it. Afterwards, he always went in and made love to Rose.

Mary Halliday described how, one day, Fred asked her if she would like to see inside their "secret room." It contained a huge four-poster bed, and there was a torture chamber with whips, hooks and chains. Then Rose brought out a pile of porno magazines showing people in black latex suits, and a suitcase with similar black suits in it, all looking well worn. The bedroom cupboard was full of whips, dildos and other "sex toys." Mary Halliday declared that she felt "out of her depth"—particularly when Fred showed her videos of young girls being tied up, whipped and tortured. Some of these videos did not seem to be commercial—one of the girls looked as if she was in agony.

Mary Halliday participated in some of the "games," allowing herself to be tied up with a pillow over her face, after which West flogged her with whips, or abused her with huge objects. But when he cut her stomach with a knife, she seems to have felt he was going too far. She broke off the relationship.

The last known victim, sixteen-year-old Heather West, had been sexually abused by her father for at least two years. As soon as she was a teenager, West began asking her when she was going to lose her virginity, and urging her to find a boyfriend; but finally, he himself took her virginity. Heather was a quiet girl, but seems to have been a less compliant character than her sister Anne Marie (possibly she inherited some of her mother's dominance). When at the age of sixteen, she announced she was leaving home, the Wests must have known that she was unlikely to keep silent about her ordeal. According to Fred West, he killed her in the hallway by strangling her, "to wipe the smirk off her face," then sawed off her head and legs with an ice saw, so she would fit into a dustbin liner.

West was arrested in August 1991 on a charge of raping and sodomizing his thirteen-year-old daughter; Rose was also implicated, but released on bail. She spent most of that year alone. But when the daughter decided not to testify, West was released. During that year, Rose had been profoundly depressed, and had attempted suicide with an overdose. For some considerable time after West's release, the children were not returned to 25 Cromwell Street—they preferred to live "in care." The Wests became depressed, convinced that it could only be a matter of time before they were caught; they spent a lot of time watching television together and holding hands.

Yet they might never have been caught if it had not been for the persistence of Hazel Savage, and her certainty that they had killed Heather. In February 1993, when they were finally arrested, West was ready to confess.

He went on to tell detectives the story of how he had killed Heather "to wipe the smirk off her face," and described exactly where her body would be found. But he insisted that the death had been an accident—he had grabbed her by the throat because she was being insultingly defiant, and was shocked when he saw that she had "gone blue." "I blowed air into her mouth and that, and pumped on her chest, but she just kept going bluer . . ." Rose, he claimed, was out at the time—he had sent her out so he could have a long talk to Heather. Rose knew nothing of Heather's death.

But his attitude toward Rose was not entirely one of chivalry. He was later to tell Dr. James McAlister that Rose had been burying girls in the cellar without his knowledge. He had been away from home for a few days, and when he came back, Rose persuaded him to concrete the cellar floor. He does not seem to have been struck by the absurdity of his story—that he would have had to be away from home at least nine times to be unaware of his wife's activities.

During his period in prison, West unburdened himself to his son Stephen, and told him that there had been many more victims—some murdered and dismembered on a deserted farm near Much Marcle. (According to Stephen he named the farm.) West was also to tell a social worker, Janet Leach, who acted as an independent observer at eighty of his interviews, that there had been twenty more victims, and there had been other people involved in the murders—his wife, "another person, and some colored men."

But then, Stephen was to describe how his father would switch between confessing, then claiming that someone else was the killer. "He blamed it on everybody but the milk man." And West told Janet Leach that Anne McFall was killed by "another person" and his wife Rena—although Rena was (as far as we know) in Glasgow at the time. Even when confessing to murder, West found it hard to stick to the truth.

The trial of Frederick and Rosemary West was due to begin some time in the autumn of 1995.

But Fred West would never face justice; he committed suicide on New Year's Day, 1995, by hanging himself in his cell in Winson Green prison, Birmingham. He had found it nerve-wracking being in prison among the "hard men"—child killers are always hated—and told his son Stephen that he had to keep looking over his shoulder. He behaved meekly, and addressed guards—and even fellow prisoners—as "sir."

Although West was being carefully watched, he took advantage of the fact that fewer staff were on duty because of the New Year holiday and that there was a change of shift at midday. He died on the twenty-sixth anniversary of the murder of his first wife Rena.

Rose West claimed to be delighted by the news. Her story was that she had been "duped" by West, and was as much his victim as any of the women he killed. After hearing of Heather's death, she claimed that if she could get her hands on him, "he would be a dead man." It is just possible that her hatred was genuine. As she saw it, she had been an innocent schoolgirl when she met West, and now she was facing a life in prison. It was Fred who was to blame.

Two days later, newspapers announced that "there is mounting speculation that the accusations against her will now be dropped." Her solicitor, Leo Goatley, declared that the case against her had always been flimsy, and that it was flimsier now.

The police had good reason to disagree. They had the testimony of Caroline Raine, Sharon Williams and Anne Marie West (now Davies) that made it very clear that Rose West was at no point a "victim," or even an unwilling participant. In fact, her part in the rapes had been *more* active than that of her husband. She was the dominant one, not the unwilling tool.

The trial of Rosemary West opened at Winchester Crown Court on October 9, 1995, before Mr. Justice Mantell. The defense was led by Brian Leveson, QC, and the defense by Richard Ferguson, QC.

The prosecutor made a grim opening speech, describing how the nine victims had all been naked at the time of death, and bound with tape—including their faces. And he hinted at even more horrific abuse when he mentioned that many of the fingers and toes seemed to be missing.

The defense team had an almost impossible task. The only point in their favor was that there was no solid evidence against Rose West; no one had actually seen her kill anyone; no one could disprove her unlikely assertion that she had lived in a tiny house, and yet been unaware that her husband was murdering girls and burying them on the premises.

In fact, the first witness for the prosecution, Rosemary West's mother, Daisy Letts, a frail seventy-six-year-old widow, made a point that was undoubtedly in her daughter's favor. She described how, in early 1971, Rose had left Fred after a quarrel, and returned home to her parents, and how, when Fred came to beg her to return, Rose had turned to her father and said: "You don't know him. There is nothing he wouldn't do." Mrs. Letts thought that her daughter had added: "Even murder."

Next, a neighbor of the Wests named Shirley Giles described how her daughter had walked into the kitchen at 25 Midland Road, and saw the baby, Charmaine, standing on a stool, with her hands tied behind her, while Rose threatened her with a wooden spoon.

The next witness was Caroline Raine—now Owens—the girl who had been abducted and raped by the Wests in December 1971, and whose failure to appear in court as a witness against them had enabled them to move on to a career of murder. She described in detail how the Wests had offered her a lift, then bound and gagged her, and taken her back to Cromwell Street. She added an interesting detail—that after they had both assaulted her, Fred West began crying and apologizing for what he had done. Her testimony made it clear that Rose was the prime mover in the kidnap and rape, and that Fred experienced some pangs of conscience about it.

Another witness, Mrs. June Gough, described how after her daughter Lynda had disappeared, she called at the Wests' home, and noticed that Rose was wearing Lynda's slippers, and that there were some of Lynda's clothes on the clothes line.

Family and friends of the dead girls gave evidence about the last time they had seen them alive. And one witness, Kathleen Ryan, described how she had called at 25 Cromwell Street, and how Fred West had remarked: "These are the children and this is my wife, and this"—pointing to Shirley Ann Robinson—"is my mistress." Another lodger at 25 Cromwell Street, Liz Brewer, revealed that Shirley Ann Robinson had been afraid of the Wests just before her disappearance, and wanted to get away from them.

When "Miss A"—Sharon Williams—gave evidence about how she was co-opted into a sex session with the Wests and two other girls, and how she had gone back to their house later with a can of petrol to burn it down, it became increasingly obvious that the defense argument—that Rose West was innocent of what was going on—was becoming increasingly unbelievable.

Anne Marie West—now Davies—went into the witness box to describe in detail how her father had deflowered her with a vibrator when she was eight, and had begun having sex with her when she was nine. She described how Rose West had often taken part in these sessions, once holding her down while Fred raped her. She also told how Rose had once forced her to perform oral sex on her. She had become pregnant by her father when she was fifteen, but had aborted. After that, she left home, and remained away for four years. Two subsequent marriages had been unsuccessful.

The defense, obviously aware that things looked bad, decided on the desperate expedient of putting Rose West herself in the dock. The accused murderess cried as she tried to convince the jury that she was the victim of a violent and brutal bully who kept her under his thumb. In an obvious attempt to gain the sympathy of the jury, she also described how she had been raped twice before she met Fred West, and how he had seduced her. They had lived "separate lives" at Cromwell

Street, she claimed—contradicting the evidence of every witness who had lived there.

By the time her testimony was finished, it was obvious that it had had the opposite effect from the one the defense intended. And when a social worker named Janet Leach, who had met Fred West during his interrogations, stated that West had told her that he was lying to save his wife, it became obvious that the defense was virtually in ruins.

The judge's summing up—beginning on Thursday November 16—was fair and balanced. He warned the jury that they needed to keep cool heads and set aside all prejudice. But he pointed out that if two people take part in murder, then both are equally guilty, no matter which of them actually killed the victim.

The jury returned from their overnight deliberations on Tuesday November 21, and the foreman stated that they had found Rose West guilty of three murders—that of baby Charmaine, of daughter Heather West, and of Shirley Ann Robinson. The next day they were back again, to announce that they had now found Rose West guilty of the murder of the other seven girls found buried at Cromwell Street.

Rose West's face was expressionless as Mr. Justice Mantell said: "If attention is paid to what I think, you will never be released. Take her down."

A few days later, the press announced that the police were looking into the disappearance of nine more girls who had stayed at 25 Cromwell Street. Rose was quoted as saying, as she was taken to prison, "God knows what will happen if they find the other nine."

The West case is certainly one of the most unusual in British criminal history—in fact, it is difficult to find a parallel elsewhere in the world. In the early 1930s, a Serbian confidence man who called himself Captain Ivan Poderjay married a

Frenchwoman named Marguerite Ferrand, and the two began a sex life that Sigmund Freud described as one of the most complex cases of sexual perversion that he had ever encountered. Both were sadists, masochists and fetishists, as well as fantasists who liked to dress up as the opposite sex. But Poderjay is remembered solely for having married—bigamously—a wealthy Scandinavian named Agnes Tufverson, whom he murdered shortly after setting out on a transatlantic crossing, then took aboard in a trunk, and disposed of by cutting her up with razor blades and feeding her to the fishes. He forced the larger bones out of the porthole by greasing them with cold cream. Poderjay was never convicted of murder, although he was sent to prison for bigamy. But he and his wife are not known to have collaborated on murder.

The case of Gerald Gallego and Charlene Williams is perhaps the closest to the Wests' in modern criminal history. Between 1977 and 1980, they abducted, raped and murdered eight young girls in the San Diego area of California—they were finally caught when a passer-by was astute enough to take their car number after they had kidnapped a young man and woman, both of whom they would murder. According to Eric van Hoffmann, the author of a book on the case, the bisexual Charlene played as active a part in the murders as her lover. But their killing spree lasted for only three years, a mere quarter of the Wests' period of collaboration. And although Charlene was a woman of high dominance, she was undoubtedly less dominant than her lover.

What makes the West case almost unique is that it was Rose West who was the more dominant of the two. Everyone who knew them acknowledged this. Fred had committed murder before he met Rose, but it was meeting Rose that turned him into a serial sex killer.

This "chemistry of dominance" throws a floodlight on the murders. In the early 1940s, the American psychologist Abraham Maslow conducted a lengthy study of dominance in women, and found that they fell into three groups: high dominance women (who were exactly 5% of the total), medium dominance women, and low dominance women. High dominance women were promiscuous, often bisexual, and adored sex. Medium dominance women tended to be romantics who wanted to find "Mr. Right," and liked the kind of lover who would take them to candlelit restaurants, and give them flowers and chocolates; they liked sex, but not to the point of obsession. Low dominance women were terrified of sex. *All three types preferred a partner within their own dominance group,* and found it hard to become personally involved with anyone outside that group. (A dominant male would happily sleep with any woman, but there would be no personal involvement unless she was also high-dominance.)

Maslow also discovered the curious fact that *all* women prefer a male who is slightly more dominant than themselves—but not too much. One woman was of such high dominance that she could never find a man to satisfy her—she felt they were all too weak, and that she was unable to give herself to them. Finally, she found a highly dominant male—but he still wasn't more dominant than she was. So she would provoke fights that ended with his slapping her violently, then throwing her on the bed. This was the only time she really enjoyed sex.

Now Fred West *was* dominant, but not quite dominant enough. That meant that Rose was the Boss. He adored her and saw her as a goddess; she probably had her reservations about him, and would have deserted him instantly if a more dominant male had come along. Yet the extreme closeness of their relationship was due to the fact that they belonged to the same dominance group.

West felt he was lucky that she put up with him. She was the master, he the slave. He kidnapped for her, presented her with victims, like a dog carrying a partridge to its master's feet.

Is this the reason that he committed suicide—hoping that there would not be enough evidence to convict her?

Unfortunately, it is hard to ascribe so much chivalry to Fred West. Those close to the family believe that Rose genuinely came to hate him after her arrest, and that her rejection shattered him. It is far more probable that he killed himself because he was deeply depressed at the prospect of a life behind bars. And Rose, who had come to regard him as a weakling, must have felt justified in her opinion.

The ultimate judgment on Fred West must be that, more than any other British serial killer, he deserves to be classified as a sex maniac. Like the Boston Strangler, he went around in a continual state of violent sexual desire. Yet he was almost certainly not sufficiently aggressive to be a rapist or—to begin with at least—a sex murderer. What *is* certain is that what made him capable of murder was the blow on the head he sustained in his teens; it meant that when he became angry or frustrated, he was unable to control his impulses of violence.

It was a million-to-one chance that a sex maniac like Fred West should meet a schoolgirl who was a potential nymphomaniac like Rose Letts. Fred West was instrumental in releasing in Rose a flood of abnormally aggressive sexual desire and dominance. She in turn deepened his own sexual obsession. All sex is based on "forbiddenness," but for someone whose adolescence had been a saga of incest, Fred West was in the grip of a compulsion to discover new degrees of transgression. Like the Victorian author of *My Secret Life*, the story of a man's lifelong pursuit of promiscuity, he felt that a life devoted to the quest for the farther reaches of sexual experiment would be a life of total and ultimate satisfaction. Unlike moors murderer Ian Brady, he was too illiterate to read de

Sade; yet he carried Sade's compulsion to extend sex into a kind of religious experience even further than Brady.

Even so, without Rose, it is doubtful that he would have been anything more than a would-be Casanova with Jekyll and Hyde tendencies. Her aggressive lesbianism made her the ideal partner. Together they could lure girls into their home and use them as playthings. Each offered the other unrestricted satisfaction of their sexual desires. They were like two Alsatian dogs that decide to kill sheep. And the fact that Fred had killed before he met her (and undoubtedly told her so at a fairly early stage in their relationship) meant that she came to accept murder as a norm, just as she came to accept "kinky sex" as a norm. Fred conditioned Rose; Rose conditioned Fred. They are a perfect textbook example of what the French called *folie a deux*.